GOVERNORS ISLAND

The Jewel of New York Harbor

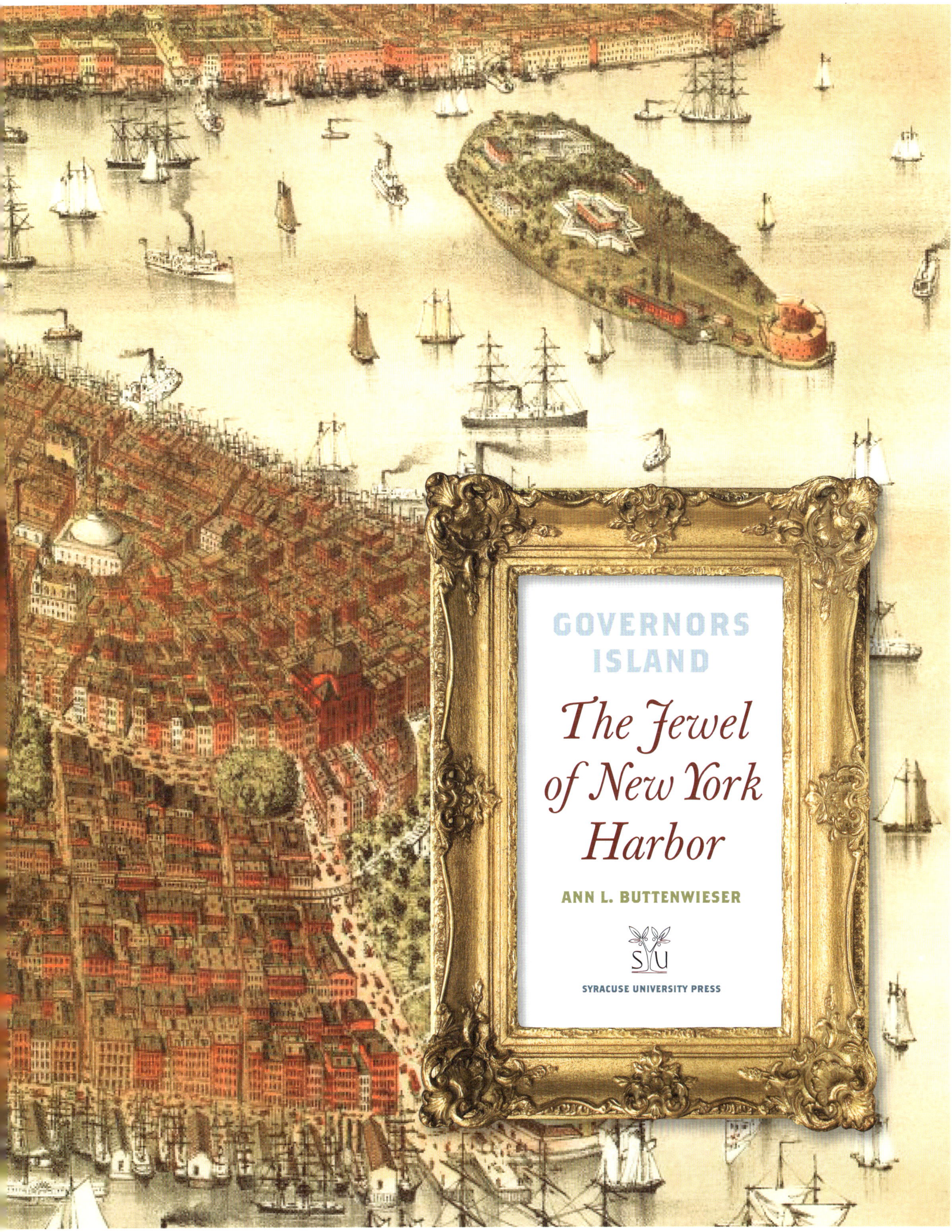

GOVERNORS ISLAND

The Jewel of New York Harbor

ANN L. BUTTENWIESER

SYRACUSE UNIVERSITY PRESS

ANN L. BUTTENWIESER, an urban planner and American historian, is the president of the Neptune Foundation and adjunct professor at Columbia University. On July 4, 2007, she opened the nation's only floating swimming pool on the industrial waterfront of Brooklyn, New York. She is the author of *Manhattan Water-Bound: Manhattan's Waterfront from the Seventeenth Century to the Present, Second Edition* (Syracuse University Press, 1999); other writings include an introduction to *The Lower Manhattan Plan* (2002), entries for the *Encyclopedia of New York City* (1995; 2d ed. forthcoming) and *Encyclopedia of New York State* (Syracuse University Press, 2005), and an article in the New-York Journal of American History (spring–summer 2005). Dr. Buttenwieser's voluntary activities include membership on the Board of New Yorkers for Parks, the New York State Archives Partnership Trust, and the Skyscraper Museum. In 2009 she was appointed to the Board of the Governors Island Preservation and Education Corporation.

Cover and title pages ii–iii: *"New York and Brooklyn," Currier & Ives, ca. 1877 New York, NY. Courtesy of the Library of Congress, Geography and Map Division, Washington, D.C.* Page vi: *"New York," J. Bachmann, illustrator, and G. Schlegel, printer, ca. 1874. Lithograph. Courtesy of Prints and Photographs Division, Library of Congress, Washington, D.C.*

First Edition 2009
09 10 11 12 13 14 6 5 4 3 2 1

Some portions of chapter 7 appeared in a different form in volume 65 (spring–summer 2005) of the *New-York Journal of American History,* published by the New-York Historical Society. Reproduced with permission.

All illustrations of Coast Guard patches courtesy of Rex M. Wessling, lieutenant commander, U.S. Coast Guard, ret., unless otherwise noted.

The paper used in this publication meets the minimum requirements of American National Standard for Information Sciences–Permanence of Paper for Printed Library Materials, ANSI Z39.48-1984.∞™

For a listing of books published and distributed by Syracuse University Press, visit our Web site at SyracuseUniversityPress.syr.edu.

ISBN-13: 978-0-8156-0936-0 (cloth)
ISBN-10: 0-8156-0936-1 (cloth)

Library of Congress Cataloging-in-Publication Data

Buttenwieser, Ann L., 1935–
Governors Island : the jewel of New York Harbor / Ann L. Buttenwieser. – 1st ed.
p. cm.
Includes bibliographical references and index.
ISBN-13: 978-0-8156-0936-0 (cloth : alk. paper)
ISBN-10: 0-8156-0936-1 (cloth : alk. paper)
1. Governors Island (New York County, N.Y.)–History. 2. Military bases–New York (State)–Governors Island (New York County)–History. 3. New York (N.Y.)–History, Military. I. Title.
F128.68.G7B88 2009
974.7'1–dc22
2008049300

Book design by Michael J. Walsh
Manufactured in the United States of America

for Annabelle, Charlotte, Jake, and Luke,
and the future of Governors Island

NEW-YORK & ENVIRONS

Contents

ACKNOWLEDGMENTS

This recital is accompanied by gratitude and affection for all who edited, educated, e-mailed, encouraged, and shared their memories and mementos.

Thanks go to Ruth Peltason, who helped me shape a vast array of documents into a story and who hounded me until I secured a publisher, all the while asking: "Are you having fun?" Jeanne Findlay took up where Ruth left off, lending encouragement, dotting the i's, and correcting endless endnotes. Annie Barva and Kay Steinmetz finished the job. Marrianna Tretiak was a trusted and creative researcher.

Elihu Rose and Jeff Freeman were the military experts who helped me distinguish a company from a regiment and a YN-1 from a W4. Mike Shaver shared photographs and his extensive knowledge of the island's history. Rob Pirani advised me on the contemporary landscape.

Countless former and existing members of the army and Coast Guard and their respective brats responded to my e-mails requesting mementos and information about life on Governors Island. Among them were Tom Clinard and Connie Freeman, who are no longer with us, as well as Georgianne Beurket, Linda Fisher, Jerry Keogh France, Wanda Hinkel, Claudia Iannucci, Admiral Richard Larrabee, Palmer McGrew, Garret Roosma, and Rex Wessling. Richard Kahan introduced me to his polo player uncle; teacher Carol Teller shared her students' art work.

The search for unusual photographs led me to a variety of fascinating institutions. Cliff Hyatt and Bob Wintermute at the U.S. Military History Institute introduced me to never-before-published treasures. Robert Browning Jr. at the U.S. Coast Guard Historian's Office, Mitchell Yokelson at the National Archives and Records Administration, David Smith at the New York Public Library, Tim O'Gorman at the Quartermaster Museum, and Barbara Romer at the Globe Theater helped mightily to fill in the rest of the pieces.

Larry Buttenwieser was the most patient and supportive individual during this process.

Foreword

IN SEPTEMBER 2010, GOVERNORS ISLAND will once again be home to hundreds of children. The Harbor School, a public high school that focuses on the study of the maritime culture, history, and environment of New York City and its surrounding waters, will become the first permanent occupant of a new, postmilitary Governors Island.

The timing cannot be more meaningful. The school will open just over four hundred years after Henry Hudson sailed into the waters of New York Harbor. One of the first places he saw was Governors Island, a ninety-two-acre wilderness just a half-mile from the southern tip of what was to become known as Manhattan and one-quarter mile from the shores of Brooklyn. For Hudson, the island, the harbor, and the great river that would bear his name were a gateway to the New World–a place of seemingly limitless potential and possibility.

For those four hundred years, though, Governors Island remained a largely inaccessible and little-understood place. Even today, few New Yorkers can accurately place it on a map despite the fact that, as Ann Buttenwieser so thoughtfully describes in this book, it can be argued that few places in America are so rich in history.

What other place can claim to have Benjamin Franklin as the author of original plans for its fortifications, which were later blessed by George Washington? In its more than two hundred years as a military base, it housed Confederate prisoners of war during the Civil War and German and Italian prisoners during World War II; its officers included some of the greatest military leaders in U.S. history, such as Generals Winfield Scott, John J. Pershing, and Omar Bradley; thousands of soldiers passed through the island, including Joe Louis, who took his army physical there, and David Rockefeller, who painted its latrines. It was the take-off and landing point of the first overwater flight in America, made by none other than Wilbur Wright (exactly one hundred years ago), which, in part, inspired a fight over its possible future as New York City's municipal airport, led for decades by Fiorello LaGuardia. And in 1986 it was the site of the summit between Ronald Reagan and Mikhail Gorbachev.

Throughout its history as a military base, Governors Island, like the city it defended, changed. The island nearly doubled in size after landfill from the Lexington Avenue subway line was added in the early twentieth century. Rebuilt fortifications, beautiful civic spaces, historic homes, and grand (or not-so-grand) facilities were added as the nation's military needs changed. Men and women stationed there played a role in times of both war and peace. They participated in every major armed conflict abroad as well as in smaller patrol efforts closer to home, protecting their city and country.

After World War II, Governors Island became increasingly irrelevant for America's defense, New Yorkers were becoming disconnected from the city's waterfront, the manufacturing economy faded, and the water's edge diminished with it. Port facilities closed, businesses left, and

piers remained vacant and neglected. Throughout New York Harbor, the teeming waterfront that in many ways defined the city had become sullen and abandoned.

A little more than a decade ago, when the U.S. Coast Guard base closed, Governors Island became part of that deserted waterfront. In 2003, the U.S. government sold the land to the State and City of New York for one dollar and the promise that Governors Island would one day fulfill its promise as the jewel of the harbor in the center of the most cosmopolitan city in the world.

All around Governors Island, the waterfront is coming back to life. New parks are being constructed along the entire waterfront of Lower Manhattan. In Brooklyn, massive passenger ships navigate the Buttermilk Channel and dock at new cruise ship facilities in Red Hook. Just to the north, construction is under way to turn abandoned piers into the mile-long Brooklyn Bridge Park, perhaps the most scenic park anywhere in the world. To the north of that, the decrepit waterfront of Greenpoint and Williamsburg is set to become home to tens of thousands of apartments and tens of acres of parkland.

Yet it is Governors Island that occupies the space in the center of it all, as it always has. Its status as the centerpiece, its views, its history, and its architecture demand not just that it become an ordinary park, residential community, or commercial center, but that it be something new and bold that impacts New York City and inspires the world.

The Harbor School is just the first small step. What emerges in nearly every subsequent step will build on the richness of the social and physical history that is described in this book. Just as the cannons that guarded the harbor were melted into bollards that prevented people from falling into it, in a few years the postwar high-rises that dominate the southern part of the island will be demolished, and the rubble will be reused to form "green" hills that will offer vis-

PROPOSED DESIGN *for Governors Island open space competition. Photographic rendering. December 2007. Courtesy of West 8 / Rogers Marvel Architects / Diller Scofidio + Renfro / Quennell Rothschild & Pertners / SMWM.*

itors to the lush, dramatic new park spectacular views of the Statue of Liberty and the entire harbor. A proposal has been made to reuse the quaint, historic buildings for a "global commons," which would bring together scientists, philanthropists, business executives, and leaders of international organizations to tackle some of the most vexing problems of our era. New York University's expression of interest in creating a new campus on the island echoes the fact that Columbia University was granted the right to Governor's Island in pre-revolutionary times.

The history of Governors Island also reminds us that little of consequence happens quickly or without cost. The original fortifications on Governors Island took four decades to build, and in 1794 the U.S. Congress appropriated $150,000 to build them–an amount equivalent to $39 billion in today's dollars! Needless to say, we will do better.

And we must. Governors Island maintains the promise today that it did four hundred years ago when Hudson first saw it. Yet it is only by being aware of its past and by capitalizing on the remarkable legacy we have been left that we will realize the vision of a jewel in the center of the harbor.

Daniel L. Doctoroff
President, Bloomberg LP
Former chairman, Governors Island Preservation and Education Corporation

Introduction

The big red ball of fire, which later resolved itself into the morning sun, had just made its appearance above Governor's Island yesterday morning, and had just received its daily welcome from the booming cannon there.[1]

OCCUPYING 172 ACRES and firmly ensconced in New York Harbor, Governors Island is historically one of the richest military bases in the northeastern United States. It's just four minutes south of Manhattan, and anyone possessing a good pitching arm and standing on the island can easily hit a ball field in Brooklyn.

The history of Governors Island is more than a chapter in military history. The island has played a vital role in the country's armed forces, including the British navy, the U.S. Army, and the U.S. Coast Guard. In wartime, it was a major administrative army center, training ground for troops, and storage yard for arms. During peacetime, civic events reigned there: receptions for dignitaries, high-level political summits, garden parties, polo games, Easter egg hunts, and open houses for Operation Sail.

The country's largest regimental dormitory, Liggett Hall, is on Governors Island and was designed by the prestigious New York firm McKim, Mead & White. By way of contrast, the world's shortest railroad, somewhere between one and five miles of track, was once on the island. The prison in Castle Williams can rightly be considered an "eastern Alcatraz," and the nation's early military "brats" were born in the small hospital on the island. The island had a museum that housed the remains of Winchester, né Rienzi, General Philip Henry Sheridan's Civil War steed, and a Burger King that served beer.

The history of this seemingly insular body of land both mirrors and contrasts with events in New York City and the world at large. The records of Castle Williams are a compilation of an evolving, national penal system, and those of the hospital are a testament to worldwide contagion and local sanitary practices. A look at individuals' lives on the island offers us a microcosm of the changing roles of women in the military and in the larger society, as well as an example of New York City's ethnic assimilation. The creation of one of New York City's largest landfills is a story of political will and state-of-the-art engineering, and the saga of developing the landfill traces the changes in twentieth-century transportation and provides examples of that period's campus planning.

Finally, the stories that reveal the changing meanings of open space and recreation on the island have particular relevance for the twenty-first century. In 2007, the Governors Island Preservation and Education Corporation announced the selection of a world-renowned team of architects and landscape architects to design a forty-acre park on Governors Island. Using a sequestered piece of property, largely unknown to the public, these designers will write the next chapter in the island's history.

Timeline

1624 Eight Dutchmen land on the island called "Nooten Eylandt."

1630 Island called "Hoogcamer Eylandt" is seen on Minuit maps.

1637 Wouter Van Twiller buys island from the Manhattas (who called it "Pagganack").

1639 Island leased out with sawmill and house.

1664 British take possession of island.

1691 Island transferred to British governor as "his majesties fort and garrison."

1699 Island is renamed "Governor"s Island" and reserved for the king's governors and councilors.

1710–1711 Island serves as a quarantine station for Palatines.

1738 Governor designates island a game preserve for English pheasants.

1745 Troops encamped on island need straw and wood.

1750 Island made part of New York County under Montgomerie Charter.

1754–1763 French and Indian War.

1756 Regimental depot established on island to house, supply, and train recruits for four battalions of the Royal Americans.

1775–1783 Revolutionary War.

1775 Continental Congress approves formation of American Continental Army.

British withdraw from island.

1776 Israel Putman drafts men from New York Continental regiments to build breastwork.

British reoccupy island.

1779 Volunteer Tory civilians help build up fortress.

1783 British troops withdraw from island, Royal Navy surrenders.

British leave convalescent hospital on island.

1784 Legislative act appropriates island for governor of New York State.

1787 State leases island to Dr. John Price.

1788 Legislative act calls for survey of island laying out two-acre lots for sale, reserving parts of island for fortifications.

1790 Alexander Hamilton establishes the Revenue Marine, the forerunner of the U.S. Coast Guard.

New York Journal advertisement for horse race on island.

1790–1794 State grants island to regents of Columbia University, which attempts to auction a twenty-one-year lease.

1791 Improvements begun to make island a "place of resort."

1793 Yellow fever pandemic in New York.

1794 First licensed ferry service begun by John Hillyer; civilians charged three cents, military personnel ride free.

Legislative act allows island to be appropriated to accommodate people with infectious diseases.

State seeks federal funds for fortification of the island.

1794–1796 Construction of fortification.

1796 Surgeon assigned to the garrison.

1798 Fort named "Fort Jay."

1800 State grants title of island to high-water line to U.S. government.

1806–1809 Fort Jay partially demolished, replaced by Fort Columbus; Jonathan Williams, engineer.

1807–1811 Castle Williams built; Jonathan Williams, engineer.

1812 South Battery.

1812–1815 War of 1812: recruitment site, outsiders trained for artillery.

1821 Army of the East headquarters established on island.

1823 Signal Station to notify New York City of ship arrivals.

1833 U.S. Army Ordnance Department arsenal moves to island.

1836 Garrison sent to Florida; only time in three hundred years that island is without a garrison.

1837–1852 Artillery station with occasional detachments of mostly German recruits.

1839 Post hospital constructed.

1843	Commanding Officer's House, Martin E. Thompson architect.
1844	Reverend John McVickar first chaplain assigned to island.
1846–1847	Mexican War: troops and supplies mobilized on island. Chapel of St. Cornelius.
1847–1868	Periodic cholera outbreaks.
1852	Ulysses S. Grant resides in officers' quarters known as Block House.
1854	Whale oil and kerosene replace candlelight.
1856	Yellow fever epidemic.
1861–1865	Civil War: island is used to receive mostly German recruits, to assemble Union troops and materials to send south, and to receive returning Union soldiers.
1861	Castle Clinton becomes prison for captured Confederate soldiers.
	Steam tug *General McClellan* provides free ferry service.
1862	Draft riots.
1865	Executions of bounty hunter James Devlin and privateer John Beall.
1870	Yellow fever epidemic.
1871	Rotten Row, the housing constructed for builders of Fort Jay, torn down.
1872	Grand Duke Alexis of Russia visits.
1878	Island becomes army headquarters (a switch from fortification to administration); recruiting moves to Fort Slocum.
1879	Officers' Club established in South Battery.
1880	Water lines from city and gas streetlights installed.
1888	Park bill in Congress.
1890	New York State grants title to low water line to U.S. government.
1895	Fort Columbus one of ten army posts housing military prisoners.
1897	Park bill in Congress.
1898–1899	Spanish American War: Thirteenth Infantry sent to Cuba from island.
1898	One hundred deserters held in Castle Williams.
1899	All guns and carriages on first and second tiers removed from Castle Williams. Three tiers used as prison.
1899–1902	Philippine-American War: troops and supplies mobilized on island.
1900–1913	Island expanded to 103 acres with ninety-acre landfill.
1900–1916	Garden parties highlight New York's social season.
1900	Young Men's Christian Association (YMCA) opens on island.
1901	McKim, Mead & White hired to redesign entire island.
1904	Fort Columbus renamed "Fort Jay."
	Electricity replaces gas.
1905–1906	New Chapel of St. Cornelius, designed by Charles Haight.
1909	Hudson Fulton Celebration.
	Flight competition between Glenn Curtiss and Wilbur Wright.
	Wilbur Wright sets record for overwater flight.
1910	Glenn Curtiss flies to island from Albany.
	Ferry *General Otis* carries horses, carriages, wagons, and motor cars.
1912	Secretary of War Henry Stimson states island is "the most valuable military property in the U.S."
1913	Ninth Disciplinary Company formed for prisoners in Castle Williams.
1917–1919	World War I: island a major supply base.
1917	Congress authorizes president to temporarily increase U.S. military establishment on island.
	Landfill becomes site of hastily erected cantonments and warehouses.
1918–1931	"World's shortest railroad" (locomotive, three flat cars, one and three-quarters miles of track) carries coal, machinery, and supplies from piers to shops and warehouses.

Timeline

1918 Influenza epidemic.

1919 Merchant's Association recommends island for municipal airport.

1921 Competitive polo field created on island.

1920s "Little Pool": island's first swimming pool built.

1922–1941 Sixteenth Infantry, "New York's Own."

1924 McKim, Mead & White present revised plan for barracks.

1925–1941 Battle over municipal airfield on island.

1925–1943 Prison named Atlantic Branch U.S. Disciplinary Barracks.

1926 War Department considers selling island to raise money for army housing.

1927 Army units on island: headquarters for Second Corps Area, one battalion Sixteenth Infantry, Enlisted Reserves, one division quartermaster training, Quartermaster Corps, Publicity Bureau, Signal Service Company, prison, Medical Department, Ordnance Department, Veterinary Corps.

1928 President Calvin Coolidge signs act making funds available for construction of Liggett Hall.

1930 Congress establishes imaginary "James Line" to determine where federal monies can be used for construction on island.

1932 Merger of Fort Totten Second Corps Area hospital with Fort Jay hospital.

Trucks, trailers, and motorcycles replace 180 mules and carts.

1932–1933 Partial reconstruction of Castle Williams.

1933 Post Hospital, McKim, Mead & White architects; and Nurses Quarters, Rogers and Poor architects.

1934 Works Progress Administration work on roads and walks.

1935 P.S. 26, Eric Kibbon architect.

Recommendations for other uses of Castle Williams: post headquarters, quartermaster's warehouse, museum, theater.

Sixteenth Infantry regiment completely motorized.

1936 Land appraised at $3,250,000.

1937 Weeklong three-hundredth-anniversary celebration.

1937–1938 Comedians Tommy and Dick Smothers born in base hospital.

1937–1939 Theater.

1940–1941 Forty-three new temporary buildings erected on landfill.

1941 President Franklin D. Roosevelt signs repeal of James Line.

1942–1945 World War II: island an induction center for a short period.

1942 Our Lady Star of the Sea built.

Army units on island: First Army Headquarters, Recruiting Publicity Bureau, Ordnance Battalion, Army Band, Signal Service Co., Battery C, Stationary Medical Detachment; Bakers and Cooks School, Military Police Battalion, Quartermaster Corps.

1943 Duke and Dutchess of Windsor visit.

1943–1966 Post takes over prison.

1944 Hospital designated a regional hospital.

Women's Army Corps (WAC) detachment in Building 101.

1944-1946 Stockade for prisoners of war located on landfill along western shoreline.

1949 Excavations for Brooklyn Battery Tunnel placed as fill on east side of island.

1949 Temporary barracks on landfill converted to "splinter village" apartments.

1950 First Armed Forces Day.

1950–1953 Korean War: troops muster out on island.

1955 Army counts 11,500 visitors to island.

1957 Diesel ferries replace steam.

Queen Elizabeth visits New York City. Island staff arranges military support and reviews.

1959 Her Royal Highness Princess Beatrix of the Netherlands visits.

1961 Three seven-story apartments constructed on landfill.

1964 Defense Department announces pending closure of island army base.

1964 Assessed value of land and buildings: $16,250,000.

1965 Mayor Robert F. Wagner suggests incorporating island into a national recreation area.

1965–1975 Vietnam War.

1966 Rear Admiral Irvin J. Stephens assumes possession of island for Coast Guard.

Prison closed. Castle Williams used for classrooms, meeting rooms, and day care.

Movie of the week: *Kisses for My President* starring Polly Bergen and Fred MacMurray.

1968 St. George, Staten Island, Coast Guard base closed.

1969 President Lyndon B. Johnson asks for increase in monthly draft.

Fifty-four hundred men, women, and children living on island.

Women's Voluntary Reserves housed in Liggett Hall.

1971 Eleven-story Cunningham Apartments constructed on landfill.

1972 P.S. 26 dedicated to former Coast Guard commander Frederick C. Billard.

1973 Island cutters respond to *Sea Witch* and *Esso* tanker collision.

1975 Open houses welcome eleven thousand visitors.

1976 Bicentennial party and Operation Sail.

1978 Cutter *Mahoning* breaks ice to Troy, New York.

1979 *Mahoning* hauls eighty-eight garbage barges during New York City tug strike.

1983 Burger King built on island.

1985 Historic district designation.

1986 U.S. president Ronald Reagan and French president François Mitterrand relight Statue of Liberty.

Liberty Village replaces Fog Horn Alley.

1988 Summit between Ronald Reagan and Mikhail Gorbachev held in Admiral's House.

1990–1991 Gulf War: troops mustered out on island.

1993 Governors Island Accord talks on Haiti.

Island cutters respond to Chinese immigrant ship aground in Rockaways.

1994 "Andes Road Man" human remains discovered.

1995 King Harald and Queen Sonja of Norway visit.

1997 Permanent closure of Coast Guard base.

U.S. Government Services Administration assesses value of island at $500 million.

2003 Portion of island transferred to the National Park Service, remainder transferred to the people of New York City and New York State via Governors Island Preservation and Education Corporation.

2007 West 8, Diller Scofidio & Renfro, Rogers Marvel, Quennell Rothschild & Partners, and SMWM selected to design forty-acre park on southern half of island.

MAP OF *Governors Island*

Courtesy of Governors Island Preservation and Education Corporation. Sandrine Dedieu.

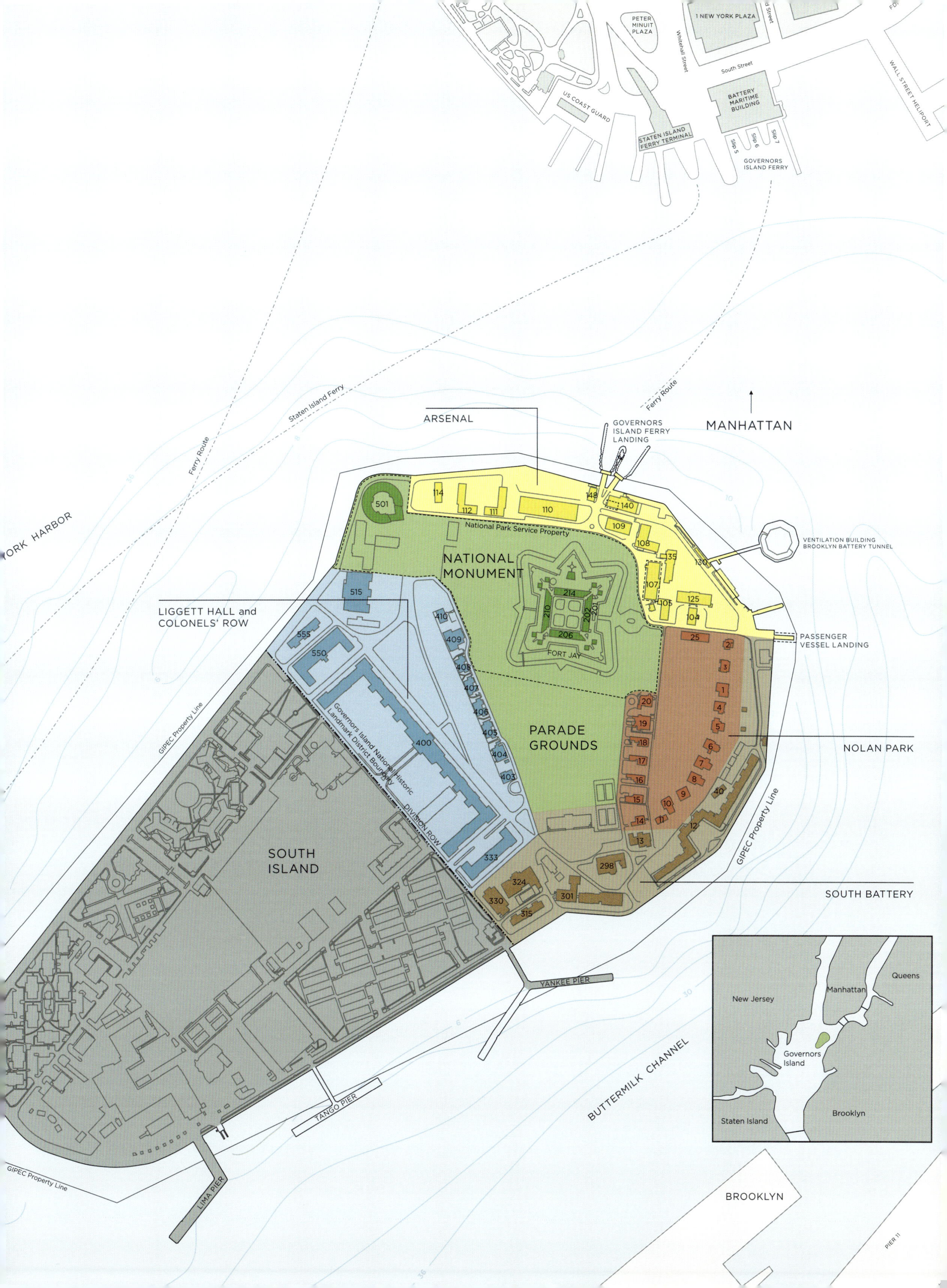
1 NEW YORK PLAZA
PETER MINUIT PLAZA
Whitehall Street
South Street
BATTERY MARITIME BUILDING
WALL STREET HELIPORT
US COAST GUARD
STATEN ISLAND FERRY TERMINAL
Slip 5
Slip 6
Slip 7
GOVERNORS ISLAND FERRY
Staten Island Ferry
Ferry Route
Ferry Route
YORK HARBOR
ARSENAL
GOVERNORS ISLAND FERRY LANDING
MANHATTAN
114
112
111
110
148
140
109
108
135
130
107
105
125
104
501
National Park Service Property
NATIONAL MONUMENT
VENTILATION BUILDING BROOKLYN BATTERY TUNNEL
214
210
202
201
206
FORT JAY
PASSENGER VESSEL LANDING
LIGGETT HALL and COLONELS' ROW
515
555
550
410
409
408
407
406
405
404
403
400
333
Governors Island National Historic Landmark District Boundary
DIVISION ROW
PARADE GROUNDS
25
2
3
1
4
5
6
7
8
9
10
11
12
13
14
15
16
17
18
19
20
40
NOLAN PARK
GIPEC Property Line
GIPEC Property Line
GIPEC Property Line
SOUTH ISLAND
298
324
301
330
315
SOUTH BATTERY
YANKEE PIER
TANGO PIER
LIMA PIER
BUTTERMILK CHANNEL
BROOKLYN
PIER 11
New Jersey
Manhattan
Queens
Governors Island
Staten Island
Brooklyn

COLORS AT OLD FORT JAY, *Governors Island, ca. 1940, Signal Office. Courtesy of U.S. Army Military History Institute, Carlisle, Pa.*

Chapter One

FIRST IN DEED AND ALWAYS READY

The Military on Governors Island

Directly or indirectly [Governors Island] has contributed to every war in our nation's life and to every peace.... Its soldiers have worn every uniform in our Army's catalogue from the homespun hunting shirt to...combat boots of today.... The Infantry, Cavalry, Artillery, Engineers, Ordnance, Medical Service, Transportation, Military Police, and Quartermaster Corps have contributed troops...not forgetting the feminine touch offered by the...WAC Detachment.... Governors Island [was] one of the most important of our military posts and one of the most interesting of our historic centers.[1]

Nothing of note would ever have taken place on Governors Island without the military. For 242 years, from the arrival of a British regiment in 1755 to the disestablishment ceremonies of the Coast Guard base there in 1997, the lifeblood of Governors Island has been the military. Without it, there would be no Fort Jay, Castle Williams, Officers' Row, Pershing Hall, or Yankee Pier; without it, the island might be only 90 acres, half its present size of 172 acres. Were it not for the military, neither the country's largest regimental dormitory–Liggett Hall, designed by the prestigious New York firm McKim, Mead & White–nor the world's shortest railroad, just more than five miles of track, would have been built. There would have been no prison or hospital or Officers' Club, no library or museum, and no Burger King that served beer.

In wartime, the island was outfitted for defense, and in peacetime it was a popular venue for civic events. Over the years, both hawks and doves have made up a long line of military personnel and civilian dignitaries going on and off the island. Some were famous, among them Ulysses S. Grant, Leonard Wood, Omar Bradley, Ronald Reagan, and Mikhail Gorbachev. Others–privateer John Yates Beall, for example–were infamous. The presence of the army and the Coast Guard on Governors Island has created centuries of stories about America, New York, and its people: stories of a fortress, a supply and storage base, a military administration, and a home base and part-time training ground for hundreds of thousands of army and Coast Guard men and women who fought wars and kept the peace.

FORTIFICATION, 1766–1860

THE REMARKABLE STRUCTURES OF FORT JAY and Castle Williams dominate the landscape of Governors Island and today form its anchor and tourist centerpiece. Inland, Fort Jay hides behind a grassy bank, a dry moat, and a massive sandstone archway. Seen from the inner harbor, Castle Williams looms as a hulking, circular brick structure that anchors the western corner of the island. Along with a third, less-visible battlement, the South Battery on the eastern

DESIGN FOR GOVERNORS ISLAND, *ca. 1766, John Montresor. Courtesy of Geography and Map Room, Library of Congress, Washington, D.C.*

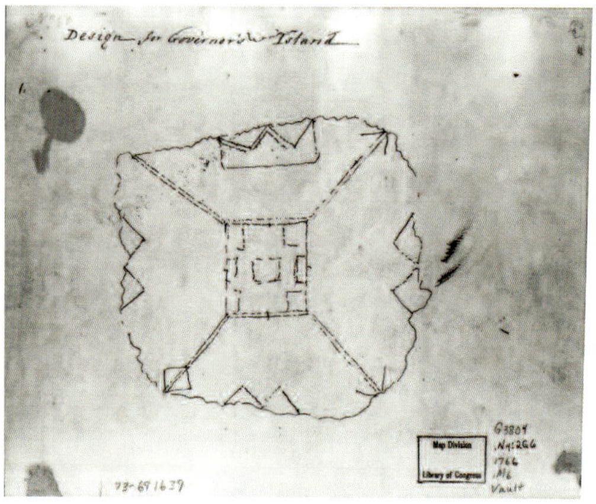

INTERIOR, OLD FORT JAY, *Fort Jay, N.Y., n.d., A. M. Simon. Postcard. Author's collection.*

side of the island, these structures are reminders that Governors Island was originally developed as one of the prime fortifications protecting New York City. It took more than four decades, from 1766 to 1812, to build these edifices, but shots were fired from them only three times, all between July and September 1776. Until the Civil War in 1860, when their use in military defense was no longer viable, these forts in the harbor were like bullies in a schoolyard, more bluff than punch.

FORT JAY, PHASE ONE, 1755–1783

THE FRENCH AND INDIAN WAR brought the first military station to Governors Island. Between July and August 1756, the British established a depot there, possibly under the leadership of Colonel Henry Bosquet. By the end of August, seasoned soldiers were training newly arrived German recruits and outfitting them to become part of the Royal Americans (shortly to become the Sixtieth Regiment of Foot). As would be the pattern during subsequent wars, the men's stay on the island was short. By November, they were posted in towns from Saratoga, New York, to the Delmarva Peninsula, helping to forestall French advances into the colonies.[2]

It is possible that Colonel John Montresor's 1755 sketch depicting several forts on the island gave the new residents a blueprint for erecting a primitive army base, but for years little was built. The first drawings were sidelined; organizing troops to fight in the north took precedence over constructing a fortification to protect the harbor. Then, in 1766, Montresor submitted a more detailed plan for a battlement, but another ten years of dormancy ensued on the island until the American Revolution.

Having successfully resolved the French and Indian situation in 1763, the British next encountered rebellion from members of their own colonies who desired independence from Great Britain. Life for British soldiers in New York became increasingly difficult after the revolution's first salvo in Concord, Massachusetts, in April 1775. Unable to quell constant anti-British demonstrations, the soldiers were also attacked in the streets and taverns. On June 7, 1775, only two months after the first major dissents, the British were no longer able to occupy and administer New York. Sir William Howe, the British commander, withdrew his troops from New York City and Governors Island to replenish them in the friendlier environment of Canada. On June 14, the Continental Congress approved the creation of an American Continental Army to oppose the British when they returned.[3]

The task of completing the first fortification on Governors Island now became a duty for the new American forces. In February 1776, Benjamin Franklin, foreseeing a return of the British and a need to protect the entrance to New York, forwarded a letter to Lieutenant

MAP OF GOVERNORS ISLAND, *1813, Joseph L. Mangin. RG 77 Fortification File, 077-HMF-Drawer 037-sheet 01. Courtesy of National Archives Architectural and Cartographic Branch, College Park, Md.*

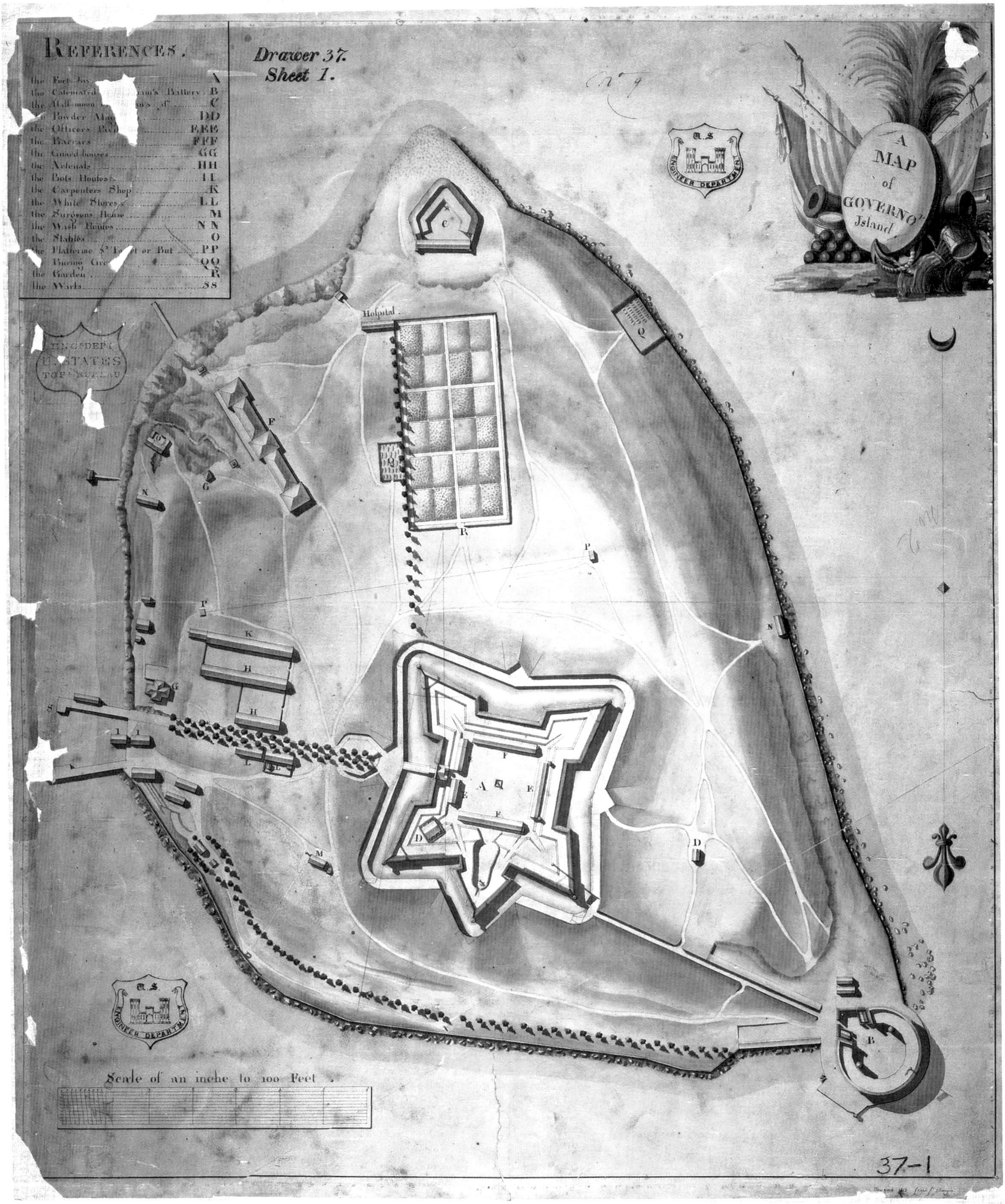

General Charles Lee of the Continental Army. Although there is no indication that Franklin was aware of Montresor's prior drawings, the letter proposes a layout similar to Montresor's 1775 plan for the British:

> [T]here is Long Island and Nutten Island well situated to place Guns, and I would imagine three or four hundred men would be sufficient to complete all the works...in one night....Batterys and Guns properly placed will soon silence them [hostile war ships]....[T]he Batterys and Guns should be fixed at a distance from the water and vessel, no nearer than 200 yards...and upon high ground enough to be out of range of her shot....[S]ink in...your platforms and guns upon the top of the summit of the hill, the muzzles...as it were peeping out of the hill....[T]he men will work their guns...with a facility and safety, and out of reach of all shot.[4]

Lee was not in New York long enough to follow Franklin's advice. In April, his successor, General Israel Putnam (of Bunker Hill fame, who said, "Do not fire till you see the whites of their eyes"), took up the cause. On April 8, 1776, Putnam took one thousand of the Continental Army's officers and soldiers stationed in New York to Governors Island to begin defense works. To bolster these efforts, on April 16 the head of the Continental Army, General George Washington, who was also in New York, ordered Colonel William Prescott and his regiment to help Putnam complete the defenses. Prescott had also been at Bunker Hill ten months earlier, and on June 17, 1775, his regiment had been narrowly defeated by British commander Sir William Howe. Now a reunited Prescott and Putnam were preparing to defend New York against the same foe.

From April to June 1776, troops under orders from George Washington built up the fortifications in New York Harbor. On May 9, Washington followed up on Franklin's earlier letter to Charles Lee. He summed up for Lee the results of the work accomplished by others: "We have done a great deal of work at this place. In a fortnight more I think the City will be in a very respectable posture of defense."[5] Five weeks later, however, according to Washington's description, men in uniform and mufti were still toiling on Governors Island:

> A working party consisting of nine hundred men properly officered to parade tomorrow morning at Six O'Clock near the Artillery park–Those of Bailey's and Read's Regiments to go to Powle's-hook–Wyllys's to Governor's Island....Brigadier General Greene and Col Prescott, will furnish, one hundred and fifty men each, as a working party on Governor's Island...men to be furnished with one days provision....On the present emergency, all working parties to work 'till Six o'Clock in the afternoon, except such as go by water, who will be allowed to leave work sooner, if the Wind and Tide make it necessary. Head Quarters, New York, June 19, 1776.[6]

Day and night, with candles to light their way and armed with small spades, pickaxes, and shovels, men from ranks high and low–hunters, farmers, bankers, and others–arrived on Governors Island and built the earthen defense.[7]

Four months after Franklin first wrote to Lee, the Americans finally turned Governors Island into a fortification. Establishing a rudimentary defense at best (the actual layout no longer exists in the records), the Americans mounted four 32-pound cannons, four 18-pound cannons, and thirty other sundry cannons on the fortifications. They sank hulks of old vessels in the channels outside the island, plunged stakes into the ground along the shoreline, and created an unobstructed line of fire by burning down the island's only existing farmhouse and barn. And they stationed the first American Continental Army garrison on the island.[8]

For a time, it seemed that the fortification did help protect New York from the British. On July 6, two months after Washington's letter, a British soldier reported on the strength of the work: "Observe the Rebels have fortified Governor's Island very strongly."[9] The battlements were initially a failure, however. On July 12, Lord Howe, back in New York from Canada, tested the waters by sending three British ships and two tenders toward the Hudson River. From Governors Island, the Battery, and Red Hook, Continental Army troops fired 196 rounds altogether at the vessels, but to no avail. Within an hour, the British had swept past the batteries. Then on August 29, George Washington, finding his troops outmaneuvered by the British on Long Island, ordered an evacuation across the East River to Manhattan. It may have been the psychological effect of the battlements on Governors Island or a nor'easter followed by a dense fog that kept the British from entering the East River that night, but whatever the case, the Americans ultimately escaped and even rescued their garrison on Governors Island.[10]

By September 1776, the British were once again in control of the island. Three years later, volunteers loyal to the British were enlisted to shore up its ruined facilities. Merchants and shopkeepers worked for free, and lower-class individuals were paid ten shillings a day plus rations, rum, and spruce beer.[11]

The British stayed for seven years, until the end of the revolution. On December 3, 1783, the Royal Navy surrendered Governors Island to the State of New York. In the list of the structures left behind, there is no mention of a fort.

FORT JAY, PHASE TWO, 1793–1812

A LEITMOTIF OF BENIGN NEGLECT in peacetime and center-stage importance in wartime runs throughout Governors Island's history. Immediately after the revolution, New York turned its attentions to rebuilding burned-out New York City and shoring up its maritime economy. Franklin, Washington, and others concentrated on writing a constitution and forming a viable national government for the new country. With attention elsewhere and no military crisis, there was little public support for maintaining Governors Island as a military defense. The plea for keeping an army post, made by Commandant Sebastian Bauman of the New York Regiment of artillery in 1788, would be repeated over the next two centuries. Writing that the sale of Governors Island would "injure the state" and that "posterity will feel the remiss of it," Bauman recommended instead the construction of a proper fort–large enough to contain five hundred men–and two water batteries.[12]

New York State however, which had become the owner of the island upon the departure of the British, saw it as a revenue enhancement for its war-depleted treasury and leased the land to private individuals. Although there were no quarantine laws to protect New York from epidemics, ships carrying passengers with contagious diseases were stopped at outlying islands in the harbor. From 1786 to 1790, passengers were quarantined on Governors Island before being allowed to enter New York City.[13]

In 1790, the New York State Board of Regents allegedly granted Columbia College a franchise for the island. In turn, the college intended to issue its own leases to gain financial support. No direct records exist of Columbia's involvement, but it is known that the state franchise contained an important caveat that would recur in future discussions over the island's use: should the island be needed for defense, the agreement would be null and void.

Indeed, military and political events abroad soon caused the government to return its attention to Governors Island, and this time it was the French who precipitated the newest anxiety about war. In 1792, George Washington sent Supreme Court chief justice John Jay to London to negotiate a treaty with the British in order to settle political details left over from the revolution. In return for agreeing to vacate western forts and to compensate American ship owners for goods and vessels lost during the war, the British were given most-favored-nation trading status via the Jay Treaty. However, the French considered this treaty as evidence of an Anglo-American alliance and in 1797 began to seize the cargo of American ships bound for British ports, whereupon supporters of both outgoing president George Washington and incoming president John Adams began demanding war against France.

Thus, in the early 1790s Governors Island was dormant, waiting for something to happen while players in New York State and Washington discussed its future. In a message to Congress on January 4, 1794, a year before the British and Americans signed the Jay Treaty, Governor George Clinton described the "naked and exposed condition of our principal seaport" (New York City) and stressed "the necessity of immediately providing for its defense."[14] Clinton must have recognized that the naval infrastructure, consisting of nothing more than congressional approval to build half a dozen frigates, was uncommonly weak. Furthermore, there was no approved navy department. The Revenue Service, authorized by Alexander Hamilton in 1790 and the forerunner of the U.S. Coast Guard, could help protect American cargo, but its putative duty was to collect customs. Land-based lines of defense were obviously also needed.

While debating the type of navy required, the House of Representatives also investigated on February 28, 1794, the cost of making Governors Island capable of defending the country's principal seaport. At this time, the authorized strength of the permanent army was about 3,300 men conscripted by individual states, and it was up to each state to train its complement of soldiers. The result of the deliberations was a defense works modeled on the congressionally authorized "First System of Defense." Initial estimates for the infrastructure were modest. For $1,727.52 (in 1794 dollars), the island could have batteries, embrasures (openings to shoot through), and platforms for twenty-four cannons.[15] An additional $2,010 could finance an earthwork with openings, a place to store gunpowder, and a fortified structure, or blockhouse, to barrack a garrison of 97 men.[16] A month later Congress appropriated a more realistic $150,000 for fortifications on Governors Island.

But who would design and build the fortifications? Because the new nation was lacking engineering schools, President Washington turned to French émigré Charles Vincent. Trained in building the earthenwork fortifications envisioned by Montresor, Vincent immediately set

PRIVATE HARVEY B. HEATH *standing in the Fort Jay quadrangle. 1898, unknown photographer. Courtesy of U.S Army Military History Institute, Carlisle, Pa.*

about constructing a fort to be named after Chief Justice John Jay, who was at the top of his career. However, sometime in 1794, when Vincent had nearly completed the fort, the secretary of war voiced qualms about its effectiveness, reporting that the works, being only sodded, would not last long.[17] Nevertheless, by January 1796 the War Department reported the completion of an earthen fort housing a garrison of one major, one captain, one surgeon, one corporal, and a cadet; two first lieutenants, three sergeants, four musicians, five mechanics for boat and artillery repairs (what would become ordnance and quartermaster detachments); and thirty-four privates (three-quarters the number anticipated by Congress three years earlier).[18] Horses and mules were available to carry the men and their supplies.

With a war against France still looming, more congressional appropriations followed for other facilities on Governors Island, and in 1797, to keep within budget and to speed the building process, another incongruous mix of volunteers was enlisted to help. The group was reminiscent of the hodgepodge that had composed past efforts to build a fortification on the island: English Republicans and Republican bankers; members of Scotch, trade, and philanthropic societies; lawyers and law students; cask and candle makers, ship carpenters, and shoemakers; hatters, wig makers, and hairdressers; and Columbia College students.[19]

As Charles Vincent had suspected, Fort Jay was short-lived. In 1800, the U.S. government took over the island from New York State, formalizing it as an army base. On January 6, 1806, President Thomas Jefferson announced that "[i]n this year, most of Fort Jay on Governor's Island was demolished, and a reconstruction known as Fort Columbus was begun on the site."[20] (The fort was called "Fort Jay," "Fort Columbus," and once again "Fort Jay" over the course of its tenure and in its various forms. To add to the confusion, these names also applied to the military post until 1966, when the entire base became simply "Governors Island.")[21] Modeled this time on European bastions, the new work was directed by Lieutenant Colonel Jonathan Williams, the army's chief engineer, who at the time was in charge of fortifying all of New York Harbor. When his job was complete, an enlarged, permanent masonry fortification sat in the same location as the first Revolutionary War battlement. A two-story brick blockhouse/barracks with a well underneath was positioned

On February 15, 1800, Governors Island was ceded by the State of New York to the United States Government, and with the bugaboo of another war with England now looming large in the immediate future, the federal authorities demolished the Island's impermanent emplacements and began to install more durable construction that would preserve the fort intact and solid for generations not yet born. Nor were the alterations all of a physical nature: John Jay's popular fame was suffering a temporary eclipse as a suspected adherent of England, so in 1810 the name of Fort Jay was changed to Fort Columbus.

(ANASTAZIO CARLOS MARIANO AZOY, *THREE CENTURIES UNDER THREE FLAGS: THE STORY OF GOVERNORS ISLAND FROM 1637* [GOVERNORS ISLAND, N.Y.: HEADQUARTERS FIRST ARMY, 1951], 35.)

The story is that a prisoner who was a stone cutter by trade was detailed to make the fine carving [that represents the War Department seal] which adorns the gateway [of Castle Williams]....[O]ne day the commanding officer's little daughter stood under the gateway with the stonecutter who was inspecting his work from below. Just then a heavy block of stone or a stone cannon ball fell and would have killed the child, but the prisoner...interposed his own body and saved her life....His reward for the gallant act was pardon.

(EDMUND BANKS SMITH, *GOVERNORS ISLAND: ITS MILITARY HISTORY UNDER THREE FLAGS, 1637–1913* [NEW YORK: EDMUND BANKS SMITH, 1913], 54.)

in the center of the fort. By 1812, the garrison included four companies of soldiers with substantial firepower at their service. However, except for live ammunition practice in anticipation of a war (what would be the War of 1812), the only cannons shot from Fort Columbus were used to fire salutes.[22]

CASTLE WILLIAMS, 1807–1860

NEW YORK'S MARITIME ECONOMY at the turn of the nineteenth century was poised to explode. The favored-nation clause in the Jay Treaty briefly increased trade with England and then brought it to a halt. Robert Fulton launched his steamboat in 1807, opening up more of the city to shipping. The Brooklyn Navy Yard, completed in 1806, began to build the much-needed vessels to defend American commerce. But the threat of war with England loomed, giving cause once again to protect New York Harbor.

Between 1807 and the outbreak of the War of 1812, engineers acting on behalf of what Congress authorized as the "Second System of Defense" constructed new, more permanent, all-masonry battlements in Greenwich Village, the Battery, and Fort Wood (the base of the Statue of Liberty).[23] On Governors Island, the newest structure was the Tower, officially named Castle Williams in 1810 in honor of its builder Jonathan Williams.

The massive edifice of Castle Williams became a model for nineteenth-century fortification construction around the country. Built with forty-foot-high walls, it was made of red stone, eight feet thick at the base and seven feet wide. The masonry construction allowed Williams to include two tiers of casemates, or gun portals, that contained arches designed to hold more than a hundred pieces of artillery. The portals not only protected the gunners during an attack (the guns were inside the walls), but also increased the number of guns able to be deployed, thereby producing an imposing array of firepower. Because there were few living quarters on the island, the upper tier of casemates served as both housing and protection from hostile fire. This solution may have been expedient, but in reality the casemates were cold, damp, and dark. The original structure had two brick buildings at each end of the circle and a well inside the castle. Still visible today is the outer walls' dovetail pattern, which prevented stone from being knocked out in one piece.[24]

Castle Williams's heyday was soon over. By the time of the Civil War, its poor location and structural vulnerability diminished its usefulness, and its firepower had been subsumed by fortifications in Brooklyn and Staten Island. Also around this time, military technology had advanced substantially, thereby making the castle's model construction obsolete. When the castle was built, it was intended to battle slow-moving, easily targeted wooden sailing ships whose cannons were incapable of inflicting much damage to its masonry walls. However, not only were the modern steam-powered ships, with their thick layers of armor plating, impervious to shots from the castle, but their cannons also fired cone-shaped explosives whose mass could now penetrate the castle's structure. The cannons of Castle Williams, like those of its sibling Fort Jay, no longer functioned as defense, but were mostly symbolic, giving salutations on formal occasions and sounding retreats at funerals. In the 1930s, they became part of the island's beautification, used as bollards and edging decor for roads and paths. In 1942, all but two of

POST HEADQUARTERS AND NEW YORK ARSENAL *with arsenal store yard in the center, n.d. Postcard. Rotograph Co. Author's collection.*

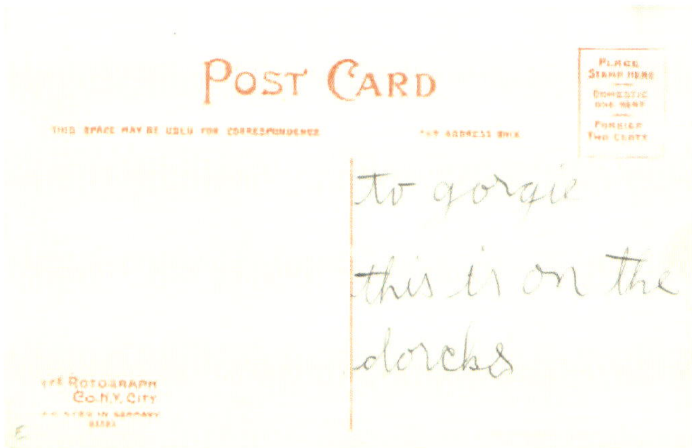

"TO GORGIE *this is on the docks."* *Message on reverse.*

the Rodman guns on Castle Williams, six cannons at Fort Jay, and 1,100 cannonballs were sold for scrap and shipped to a Pennsylvania steel mill to be melted for use in another war.[25]

THE ARSENAL, 1833–1920

AN OFFICER OR ARTILLERYMAN assigned to fire the cannons on Governors Island after the War of 1812 lived either in barracks in Fort Jay or in the musty, upper-tier casemates of Castle Williams. But he had few places in either location to keep the armaments viable. Yards and buildings were necessary to store ammunition, parts, and tools, and to keep weapons battle ready. The army in its early stages had depended on contractors to supply the weapons and accoutrements required to outfit the soldiers, but as it grew larger and war seemed closer, contractors took advantage of war fever by overcharging and supplying faulty goods. As a result, the government created its own system of arsenals for arms manufacture and warehousing.

Founded upstate in 1813, the Watervliet Arsenal was the first arsenal in New York State. It was used primarily to manufacture such military equipment as caissons, tools, and ammunition to be sent to storage sites elsewhere. Subsequent arsenals (or armories) were constructed in New York City: on Bridge Street, at the foot of West Twelfth Street, and on the site of what is now Madison Square Park. Each was used for military exercises, to store munitions, and to assemble forces when needed to guard the city.

By 1833, open space was becoming expensive and scarce in the city, and one of the armories, the New York Arsenal, was looking for a new home. A location was needed with room to store ammunition, armaments, food, and clothing, and to

The general order of 1851 directed a radical change in the uniforms of the period, being for commissioned officers a frock coat of dark-blue cloth, the skirts to extend from two-thirds to three-fourths of the distance from the waist to the knee, single-breasted for captains and lieutenants, double-breasted for all other grades....For enlisted men the uniform coat was a single-breasted frock of dark-blue cloth, the skirt extending one-half the distance between the waist and the knee. The uniform trousers for officers and enlisted men were of cloth of sky blue mixture, to be worn throughout the year, "made loose and to spread well over the boots." For enlisted mounted men they were reinforced....The general order of 1857 prescribing the uniform dress of the Army made no particular change except as regards the hat for officers and enlisted men. This was to be of best black felt....For officers it was bound with black silk, and for enlisted men stitched. The trimmings for general officers were the gold cord with acorn-shaped ends, eagle and three black ostrich feathers...below the rank of field officers two ostrich feathers were allowed. The enlisted men were still allowed to have one feather....In 1853 the order [prohibiting]...whiskers was rescinded, and in the service now the beard may be worn at the pleasure of the individual, but to be kept short and neatly trimmed.

(OSCAR F. LONG, A.Q.M., U.S.A., *CHANGES IN THE UNIFORM OF THE ARMY, 1774–1895* [WASHINGTON, D.C.: U.S. ARMY QUARTERMASTER'S DEPARTMENT, 1895], AVAILABLE AT HTTP://WWW.QMFOUND.COM/CHANGES_IN_THE_ARMY_UNIFORM_1895.HTM.)

THE SOUTH BATTERY, *n.d., unknown photographer. During the War of 1812, the South, or Half Moon Battery, had thirteen cannons mounted on an open parapet to protect Buttermilk Channel. Courtesy of U.S. Coast Guard Historian's Office, Washington, D.C.*

provide quarters for officers and staff. Governors Island was a fitting site: it was secure, land was available, and it was rent free. Furthermore, it was a new base looking to establish itself.[26] Given that the artillerymen in Castle Williams were needed for defense, who would manage the arsenal's operations? On May 14, 1812, Congress created the Ordnance Department, which, like the Corps of Engineers, was a distinct branch of the military. The chief officer of each unit was authorized and given funds to establish ordnance depots; to enlist artisans and laborers; to direct the inspection and proof of all cannon and small arms; to direct the construction of gun carriages, equipment, implements, and ammunition; to make estimates of, contracts for, and purchases of ordnance supplies and stores, and to issue them to the army.[27]

The Ordnance Department, with its own staff and boats, would remain a distinct department on Governors Island for eighty years. Among its responsibilities was management of the New York Arsenal, which was situated on a triangular piece of land west of today's Andes Road and away from Fort Jay's powerful line of fire.

HEADQUARTERS AND NEW YORK ARSENAL, *with arsenal store yard in the center, n.d., Rotograph Co. Postcard. Author's collection.*

NEW YORK ARSENAL, *ca. 1909, Post Exchange.* Left to right: *Arsenal storehouse, officer's quarters, carpenters' shop, guard house. Postcard. Author's collection.*

The arsenal expanded over time, eventually reaching west of today's ferry terminal. The first expansion occurred in 1850, following the Mexican-American War (1846–48), when supplies needed for the troops moving out to the Texas border surpassed the limits of the arsenal's boundary. Two years later the arsenal property was expanded to include all of the land north of Andes Road. By the time of the Civil War, the arsenal's twelve buildings were simple one- and two-story red brick structures that held offices, limited quarters, workshops, and arms and ammunition stores. In addition, there were outside shell yards and stables. As the chief of ordnance at the time recollected, the extra space came in handy during the Civil War, allowing several vessels to be loaded in a single night.[28]

After the Civil War, and at a time when the armaments on the forts had already stood idle (save for salutes) for nearly a century, the army recognized that direct access to the harbor from the gun batteries at Fort Jay and Castle Williams was no longer required. The arsenal, meanwhile, was growing increasingly crowded—no longer with the newest equipment, but with used stores arriving from all over the country. Additional buildings were finally constructed along the water, much to the arsenal overseers' relief.

But the overcrowding persisted. Unused and outdated munitions from army posts nationwide usurped the landscape and overloaded the arsenal's coffers. To provide some space, sixty worn-out battery wagons were sent north in 1889 to Watervliet to be sold as junk at public auction.[29] An 1895 War Department survey describes the collection thus: "Here is a vast accumulation of obsolete war material, and nearly all the available ground [in the arsenal compound], save a vegetable garden, is thickly piled with obsolete shot, shell, guns and mortars."[30]

In the next quarter century, several wars and technology would change the nature and the amount of arms and ammunition the army used. The island no longer had the capacity to adjust to changes. By 1920, the Ordnance Department had moved its personnel and stores to the Raritan Arsenal in Metuchen, New Jersey, and had turned its buildings on the island over to the commanding general of the army's Second Corps Area.[31]

ARMY HEADQUARTERS AND LEADERS

GOVERNORS ISLAND WAS NOT JUST A STOREHOUSE for arms and a bastion of fortifications; it became a major military administrative center. The transition from battlement to management began in a small way in 1821. As part of a periodic restructuring of the army, local offices known as the U.S. Third Military District, under the command of Brigadier General Winfield Scott, were transferred from Castle Clinton in Manhattan to the island. On March 2, 1821, faced with an outbreak of Indian warfare on the border between Georgia and the Spanish province

PLAN OF NEW YORK ARSENAL, *March 3, 1875, Board of Arsenals. Author's collection.*

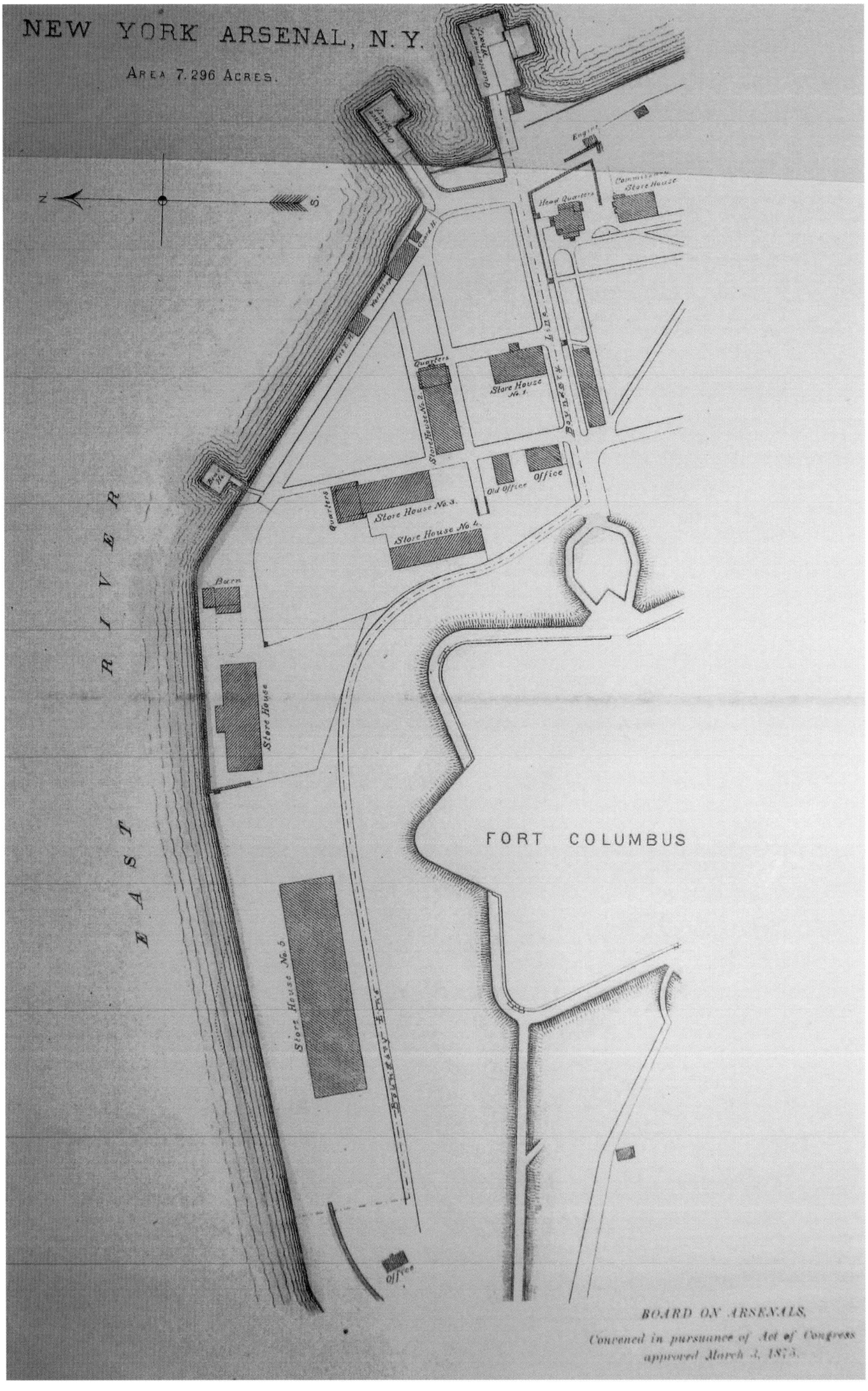

GENERAL'S ROW AND POST HEADQUARTERS, *ca. 1910, Post Exchange. Postcard.* Left to right: *General's Row, Dutch House, post headquarters. Electric lines are in evidence. Author's collection.*

POST HEADQUARTERS, *Fort Jay, N.Y., n.d., A. M. Simon. Postcard. Author's Collection.*

of Florida, the army also reorganized its nine northern and southern territorial divisions into eastern and western departments. Scott was placed in command of the short-lived Eastern Department, which for a time was headquartered on Governors Island. In 1827, Scott's successor moved army headquarters back to Manhattan.

The island made the final transition from military fortress to army administrative center after the Civil War, on July 1, 1878. As the pendulum had swung from war to peace, pressures for military preparedness lessened. The island became a ghost town, but it nevertheless provided a secure location where northeastern army activities converged. Aware of the benefits of reviving this sleepy site, the army, in another round of reorganization, established one of three major territorial commands, the Division of the Atlantic, on Governors Island. As in the past, to better manage the vast territory from Maine to Florida and from Wisconsin to Mississippi, the army broke the commands of this territory into eastern and western units; a new Department of the East joined the Division of the Atlantic on Governors Island. In the next eighty years, tied to reorganization of the army and its commanders, the name of the island's headquarters would change five more times.[32]

Following the 1878 reordering, the army placed Major General Winfield Scott Hancock (named after but not related to Winfield Scott, the 1821 divisional commander) in charge of the dual commands of the East and Atlantic Divisions. Hancock was notable, but the names and exploits of other Governors Island headquarters commanders and officers are also memorable. Many had exceptional army careers. Winfield "Fuss and Feathers" Scott served fourteen presidents over a period of fifty-one years, twenty of them as general in chief of the army, and during the Civil War he oversaw recruiting and training for the defense of Washington, D.C. Later commanders, such as Leonard Wood, John J. Pershing, Hugh A. Drum, and James Van Fleet, served with distinction in Cuba, the Philippines, Europe, Japan, and Korea.

Some men are remembered for their family ties to Governors Island. Three generations of Grants served on the island in the eighteenth and nineteenth centuries. Major General Frederick D. Grant was the son of Ulysses S. Grant, also a Governors Island alumnus. Frederick's son, Ulysses S. Grant III, was Second Corps Area chief of staff. Major General Arthur MacArthur Jr., who was commander of Governors Island briefly in 1902, was the father of Douglas MacArthur, the renowned World War II military leader (who was assigned to unspecified active duty on Governors Island in 1952, but preferred to headquarter at the Waldorf Tower).

COMMISSARY BUILDING, *September 28, 1864, unknown photographer. Known as the Dutch House, this 1847 building was also the quartermaster's storehouse for food and uniforms. Courtesy of Still Pictures Branch, National Archives, College Park, Md.*

TEMPORARY ONE-STORY OFFICE, *November 14, 1918, unknown photographer. Scrapbook photograph. The entrance to Fort Jay is on the left. Courtesy of National Archives, College Park, Md.*

REGIMENTAL HEADQUARTERS *Administration Building, ca. 1918, unknown photographer. Scrapbook photograph. Courtesy of National Archives, College Park, Md.*

Many others with ties to Governors Island are known for their careers in government service. Leonard Wood was Grover Cleveland's White House physician and military governor of Cuba prior to coming to Governors Island. Omar Bradley became administrator of the Veterans Administration and a member of the Joint Chiefs of Staff. Walter Bedell Smith served as U.S. ambassador to the Soviet Union, director of the Central Intelligence Agency, and undersecretary of state. And three commanders had presidential aspirations: Winfield Scott ran for president as a Whig but was defeated by Franklin Pierce in 1852; Democrat Winfield Scott Hancock was still the commander in charge at Governors Island when he was narrowly defeated by James Garfield in the 1881 presidential race; and Leonard Wood lost to Warren Harding in the 1920 Republican presidential primary.

THE ARMY POST

THE FORT JAY POST established in 1800 was initially under a command separate from headquarters. Whereas the latter managed the island's involvement in national and international affairs, the post's leaders, most often full colonels, took care of the day-to-day operations on the island as well as in the regiment (or, in later years, the garrison).[33]

The most illustrious of the colonels may have been Ichabod B. Crane. Army historians say that Washington Irving met Crane during the War of 1812 and later used his name for the character of the schoolteacher in *The Legend of Sleepy Hollow*. Crane began his first command in 1819 at Fort Wolcott, then the primary fortification protecting Newport, Rhode Island. He was post commander of Fort Jay twice, first in 1828 as a thirty-nine-year-old major, and then again as a colonel twenty years later. One of his troops at that time, Abner Doubleday (who allegedly founded the game of baseball), described him as "an old soldier, a thorough gentleman."[34]

COLONEL JOHN S. ROOSMA, *Deputy Post Commander. Also a sports star, Colonel Roosma was a champion high school and college basketball player, and was later inducted into the Basketball Hall of Fame. 1953. Photographer unknown. Courtesy of Garret Roosma.*

SHELTER TENT DRILL, *ca. 1912, Rotograph Co. Postcard. Brick Row is in the background. Author's collection.*

THE GARRISON

FROM THE DAYS OF BRITISH occupancy, Governors Island has been home to cadres of soldiers. Here they lived, trained, and went off to war. Three types of combat forces were stationed on Governors Island as its permanent force: the artillery, the infantry, and the Coast Guard. Their numbers ranged from the first 1,000 Continental troops ready to fight in 1776 to a low of 400 soldiers rounded up in an unpopular draft during the Civil War to an all-time high of 4,600 Coast Guard members and families in the early 1990s. In keeping with the island's fortification function, the artillery came first in 1794. Save for brief hiatuses when the garrison went off to fight the Seminole in Florida and before and after the Civil War, various companies of artillery troops remained on the island for a century.

Life on the island was of course regimented and followed a manual that General Winfield Scott had prepared in 1821 detailing every aspect of a soldier's life, including the ingredients of his soup. Lieutenant Thomas Sparrow, Confederate prisoner, described daily drill parades in his 1861 diary: "The men and officers of the garrison usually are in drill in companies and squads on the lawn in front of Col. Loomis's house" [the commanding officer's quarters, later the Admiral's House, or Building 1].[35] Soldiers also had classroom training in military skills, and weekly attendance at religious services was mandatory. Even so, this strict regimen had some breathing space for hops and romance with the Irish maids and laundresses who worked on Governors Island.

By 1894, artillery had moved to harbor defense posts elsewhere, and field army or infantry units made up the major portion of the Governors Island garrison. The 1900 census indicates 208 men attached to the K and L Companies of the Fifteenth Infantry Regiment. There were 2 captains, 12 sergeants, 3 lieutenants, 24 corporals, 157 privates, 4 cooks, 2 artificers, and 4 musicians. Twenty-four percent of the infantry was foreign born, immigrants mainly from Ireland and Germany, but some also from Austria, Canada, and Scandinavia.

By 1920, World War I had made an impact on the island, and the number of infantry soldiers nearly tripled. The increase in the regiment's size, technological change, and new demands from headquarters added to the type of adjunct military activities on Governors Island: the Signal Service was added probably sometime between 1913 and 1920, and the Intelligence Department and War Risk Insurance Agency were added in 1917. The 1920 census lists motor transport companies, an indication that cars and trucks had replaced the pack- and carthorses previously used on the island. Seven years later the

WANTED: For the First Regiment of Artillery U.S. Army, able-bodied, unmarried men between the ages of twenty-one and thirty years, of good moral character and temperate habits. Apply in person or by letter...to the Recruiting Officer, CAPTAIN MERRILL, Governors Island, N.Y.

(DISPLAY AD 13, *NEW YORK TIMES*, APRIL 5, 1894, 7.)

EASTERN DEPOT BARRACKS, *ca. 1918.*
Photographer unknown. Courtesy of U.S. Coast Guard Historian's Office, Washington, D.C.

New York Times found a total of 849 soldiers in headquarters and the Sixteenth Infantry. In addition, 233 officers and soldiers had been assigned to support services as well as to the newly acquired Publicity Bureau.[36]

By the 1950s, the island had made a complete transition to an administrative headquarters. The only troops that remained were for show and in support companies.[37]

At the outset of the Civil War, Congress mandat-ed] that the Army ration shall be increased as follows viz: Twenty-two ounces of bread or flour, or one pound of hard bread, instead of the present issue; fresh beef shall be issued as often as the commanding officer of any detachment or regiment shall require it, when practicable, in place of salt meat; beans and rice or hominy shall be issued in the same ration in the proportions now provided by the regulation, and one pound of potatoes per man shall be issued at least three times a week, if practicable, and when these articles cannot be issued in those proportions, an equivalent in value shall be issued in some other proper food, and a ration of tea may be substituted for a ration of coffee upon the requisition of the proper officer....Condiments and flavorings were sanctioned in the Act of March 3, 1863, which stated that "the Army ration shall hereafter include pepper, in the proportion of four ounces to every hundred rations."

(FRANZ A. KOEHLER, "EARLY ARMY RATIONS," CHAP. I OF *SPECIAL RATIONS FOR THE ARMED FORCES, 1946–53*, IN *QMC HISTORICAL STUDIES*, SERIES II, NO. 6 [1958], AVAILABLE AT HTTP://WWW.QMFOUND.COM/ARMY_RATIONS_HISTORICAL_BACKGROUND.HTM.)

SOLDIERS CLEANING THEIR EQUIPMENT, *ca. 1918, unknown photographer. Courtesy of the Collection of the Prints and Photographs Division, Library of Congress, Washington, D.C.*

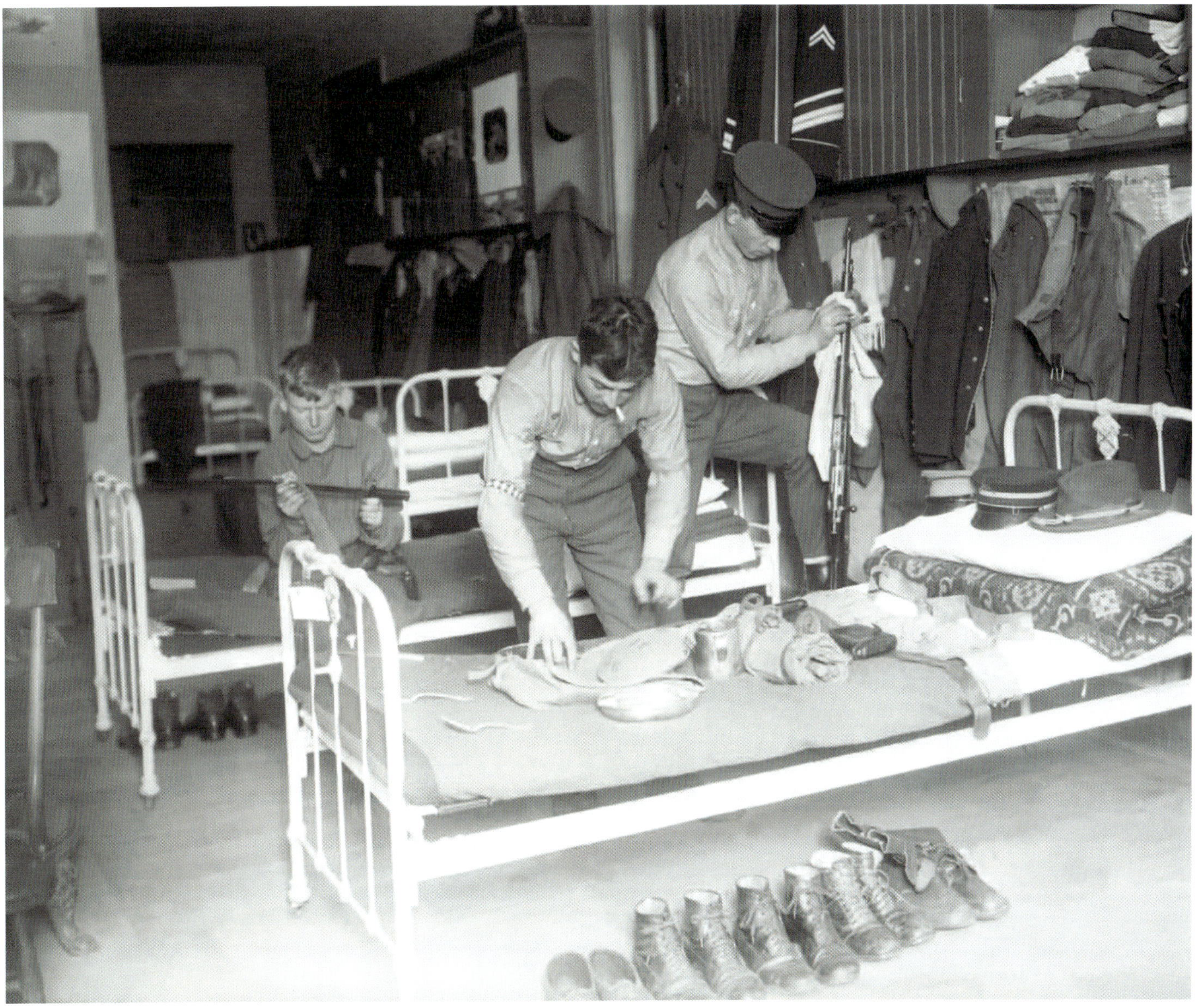

EASTERN DEPOT MESS, *Governors Island mess, n.d., unknown photographer. Courtesy of U.S. Army Military History Institute, Carlisle, Pa.*

MAJOR GENERAL T. A. TERRY *inspecting the mess hall before dinner, n.d., unknown photographer. Courtesy of G. S. Grunert Collection, U.S. Army Military History Institute, Carlisle, Pa.*

THE LABOR BATTALIONS

ENCOUNTERS WITH MEMBERS OF THE GARRISON or headquarters were probably few and far between for the labor battalions because the latter lived and worked in segregated conditions. These units, made up entirely of African Americans, apparently were assigned to Governors Island during periods of construction. Poorly trained and historically excluded from combat, men in these battalions held such menial positions as wagoners, scouts, laborers, and servants. In an entry to his diary while his Confederate regiment was imprisoned on Governors Island, Edward Drummond writes about his fears after the army freed the regiment's young "Negro" servant, who had been imprisoned with them. "A dark cloud," he wrote, "passed over all hands in consequence of an order coming from the War Dept. ordering all of our Negro Boys to be sent to New York and turned loose in the City" with no backup or support.[38]

The first reference to African American soldiers on Governors Island appears in Anastazio Carlos Mariano Azoy's *Three Centuries under Three Flags*. He describes the island garrison as composed of "Companies A, B (the 'music Boys'), C (the 'Permanent Party')...and the 'Coloured Infantry' Company H."[39] This period was a very active time for construction on the island, and it is likely that these men were brought in to unload materials, dig ditches and foundations, and repair wharves.

Records from World War I give a fuller picture. By 1917, still only a small fraction of blacks were assigned to combat duty.[40] The only recourse for black men who wanted to perform patriotic service was the Labor Battalion. The confluence of Governors Island as a major trans-shipment point for the war in Europe and the availability of this manpower brought Captain E. S. Jones, his six-member staff, and an unknown number of African American soldiers to Governors Island to help with the war. Details of their lives are scanty. The men attached to the Labor Battalion lived in segregated housing–first in tents, sometimes without floors, and by November 14, 1918, in wooden barracks that they had erected in little more than seven weeks. Photographs show that their barracks were bare bones in comparison to the regiment's barracks. Beds were without sheets or pillows. Space to hang their clothing and shelves for such necessities as a razor were minimal. A homemade, low table provided the only venue for games. The battalion also ate and worked under segregated circumstances. Other images show the men in line outside the segregated dining hall and grouped together working on construction of the cantonments for housing, offices, and warehouses.

By the time the United States entered World War II, African Americans were represented in all branches of the military service, but few were integrated into white units.[41] Claudia Iannucci, the daughter of Staff Sergeant E-6 Harvey L. Thompson, an African American enlisted man, describes her father's position when he first entered the army in January 1945: "black soldiers would be housed in separate barracks and would not be allowed to eat and sleep with white soldiers." By the time Thompson retired in 1966, he had received countless medals and citations and had led many units regardless of color.[42] It had taken such luminaries as boxer Joe Louis and such events as the Korean War for African Americans to gain parity on military posts.

ONE OF THE OFFICERS IN CHARGE *of the Labor Battalion working on Governors Island, November 18, 1918, Lieutenants Barasanti and Layer (no first names given). Courtesy of Still Pictures Branch, National Archives, College Park, Md.*

STAFF SERGEANT HARVEY L. THOMPSON, *n.d., unknown photographer. Born a sharecropper, Thompson served in the U.S. Army for twenty-one years, seven months. Courtesy of Claudia Iannucci.*

VIEW OF LABOR BATTALION'S BARRACKS, *November 18, 1918, Lieutenants Barasanti and Layer (no first names given). Courtesy of Still Pictures Branch, National Archives, College Park, Md.*

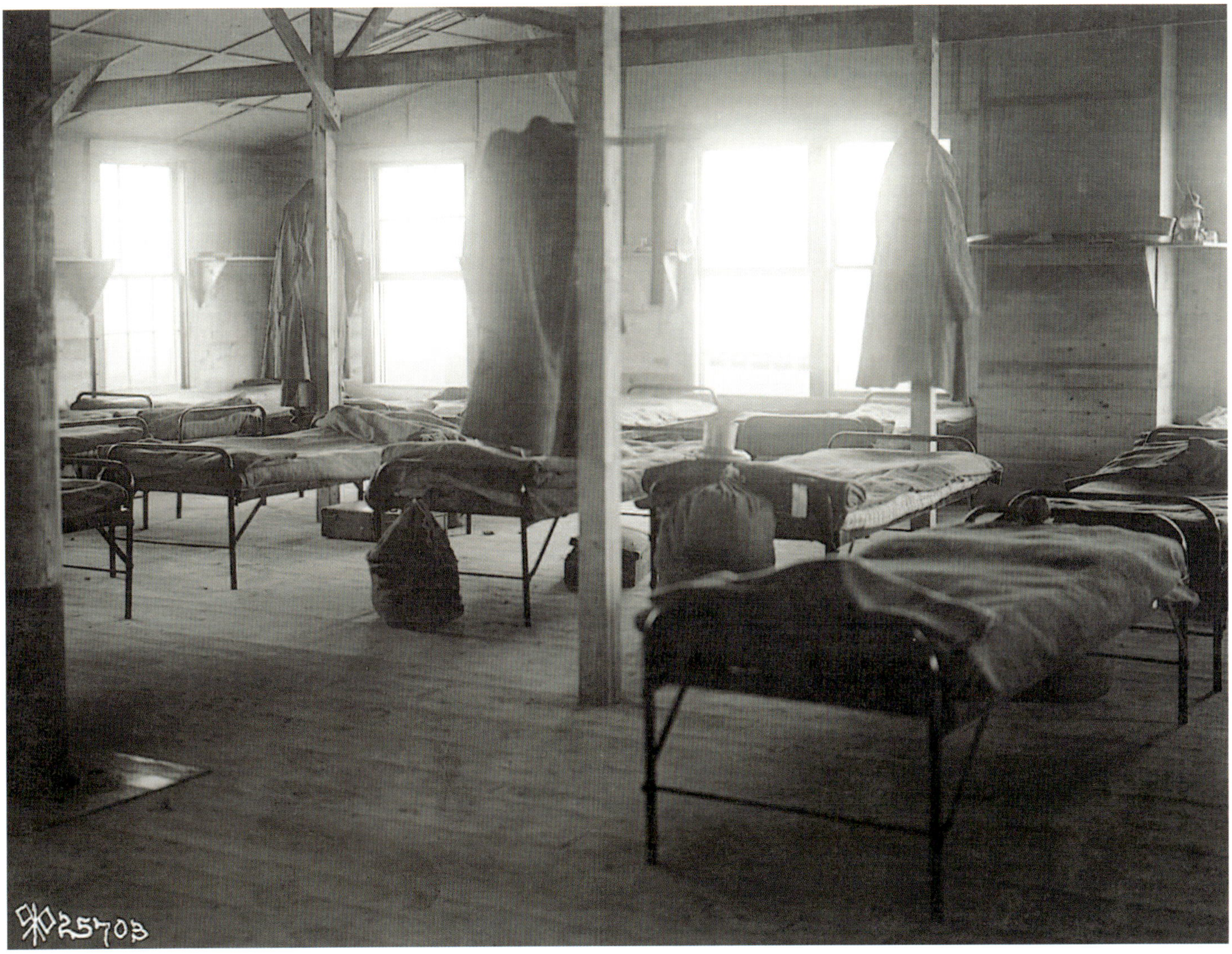

25693

MEN OF THE LABOR BATTALION *in a segregated barracks, November 18, 1918, Lieutenants Barasanti and Layer (no first names given). Courtesy of Still Pictures Branch, National Archives, College Park, Md.*

LABOR BATTALION LINED UP *outside the segregated mess hall, ca. 1918, unknown photographer. Courtesy of Still Pictures Branch, National Archives, College Park, Md.*

LABOR BATTALION INSIDE *segregated mess hall, ca. 1918, unknown photographer. Courtesy of Still Pictures Branch, National Archives, College Park, Md.*

JOE LOUIS *receiving army physical exam, January 12, 1942, unknown photographer. Louis was measured by Sergeant William Chrastina at Fort Jay. Courtesy of @Bettmann/CORBIS.*

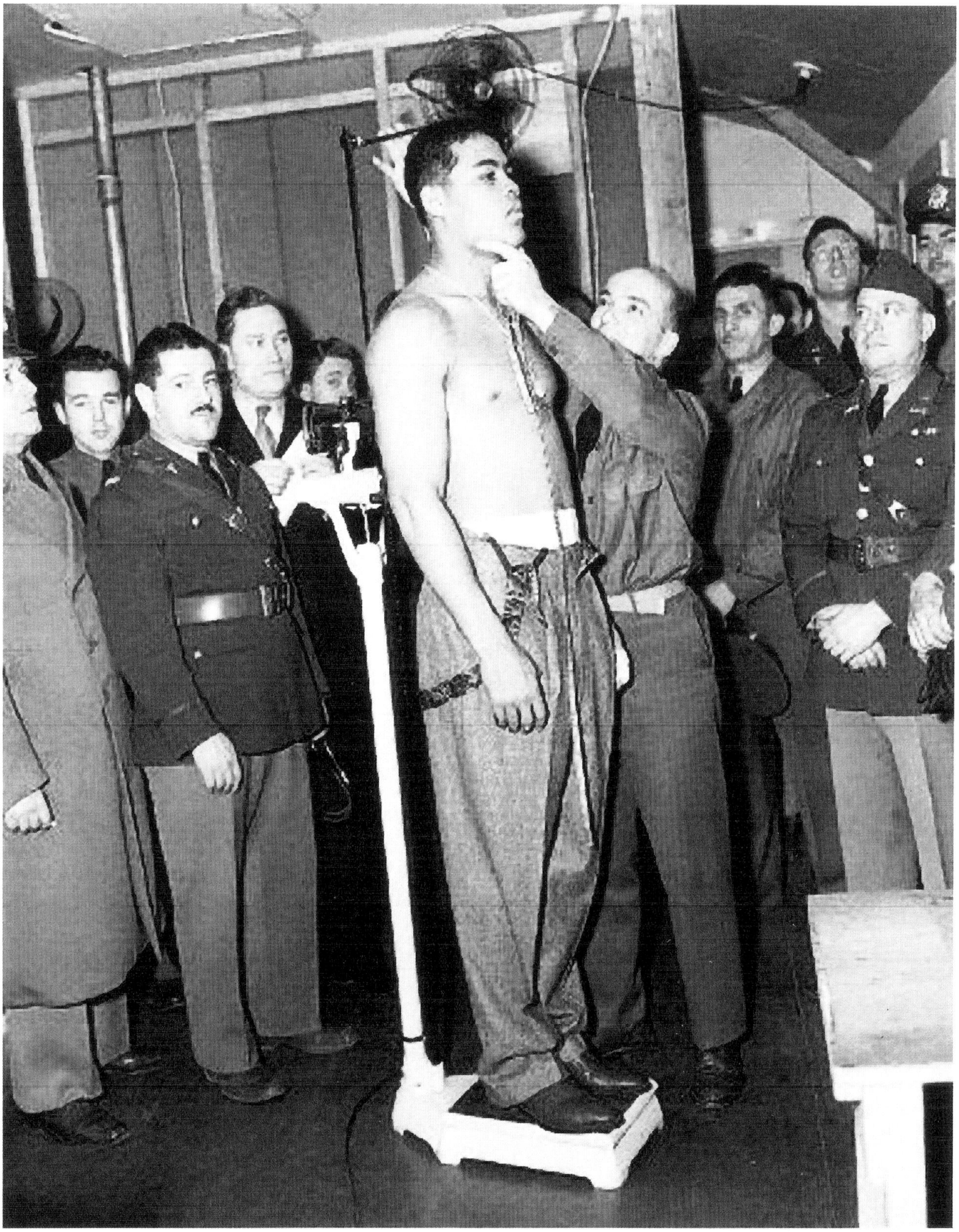

PART-TIMERS

IN ADDITION TO THOSE STATIONED as part of a regiment, tens of thousands of other men and women passed through Governors Island. Some went off to war or to duty protecting the frontier. Others were stationed on the island after having honorably served their country. Recruits were a familiar sight during the wars of the nineteenth century and again prior to World War II.

Many of the recruits were famous. Private Winthrop Rockefeller, who would one day become governor of Arkansas, was received at Fort Dix, spent a few hours assigned to the Military Police Battalion on Governors Island, and was promptly sent by railroad to join a training regiment in Plattsburgh, New York. Boxing great Joe Louis had his physical on Governors Island prior to reporting for induction into the army.

Some citizen-soldiers received specialized short-term training on the island. During World War I, volunteer flyers took lessons at a makeshift airstrip on the 1900s extension of the island. Between the wars, regular army soldiers ran summer programs in the Citizens Military Training Camp for National Guard units, college Reserve Officers' Training Corps (ROTC) cadets, and high schoolers. Some prominent New Yorkers who were former military helped out. Among them were Cornelius Wickersham, a lawyer with the firm of Cadwallader, Wickersham and Taft, and Julius Ochs Adler, general manager of the *New York Times,* who assisted with army investigations, raised money for military causes, and gave advice to prospective soldiers.

UNKNOWN OFFICER *in a typical Governors Island office, August 9, 1920, Sergeant J. H. Saum, Signal Corps. Courtesy of Still Pictures Branch, National Archives, College Park, Md.*

CIVILIANS BOARDING THE GOVERNORS ISLAND FERRY, *n.d., unknown photographer. Courtesy of U.S. Coast Guard Historian's Office, Washington, D.C.*

Members of notable families also trained on the island in the 1910s and again in the 1940s. A 1917 *New York Times* photograph shows "rookies, sons of prominent Americans" on the "air-field" south of Liggett Hall. These men of all ages were seeking commissions as officers in the reserves. The photograph shows them marching in lockstep and holding sticks that mimic rifles. These sessions were also great equalizers: draftees from disparate professions met on the island in afternoon drills, while factory managers, bank clerks, engineers, policemen, carpenters, bricklayers, and a film director performed sit-ups and learned together how to handle rifles.[43]

In his memoirs, David Rockefeller describes his basic training on Fort Jay in 1942 and his concern about his "ability to cope with [the army's] rigors physically or to adapt socially." But his work ethic was intact, a quality that impressed his fellow enlisted men. About painting the kitchen of the Officers' Mess, he wrote: "They were amazed that a Rockefeller was willing to do manual labor. I soon realized that I wasn't as inept as I had feared; that I could get along and even become friends with people with whom I had few things in common."[44]

TRANSITION

IN THE TWENTIETH CENTURY, finances often threatened the military's stay on Governors Island. Money during wartime was fairly plentiful, but in peacetime the island fought for funds to subsist. As early as 1912, there was talk of selling the island along with twenty-eight other army posts—a conversation that would be repeated many times in years to come. The value of all posts was assessed that year and then again prior to World War II, and Governors Island came in somewhere between $4,070,000 and $6,280,000. Secretary of War Henry Lewis Stimson used the numbers to rationalize keeping Governors Island, which he deemed "the most valuable military property in the United States."[45]

THE LAST SHOW OF FIRST ARMY COLORS *before its transfer to Fort Meade, 1965, unknown photographer. Courtesy of Thomas W. Dunn Collection, U.S. Army Military History Institute, Carlisle, Pa.*

Ironically, a high assessed value was an enticement to sell the island: Perhaps the army should indeed cash in and use the proceeds elsewhere? In 1926, the War Department again considered selling. One offer came from Charles C. Nicholas Jr., vice president of Schulte Cigar Stores, who wrote to Secretary of War Dwight Filley Davis: "I have had some correspondence with Senator James Wadsworth Jr. of New York in reference to the purchasing of Governors Island by our company....If you think it is advisable for the War Department in order to raise necessary funds to sell Governors Island, I would be very pleased to hear from you and secure from you the proper method to proceed."[46] Correspondence among army officials suggests there was an ongoing debate about using the island's estimated $18–25 million income to build housing elsewhere for the army rather than build much-needed billeting for officers and families on the island. President Calvin Coolidge's supplemental appropriation for fixing up barracks settled the matter, opening new housing on the island.

By the 1960s, however, the bustling wartime life on Governors Island was long forgotten. Though picturesque, the now sleepy town had once again become a financial burden on the government. Was it time for the army to move on? In 1964, the total assessed value of land and buildings on Governors Island was $23,250,000, and Secretary of Defense Robert McNamara was finally ready to close down the island, the Brooklyn Navy Yard, and the Brooklyn Army Terminal as an economic move. For the U.S. Coast Guard, however, the timing was propitious. With operations scattered around the Northeast and in dire need of housing and improved morale, the Coast Guard successfully bid to move in. The fit was ideal: land was cheap, the area was secure in the nation's busiest harbor, and the Coast Guard could comfortably accommodate its force on the island.

THE COAST GUARD COMES TO GOVERNORS ISLAND, 1965–1997

THUS BEGAN THIRTY YEARS OF COAST GUARD service on the largest military base in New York City.[47] A military pageant opened the ceremony. After army retreat, Colonel Arthur M. Murray transferred Governors Island to Commander Third Coast Guard District Rear

SIXTEENTH INFANTRY LINEUP, *February 1939, unknown photographer. "New York's own" was the last of the regiments to be garrisoned on Governors Island. This select contingent is shown here practicing to garrison at the New York World's Fair. Courtesy of U.S. Army Military History Institute, Carlisle, Pa.*

Admiral Irvin J. Stephens. Following the raising of the National Ensign, a seventeen-gun salute honored Assistant Secretary of the Treasury True Davis, who was a guest at the handover, as three search-and-rescue helicopters flew overhead in salute. At the end of the hour-long ceremony in blistering heat (during which some men—especially those who were required to stand at full attention the whole time—actually fainted), Rear Admiral James A. Alger became the island's first Coast Guard base commander. Henceforth, ships would replace sleepy forts for harbor protection; admirals would replace generals; bulkheads, decks, and ladders would replace walls, floors, and stairways; and, symbolically, blue would forever replace khaki.[48]

Like the army before it, the Coast Guard had several commands on Governors Island. The Third District encompassed thirty-nine states from the Canadian border to the Gulf of Mexico and westward to the Grand Tetons in Wyoming. It was also in charge of the Atlantic area, which covered the Port of New York and the east coast from Greenland to the Gulf of Mexico.

A variety of large and small cutters, buoy tenders, and tugs were based at Governors Island. The larger vessels, such as the *Dallas* and the *Gallatin*

The United States Coast Guard had a hand in another important event in the island's history. Eighteen minutes after Congress declared war against Germany at 3:12 A.M., April 16, 1917, a battalion of the 22nd Infantry set out in Coast Guard furnished boats to seize enemy ships and their crews at anchor in New York harbor.

(JEFF BLINN, "GOVERNORS ISLAND—A SKETCH OF HISTORY," *TOW LINE* 20, NO. 5 [FALL 1969], 13).

THE LARGEST U.S. COAST GUARD BASE *in the world was commissioned following the transfer of Governors Island from the U.S. Army, 1500 hours, Thursday, June 30, 1966, unknown photographer. Courtesy of U.S. Coast Guard Historian's Office, Washington, D.C.*

(named for Albert Gallatin, the fourth secretary of the Treasury), left the island for months on end to run border patrols and vessel inspections. The buoy tenders *Sassafras* and *Red Beech,* named for local trees, made sure that harbor entries and rivers were well marked for safe navigation. The smaller cutters and tugs, with names of lakes (the *Manitou*), forts (the *Mahoning*), and naval equipment (the *Hawser*, the *Line*, and the *Wire*), kept the harbor open in winter and performed search-and-rescue and disaster-response duties. During the winter deep freeze of 1978, the buoy tender *Red Beech* broke forty-eight miles of ice in the Hudson River from West Point to Silver Point, New York.[49] In 1996, Coast Guard units responded to the crash of TWA Flight 800 off the Rockaways, unfortunately to no avail.[50]

In 1981 I reported back to Governors Island as a warrant officer. I was standing...near the ferry terminal. It was a gorgeous morning and the New York City skyline was just *sparkling!* Ships were going by and seaplanes were taking off....For me, it was as if they were welcoming me home to a very special place.

("FROM SCARY TO HAPPY TO STRANDED ON GI," *THE COAST GUARD RESERVIST*, DECEMBER 1997, 12, EMPHASIS IN ORIGINAL.)

The largest command on the island was the Coast Guard Training Center. It opened in Liggett Hall in October 1967, having moved there from Groton, Connecticut, over the objections of Senator Abraham Ribicoff, who was loathe to lose the center's economic benefits to his neighbor New York. Just as the army had trained troops to march and carry arms, for the next twenty years the Coast Guard would train the specialists needed to run the ships, the advanced technological systems, and the computers that are its hallmarks.

In October 1970, I graduated from SK Class "A" School on Governors Island. I was one of two African Americans graduating. GI [Governors Island] was a place that captured the imagination....As you fell into ranks on the parade grounds outside the huge archway, you wondered of medieval times.

(SKC KENNETH G. MCGRUDER SR., U.S. COAST GUARD, RET., "THE WHITE HATS CLUB," *THE COAST GUARD RESERVIST* [DECEMBER 1997], 8.)

However, a reminiscence from a Coastie (the nickname given to a low-ranking Coast Guard member) indicates that much of the equipment the army had left behind was never upgraded and was fairly outdated when Governors Island was transferred. The Coastie wrote in 2004, "Back in 1968 when I went to the Radioman School, we learned Morse Code, transmitter and receiver use and repair...and typing of course on manual typewriters (old Olivetti and Remingtons as I remember). Messages continued to be sent from the island in Morse Code until 1995," a year before the base closed.[51]

The Coast Guard replaced the army's Fort Jay post with Support Center New York, landlord of the world's largest Coast Guard facility. The center was involved with neither training nor waterway search and protection;

TWO HIGH-ENDURANCE CUTTERS *are berthed at Yankee Pier in the early 1970s, seemingly at the base of the partially completed World Trade Center, n.d., unknown photographer. Courtesy of U.S. Coast Guard Historian's Office, Washington, D.C.*

RADIO STATION, *Governors Island, n.d., unknown photographer. This photograph is probably vintage army. Courtesy of U.S. Coast Guard Historian's Office, Washington, D.C.*

GOVERNORS ISLAND'S DISASTER RESPONSE UNIT *prepares to deal with harbor oil spills, ca. 1981, unknown photographer. Courtesy of U.S. Coast Guard Historian's Office, Washington, D.C.*

Our only residents now are the Canada Geese that have taken over the baseball fields, playgrounds, and golf course. Hopefully something will happen soon to get people back out here.

(LIEUTENANT WILL AGEN, HEAD OF THE U.S. COAST GUARD CARETAKER DETACHMENT, SEPTEMBER 30, 1997, IN "LOOKING AHEAD...," *THE COAST GUARD RESERVIST*, DECEMBER 1997, 20.)

instead, it had charge of the common facilities that army ordnance and quartermasters had run in the past, plus the medical facilities and public works. It also maintained the residential and administrative structures, open and recreational spaces, stores, and transportation systems. The center's commanding officer had such a pivotal role in the island's life that he was known as the "mayor of Governors Island."

Perhaps the role most favored by the Coast Guard and most enjoyed by its residents during its thirty-year tenure on Governors Island was that of host to famous events. Operation Sail 1976, celebrating the nation's bicentennial, was the first showcase. Ten years later the island hosted President Ronald Reagan, who lit the torch of the Statue of Liberty during its centennial celebration.

Some of these "famous events" were political. Former residents fondly remember President Reagan using the Admiral's House in 1988 for a summit meeting with Mikhail Gorbachev. Five years later Jean Bertrand Aristide, the ousted president of Haiti, met on the island with State Department officials to discuss his return to power. And in 1995, the Coast Guard greeted King Harald and Queen Sonja of Norway with a parade similar to one the army had given the king's parents in 1909. Other events recognized wartime service. In 1991, troops from the Gulf War were mustered out and met their families on the island, celebrating with baked goods, barbecues, and fireworks.

And then came the final closing ceremonies on September 27, 1997. Much like the army, the Coast Guard had to respond to a presidential mandate to identify recurrent savings: looking at a $30 million annual tab for the Coast Guard center, military officials deemed it wise to move out. The disestablishment ceremonies, with two hundred onlookers, were "low key but nostalgic."[52] Nearly two and a half centuries of military rule on Governors Island had come to an end.

ISLAND HIGHLIGHTS *Early Island Engineers*

"Delivered to the Comm" in Chief...a plan of Governors Island to a large scale with a fair draught of my design the whole approved by the General and received his orders to make an estimate to accompany my design.[1]

Two men, John Montresor and Jonathan Williams, were the earliest architects of Governors Island. Both engineers—one British, the other a European-trained American—were highly respected in their time, and both had a hand in the design of Fort Jay. Williams was fortunate enough to oversee the inland fort's construction as well as the design and implementation of the island's most visible and photographed structure, Castle Williams.

John Montresor, born in Gibraltar in 1763, was an engineer and officer for the British. His work included the earliest designs that have been found to date for fortifications on Governors Island. Montresor accompanied his father, James Gabriel Montresor (1702–76), to America in 1754. Father and son initially surveyed outposts for the British, who were then engaged in battles against the French and their Indian sympathizers. The British goal was to acquire New France, the land extending from west of the Allegheny Mountains to the Mississippi River. The Montresors were working in the vicinity of Fort Duquesne near Pittsburgh when the first battle of the French and Indian War erupted in 1754.

That same year, the British commissioned John Montresor to be chief engineer in the American colonies. In this role, he focused on three important military areas along the east coast: Boston, Philadelphia, and New York. While in New York, Montresor became a landowner; in 1772 he purchased an island in the East River off Manhattan, known as Montresor's Island, where he lived with his New York–born wife, Frances Tucker, and their family. Although Montresor owned the property until the British evacuation in 1783, his home was burned to the ground during the Revolutionary War. Jonathan Randall purchased this island in 1784, giving it his name, still in use today.[2]

In the eleven years between 1755 and 1766 before moving to New York, Montresor produced designs for many of the colonies' coastal fortifications–designs that were used by both the British and the Americans. Among these drawings, at least two plans for Governors Island have survived; however, no remnants of the depicted battlements have been found in the island. The challenge of constructing Governors Island's principal edifices would fall to Jonathan Williams forty years later.

Despite a stormy personal history related to his time on the island, between 1806 and 1812 Jonathan Williams was responsible for completing a regimental headquarters and bastion that had been constructed in fits and starts since before the Revolutionary War. Using techniques learned abroad, he also designed and supervised the construction of the castle named after him, the first casemated battery to be built in America.

Born in Boston in 1750, Williams was a grandnephew of Benjamin Franklin. Under Franklin's aegis, Williams spent most of the years between 1750 and 1785 in England and France. There he learned diplomacy and became an agent for U.S. markets abroad. In France, a country known for its bastions, Williams also studied military science, specializing in fortifications. This knowledge, coupled with his scientific publications, soon catapulted him to the top of the nascent engineering establishment in the United States.

Williams was in the sights of several presidents. In February 1801, John Adams appointed him to be a major of the Second Regiment of Artillerists and Engineers. Absent formal schools, this regiment was where engineering was taught (mostly by practice) in the field for the building of forts and roads and for the calming of rivers. Williams also came to the attention of Thomas Jefferson, who appointed him the following December to be the inspector of fortifications. He was stationed at an army post at West Point, where he taught engineering to the soldiers. When Jefferson established the nation's first military academy at West Point in 1802, he

COLONEL JOHN MONTRESOR, *ca. 1771, John Singleton Copley. Photograph of painting, 2001. Courtesy of Founders Society Purchase, Gibbs-Williams Fund, Detroit Institute of Arts.*

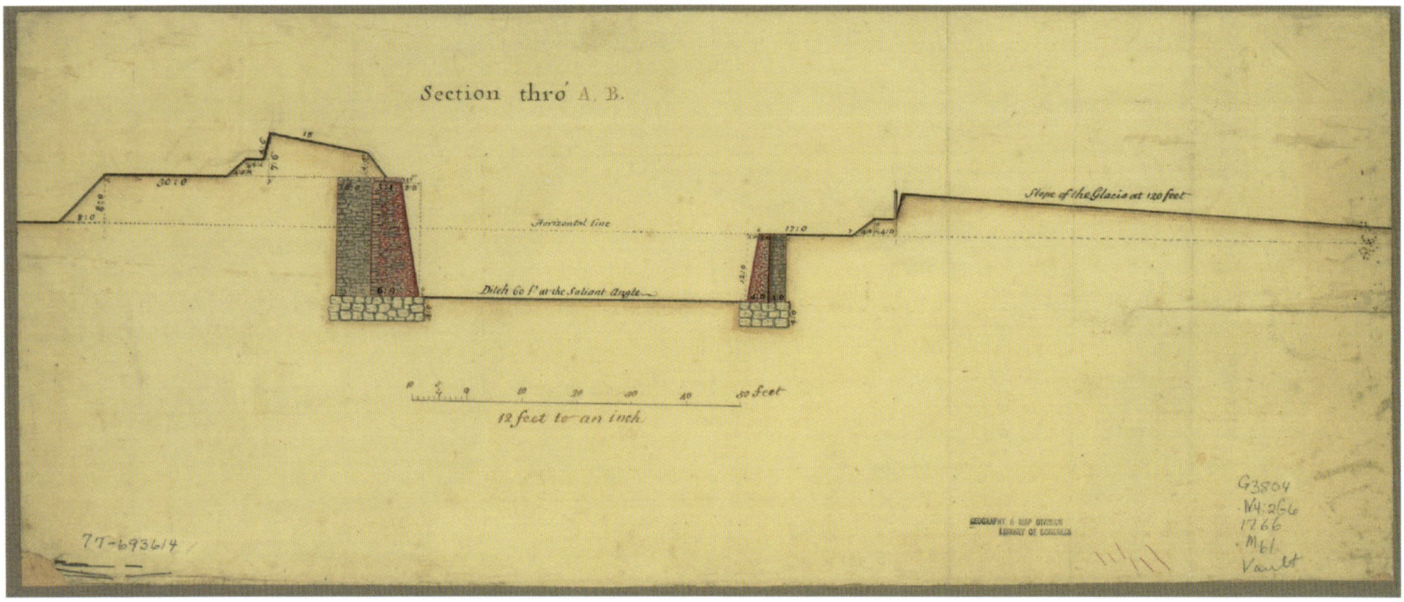

DESIGNS FOR FORTIFYING *Governors Island near New York, ca. 1766, John Montresor. Plan elevation. Courtesy of Geography and Map Room, Library of Congress, Washington, D.C.*

appointed Williams as its first superintendent. Engineering finally became a recognized subject.

That same year Williams was also appointed to head the newly created Army Corps of Engineers, singling out that cadre of soldiers from the artillerists. In 1806, he was back in charge of the U.S. Military Academy, but he also brought his engineering talent to New York and Governors Island. Fort Jay, Castle Clinton, and the castle's twin–temporarily named the "Tower"–rose in the harbor over the next four years. In 1810, the latter structure was renamed Castle Williams.

In hindsight, Jonathan Williams's personal glory from the design and construction of Castle Williams was short-lived. By 1812, artillery companies made up half of the Governors Island garrison.[3] The War Department, in recognition of his service, assigned Williams–who was still a member of the Army Corps of Engineers–to command the regiment. But long-standing notions of military hierarchy crippled his commands. Disaffection and a potential intramural dispute ensued, and in less than a month Williams resigned his commission in the army. Two years later he was elected to Congress from Philadelphia, but he died before he could take his seat.[4]

ISLAND HIGHLIGHTS *Island Vessel*

The cutter Mahoning, *equipped with sonar, began covering a five-square-mile area between Brookhaven, L.I. and Old Saybrook, Conn., where it is believed that the pleasure boat, the* Karen E., *and a barge under tow by a tugboat collided on the night of August 9 [1981].*[1]

Underwater searcher, firefighter, garbage hauler, narc, and escort, the Coast Guard cutter *Mahoning* plied her many trades from her home base on Governors Island from the 1960s to 1984. Her career was illustrious and distinguished. She hobnobbed with a queen and helped to clean up a 2.5-million-gallon oil spill. She conveyed U.S. Customs inspectors to and from passenger liners that were awaiting entry into New York and occasionally helped the *Wire* and *Red Beech* keep the Hudson River free of winter ice. For her work, the

ANTHONY RAVEILLE MURAL, *November 1944, U.S. Army Signal Corps. This mural, painted in the 1930s, hung in the Officers' Club. It shows Jonathan Williams (hands behind his back) standing on a hill overlooking the castle named after him. Courtesy of Garret Roosma.*

Mahoning was awarded four Coast Guard unit commendations and two National Defense Service medals, and received sundry other recognition.[2]

The *Mahoning*'s early history was uneventful. She was built in Mississippi at the Gulfport Works in 1938 at a cost of $309,000 and launched at Port Arthur, Texas, in August 1939. According to the Coast Guard Historian's Office, she was one of four tugs (the terms *cutter* and *tug* are used interchangeably for this type of vessel) built for the Coast Guard at that time. Weighing in at 328 tons, she was 110 feet long–half a block–and more than 26 feet at her widest point. When under way, she could travel as fast as twelve knots and could cover a distance of four thousand miles.

THE *MAHONING* *cutting ice in the Hudson River, n.d., unknown photographer. Courtesy of U.S. Coast Guard Historian's Office, Washington, D.C.*

On board, the cutter had twenty in personnel. The crew's quarters, with multiple berths, were on the "port side facing the bow...one ladder down."[3] Captains and other officers were on the starboard side. There was also space in the stern for such passengers as divers and inspections officers. The *Mahoning*'s ice-breaking bow was capable of plowing through three-foot-thick ice, and when called upon, her two fire monitors produced approximately two thousand gallons of water a minute.[4] She also packed an electronic radar device that was crucial for search-and-rescue operations.

When christened in 1939, she was named after a vessel built for the U.S. Revenue Service in 1863 that had patrolled the East Coast for more than fifty years. The Delaware word *mahoning* means "at the salt lick" and referred to a river where the tribe lived near what became Youngstown, Ohio.[5] From Gulfport, the new *Mahoning* sailed immediately to New York, where she was stationed first at Staten Island and, after the Coast Guard moved in, at Governors Island.

Her time at the island was eventful, to say the least. The bicentennial in July 1976 gave the *Mahoning* the opportunity to be a first-class escort ship. She accompanied many of the tall ships in the Operation Sail parade in New York Harbor. That same month, she escorted Her Majesty's yacht *Britannia* with none other than Queen Elizabeth II aboard.

But not all the *Mahoning*'s service was glamorous. Fighting dangerous fires and an illegal narcotics trade was an important part of her mission. In the 1970s, she helped combat a mas-

HOLIDAY GREETINGS CARD, *n.d., James Melnick. Courtesy of James Melnick.*

sive fire caused by an oil terminal explosion near the Gowanus Canal in Brooklyn. In another operation, she doused a fire in a tugboat that was towing an empty naphtha barge, thus avoiding an imminent explosion (at risk on the neighboring shore was Tarrytown).

Beginning in 1980, the *Mahoning* patrolled the eastern coastline from New Jersey to southern New England seeking vessels with hidden caches of marijuana, heroin, and other controlled substances aboard. In 1981, however, the cutter performed a search far different from her narcotics runs. With sonar that, according to the *New York Times,* "would pick up rocks, old cars, anything," she was assigned the task of locating a sunken cabin cruiser, the *Karen E.* The results of the search were crucial to a lawsuit alleging misconduct on the part of a prominent towing company. Aboard the *Mahoning* were four Coast Guard divers who were prepared to look for scrape marks or other evidence of how and why the recreational boat had sunk, as well as to recover three of the five bodies lost in the wreck. From dawn to dusk for two weeks during a foggy September in 1981, the cutter meticulously scanned a five-mile-long, one-mile-wide area in Long Island Sound. The records do not indicate whether the yacht was found, but because of the legal implications, the operation was fairly unique for the Coast Guard officers involved.[6]

MAHONING, *1939–80, n.d., unknown designer. U.S. Coast Guard patch.*

Probably the most noxious job for the *Mahoning* came during New York City's 1979 tugboat strike. Three months' worth of garbage piled up at piers in Brooklyn and Manhattan, with no vessels to move it to the Fresh Kills landfill on Staten Island. A health emergency was in the works. To the rescue came the tug. She performed yeoman service, hauling a string of eighty-eight barges to the landfill, thirty-six of them loaded with city refuse.

On October 1, 1984, the Coast Guard decommissioned the forty-six-year-old *Mahoning.* Attending the ceremony was her last commanding officer, Chief Warrant Office 3 Craig A. Reynolds.

HOSPITAL STEWARD *in dress uniform, n.d., unknown photographer. The steward's green and yellow half-chevron is visible on his sleeve. Hospital stewards were the only enlisted men who wore the metallic wreath and the letters "U.S." on the front of their Jeff Davis (Hardee) hats. Courtesy of USA Quartermaster Museum, Fort Lee, Va.*

Chapter Two

HOSPITAL CARE
From Rudimentary to Necessary

Fort Columbus, New York Harbor, 1868. Mean strength: 584.41; Number taken sick: 1,428; Typhoid fever: 1; Malarial fevers: 44; Diarrhea and dysentery: 369; Venereal diseases: 143; Rheumatism: 65; Phthisis (pulmonary tuberculosis): 4; Catarrhal affections: 171; Number of deaths: 2.[1]

From the eighteenth century up to World War I, diseases rather than wounds were the main cause of death in the U.S. Army.[2] It's no wonder, then, that Governors Island–a post that was never actively in the line of fire–has a long history of providing medical care to army (and later Coast Guard) personnel. This care was provided in very rudimentary facilities in the eighteenth century. Beginning in 1839, dysentery, malaria, cholera, yellow fever, venereal diseases, and influenza were among the illnesses treated in a free-standing "post hospital." War wounds were added a century later to the list of cases treated in a "regional hospital" on the island that was designed by the architectural firm of McKim, Mead & White. Although patients came from near and far, Governors Island was never a pioneer in hospital design or medical treatment. Over the years, however, this hospital was where babies were born, appendixes were removed, and induction and discharge physicals were performed in structures that were known only by the size of the area they served. At the time of the island's closure in 1998, only a brand-new dispensary remained as a memory of the island's medical history.

BEGINNINGS, 1783–1832

THE FIRST INKLING OF A MEDICAL FACILITY on Governors Island was found in the inventory of structures that the British submitted to the New York State governor when they left the island in 1783 at the end of the Revolutionary War. Besides mentioning a hospital, this bare-bones list indicated the hierarchical order of living quarters that were reinforced in each new building period: "A Captain's barracks, kitchen and cellar and well; a Lieutenant's barracks and kitchen; a gardener's house, guard house, and summer house; a wharf; well with pump; cattle barn; a convalescent's hospital and a hospital kitchen and well."[3] Although this inventory and existing letters do not provide a physical description of the facility, they do indicate that the hospital was run by the navy and probably served British soldiers and sailors. Shortly after the British had shored up Fort Jay with the help of Loyalist New Yorkers, Major General Pattison wrote to an admiral that he was "justly sensible of his kind disposition to contribute to the Comfort of the Army and...the Sick of the Troops will be removed to Governor's Island tomorrow."[4] The sick troops came from British vessels that surrounded the island, as well as from the mainland city. But four years later the British were no longer receiving care at Governors Island. In 1783, naval captain James Duncan wrote to George Clinton, governor of New York: "Having received orders...to withdraw the Guard together with the whole Naval Hospital from this Island...at the hour of eleven A.M. this day [both] will be withdrawn."[5] It took fifty years for another hospital to appear on the island.

Nevertheless, medical care continued to be provided for the military, this time by the U.S. Army. The ratification of the Constitution in 1788 allowed for the creation of a military force. Understanding that an army required medical support, ensuing congressional legislation created the Medical Department. This organization was headed by the surgeon general in Washington, D.C., who had the power to assign doctors and staff to army hospitals, frontier posts, and coastal fortifications. Thus began the practice of assigning one surgeon and two surgeon's mates to each regiment. In the case of Governors Island, one surgeon was assigned to the garrison sent to reconstruct Fort Jay in 1796.

From the outset, medical care went beyond the island's boundaries. The surgeon, who probably practiced in a tent, treated sick and wounded soldiers from the post and from a larger population of troops sent in from nearby military installations in Staten Island, Brooklyn, and Queens.[6] He was also charged with preventing disease by ensuring that the well water was uncontaminated and the food was properly cooked. The surgeon was allowed, but not encouraged, to send intractable cases to a "general hospital," or a formal, multibed facility (such as the Smallpox Hospital on Montresor's Island in Manhattan) that treated contagious and chronic illnesses, severe wounds, and overflow cases from local army posts.

A surgeon's mate finally arrived on Governors Island in the spring of 1802. He was a full-fledged physician whose duties included accompanying the surgeon on visits to patients, carrying out the surgeon's prescriptions, dressing wounds, and enforcing discipline. In fact, this mate probably replaced the original surgeon. However, a court-martial about eight years later revealed that the mate lived and practiced medicine in Manhattan and was not readily available to the garrison on Governors Island.[7] This case and others on various army posts prompted new legislation requiring garrison physicians to live and practice at their posts full-time.

By 1815, the construction of Castle Williams was complete, and the casemates (the gun portals in the walls of the castle) of the upper two floors housed enlisted men. Absent an officially sanctioned hospital building on the island, several of the damp casemates on the second tier were used for the sick. Insalubrious for healthy soldiers, these spaces were unbearable for the sick because the conditions tended to spread disease rather than provide sanctuary for rest and recovery of health.[8] It is likely, therefore, that more patients were transferred elsewhere. A "four-oared green boat" had even been reserved for taking patients to the "Gen. Hospital" located on the mainland.[9]

THE FIRST HOSPITAL, 1832–1842

IT IS POSSIBLE THAT AN OUTBREAK of cholera hastened the arrival of a proper hospital on the island. On June 6, 1832, the disease appeared in Montreal; eight days later it had reached upper New York State. On June 26, an Irish immigrant family, newly arrived in Manhattan via Montreal, became ill. By August, the disease had disappeared, but in less than three months it had caused more than three thousand deaths in New York City.[10] Although the epidemic is known to have spread to Governors Island, the number of people infected there is unknown. Conditions on the island surely contributed to its presence: unfettered swine used as the only means of "garbage removal," insect-breeding cisterns, animals watering at the drinking well, privies flushed by the tides, washing stations in the river, and Irish maids and laundresses going back and forth from the island to their families in city tenements were all factors in the epidemic.

From 1832 to 1866, there were three cholera outbreaks. In the fall of 1848, cholera reappeared on Governors Island and other New York Harbor posts. This time the disease killed twenty-nine of the seventy-nine people who contracted it on the posts. In 1866, it again took its toll from the garrison, for the last time, though.

In 1839, when a hospital building was finally in the works on Governors Island, the combination of a war in Florida and contemporary medical practices immediately overtaxed the island's first formal medical facility. When Florida became a territory in 1821 after its purchase from Spain, its seven thousand Seminoles were considered a handicap to its development. In 1830, Congress passed the Indian Removal Act and negotiations began with the Seminoles to leave Florida. A treaty ensued in 1832, and the Seminole chiefs agreed to move to land west of the Mississippi River. Three years later, when U.S. troops arrived in Florida to enforce the treaty, the Seminoles rebelled, beginning what is known as the Second Seminole War. From 1835 to 1842, U.S. Army troops fought in Florida, and more than fifteen hundred soldiers and civilians died.

In theory, the newly constructed "general hospitals" in the South should have kept patients close to the battlegrounds during the Seminole War, but those hospitals were actually already inundated with patients who had dysentery and recurrent fever. Doctors believed that a change of climate would benefit these patients and consequently evacuated many of them to the cooler North, specifically Fort Jay and Fort Hamilton.[11]

In June 1839, fifty-seven patients arrived in Fort Jay from Florida duty. In the absence of available records, we can assume that they were put up wherever space could be found; a single room in a post building, casemates in Castle Williams, and even tents probably served as hospital wards. As would be the case with most new construction on Governors Island and on army posts in general, a congressional appropriation–this time for upgrading the standards of various post hospitals scattered about the country–finally arrived for Governors Island.[12] But by this time it was too late for the Seminole War patients, who were probably shipped back to battle before the new hospital could receive them.

In June 1839, the new post hospital was finally under construction on the south edge of Nolan Park, sixty yards north of the South Battery. The task of designing the two-story structure probably fell to the post quartermaster, given that standardized plans for army medical buildings came later.[13] He also contracted local mason Stanley Pitcher and local carpenters A. Mackay, Joseph F. Donnel, and John P. Angovino to supply materials and build the hospital. Well out of any line of fire and, more important, far enough away from residential quarters and administrative buildings, the hospital was sited to protect the officers from contagion and unpleasant odors. Soldiers and support staff were not as well protected. If a patient was healthy enough to look out of the ill-ventilated ward, he would have seen a long row of one-story wooden houses known as Rotten Row. These houses began just north of the hospital and

MAP OF GOVERNORS ISLAND, *1859, J. G. Barnard. RG 77 Fortification File, 077-HMF-Drawer 037-Sheet 15. Courtesy of National Archives Architectural and Cartographic Branch, College Park, Md.*

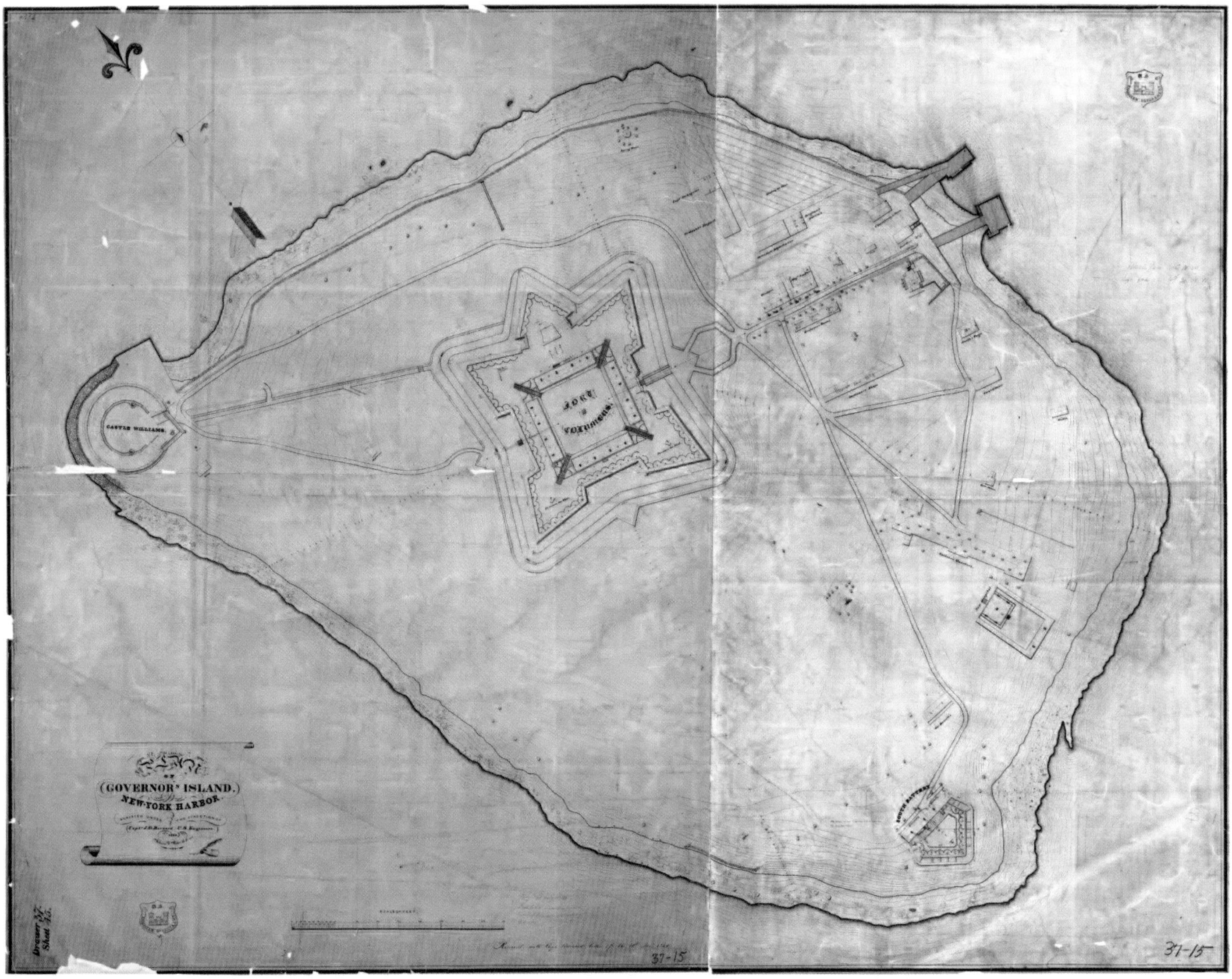

stretched westward to the area that years later became Colonel's Row. These primitive structures were possibly first used by the builders of Fort Jay and later sheltered the sutler, his store, and soldiers and their families.[14]

In the fall of 1839, Dr. Joseph P. Russell, the first known hospital chief on Governors Island, wrote to the U.S. surgeon general expressing his pleasure that the hospital was nearing completion and saying that he hoped to furnish it with new, sturdier, lice-free iron bedsteads commissioned by the secretary of war.[15] Russell's patients included officers and soldiers from the regiment as well as local recruits and men from the Seminole War. Russell also cared for post families, even though it was against military policy.

Two rectangular wards, each forty-eight by twenty feet, were separated by a central hallway on the first floor and three smaller wards sat on the second floor. Approximately sixty patients lay in iron or wooden beds in these wards. (Records do not indicate the hospital's capacity. This "sixty patient" figure is therefore derived by allotting sixty square feet per bed, the number considered to be beneficial to health, as indicated in later reports.) The federal government required the beds to have straw mattresses because of the difficulty in cleaning feather beds. The offices, kitchen, storerooms, dispensary, and stewards' quarters were in the basement. The only bathroom in the building was on the second floor, and there is no mention of hot water or an operating room. A small one-story structure in the rear of the hospital had rooms for the hospital matrons and the "dead house," or morgue.[16]

At the time the hospital on Governors Island opened, it was modestly staffed, probably consisting of two privates serving as ward master and steward, one nurse for every ten patients, a matron for every twenty patients, and at least one female attendant. The ward master was responsible for the cleanliness of the patients and the wards, as well as for care of the chamberpots. Congressional legislation set the pay rates for the hospital staff, although the ward master received his regular army pay. The matron, who oversaw cooking, nursing, washing, and cleaning, earned $5 a month, and the attendant, who was assigned the menial tasks of washing the bunks, floors, bedding, and cooking utensils, earned no more than $6 a month, plus one ration a day.[17]

The new hospital immediately became a nexus for training stewards for the army. The hospital steward had a position of responsibility, reflected in a salary of $10 to $16 a month in the 1840s and rising to $30 a month in the Civil War. The steward was in charge of all hospital provisions, including food, furniture, and utensils, and the ward master reported to him. Because most stewards had limited medical backgrounds, in 1840 the U.S. surgeon general attempted to professionalize them by establishing a training school on Governors Island. Little is known about the classes except that an assistant surgeon trained the men and that within six months of the school's establishment, twenty had graduated. Upon request, the stewards were sent to aid surgeons in far-flung posts in the West and along the Canadian border.

But Commanding General of the Army Winfield Scott, who had previously served on Governors Island as top military commander of the East, closed the school. He insisted that the stewards remain with their regiments instead of being sent wherever they were needed—which ironically led to the extraordinarily long and distinguished service of steward David Robertson on Governors Island. Although very little personal information about Robertson exists, the length of his service makes him memorable. Born in Edinburgh, he was assigned to the Hospital Corps on Governors Island in 1854 at the age of twenty-one and remained there for fifty-nine years.[18] Including the required business duties, he also made rounds, dressed wounds, and dispensed medication as the putative assistant surgeon. He was a much-beloved man who cared for soldiers and prisoners through cholera, measles, and yellow fever epidemics, and nursed them through wounds acquired in the Civil and Cuban Wars. Roberts and his wife, Mary Moore, the daughter of bandmaster Michael Moore, became pillars of the island community, were active in the church, and had a splendid garden.[19]

Joseph Russell, post surgeon on the island in the 1830s and 1840s, was an experienced doctor. His wages—which included eight rations and forage for three horses—were equivalent to an army major's, even though he had no rank. Among his nonmedical duties, Russell served as the "weatherman": like doctors at many army posts, he was charged by the surgeon general to collect and report on meteorological data. What better place to gather this information than an island in the middle of New York Harbor? At the beginning of the 1840s, Russell kept a barometer, thermometer, rain gauge, and wet bulb in his black bag to record sudden changes in temperature, barometric levels in a storm, and the amount of rain in a given period. He, or an assistant (foreshadowing the twentieth-century work of Governors Island Boy Scout

Governors Island Meteorological Report

MONTH	1870–71 TEMPERATURE Mean	Max	Min	Rainfall in Inches
July	76.03	93	60	3.93
Aug	74.96	90	62	3.98
Sept	68.16	82	56	1.79
Oct	57.53	74	37	5.88
Nov	45.14	63	30	2.97
Dec	34.67	56	10	1.97
Jan	28.41	49	4	2.76
Feb	29.43	50	-3	3.95
Mar	42.74	65	32	5.39
Apr	51.80	77	35	2.66
May	59.78	87	45	3.83
Jun	68.31	87	58	6.25

(SURGEON J. J. MILHAU, UNITED STATES ARMY, "FORT COLUMBUS, GOVERNORS ISLAND, NEW YORK HARBOR," DESCRIPTIONS OF MILITARY POSTS, IN *SURGEON GENERAL'S REPORT* [WASHINGTON, D.C.: U.S. GOVERNMENT PRINTING OFFICE, 1874], 19.)

Troop 100 and the National Weather Service), also monitored cloud formations, direction and force of the winds, and the passage of flocks of migratory birds.[20]

The Medical Department's regulations assured Russell and his assistant assigned quarters on the post, perhaps near the arsenal or in Rotten Row, but this was no guarantee of an available–or even an acceptable–room. On a busy post, it was nearly impossible to keep rooms empty. One's rank also affected the choice and quality of domicile. Upon return from service in Florida a year before the new hospital opened, Russell discovered that a major from the Corps of Engineers had appropriated his quarters. He subsequently found an alternate space, but it was already occupied by a post clerk. Because Russell lacked a formal rank, it took an appeal to the secretary of war to allow him to bump the clerk.[21]

No sooner was the new hospital opened in early 1840 than it was crammed to capacity with sick troops arriving from duty in the Second Seminole War. In addition to the patients already on the island at the time, another three to four dozen men arrived from Florida, causing Russell to question the army's recommended mode of healing. Removing invalids from a warm climate to a cold one was "extremely injudicious and ill advised," he wrote to the surgeon general. After a difficult journey by water, the men arriving at Fort Jay presented "a most pitiable spectacle, were generally in a very filthy and lousy condition, two of them had involuntary and unconscious discharges and were literally wallowing in their excrement."[22]

The surgeon general's rules added the requirement that, besides treating the sick, post surgeons conduct preinduction and discharge physicals, which meant that Russell examined new recruits who were training at the base on Governors Island for active duty in the Seminole War.[23] He was justifiably concerned that these new soldiers would be adversely affected by the condition of the patients around them, whose illnesses included gonorrhea, syphilis, skin infections, malaria, scabies, respiratory problems, scurvy, and rheumatism. Moreover, the stream of Florida invalids continued to flow in, seventy-three in June 1841 and fifty-six only a month later, which probably disheartened the new recruits about their upcoming service in the Florida Everglades.

YELLOW FEVER AND MEASLES, 1856–1874

IN JULY 1856, YELLOW FEVER BROKE OUT on the southern part of the island that bordered Buttermilk Channel. It afflicted the young and working-class population: teenage soldiers living in the South Battery who had enlisted in the Army Band School to learn music and civilian men and women working in the nearby cookhouse. Officers and soldiers living in Fort Jay and Castle Clinton some distance away from the shore were not affected. Within days, ten had died, and thirty-four were ill, twenty-four of whom were hospitalized. Knowing no other etiology, officials blamed the cause of the contagion on contaminated mattresses that had washed up on the unprotected riverbank.

In 1861, the Governors Island medical staff and hospital were called upon to meet the exi-

NEW HOSPITAL, *September 28, 1864, unknown photographer. The "General" Hospital constructed in 1862 was able to hold ninety-six patients. Courtesy of Still Pictures Branch, National Archives, College Park, Md.*

gencies of another armed conflict, the Civil War. Between 1861 and 1865, thousands of Confederate prisoners of war were incarcerated on the island for months at a time, pending shipment to longer-stay facilities farther north. Accommodating them engendered new medical problems and overtaxed the modest post hospital, which had originally been designed to serve only the resident regiment.

A deluge of troops—ten times the size of the consignments during the Second Seminole War—swelled the ranks at Governors Island beyond capacity in 1861. This time, nearly seven hundred men arrived at once, including entire companies of Confederate officers and soldiers who had been captured by the Union army in North Carolina and Georgia. The diary of Lieutenant Thomas Sparrow, a prisoner of war from North Carolina, gives an account of the conditions. According to Sparrow, the officer cadres were crowded into a section of Fort Jay, and the six-hundred-odd enlisted men were crammed into the casemates on the top two floors of Castle Williams.[24]

A combination of cramped conditions, the change of climate from hot to cold, and—for those from the backwoods—a lack of prior exposure to certain childhood diseases, quickly led to outbreaks of respiratory infections and measles among the prisoners. Not daring to risk the spread of measles to the post, hospital staff confined contagious officers to their rooms in Fort Jay. Those prisoners who could be accommodated were treated in the twenty-year-old post hospital. As in the past, a makeshift hospital was set up for the overflow in a few of the casemates in the castle, where mosquitoes coming through unscreened windows added to the sick prisoners' discomfort.

William J. Sloan, Governors Island's hospital surgeon, complained repeatedly to Washington of the crowding, illness, and unhealthy living conditions among the prisoner population that by then had swollen to 707. "There are no conveniences for cooking," Sloan wrote, "except in the open air, no means of heating the lower (second) tier of gun rooms and no privies within the area."[25]

By 1862, spurred on by both the lamentable deficiencies reported by Dr.

Of six hundred & fifteen men, prisoners in castle Williams, one hundred, more than one fifth, are sick. Two of the casemates on the third floor, used as sick wards, are filled....Some few have been taken to the Post Hospital on another part of the island....I took a walk with Coln. Martin this morning through the lower casemates. The sick were lying on the floor, in the corners, in every stage of the measles. Cheerless & comfortless enough.

(THOMAS SPARROW COLLECTION, NO. 1878, FOLDER 7, VOL. 1, SEPTEMBER 30, 1861, 201, TRANSCRIBED BY ALEX CHRISTOPHER MEEKINS, UNIVERSITY OF NORTH CAROLINA—CHAPEL HILL SOUTHERN HISTORICAL COLLECTION.)

THE RENAMED "POST" HOSPITAL ADDITION, *ca. 1874, unknown photographer. The addition was constructed by soldiers under the supervision of Assistant Surgeon A. H. Hoff. Courtesy of Still Pictures Branch, National Archives, College Park, Md.*

Sloan and the need to serve the growing New York City–area population of Union war casualties and Confederate prisoners, a new hospital facility was finally added, several feet west of the old one.[26] Coming twenty-three years after the original structure was built, the new building was promoted to the category of "general hospital," giving formal recognition to the fact that an island medical facility had long served both the post and the larger army population outside. The hospital included a few modern conveniences, notably an operating room for the surgeon and four large wards, now on a single floor, arranged in a horseshoe pattern that was becoming common for military hospital design. The wards (two each, measuring fifty-seven by twenty-four feet and seventy-eight by twenty-four feet, respectively) were double the size of those in the 1840 hospital, capable of handling a total of ninety-six patients, and had openings in the ceilings for ventilation. Patients in at least one of the wards now had direct access to the only washroom, which was supplied with hot water from a basement laundry. On sunny days, a patient might recuperate on a small veranda and view the grassy courtyard.[27]

The postwar years provided a respite for the medical staff, but in August 1870 what appears to have been yellow fever struck the island again, sorely testing the hospital complex. This time, hierarchical living spaces were no protection. From August 16 to October 25, between 105 and 157 cases were recorded, with 50 deaths.[28] They included enlisted men, recruits, corporals, privates, and a sergeant major; musicians, carpenters, a gardener, and a hospital matron; and a three-year-old boy and girl. Neither rank nor age made an apparent difference in who lived and who died, but ethnicity or geographic roots might have. The "Sick Reports" prepared by the post surgeon for the surgeon general listed whites and blacks separately for the first time and show that the latter were not affected by the disease.[29]

The cause of yellow fever epidemics was still a matter of speculation, and the solution at the time was to burn any infected material. Even more radical–and also wrong–was the decision a year later to tear down the wooden houses adjoining the hospital on Rotten Row that had been used for patient overflow. Not until three decades later would mosquito eradication and inoculation become the recognized cure for yellow fever.

THE POWDER MAGAZINE, *n.d., unknown photographer. The magazine was located behind the hospital. Courtesy of Still Pictures Branch, National Archives, College Park, Md.*

Twelve years after opening as a general hospital, the medical complex on Governors Island reverted back to a post hospital, probably because it was no longer needed to serve a large off-island population. Even so and in keeping with contemporary military design, the army created a fenced complex in which two new wings were constructed, some material and space in the original two hospitals were recycled, and a barn and stable were built. Like cholera in the 1830s, the yellow fever epidemic in 1870 perhaps caused the army to recognize the need to revamp the hospital. The patient numbers also lent support for expansion: in 1871–72, the hospital treated roughly 650 officers and enlisted men. A year later, with the addition on the island of the new home for the Department of the East, that number rose by 8 percent. Ironically, the hospital patient count grew in relation to the very unit that vied with it for additional space: the purely administrative Department of the East required additional office, residential, and interior recreational rooms.

In 1874, the solution to overcrowded and less-than-ideal conditions for patients, medical personnel, and army administrative staff was to revamp the original 1840 hospital into an administration building. It was used to house visiting medical officers and treat special cases. The basement was retrofitted to accommodate the surgeon's office, a dispensary, and the hospital kitchen and mess hall. In an odd juxtaposition that illustrates just how crowded the entire island had become, one of the old wards became the Catholic chapel, and the other ward adjoining it was used for courts-martial and lectures. A third ward was recycled into an examining room for recruits during the day and then was used at night for more frivolous matters, including balls and concerts.

The 1840 and 1862 wards were replaced by two long wings, attached to the rear of the administration building, which stretched nearly to the banks of Buttermilk Channel. Two water closets and the "dead house" sat in close proximity to the seawall. Verandas, now an essential element of military hospital design, covered three sides of the horseshoe layout. Inside ventilation and plumbing were vastly improved, with two stoves heating each

Each ward proper is 77 by 24 feet, with twelve full-sized windows, admitting favorable location for 24 beds; but it is the intention to limit the number of patients to twenty, so that each may enjoy an air-space of over 1,100 cubic feet and an area of 92 [square] feet. Each ward is heated by two stoves....In the west ward there is, in addition, a smoking room. The water closets and lavatories are in a projection of 9 by 8 feet at the southern end [facing Buttermilk Channel].... Drain pipes connect the water closets and privies with tide water....Quarters for the steward and for the two matrons have been very comfortably fitted up in a building which formed part of the old [1862] Hospital.

(SURGEON J. J. MILHAU, UNITED STATES ARMY, "FORT COLUMBUS, GOVERNOR'S ISLAND, NEW YORK HARBOR," DESCRIPTIONS OF MILITARY POSTS, IN *SURGEON GENERAL'S REPORT* [WASHINGTON, D.C.: U.S. GOVERNMENT PRINTING OFFICE, 1876], 17–18.)

ARRIVAL OF THE DEAD *at the hospital, August 18, 1884, Schell and Hogan (no first names given). Drawing from* Harper's Weekly. *These men from the Army Signal Corps died while trying to establish meteorological stations in the northernmost regions of Greenland. Author's collection.*

ward. Hot water was readily available for the basement laundry and bathroom.

Generous in war but abstemious in peace and hampered by a national treasury depleted by the Civil War, Washington provided little money for renovating the Governors Island hospital in 1874. The new wings were reconstructed using wood recycled from the demolition of the 1862 hospital additions. Soldiers were the workforce for doing everything but plumbing and roofing and were supervised by the assistant surgeon, A. H. Hoff.[30]

INFLUENZA, 1918

DESCRIPTIONS OF GOVERNORS ISLAND in the nearly half-century between the 1870s and World War I omit mention of the medical facilities. In 1898, however, the outbreak of war to free Cuba and the Philippines from Spanish rule probably put Governors Island's doctors to work. The island was an embarkation point for both supplies and New York–area soldiers who were drafted to fight on the Cuban front. It seems likely that the Governors Island medical staff continued to give physical examinations to the inductees upon their departure and return.

From the turn of the century to the buildup for World War I, the island went through a period of relative quiet. It continued to operate as an administrative center, and new land was added to the south, tripling the size of the military holdings. The complaint most often heard concerned the omnipresence of swarms of mosquitoes during the warm-weather months.

HOSPITAL STEWARDS' QUARTERS, *1908, unknown photographer. Courtesy of Still Pictures Branch, National Archives, College Park, Md.*

But it was not World War I that finally tested Governors Island's medical facilities: it was disease. In the latter part of 1917, influenza, accompanied by a virulent pneumonia, hit the United States and Europe in epidemic proportions. It declined by the following spring, only to peak again in the fall of 1918. Army bases throughout the country were severely afflicted, with death rates higher than those of the first two years of the Civil War and both of the wars in Cuba and the Philippines.[31] Fortunately, the outbreak of influenza on Governors Island came at the end of the epidemic, and the medical care, though somewhat primitive, curtailed the number of deaths.

A monthly average of 3,035 officers, enlisted men, and prisoners were crowded on the island in 1918 as part of the war effort–all of them living and working in poorly heated, nineteenth-century brick or newly prefabricated wooden structures. The possibilities for contagion were many. On September 15, 1918, three prisoners from Castle Williams–which now housed military felons and men sentenced by court-martial for various misdeeds–were admitted to the post hospital with influenza-type symptoms. They were immediately placed in isolation, but within two weeks the influenza had become an epidemic, and the hospital was filled to capacity with the sick. By requisitioning space wherever it could be found, the chief surgeon succeeded valiantly in giving every patient in the hospital building the prescribed one hundred square feet of floor space that was believed needed to treat such a scourge. As in prior epidemics, however, those men in the prison without the luxury of the extra space suffered the most.[32]

Given the large numbers of civilian and military commuters, it was impossible to quarantine the island. Fortunately, by November 5 the wave of influenza had subsided. Up to this point, though, 516 island residents had contracted the disease, and 39 had died. Although only a small number of African Americans were stationed on the base, the proportion of those who died from influenza (unlike in the yellow fever epidemic) was more than double that of the whites.[33]

Provisions were made, by placing men in tents, [for] an early expansion of the Post Hospital into temporary Hospital buildings [in] the West and South Barracks of Fort Jay...and the Y.M.C.A. Auditorium. Into the Y.M.C.A. were placed all patients in Hospital not infected with influenza. Through this isolation all of these men, about 40 in number, escaped the disease. The patients...were placed with heads and feet alternating, and cubicled by means of sheets strung on wires.

(MEMORANDUM FROM THE SURGEON [FREDERICK K. HERPEL, FIRST LIEUTENANT, MARINE CORPS], FORT JAY, NEW YORK, TO THE SURGEON GENERAL, U.S. ARMY, WASHINGTON, D.C., OCTOBER 1918, REPORT ON THE INFLUENZA AND PNEUMONIA EPIDEMIC, RG 112, 153/710.1, NATIONAL ARCHIVES, COLLEGE PARK, MD.)

VIEW FROM CASTLE WILLIAMS *showing a track for unloading supplies for the prison* (on left), *ca. 1910–20, unknown photographer. The hospital to the right of the tracks is little changed. 90.44.1.33. Courtesy of the McKim, Mead & White Collection, Museum of the City of New York.*

THE POST HOSPITAL, 1918–1965

IN THE SAME MONTH THAT INFLUENZA overburdened the post hospital, Frederick K. Herpel, the hospital surgeon, began the process of securing a modern facility and living quarters for his staff. At the time, patients were housed either in the hospital that was nearly fifty years old or, as in the early nineteenth century, still in tents. Medical staff were overworked and inadequately housed, with eighty-three men quartered in a mosquito-infested barracks intended for thirty-two.

An inkling of the specialization that would come to the practice of medicine appeared on Governors Island at this time. Soldiers, officers, and families now sought care from two surgeons on the hospital staff: Dr. Herpel, who practiced general medicine and performed various types of operations, and an orthopedic surgeon. Support staff assisted the doctors in performing routine medical work, delivering babies, and treating other conditions that required hospitalization. In addition, they performed the routine physical examinations and inoculations that were now required for the six hundred men of the Governors Island battalion and the five hundred prisoners in Castle Williams, a group in constant flux. From the city and other nearby army medical facilities, new recruits still came for checkups, and seasoned soldiers came for discharge papers. Also adding to the caseload were men disabled in the war who were sent to the hospital for aftercare.[34] Although the need for proper accommodations was plain, it took seventeen years to complete the installations.

At the end of 1930, Governors Island was finally the beneficiary of congressional largesse. As part of a general improvement

Inspection of Station Hospital by the Adjutant General, April 19, 1930

DEFECTS:

a. General uncleanliness of the hospital in all rooms...soiled walls and windows.

b. Insanitary condition of kitchen, kitchen equipment and cooking utensils.

c. Obviously poor basic training of the Medical Detachment and non-commissioned officers.

d. Uncleanly condition of ambulance and ambulance equipment.

COMMENDABLE FEATURES:

a. A sufficient strength of apparently intelligent personnel in the Medical Detachment capable of being properly trained in assigned duties.

b. Ample equipment.

c. Competent professional treatment of patients.

(MEMORANDUM FROM COLONEL J. E. WOODWARD TO STATION HOSPITAL ADMINISTRATION, RG 112, 434/333.1-1, NATIONAL ARCHIVES, COLLEGE PARK, MD.)

FORT JAY, POST HOSPITAL, *Governors Island, ca. 1934, A. Mainzer. Postcard. Following standard military hospital design, the three-story McKim, Mead & White structure is built on a central block with flanking wings. The traditional long verandah has been replaced with smaller sunrooms. Author's collection.*

NURSES' QUARTERS, *Governors Island, ca. 1935, A. Mainzer. Postcard. Army nurses finally had their own free-standing residence. Author's collection.*

of army hospitals and the availability of Public Works Administration (PWA) dollars to fight the Depression, architects were now on board. War Department policy actively encouraged distinguished architecture on permanent military bases, which meant that a new hospital and nurses' quarters were not designed in-house, as had been the procedure previously. Instead, the army hired two New York City firms for the tasks: McKim, Mead & White, which had recently completed Building 400, the island's gigantic regimental quarters; and Rogers and Poor, which was working on Buildings 111 and 112, the new officers' quarters.

The new hospital finally opened on January 14, 1934. Despite the opportunity for honoring an army dignitary, the building was never given a formal name; rather, in recognition of the wide area it encompassed, it was always simply called "Station Hospital, Fort Jay" (even as the building was enlarged and updated over the years to handle more complicated cases, its name remained unchanged). In addition to serving Governors Island, the 162-bed facility was now also the Second Corps Area hospital, replacing the original one located at Fort Totten in Queens. Immediately after its opening, an average of 135 beds were filled, including all of the Fort Totten caseload as well as soldiers and their dependents from other posts in New York, New Jersey, and Delaware. The hospital also served a new cohort, giving youths from Civilian Conservation Corps (CCC) camps their enrollment and discharge examinations.[35]

The array of specialized services provided by Station Hospital was on a par with other public or private hospitals in the region. In its first year of operation, its staff consisted of five chiefs of services (for medical; surgical; eye; ear, nose, and throat; and dental care), a part-time psychiatrist who was shared with the prison in Castle Williams, twelve officers with medical or dental training, fifteen army nurses, four CCC nurses, ninety-one enlisted men, and twenty-nine civilian employees. Together they treated and cared for 2,945 patients in one year. A soldier might be hospitalized for pneumonia or typhoid or for removal of his tonsils, adenoids, or mastoids. Hydrotherapy and massage helped to rehabilitate his body, and the psychiatrist attended to his mental health. The surgeon, Major Hertel P. Makel, and his two assistants performed 1,129 operations in 1934, without benefit of a subspecialist. They were well versed in everything from appendectomies, hernias, and circumcisions to fracture repairs and

GARRET AND WILL ROOSMA, *the first twins born in the new hospital, n.d., unknown photographer. Courtesy of Garret Roosma.*

TOM AND DICK SMOTHERS, *n.d., unknown photographer. The brothers were born in the Regional Hospital in 1937 and 1938 while their father was stationed on Governors Island. Courtesy of Knave Productions Inc.*

amputations. That year they also delivered 108 babies whose mothers were army wives or other women working on the post.

Under the leadership of an attending surgeon, the hospital's outpatient service burgeoned. In 1935, the medical staff treated more than 900 army personnel and 1,200 civilians. A year later the numbers had grown to 1,100 and 5,000, respectively. The hospital statistics also give an indication of the size of the dependent population now associated with Governors Island. In 1936, the civilians treated in the outpatient department included 145 men, more than 3,000 women, and more than 2,000 children.

An Army ferryboat plying between Manhattan and Governors Island was the setting for the birth of Rudolph John Arnold Powell Jr. whose father is stationed in Germany....Mrs. Powell who lives on St. Nicholas Avenue...called the Fort Jay Hospital and an ambulance rushed to her home and took her aboard the ferryboat to go to the hospital on GI [Governors Island]....Before the boat reached the island...the boy was born with the aid of an obstetrical technician who happened to be aboard.

("BABY BORN ON FERRYBOAT," FROM *NEW YORK TIMES*, NOVEMBER 29, 1952, 19.)

At the onset of World War II, the Station Hospital capacity nearly doubled to 256 beds. Excellent care provided in a centrally located, secure facility doubtless brought more patients. At the same time, improvements in the understanding of the cause and spread of disease and an increased use of disinfectants allowed doctors to justify the expansion of the bed count. They merely reduced the recommended sixty-square-foot space per bed to forty square feet when "an emergency" occurred. There must have been many emergencies that year because the average number of occupied beds was 335 per month. Colonel S. M. Corbett, the presiding medical officer, requested the use of additional buildings for 200 more beds.[36]

As in the past, the expansion of medical facilities vied for space with the military establishment, which was also growing in order to deal with the war effort. By 1943, one ward of the hospital had been set aside for the use of 150 newly arrived Italian prisoners of war. The doctors were allowed to turn five vintage cantonment buildings into four wards, an outpatient and dental clinic,

CHAPLAIN FISHER *conversing with patients in the ward at the Fort Jay Regional Hospital, December 8, 1942, unknown photographer. Courtesy of G. S. Grunert Collection, U.S. Army Military History Institute, Carlisle, Pa.*

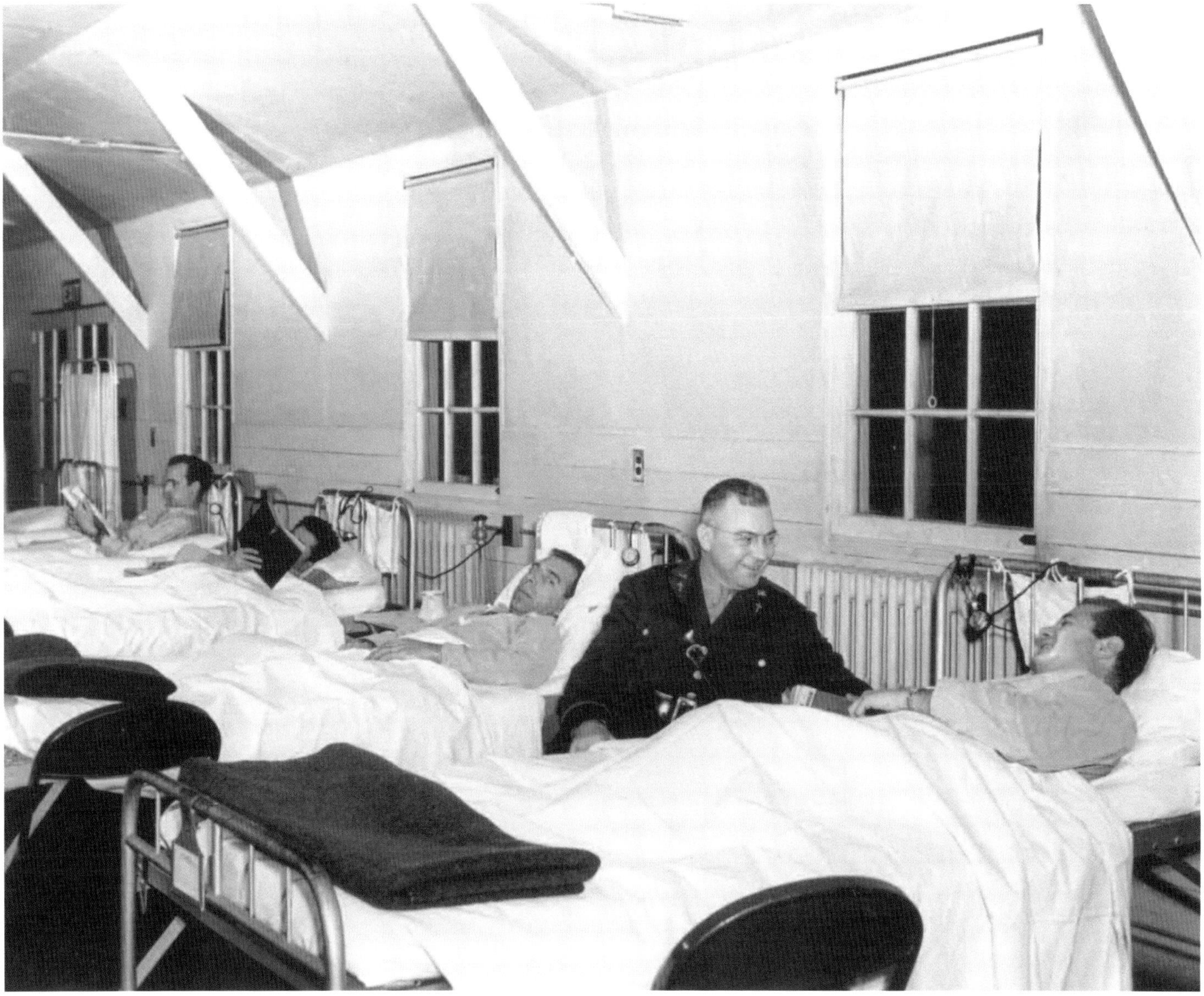

and space for "sick call." In addition, the hospital appropriated two floors in a nearby building to treat inductees referred for overnight stays. The facilities were clearly performing services beyond the usual station hospital.

The return of wounded soldiers from the European theater of war created a demand for even more specialized services than had been provided in the past. In May 1944, the Station Hospital treated 3,031 military men (three times greater than the number treated nine years earlier). In June, the facility was upgraded to the status of "regional hospital," its unofficial name since at least 1942. In addition to general surgery, specialists now performed major surgery in orthopedics, urology, ophthalmology, and otolaryngology. Only an anesthesiology department was missing.[37] At the end of the war, services were once again adjusted, this time to treat returning veterans with lasting disabilities by adding a reconditioning program headed by full-time physical and occupational therapists.

The social welfare of patients took on greater importance in medicine after the war and was supplied primarily by the Red Cross, Gray Ladies, and nurses' aides. These devoted women shopped for hospital patients, ran book carts, taught arts and crafts, and organized parties.

A Typical Daily Radio Broadcast

May 1946

TIME	PROGRAM
0800–1300	Music and News: Make Believe Ballroom
1300–1400	Off
1400–1700	Ball game
1700–1730	Recordings
1730–1930	Make Believe Ballroom; Music and News
1930–2000	WEAF—Bob Burns
2000–2030	WEAF—Burns and Allen
2030–2100	WEAF—Dinah Shore Show

16MM FILMS SHOWN IN APRIL, 1946:

We Do It Because; Welcome to Britain; Victory Quiz; How to Sleep; The Old Army Game; West Point; Army's Outstanding Football Games, 1944; Cadet Cagers; Pete Smith Scrapbook; World Series of 1944; World Series of 1945; Circling the Bases; American League Inside Information; Bull Fighting; Shark Hunting; Hurling; Sportscope-Bowling; Sing with the Stars, Marion Hutton; Sing with the Stars, Alex Templeton; That Interior Feeling; Swing High, Swing Low; Flicker Flash-backs; California Boom Town; Guest Pests; People on Paper; People Personalities; Passing Parade Information Please; Magic on a Stick.

(MEMORANDUM FROM JAMES D. BERRY TO SURGEON, SECOND SERVICE COMMAND, ARMY SPECIAL FORCES [ASF], GOVERNORS ISLAND, NEW YORK, MAY 28, 1946, TECHNICAL REPORT ON THE RECONDITIONING PROGRAM, FORT JAY REGIONAL HOSPITAL, FORT JAY, NEW YORK, RG 112, 33/353.9, NATIONAL ARCHIVES, COLLEGE PARK, MD.)

They also eased the hospital staff's paperwork burden by helping patients complete forms for government benefits and leaves. Two Women's Army Corps (WAC) members (part of a small contingent now stationed on Governors Island) ran daily popular broadcasts over the hospital's intercom and showed movies (mostly on sports subjects) on the wards. Under this reconditioning program, those who were well enough were also taken to Manhattan to see such plays as *Carmen Jones* and *Call Me Mister,* attend the Barnum & Bailey Circus, and dine at Reuben's, a famous Manhattan delicatessen.

In the early 1950s, Governors Island continued to be a crucial part of the army's local and New York medical system, although cost-saving measures were always in the forefront. Beginning in 1950, the Korean War brought new inductees from the Whitehall recruiting station in Manhattan to the island for physicals. The hospital, with two hundred beds and a free-standing clinic, continued to treat soldiers, administrative personnel, and dependents living on and off the island, as well as patients sent from nearby bases such as the Brooklyn Army Terminal, Fort Hamilton in Brooklyn, Fort Wadsworth in Staten Island, and Miller Field in Queens. Patients even came from as far away as Buffalo, Syracuse, and Watervliet, near Albany.[38] Despite what appeared to be a heavy caseload, however, the hospital's annual report a few years later recommended reducing the hospital staff to save money.[39] And the ferry that brought patients to Governors Island ran in two directions: those needing care beyond the hospital's capacity were sent away from the island to facilities in St. Albans, Queens; Valley Forge, Pennsylvania; and Fort Dix, New Jersey.

Fort Jay Station Hospital

THANKSGIVING MENU

November 24, 1949

Shrimp Cocktail
Celery Hearts — Stuffed Olives
ROAST YOUNG TOM TURKEY
Giblet Gravy — Oyster Dressing
BAKED VIRGINIA HAM
Cranberry Sauce
Snowflake Potatoes — Maple Yams
Buttered Green Peas
Cape Cod Salad — Cloverleaf Rolls
Mince Pie — Pumpkin Pie
Pistachio Ice Cream
Fresh Fruits — Mixed Nuts
Coffee — Apple Cider — Tea
Cigarettes — Cigars — After-Dinner Mints

(ARMY MEDICAL RECORDS, FORT JAY, RG 112, 49/319. 1, NATIONAL ARCHIVES, COLLEGE PARK, MD.)

In addition to giving physicals to workers from the post's barber and beauty shops, the Outpatient Department handled the same type of activities found in any medium-size town in 1950. Its staff performed the medical tests required for ninety-three marriage certificates, 101 life insurance applications, and sundry food service and civil service exams. The island's century-old mosquito problem was addressed during this period by liberal spraying of DDT, in use throughout the United States and abroad for insect eradication.

By 1953, outpatient care had reached a tipping point. Despite recommended cutbacks for the hospital, officials requested and eventual-

Eighty-five percent of the insane cases in this hospital are from stations or posts other than Fort Jay...less than 50% of all cases [are] from Governors Island. It is also necessary to send all venereal cases to Fort Hamilton for hospitalization, due to lack of suitable space here.

(MEMORANDUM FROM S. M. CORBETT, COLONEL, MEDICAL CORPS, COMMANDING MEDICAL OFFICER, TO COMMANDING GENERAL OF THE SECOND CORPS AREA, GOVERNORS ISLAND, NEW YORK, APRIL 30, 1942, THE STATION HOSPITAL SERVICE AREA, HOSPITAL FACILITIES AT FORT JAY, RG 112, 753/721-5.1, NATIONAL ARCHIVES, COLLEGE PARK, MD.)

ly secured more space. Soldiers returning from Korea were examined for release from the army. These examinations and continuing support of day-to-day medical issues brought the total annual outpatient services to 9,888 cases. In 1957, a requested "modern building to house (outpatient) things that are now in various buildings" was finally completed.[40]

New demands reflecting the shifting population on the island and changes in hospital practice came at the end of the decade. As in the past, Governors Island medical officers sought and sometimes found the means to keep the facilities up to date. The dental clinic was renovated, and the staff now examined the entire population of schoolchildren attending P.S. 26. In addition, the doctors requested, but did not succeed in securing, a new maternity facility to serve the continually growing number of families living on the island. They also hoped for both an intensive care unit to better manage postoperative patients and a neuropsychiatric clinic that would recognize the importance of mental health to military personnel and their families. It is unknown whether these facilities were added by the time the army departed the island in 1965. However, by then the so-called new hospital was more than thirty years old.

THE DISPENSARY, 1965–1998

WHEN THE COAST GUARD took over the command of Governors Island, instead of applying Band-Aids to save money, officials made the radical move of closing the hospital entirely. Medicine and surgery had become highly specialized, and the overall Coast Guard budget was very tight. Sufficient Veterans Administration, city, and private hospitals were within close enough range in Staten Island, Manhattan, and Queens to serve the new population on Governors Island efficiently. Never wasteful, the military once again recycled: the Coast Guard turned the emptied hospital wards into barracks.

As in 1874, the new tenants transformed the basement of the old army hospital, turning it into the Coast Guard's second-largest medical center and dispensing treatment to more than four thousand people a month. Now known as "sick bay," it contained medical and dental outpatient clinics, a twenty-four-hour emergency room, a laboratory, a pharmacy, and an X-ray center. The Coast Guard had doctors on staff, as well as contracts with various specialists in orthopedics, psychiatry, adolescent psychology, optometry, and dental hygiene. Those needing hospitalization were sent off island.[41] The clinic no longer treated critical cases, but many residents delight in remembering that it was used in the filming of *Critical Condition* with Richard Pryor. Three years before the base closed permanently yet another recycling took place–the opening of a new clinic in the former Electronics Technicians' School.[42]

There was a tiny building behind the dispensary and across from [Building] #555 that was green and it was the dentist. Each year kindergarten through 4th grade at PS 26 took a visit to the dentist for a yearly check-up. Most of us were terrified but we didn't mind because it was a half-day out of school. In the 90s it was moved in with the dispensary. If you were pregnant you had the baby at a hospital in NYC. If your wife was going into labor you would first call security at the ferry, tell them and they would hold the ferry, put you on and off first....A coworker of mine...ended up having her baby delivered by its father on her kitchen floor in brick village.

(E-MAIL TO AUTHOR FROM FORMER PATIENT NANCY COPPOLA, SEPTEMBER 13, 2004, CONCERNING THE COAST GUARD DISPENSARY.)

CASTLE WILLIAMS, *Governors Island, n.d., unknown publisher. Postcard. A view of prison life by a guard, written on the front of the postcard: "This is the Prison where I do Guard. There is 301 Prisnors here at Present. Some of them with ten years to do." Collection of Barbara Romer.*

Chapter Three

AN EASTERN ALCATRAZ

After arriving by mistake on Bedloe's Island, the prisoners of war...then embarked again and came to Governor's Island, where our comrades had preceded us on another boat. Governor's Island is a very pretty place. When we were coming on the Minnesota I cast my eyes to this island and told the boys that I wish we could have it for our home while we were in captivity.[1]

PRISONERS OF WAR, 1861–1865

GOVERNORS ISLAND NOT ONLY WAS A NEXUS for military training and administration and medical care, but beginning with the Civil War was also central to the U.S. Army prison system. As in the early American penal facilities scattered haphazardly across the nation, care of military prisoners had traditionally been the responsibility of local army posts and coastal fortifications. In this regard, Governors Island was not unusual in maintaining a place to guard its unruly or disobedient residents. A guardhouse that typically served as both a post prison and office of the guard was among the structures the British had left on the island in 1783. Fifteen years later, in 1798, a guardhouse was among the American-built improvements.[2]

By the nineteenth century, army guardhouses were gradually augmented by large, secure facilities to hold a changing population of felons and men captured in war. Although for the most part constantly overcrowded, the facilities on Governors Island adjusted to these changes.

At the onset of the Civil War in April 1861, Governors Island was a serious contender as a site for a formal army prison. The question for army officials at that time was not whether certain sites would house ordinary army miscreants; rather, it was where to put large numbers of Confederate prisoners of war. The army shipped these men north for incarceration until they could be exchanged for a like number of captured Union soldiers. Officials discussed using the dated Governors Island forts to hold prisoners, but concern that the men would storm the parapets and blow up the base led to paralysis in making the decision.

HEADQUARTERS AND GUARD HOUSE, *Governors Island, September 28, 1864, unknown photographer. The guard house was located under the headquarters' offices (the rear of the Governor's House). Courtesy of Still Pictures Branch, National Archives, College Park, Md.*

By September 1861, however, in addition to the traditional post guardhouses for army prisoners,

CASTLE WILLIAMS, *ca. 1860s, Mathew Brady. Courtesy of Still Pictures Branch, National Archives, College Park, Md. Thomas Sparrow's September 4, 1861, description of Castle Williams, where his soldiers were imprisoned during the Civil War, is faint praise indeed: "A round work three stories high, near the water on the northwest of the island. A prominent object in the scenery around the bay of N. York but not a very imposing one" (Thomas Sparrow Collection, no. 1878, folder 7, vol. 1, September 4, 1861, transcribed by Alex Christopher Meekins, University of North Carolina–Chapel Hill Southern Historical Collection).*

twelve formally designated military prisons for captured blockade runners and privateers, or "political prisoners," were scattered in forts in Baltimore, Boston, and New York: Fort Lafayette (now the anchorage of the Verrazano Bridge) was one, and Castle Williams was another. The army finally recognized that the military prison population had not only become different in type, but also larger in number, and so it recommended the establishment of special camps only for prisoners of war.[3] The suggestion was never implemented. Instead, Castle Williams, which for years had been housing troops and overflow hospital patients in its damp casemates, became what Civil War prison historian Lonnie R. Speer termed one of the "portals to hell."[4]

We landed at the wharf between 10 and 11 o'clock....The officers were all marched up to the interior of Fort Columbus....In the interior of the work are four buildings fifty feet long each having a basement & two stories facing on a square....The square is divided into four grand plots by walks crossing at eight angles in the centre, where stands a pump. Shade trees surround each plot of grass so that the place has a green & cheerful aspect....Quarters. We are assigned to part of the North building, facing southward. The upper piassa [*sic*] overlooks a part of the bay & the upper back windows overlook N. York City, East River, Jersey City & Brooklyn. [Forty-seven officers and a waiter boy are quartered on two floors in six out of the eleven rooms.]...The dinning [*sic*] room is in the basement. There are six tables with benches. We have tin plates & cups & Army rations–beef, pork, potatoes & light bread, rice & beans occasionally, coffee & sugar, bread & coffee only at night.

(THOMAS SPARROW COLLECTION, NO. 1878, FOLDER 7, VOL. 1, SEPTEMBER 4, 1861, 110–14, TRANSCRIBED BY ALEX CHRISTOPHER MEEKINS, UNIVERSITY OF NORTH CAROLINA—CHAPEL HILL SOUTHERN HISTORICAL COLLECTION.)

GARRISON QUARTERS, *September 28, 1864, unknown photographer. One wing of the garrison's quarters in Fort Jay housed imprisoned Civil War officers. Courtesy of Still Pictures Branch, National Archives, College Park, Md.*

THE QUEEN MARY *passing Governors Island, 1965, unknown photographer. Civil War soldiers imprisoned in Castle Williams might have seen an earlier passenger ship, the* Leviathan, *journey in and out of the harbor. Tenants in the high-rises of the 1960s had equally exciting views. Courtesy of Claudia Iannucci.*

For the next four years, the big "cheesebox with a lot of holes punched in the side"[5] held both the sick and prisoners of war, who would stay for a month or more and then were replaced immediately by another inundation of men.

On September 4, 1861, the first bedraggled Confederate officers and troops arrived on Governors Island. Among them were North Carolinians Lieutenant Thomas Sparrow and Lieutenant Alonzo Etheridge Bell, both of whom had been in transit since the Union capture of the forts in Hatteras Inlet, North Carolina, several weeks earlier.

According to Bell and Sparrow's recently discovered diaries,[6] which provide rare "insider" views of the Governors Island prison, their two-month stay began in a rather civilized manner. More than six hundred Southern prisoners were marched from their ships into Castle Williams, whose official capacity was five hundred men. Conditions were initially tolerable. On his second day on Governors Island, Sparrow reported that his men "occupy two casemates on the third floor near a right hand round tower & are very comfortable."[7] When they looked out of the portals, they saw the activity in the harbor, including the passage of the 692-foot passenger ships the *Great Eastern* and the *Leviathan,* which dwarfed all other vessels.

The more fortunate captive officers were not assigned to Castle Williams, but were marched in a separate group to quarters assigned to them in the north building of Fort Jay, thus setting a pattern for later use of this wing for a prison. The remaining three sections of Fort Jay continued to house officers of the Governors Island regiment.

Even in prison, the military hierarchy had its place. In September 1861, the three highest-ranking Confederate officers held in Fort Jay employed a woman from the garrison to cook for them and were served by a prisoner from Castle Williams. Accoutrements for the other forty-four officers were more meager, but all men had the luxury of "hiring out" their washing to the fort's Irish women for "sixty cents a dozen." To their compatriots' amusement, some men washed their own socks and handkerchiefs.[8]

We have in our rooms neither tables, chairs, nor benches. The only furniture is a camp garrison bedsted made of four boards with a headboard [according to Alonzo Bell, "about 18 inches from the floor"]. We do our writing by taking out one of these headboards & laying it across our laps as I am now doing. We sit upon the beds & the few trunks in the room. Our bedding consists of cotton sacks with a slit in the middle filled with long wheat straw. Our covering a simple coarse gray Army blanket with "U.S." wrought in the centre of each. [There are no sheets.] I have the benefit of a blanket shared & over-coat [both of which he brought from North Carolina] under my head.

(THOMAS SPARROW COLLECTION, NO. 1878, FOLDER 7, VOL. 1, SEPTEMBER 25, 1861, 176, TRANSCRIBED BY ALEX CHRISTOPHER MEEKINS, UNIVERSITY OF NORTH CAROLINA–CHAPEL HILL SOUTHERN HISTORICAL COLLECTION. SEE ALSO ALONZO E. BELL, DIARIES, SEPTEMBER 15–NOVEMBER 11, 1861, MF.P. 48.1, TRANSCRIBED BY ALEX CHRISTOPHER MEEKINS, OFFICE OF ARCHIVES AND HISTORY, DIVISION OF HISTORICAL RESOURCES, ARCHIVES AND RECORDS, NORTH CAROLINA STATE ARCHIVES, RALEIGH.)

CONFEDERATE OFFICERS *inside Fort Jay Barracks, n.d., unknown photographer. These men had comfortable and heated quarters, unlike the soldiers imprisoned in the castle. Courtesy of Still Pictures Branch, National Archives, College Park, Md.*

Reveille, taps, and mealtimes regimented daily life for the Confederate officers. Rations were supplied in a raw state to a Confederate soldier who acted as commissary manager. Meats were boiled in the basement level (first tier) by "some few Negroes along[,] who officiate as cooks."[9] After a seven o'clock breakfast, officers cleaned their rooms, wrote, and played board and card games. Afternoons were much the same, with perhaps a nap added.[10] Daily ablutions that autumn and certainly for the next four winters required a certain amount of fortitude. Outhouses were located in separate pyramidal structures in the corners of the Fort Jay complex. A cistern in the center of Fort Jay provided water for shaving, but bathing, a cold affair, took place in the bay outside Castle Clinton.

Religion was an important part of the officers' routine. The Bible Society of New York supplied a Bible from which Lieutenant Sparrow read every night before taps. The Presbyterian Board sent books to distribute to the prisoners, and ministers from New York offered to deliver sermons. Sparrow wrote in his diary that prisoners in the first years of the war required special permission to attend services at the island's St. Cornelius Chapel and even then only under guard. By 1862, however, mandatory church attendance was part of the weekly routine.

The garrison postmaster's daily delivery of the *New York Tribune*, *New York Herald*, *New York Times*, and *New York Morning Express* provided Sparrow and his men with much-sought-after details of the war.[11] A weekly newspaper was also another way to pass the time and add some levity to an otherwise depressing situation, even though

Sept. 22, Sunday. Went to church today at 10 A.M. A great Episcopal Church on the South of the Island beyond our bounds...[according to Alonzo Bell, "a small building in the Gothic style as the Episcopalians generally are"]....The permission to attend was granted by Coln. Loomis at my own request.... Hymns & tunes all good & solemnizing [by the chaplain, Reverend John McVickar] Dr. M Vicar [*sic*] is a plain good man. I like him. I like the devotion of the Litany & prayers. I like the beautiful psalms & hymns he selects & the old familiar tunes. I like the neat little chapel. I derive benefit from the services.

(THOMAS SPARROW COLLECTION, NO. 1878, FOLDER 7, VOL. 1, SEPTEMBER 22, 1861, 161, AND VOL. 2, 6, TRANSCRIBED BY ALEX CHRISTOPHER MEEKINS, UNIVERSITY OF NORTH CAROLINA—CHAPEL HILL SOUTHERN HISTORICAL COLLECTION. SEE ALSO ALONZO E. BELL, DIARIES, SEPTEMBER 22, 1861, MF.P. 48.1, TRANSCRIBED BY ALEX CHRISTOPHER MEEKINS, OFFICE OF ARCHIVES AND HISTORY, DIVISION OF HISTORICAL RESOURCES, ARCHIVES AND RECORDS, NORTH CAROLINA STATE ARCHIVES, RALEIGH.)

September 23, 1861. There is much sameness in our life at Fort Columbus....We sup usually before dark...assemble in front of our quarters or in the piazzas to discuss the political topics of the day & and promenade for half an hour...reading and writing [and an occasional pillow fight] take place before lights out at 10 pm.

September 24, 1861. On the second day of our captivity here we all signed a parole, which gives us the freedom of most of the island, except between tattoo [the evening drum that signals soldiers to go to their quarters] and reveille. We agree not to escape nor to converse with the soldiers on the Island. [They were also forbidden to render salutes.]

(THOMAS SPARROW COLLECTION, NO. 1878, FOLDER 7, VOL. 1, SEPTEMBER 24, 1861, 169, 174, TRANSCRIBED BY ALEX CHRISTOPHER MEEKINS, UNIVERSITY OF NORTH CAROLINA—CHAPEL HILL SOUTHERN HISTORICAL COLLECTION, RALEIGH.)

CASTLE WILLIAMS, *New York, n.d., Carter & Dut, Publishers. Postcard. The image of the prison was marketed on popular postcards as an "eastern Alcatraz." The accompanying messages are amusingly out of context. Courtesy of Print Archives, Museum of the City of New York.*

the first edition always arrived late. Two weeks before being shipped out of Governors Island, the officers in Bell and Sparrow's prison contingent debuted the in-house *Weekly Transcript* on October 19, 1861. The sheet was read aloud on only one Saturday before their departure. This was the genesis of prisoner-produced broadsheets: with each prisoner turnover, new officers would start another newsletter. In 1862, shortly before being transferred to Johnson's Island prison in Sandusky, Ohio, a new group of Confederate prisoners started the *Dixie Discourse,* to the amusement of the assembled officers.[12]

Part of an officer's daily routine was to visit soldiers imprisoned in the castle. The set time was hardly convenient for the officers. As Sparrow writes, "From 9 to 10 A.M. and from 4 to 5 P.M. are our hours for visiting the Castle. The mail in the morning and the music [in the bandstand in Nolan Park] in the afternoon interfere with both hours. I am seldom behind the times however & never fail to make two visits a day."[13] Sparrow brought with him extra food, the newspapers, pies, tobacco, ink, and paper purchased from a young peddler from the city, as well as clothing donated by sympathetic New Yorkers. He also attended to the prisoners' cleanliness: "Remonstrated with a Lieut. Buel about the lack of facilities among the soldiers at the Castle for washing....I had all my well men mustered in the yard & they were then marched to the West shore of the Island & allowed to bathe."[14]

We had a rich time tonight. We have started a weekly paper for our own amusement....All kinds of paragraphs were brought forth and infused somewhat with Poetry of an Elegant style and much to the point. There were communications from the dining hall and from headquarters of a character calculated to make the most moody joyous....The names of our most prominent were brought frequently into requisition and in a manner that brought roars of laughter from all present. A scientific article on Poker was introduced....Advertisements of a very rich character were out in abundance.

(EDWARD WILLIAM DRUMMOND, JOURNAL, IN ROGER S. DURHAM, ED., *A CONFEDERATE YANKEE: THE JOURNAL OF EDWARD WILLIAM DRUMMOND, A CONFEDERATE SOLDIER* [KNOXVILLE: UNIVERSITY OF TENNESSEE PRESS, 2003], 58.)

The imprisoned soldiers' daily life was much more proscribed. They were not allowed outside the castle walls. Except for the few who were assigned to cooking and serving duties at Fort Jay or to picking up the daily ration of bread from the bakery, they spent the day largely in the casemates. They passed the time playing sedentary games and reading secondhand newspapers, Bibles, or books donated by religious groups. Church services were held weekly in a small room on the second tier of the castle. The soldiers were occasionally allowed to get some air in the castle's courtyard, a space too small for anything but tossing a ball.

By September 20, 1861, a little more than three weeks after the arrival of the first Confederate prisoners, conditions inside Castle Williams had deteriorated considerably. New prisoners had arrived weekly, swelling the population to 707. The second and upper tiers of the castle were now fully packed. Sparrow describes the situation: "Those in the upper casemates are comparatively comfortable, tho' terribly crowded. Those in the lower cases are destitute of almost every comfort. They are crowded in the corners to avoid the cool winds, with a straw sack and one blanket, covered with dirt & with not a change of garments. It is a disgrace to humanity."[15] Adding to these deplorable conditions was an outbreak of twenty-five cases of measles. By the beginning of October, at least twelve of Sparrow's men had died. Nothing was done to improve conditions. Instead, on October 30, with the measles epidemic concluded, all of the Hatteras Inlet prisoners were shipped off to reconditioned facilities at Fort Warren in Boston Harbor. The next day new Confederate prisoners arrived at Governors Island.

For the duration of the Civil War, Governors Island continued to house prisoners of war, serving as one of twenty-four such army facilities. The island's experiences in this capacity were similar to those of other such makeshift wartime institutions. Conditions were crowded and primitive, although after the initial onslaught in 1861, the number of Confederate soldiers—ranging from a high of 486 in 1862 to none at war's end in April 1865—stayed below the castle's maximum capacity. Illness was an everyday occurrence, although the death count was low, with forty-seven fatalities recorded, proportionately the same as in larger Delaware and Illinois facilities.[16] Eleven of these dead soldiers, all from North Carolina, were buried on Governors Island.[17]

PUNISHMENT FOR MILITARY INFRACTIONS, 1865

DURING THE WAR, A SMALL SOLITARY CONFINEMENT area in the basement of the east building of Fort Jay (Building 202) was set aside for political prisoners. The space was insignificant compared to other military facilities holding bounty jumpers and traitors to the North, but the severity of the crimes and the dire sentences handed out to those imprisoned in Fort Jay were made very public. After trial by court-martial or military commission, it was not unusual for men accused of desertion or plotting against the Union to be shot or hung.

February 1865 was a notorious month for executions on Governors Island. James Devlin was one of many soldiers who made a living from the bounty the army offered for joining the war effort. By enlisting, deserting, and then reenlisting under another name, men such as Devlin filled their pockets and sometimes solved marital problems as well. From the army's point of view, the death sentence for these crimes conclusively stemmed such rampant desertion; it also made clear to other potential offenders the army's "zero tolerance" of this behavior.

In order to set a forceful example, the procedures for executions were laid out in the *Manual of Arms,* and the commandant of the island directed the event. At a proscribed time, troops were paraded in front of Fort Jay and formed three sides of a square: artillery on the right, infantry on the left, and execution party in the center. The prisoner was brought to the square, preceded by fifes and drums from the post band playing "Roslyn Castle," one of the dirges reserved for military executions. Devlin met his end under similar circumstances. On February 3, 1865, the order "Forward" was given, and to the tune of the "Dead March" deserter Devlin and his attendant procession moved from Fort Jay to the beach below Castle Williams, where they lined up facing the bay. After a time, Devlin kneeled on his coffin in the center of the group, and upon Captain Ryer's signal, ten soldiers of the twelve-man execution party fired their muskets at him.[18]

During the eighteenth and nineteenth centuries, spying was also a significant enough offense

CASTLE WILLIAMS, *Governors Island, 1896, Alfred S. Campbell. Advertisement on postcard. Author's collection.*

against the country to warrant the death sentence. Three weeks after Devlin was shot, John Beall, a notorious privateer and alleged spy whose appeals to stay a death sentence had been turned down by President Lincoln, was executed by hanging. It had been 111 years since similar military punishment had been meted out to a more famous spy, Nathan Hale.

FORT JAY, 1875–1930

BY THE END OF THE NINETEENTH CENTURY, Fort Jay had long reverted to housing for officers and soldiers. An 1870 report from surgeon Charles Page listed four 2-story brick and stone buildings situated within the fort, surrounding the original parade ground or central square. Three of these buildings were outfitted as barracks, each with dormitories in five large rooms and six small rooms, similar to those described by Sparrow. The basements in the barracks had two sets of kitchens and mess halls, accessed by exterior staircases, each serving one company. Officers' quarters were located on the west side of the compound. Interior hallways and staircases increased the privacy of the eight sets of quarters, with interior connections to basement kitchens.

Water was supplied to the four structures from cisterns or wells, and heat was conducted through fireplaces in or between the rooms. But privies were still located in the small triangular outbuildings, their refuse seeping into the ground and probably into the nearby wells. In 1920, the barracks were converted to family housing for officers. Using Works Progress Administration (WPA) funds in the 1930s, the apartments were renovated and garages were added, making the former prison one of the most desirable places to live on the island.

CASTLE WILLIAMS, 1875–1925

CASTLE WILLIAMS SOON RETURNED to its pre–Civil War sleepy state. By 1875, prisoners and their guards occupied only five of the casemates in the upper tier. Each casemate was assigned sixteen single bunks, providing space for a maximum of eighty men, one-sixteenth of the capacity recommended for the

The castle has a formidable look to passengers by the Staten Island ferryboat...but it is in a condition of crumbling decay....The crust of whitewash is falling off the stone walls in flakes which spot the floors, and the buildings have an air of untidiness. The heavy doors of the cells are grated, and the windows are set in port holes pierced six or seven feet through the walls of the castle. The bedding is rolled up, and on a center-table of common boards a small Bible and a prayer-book are swamped in a superabundant assortment of sensational periodicals....[T]he prisoners...spend their evenings largely in card-playing or in reading the sensational literature aforesaid.

(WILLIAM H. RIDEING, "GARRISON LIFE AT GOVERNOR'S ISLAND N.Y. HARBOR," *SCRIBNER'S MONTHLY* 21, NO. 4 [FEBRUARY 1881], 595–96.)

CASTLE WILLIAMS, *New York Harbor, ca. 1905, unknown publisher. Fabric postcard. Author's collection.*

entire structure during the war. The remaining casemates housed recruits, just as they had prior to the war.

A few years later *Scribner's Monthly* provided an elegiac view of prisoner life.[19] Reality, however, suggested otherwise in the form of peeling paint and unkempt conditions. In a paper presented in 1884 to the Military History Institute housed on Governors Island, Egbert Veile, New York City Parks president and former parks chief engineer, alluded to worsening conditions. An examination of Castle Williams, Veile remarked, would be tantamount to "examining a pig sty."[20]

Improvements were eventually made, and by the turn of the century all of Castle Williams had reverted back to a strictly penal institution, becoming a permanent part of the U.S. military prison system. By 1898, all guns and carriages had been removed from the second and upper tiers. The squalid second-tier dormitory was replaced with a guardroom and washroom, a kitchen, a dining room, and a large open area with barred windows to hold the general prisoner population. These changes supposedly alleviated the crowded conditions because the refurbished castle could now house a maximum of four hundred deserters and felons. Administrators began to focus on the work assigned to prisoners rather than on their living conditions.

Prisoners had always been assigned maintenance tasks in the castle compound and on the grounds of the post as part of their daily routine. They worked eight hours a day under guard as prison cooks and barbers, and provided tailoring and shoemaker services to both the inmates and the army regiment. The free labor helped to offset the costs of running the penal facility and provided rudimentary training in work skills for prisoners after release.

However, deserters, first encountered during the Civil War, continued to be a gnawing problem for the army. Leonard Wood, a Department of the East commander on Governors Island, had experience with them while serving as commander in Cuba in 1898: men who disliked the idea of serving in the tropics simply fled their posts. When they were apprehended, they were dishonorably discharged (a change from the use of execution as the punishment meted out to deserters three decades earlier). So Wood tried to address the desertion problem

MESSAGE ON REVERSE *of Castle Williams fabric postcard: "This is the Prison on the Island at Fort Jay."*

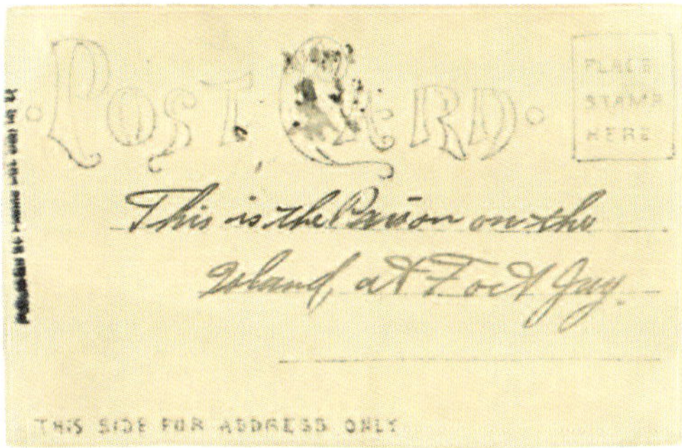

CASTLE WILLIAMS, *Governors Island, ca. 1905, H. C. Leighton Co. Postcard. Author's collection.*

in a new way. On July 1, 1909, he walked the secretary of the army through the castle and noted in his diary: "I tried to impress upon him the necessity of establishing the prison on modern lines; namely with a view to the reformation of the men, giving them a chance to re-enter the service and make good....Under the present law there seems to be no way for a man once dishonorably discharged to re-enlist."[21]

Four years later Governors Island was in the forefront of a new approach to handling deserters. The army ordered the establishment of disciplinary companies at Fort Leavenworth, Alcatraz, and Castle Williams to retrain such military offenders with an eye toward reenlistment in the army. Under this new system, from thirty to forty men in this "elite" group were housed and fed in a special section of Castle Williams; they wore modified military uniforms rather than prison uniforms; and, unlike felons, they were allowed to render salutes and talk among themselves while at work. Each morning members of the Disciplinary Company received military training while carrying rifles with the firing pin removed; in the afternoons they worked in segregated jobs, their performance observed by special personnel hired from the Governors Island garrison. Thus, the prison work program operated on two tracks, military and vocational.

The shift in focus from penitence and punishment to individual treatment through jobs, education, and–in the case of the Disciplinary Company–military retraining was in line with state and national Progressive Era prison-reform movements. Incarceration at Governors Island, however, harbored a decidedly nineteenth-century moral undertone.

GOVERNORS ISLAND, *N.Y. City, showing tug and Castle Williams, ca. 1906, Rotograph Co. Postcard. Author's collection.*

In August 1919, records indicate an all-time high of 956 prisoners, of whom 163 were living in tents. By this time, the mental and moral health of Governors Island's prisoners was in the hands of the chaplain and the psychiatrist, whose tasks were to compensate for the enervating conditions. The former was in charge of religious affairs, making sure that there were services for all denominations–a clear improvement on the offerings for prisoners during the Civil War.

The chaplain was also part of a proselytizing "welcoming committee," advising the newly arrived detainees of the "opportunities for self-improvement...the advantages of industry and good conduct...the evil effects of bad habits, etc."[22] And he was an educator, helping with letter writing and with newly instituted family visits designed to reintegrate prisoners into their communities. He even helped some of the inmates produce a newspaper called *The Castle,* believing that writing, editing, and printing skills would be useful upon their release. One chaplain, however, lamented the lack of creativity, saying that these men (unlike the Confederate prisoners) were "rather unwilling to contribute anything of their own composition."[23]

The psychiatrist, in addition to his medical duties in the prison and the post hospital, classified prisoners as to their "mental and moral characteristics."[24] In keeping with a military policy of preparing prisoners for life after their release, the psychiatrist had a pedagogic role and ran a mandatory school for those inmates who were illiterate and a voluntary grammar school for those who had not progressed to the eighth grade.

The entertainment programs begun during this period were also designed to improve self-image and were a far cry from the desultory card games and ball tossing that occurred during the Civil War. The inmates organized baseball and soccer games and were allowed to play against civilian teams from around the harbor. They put on vaudeville shows for the post and purchased a Victrola with funds earned by taking in laundry. The prison band was extremely popular, vying with the post band for Saturday night gigs at the Officers' Club.[25]

Prisoners may have had more pastimes, but they still wanted to escape this "eastern Alcatraz." One man dressed himself in women's garb and slipped away on the ferry. Another was caught hiding in the trunk of a car. Those who escaped by swimming captured the imagination of both fiction writers and the press.[26]

U.S. DISCIPLINARY BARRACKS, 1925–1943

IN 1925, THE PRISON FACILITY, which now had a new name, the U.S. Disciplinary Barracks, was placed under the control of the adjutant general of the army in Washington, D.C. The underlying moral tone continued to prevail, as seen in the barracks mission statement: "[I]t is clear that the Disciplinary Barracks were established and are to be maintained as an institution whose main object is the reformation and rehabilitation of its inmates. The Commandant endeavors, therefore, to adopt such policies and apply such measures as will tend to correct faulty habits and evil inclinations of prisoners, improve their economic prospects, and increase their respect for social and moral laws."[27]

In 1928, officials used for the first time the chronically crowded conditions at Castle Williams to justify its expansion or its closure. Castle Williams was still considered a "temporary plant," even though it held an average population of 500 inmates, roughly 100 more than its recommended capacity at the turn of the century. The men in the Disciplinary Barracks, mostly in their twenties, were from all over the country, as well as from England, Ireland, Russia, and Poland. During this period, they were serving terms for offenses such as assault, sodomy, larceny, and embezzlement—crimes far removed from the wartime offense of desertion or from prisoner-of-war status. The need for more space had become evident, but the scant funds designated for the post were being put toward the hospital and administration buildings. Castle Williams was suddenly highly desirable for other uses. Officials mounted a campaign to keep the prison as such, noting that a reversion to the early-nineteenth-century system of scattering inmates among other army guardhouses

Castle Williams Merry Christmas!

MENU

December 25, 1901

Roast turkey		Cranberry sauce
Oyster dressing		Celery
Roast beef		Brown gravy
Mashed Potatoes		Mashed turnips
Bread	Stewed Corn	Butter
Mince Pie	Apples	Apple Pie
	Coffee	

("FIFTEEN PRISONERS SET FREE BY GEN. BROOKE," *NEW YORK TIMES*, DECEMBER 29, 1901, 20.)

PRESS PRINTING ROOM, *n.d., unknown photographer. As part of a vocational training program, prisoners housed in Castle Williams often helped the soldiers supply reams of informational material used by army recruiting stations in the United States and overseas. Courtesy of U.S. Coast Guard Historian's Office, Washington, D.C.*

would be too costly. In fact, more beds meant more money. For only twenty-five cents a day per man, the castle "should be used to capacity," wrote a reviewing officer. And to make the system even more efficient, "Our average population is about 500; it is recommended that it be kept up to 575."[28]

But refurbishment did not ease crowding in the castle. The rooms were designed to house 12 men each, in bunk beds, so the twenty-six rooms, for a total of 318 men, would not have accommodated either the population in 1928 or the recommended increase. Perhaps enough food, improved working conditions, and a wider choice of recreation programs were mitigating factors. A commissary on the first tier had small tables and served the same rations as those given regular soldiers. Ironically, because the food was cooked in smaller portions, it reportedly tasted better. Prison labor helped to convert temporary World War I supply houses and storehouses (to the south of the castle, but within the barbed-wire compound) into much-needed workshops, and inmates helped to provide special holiday recreation programs.[29]

The work program also took on greater importance at this time, expanding to meet the growing demands of a post with larger acreage, aging buildings, and an increasing number of residents. The men continued to work as barbers, and there were also opportunities for cooks, painters, laborers, firemen, laundrymen, waiters, and librarians. In addition, a concerted attempt was made to have military prisoners fabricate items that the army could use; this effort also provided prisoners with a vocation that would deliver a living wage upon their release. WPA professionals were brought in to teach the men, and a furniture school was even set up in Pier A across the river in Manhattan.[30]

By 1936, certain prisoners were paid for their labor. Laundry workers earned forty-eight cents an hour; landscaping and care of the golf course and polo fields netted fifty cents; and workers on island utilities and furnaces earned the top salary of sixty cents.[31] "Local paroles," or men with records of exemplary behavior, were assigned to work in public buildings and officers' homes, where they earned gratuities of $5 per month from each officer. Officials set aside these earnings and doled them out for the purchase of cigarettes and sundries. The remainder was issued to the prisoner on release.

In 1943, the Atlantic Branch of the U.S. Disciplinary Barracks and its felons were subsumed into more modern facilities at Fort Leavenworth and Alcatraz. The post then took over Castle Williams (calling it "the guardhouse," but post residents knew it affectionately as "Castle Bill") to handle draft dodgers, deserters, and regimental disciplinary problems. The facility was reduced to a local post prison, but research indicates that it continued to handle cases from outside of Fort Jay, although it is unclear where these men came from. In 1944, creaky nineteenth-century Castle Williams experienced a turnover of 1,500 men per month–rivaling the number counted in the Civil War census.

Regulations for Local Parole:

—A 'Local Parole' is a general prisoner who has been assigned to individual work on Governors Island, without guard, but under the supervision of an officer.

—A parole eligible roster is maintained from which paroles are chosen in order of date of entry...and it is therefore requested that paroles not be asked for by name.

—The duties of paroles who are detailed as janitors in public buildings and quarters include the following: operate furnaces... supply coal and kindling wood for kitchen ranges and laundry stoves and build fires in them as required by the occupant; remove ashes; police furnace rooms and hallways leading to the kitchen; police grounds and sweep walks once daily; wash porches and steps and water lawns as directed by occupant; other work on first floor, in basement, or about the grounds.

—Paroles are prohibited from: carrying letters or packages, exercising dogs, riding in automobiles or running errands.

—Paroles will not be allowed to make personal use of a telephone.

(T. A. BALDWIN JR., COMMANDANT, AUGUST 1, 1932, GENERAL CORRESPONDENCE, 1925–1940, RG 94, 7/253.2, NATIONAL ARCHIVES, COLLEGE PARK, MD.)

The Germans arrived in their desert khaki uniforms. They were housed in barracks along the west side of the athletic field which was used for polo games on Sunday and football games on Saturday up until the war started. They were enclosed in a high barbed wire fence complete with the usual MG [Military Guard] towers at each corner. They weren't kept there very long as it was only a way-stop to camps in the Middle West and the [S]outh.

(E-MAIL TO AUTHOR FROM JOE VINCENT, MILITARY RESIDENT ON GOVERNORS ISLAND IN THE 1940S, SENT JANUARY 14, 2005.)

NEW PRISONERS OF WAR, 1943–1946

The Allied defeat of Erwin Rommel's Afrika Korps brought foreign prisoners of war to Governors Island for the first time. A former army resident on the island recalled that the Germans were the first to arrive.[32]

Then, a year after the outbreak of World War II, 150 Italians landed on the island on December 3, 1943. Ironically, like their Civil War predecessors, they too were shipped from North Carolina, but the conditions of their stay were vastly different.[33] Most of the men were soldiers from the Italian infantry, along with a fair sampling of corporals and sergeants. Some of them had served in the Quartermaster Corps or the navy. Their spokesman was Staff Sergeant Pasquale Caruso, a senior officer with a good command of English. The Italians were incarcerated on the island at least until 1946, and for the years they were there, they lived in three 2-story barracks cordoned off by cyclone fencing and topped by barbed wire.

The self-contained compound just south of the polo field between Gresham and Craig Roads included the same adjunct facilities found in Castle Williams. A recreation room, canteen, and barbershop were fashioned out of a former supply warehouse. A mess hall and kitchen served "excellent" food "prepared according to the Italian

POW STOCKADE, *n.d., unknown delineator. Sketch plan of layout. On December 3, 1943, 150 Italian prisoners of war landed on Governors Island. The army constructed a self-contained compound for them just south of the polo field between Gresham Road and Craig Road. Courtesy of National Archives, College Park, Md.*

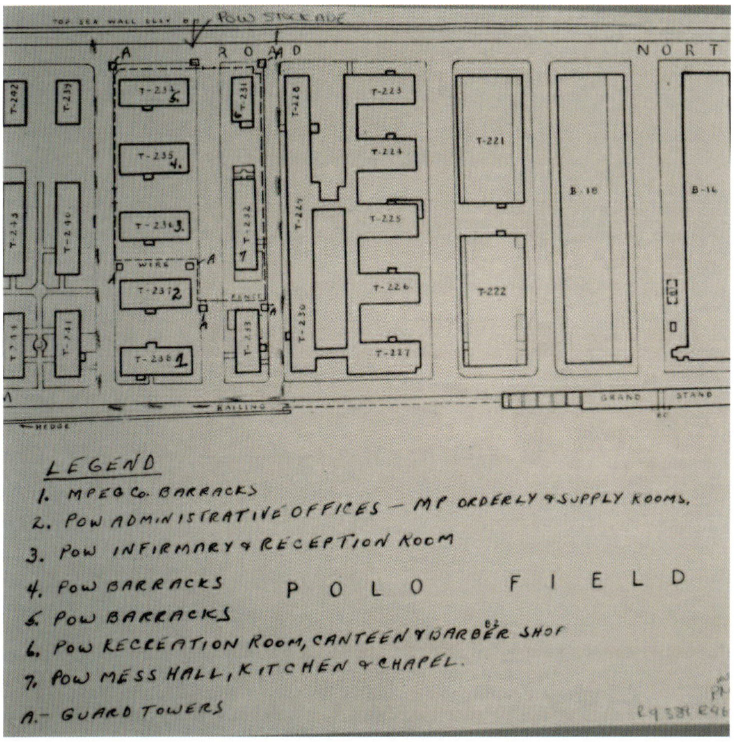

taste." This hall, the walls of which were decorated by the prisoners' artwork, doubled as a chapel. On weekends, prisoners formed small orchestral groups.[34] Health matters were cared for in a ward set aside in the hospital and in a small infirmary, the ground floor of which doubled as a reception hall for Sunday visitors. Administrative offices and barracks for the military police that guarded the prisoners were just outside the wire fence, adjacent to Gresham Road.

As part of their treatment under the Geneva Convention and to help overcome the shortage of American-enlisted manpower, prisoners were given daily labor assignments. Thirty-seven men were assigned to the Second Service Command salvage depot at the Brooklyn Army Terminal. Here they sorted such war materials as empty shell cases, tanks, combat vehicles, and scrap metal that had been used by the German, Italian, and American armies. The prisoners were also assigned to various jobs on Governors Island. In the Recruiting Publicity Bureau, for example, they had the dubious role of helping to print and publish advertising brochures that encouraged enlistment in the American army to fight the Italians and Germans.[35]

The Italian prisoners were a great help in maintaining the post. Some of them were assigned to assist parolees from Castle Williams in caring for officers' homes and gardens. One man who had been a barber prior to the war had a busy side job cutting his compatriots' hair. As one report on the Fort Jay prisoner-of-war camp noted, these men were "much more trustworthy and efficient in their work than the American garrison and general prisoners in the Castle Williams guardhouse."[36]

After the end of the war, German prisoners were sent to several camps in the New York region, including Fort Dix in New Jersey, Mitchell Field in Queens, and Fort Hamilton in Brooklyn, pending repatriation. Around February 1, 1946, a transfer of 126 German prisoners took place from Pine Camp in the Thousand Islands region of upper New York State (also known as Fort Drum) to Governors Island. This group included enlisted men and noncommissioned officers from the German army, navy, and air force. Nothing is known about their stay except that three months later, on April 26, 1946, the prisoner-of-war camp in Governors Island was deactivated. The remaining Germans were sent to a stockade at Camp Shanks in Rockland County, New York, to be processed for return to their native land.

This POW camp was the best in appearance, organization, and administration of all the camps, temporary and permanent, visited by this officer on his tour of the Second Services Command. The commanding officer of this camp inspired confidence in his ability, initiative and grasp of POW affairs....This officer was given to understand that the POW camp at Fort Jay is somewhat in the nature of a "show camp." All visiting dignitaries usually include a tour of this installation while on Governors Island. Nevertheless it was a model which other camps in the Second Service Command would do well to follow.

(MAJOR FRANK L. BROWN, REPORT OF VISIT TO POW CAMP, FORT JAY, NEW YORK, TO CHIEF, OPERATIONS BRANCH, POW DIVISION, OFFICE OF THE PROVOST MARSHALL GENERAL, WASHINGTON, D.C., FEBRUARY 24, 1944, [RECORDS OF] PRISONER OF WAR CAMP FORT JAY, RG 389, 461/2664.3, NATIONAL ARCHIVES, COLLEGE PARK, MD.)

THE CASTLE WILLIAMS COURTYARD, *n.d., unknown photographer. Showing casemates that housed prisoners from 1861 to 1965. Here, rabbits appear to be the only residents. Courtesy of McKim, Mead & White Collection, Museum of the City of New York.*

RIOT AND RESOLUTION, 1950–1965

BY 1951, THE PRISON CENSUS showed four hundred men captive, all housed in Castle Williams. It could have been a quiet time, but a change of command that year brought harsher discipline and revolt. Prisoners had their rations cut to one pack of cigarettes a week, although many of them had prior drug convictions and were used to receiving ten packs a week; razor blades were given out only once a week, and other privileges, such as seeing movies, were also curtailed. On September 17, the prisoners rioted.

The penalties meted out as a result of the ensuing courts-martial were far less dire than those of the nineteenth century. Though the maximum penalty for mutiny was death, the nine-member court sentenced the seven alleged ringleaders to nine to fifteen years of hard labor. They were also given dishonorable discharges and lost their pay and allowances. First Army commanding officer Willis D. Crittenberger subsequently reduced these sentences to six to ten years' hard labor. What became of the bulk of the prisoners who rioted but who were not brought to trial is unknown.[37]

CASTLE RECYCLED, 1965–2005

THE CASTLE WILLIAMS PRISON finally closed in 1965, before the transfer of the island to the Coast Guard, and like the hospital and many other buildings on the island it was quickly recycled for various uses. Parents who lived on the island under the auspices of the Coast Guard remember taking their children to the daycare center housed in the castle,[38] and former teens fondly recall the club rooms on the first tier.[39] The Enlisted Men's Wives' Club found another use for the castle. Capitalizing on the fortress's disquieting past, they turned it into a Halloween haunted house, invoking the spirits of long-gone soldiers and headless prisoners "stalking" the empty casemates. In 1976, as part of the island's bicentennial celebration, the castle underwent rejuvenation as a historical monument. Coast Guard officials and families, clothed in homemade eighteenth-century dress, gave guided tours to visitors.[40]

On January 31, 2003, Castle Williams became part of the Governors Island National Monument, with the former prison transformed into a tourist attraction. In 2005, seeking income to maintain the decaying structure, the U.S. National Park Service sought ideas for new uses. Among them was a proposal to build a copy of Shakespeare's Globe Theater within the confines of the castle walls. It's not farfetched to think that in the future the ghosts of Alonzo Bell and James Devlin might be joined by the ghosts of Banquo and Hamlet's father.

ISLAND HIGHLIGHTS *Island Music*

There are also on the Island, schools, wherein the boys attached to the station can receive an excellent English education, and are taught the use of fife and drum.[1]

A soldier in the vicinity of the South Battery in the 1850s doubtless heard the strains of flutes, oboes, bassoons, clarinets, and French horns mixed with the beats of serpents, bass drums, and tambourines. This cacophony differed markedly from the rudimentary fife and drumming used for military drills and parades when the English had occupied Governors Island. It was not a call to arms; it was band practice, emanating from the newly instituted School of Practice for U.S.A. Field Musicians.

According to the U.S. Army Band Web site, musical units have always been an important component of military life in the United States. Both the English and colonial regiments had bands that performed for special occasions and ceremonies. Their field units sounded signals for daily routines and for action in battle. Drummers gave the cadence for marches, and bugle calls signaled troops when to go to bed, wake up, eat, attack, and retreat.[2] There were stable calls, water calls, drill calls, sick calls, and church calls on Sunday. During the Revolutionary War, nine- to fourteen-year-old Continental drummers and fifers also performed soldierly duties. They were paid $7.33 a month, and their superiors received $8.33 a month.[3]

THE MUSIC BOYS CONGREGATING *outside of the band quarters in the South Battery, September 28, 1864, unknown photographer. One can imagine the boys taking a break from their lessons and practice. Courtesy of Still Pictures Branch, National Archives, College Park, Md.*

Musicians were a part of the earliest military companies on Governors Island. In the 1750s, the Loyal American Provincial Regiment battalion included a band. When the combat troops were removed from the island during the revolution, this largely ceremonial group remained to entertain Loyalists in New York City.[4] As music

GUARD MOUNTING, *Fort Jay, n.d., Rotograph Co. Postcard. Author's collection.*

BUGLERS LEADING THE BATTALION *from the sally port of Fort Jay, August 25, 1888, unknown artist. Cover illustration for* Harper's Weekly. *Courtesy of G. S. Grunert Collection, U.S. Army Military History Institute, Carlisle, Pa.*

became a recognized part of army routine and culture, Governors Island's musical rolls increased. In the 1780s, the fifty-seven-man American garrison stationed on the island contained only four musicians,[5] but by 1832 the regiment probably had a band composed of up to ten enlisted musicians with the rank of private, a chief musician, and a bandmaster. The bandsmen's pay was $8 per month, not a significant change from that of the revolutionary fifers three-quarters of a century earlier. The chief musician received a little more than double that amount, or $17.[6]

It is the drill that induces discipline, and no intelligent leader will ever forgo that which helps to give him firmer musical command over his bandsman.

(WILLIAM C. WHITE, ED. AND COMP., *UNISONIC CHORDS, SCALES, AND RHYTHM STUDIES FOR BANDS* [NEW YORK: CARL FISCHER, N.D], 2.)

The army band's professionalism was bolstered by the creation of the Sixth Infantry Band School. Why Governors Island was the site chosen for the school is unknown; perhaps it was the proximity to New York City's cultural life. It might also have been the persistence of the beloved bandmaster, Sergeant Michael Moore, who became a long-time island resident along with his daughter Mary, wife of steward David Robertson. Students received training in woodwinds, brass instruments, and drums. When their studies were complete, many men were sent to West Point, where they became part of that school's now famous military band.[7]

Along with the band school, the army had General Winfield Scott's manual of infantry tactics that described not only the details of daily life, but also musicians' roles in army life, the placement of bandsmen, and the signals for maneuvers. According to the directive, "The field

MUSICAL DRILL—*Twelfth Infantry (2d Battalion), early 1900s, George Grantham Bain. Courtesy of George Grantham Bain Collection, Prints and Photographs Division, Library of Congress, Washington, D.C.*

BAND QUARTERS, *Governors Island, September 24, 1864, unknown photographer. An 1870 retrospective report indicated that the army had moved the Music Boys to a one-story frame building twenty-five yards east of the South Battery. Courtesy of Still Pictures Branch, National Archives, College Park, Md.*

AMERICAN LYRIC SOPRANO ANNA FITZIU *performing in the Governors Island band shell with the army band, ca. 1908, George Grantham Bain. Ms. Fitziu was probably around twenty at the time. In 1916, she performed with the Metropolitan Opera and later toured with the San Carlo Opera Company. Courtesy of George Grantham Bain Collection, Prints and Photographs Division, Library of Congress, Washington, D.C.*

music will be formed in two ranks, the drummers in the rear, ten paces in the rear of the left center company."[8]

By 1836, the field music detachment on Governors Island–which had probably been housed either in tents or with the regiment in Fort Jay–was given a home in the casemates on the Buttermilk Channel side of the South Battery. This group of between fifty and ninety boys, called the Music Boys, became part of the permanent two-hundred- to five-hundred-man detachment on the post (soldiers who provided a special service and who were not transferred when others left). The publication *U.S. Army Bands in History* references a book about the band school–renamed the School of Practice for U.S.A. Field Musicians–written by twelve-year-old Augustus Meyers. According to this young musician-soldier, the sparse living conditions included crowded double bunk beds made of straw sacks reminiscent of the period's hospital beds. The food was common army supply: "boiled salt pork and beef, rice soup, bread, potatoes, bean soup, and coffee." In addition to board, lodging, and musical training, the boys received only $7 a month.[9]

Young Meyers's diary also provides a glimpse of the Music Boys' daily schedules. The fife and drum players began their day at one of Fort Jay's south corners, where they performed reveille.[10] At 0800, the boys played at the guard mount ceremony, which was followed by lessons on uniform and equipment maintenance. Academic classes ran from 0900 until 1100 hours. Musical training–based on *The Drummers and Fife Guide* by George G. Bruce, the official text for the school–followed until 1600 hours, with a break for lunch and perhaps leisure. The day ended when the young drummers and fifers played retreat.

The 1860 census confirms the large number of men and boys stationed on Governors

With the Castle Williams band playing "Auld Lang Syne" and the 225 young prisoners who were left behind shouting words of farewell to them, seventy-four army prisoners ...marched out of the old castle...departing for the federal penitentiary at Fort Leavenworth.

("74 YOUNG SOLDIERS TAKEN TO PRISON," *NEW YORK TIMES*, FEBRUARY 25, 1907, 7.)

Island who were involved in music. Twenty-eight musicians (probably teachers and bandsmen) were largely older men, some with wives and several small children. Thirty-four-year-old Charles Reham is listed as the bandmaster. The men's ethnicity was largely European. More than half were from Germany, where band training was an art. Five men were Irish, and only two were American born. The sixty Music Boys had a far different profile. They were very young, their ages ranging from thirteen to twenty-six; two-thirds of them were between thirteen and sixteen. More than half were American born. Probably because immigrant families recognized the benefits of the nearby training facility, and recruiters found a handy resource in them, twenty-eight of the boys were from New York.[11]

With these improvements carried into effect, no pleasanter lounging-place of a Summer twilight can well be imagined than the pretty but ample green between the fort and the light villa structures. There is talk about organizing a band for Summer-night concerts.

("IMPROVING A PLEASANT RESORT," *NEW YORK TIMES*, MARCH 16, 1879, 12.)

From the mid–nineteenth century on, the band was an integral part of life on Governors Island, performing everything from daily bugle calls to funeral taps. In addition to announcing the normal military routine, members performed at daily dress parades and greeted such visiting dignitaries as Grand Duke Alexis, brother of the Russian czar (1872), and Grand Admiral Von Koester from Germany (1909). The band's performances provided a nostalgic respite to Civil War prisoner Thomas Sparrow, who in his diaries described its playing "Still So Quietly o'er Me Stealing" in front of Colonel Gustavus Loomis's residence in Nolan Park at 3:30 every day while men were in drill on the lawn.[12] In 1865, the band played the "Dead March" at the executions of John Beale and James Devlin, and in 1886 it performed retreat as General Winfield Scott Hancock's body was removed from Governors Island for burial. Later in the nineteenth century and well into the twentieth, the band was central to such social functions as summer hops, weddings, and garden parties.

The Music Boys' living conditions changed little between 1830 and 1870. Possibly because of crowded, unsanitary conditions, at least four boys[13] and men succumbed to the yellow fever epidemic in 1870.[14] That year, half of the boys were living in tents, but perhaps not for long: a contemporaneous report to the surgeon general lists a "band quarters" consisting of a one-story frame building located twenty-five yards east of the South Battery. Inside was one dormitory, measuring nineteen by fifty-four feet on the first floor and holding twenty single bunks; and a basement with a mess forty-two by eighteen and a half feet and a kitchen with a cooking range.[15] But the boys' days in the South Battery were numbered. In 1879, as part of the island's overhaul, General Hancock established the Officers' Mess in the space occupied by the Music Boys, who were moved out to unknown quarters.[16]

Not until 1911 did the Governors Island's music school once again rise to prominence. In response to the army's desire to improve morale and to instill a fighting spirit into the men, Congress authorized the Army Music School to train bandleaders.[17] Dr. Frank Heino Damrosch was put in charge. Damrosch, an esteemed professional musician, was a founder and director of the Institute of Musical Art (which in 1926 would become the Julliard School of Music) as well as a former assistant conductor of the Metropolitan

Had a lovely day, it is a very beautiful spot. Saw everything that was to be seen...and stayed for the band concert.

(POSTCARD FROM SADIE [NO LAST NAME GIVEN] TO MAMIE FURMAN, JAMAICA, L.I., OCTOBER 12, 1907.)

COVER OF Unisonal Scales, Chords, and Rhythmic Studies for Military Bands *by William C. White, n.d. Author's collection.*

WARRANT OFFICER WILLIAM J. STANNARD, *April 24, 1925, unknown photographer. Stannard was the first official leader of the Sixteenth Infantry Band. Courtesy of Still Pictures Branch, National Archives, College Park, Md.*

THE SIXTEENTH INFANTRY BAND *with Lower Manhattan in the background, April 24, 1925, unknown photographer. Courtesy of Still Pictures Branch, National Archives, College Park, Md.*

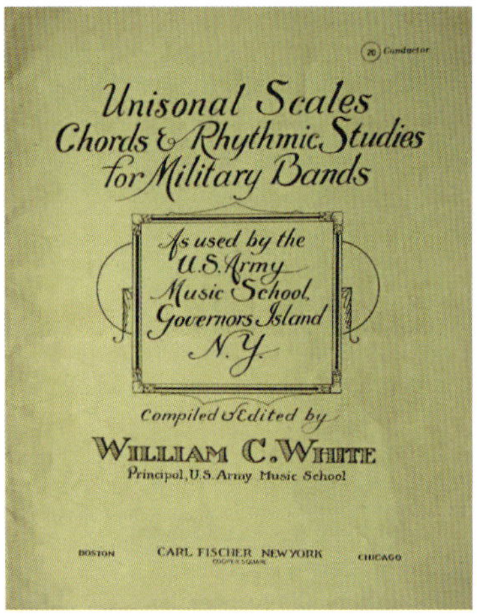

Opera and conductor of both the Oratorio Society and the Young People's Concerts. He filled his army mandate by establishing a branch of the institute on the island.

The Governors Island music school was initially highly selective, and the curriculum was vastly different from the brass and percussion training once led by Michael Moore. Only five army bandsmen out of seventy-five applicants gained acceptance into the program in the first year. Using methods from European bandleader-training schools, instruction now included musical form, applied acoustics, music history, band instrumentation and arranging, ear training, and conducting.[18]

William C. White, an army bandleader and composer, was among the recruits who came up through the ranks of the Army Music School. A student at the New England Conservatory of Music, White joined the U.S. Army in 1907. He began his band studies on Governors Island around 1912 and two years later graduated as a bandmaster. By 1914, twenty-five army recruits had joined White at the music school, and the Recruit Practice Band performed twice weekly at a pay scale ranging from $75 for the bandleader to $40 for the bugler, and from $24 to $36 for musicians.[19]

THIRTY-SEVENTH ANNIVERSARY *of First Army–Organization Day, August 10, 1955, unknown publisher. Postcard. Author's collection.*

MESSAGE ON REVERSE *of 37th anniversary postcard: "This is a good view of what we see from our bedroom windows & you'll enjoy the drill here which they have every Wed. afternoon. We can see it all. Band too, Mom."*

As World War I approached and the number of regiments increased, the demand for army bands grew. On Governors Island, the prison—where efforts were being made not only to improve morale, but also to provide vocational training to make prisoners more useful citizens after their release—was a beneficiary of congressional legislation that broadened the establishment of bands. On July 21, 1916, the War Department ordered the formation of the Third Disciplinary Band. Six enlisted men were authorized to teach music to twenty-one prisoners. The program, run by the Army Music School, was so successful that within a few years 115 general prisoners were at one time or another members of the prison band. In a memo requesting a doubling of the enlisted men (two band sergeants and four band corporals) to teach forty-two prisoners, William C. White informed the Castle Williams prison commandant that of those men restored to duty or allowed to reenlist, about 90 percent had qualified for assignment to a military band.[20]

The prison band not only succeeded in its vocational training, but also became so popular that it was in competition with the island's famed Sixteenth Infantry Band, and the Officers' Club began to avail itself of both bands for Saturday night dinners and holiday parties. Although the club tried hard to give each group the same number of gigs, in the first six months of one year the castle band performed on ten occasions, receiving a total of $210, whereas the Sixteenth Infantry Band performed nine times, for $175. A letter from the chair of the club's entertainment committee indicated that he preferred to choose the most popular band, regardless of the number of performances; it appears that the castle band had the advantage.[21]

In 1917, World War I was under way, and the demand for army bands was even stronger. The Recruit Band, now known as the Governors Island Practice Band, had grown to forty-nine men, who were being trained and then sent to perform their patriotic duties in army bands at home and abroad.[22] The Army Music School's heyday was short-lived, but the band played on. In 1921, the school was relocated to the Army War College in Washington, D.C., where White remained in charge until its closure in 1928.[23] The following year, army chief of staff General John J. Pershing ordered the formation of the U.S. Army Band. Many of its members were most likely graduates of the Music School.

The music school never returned to Governors Island, but bands remained an important part of the island's military and social life until the army left the island in 1965. The regiment's Sixteenth Infantry Band was a favorite of New York City's mayor Fiorello LaGuardia, and until ordered to inactivate on January 6, 1941, it often welcomed assorted heroes in Wall Street parades. Other groups came to the island for special occasions. In 1951, thirty-three women from the WAC's Fourteenth Army Band played "When the Saints Go Marching In" and "Colonel Bogey" at a solemn retreat.[24] The U.S. Army Band traveled the world from its home in Liggett Hall until 1965, when it moved to Fort Meade, Virginia.[25]

The Coast Guard carried on the musical tradition. Although its official band was not based

MAP SHOWING *the position of all buildings on Governors Island, December 1, 1867, John G. Bernard, surveyor. Author's collection.*

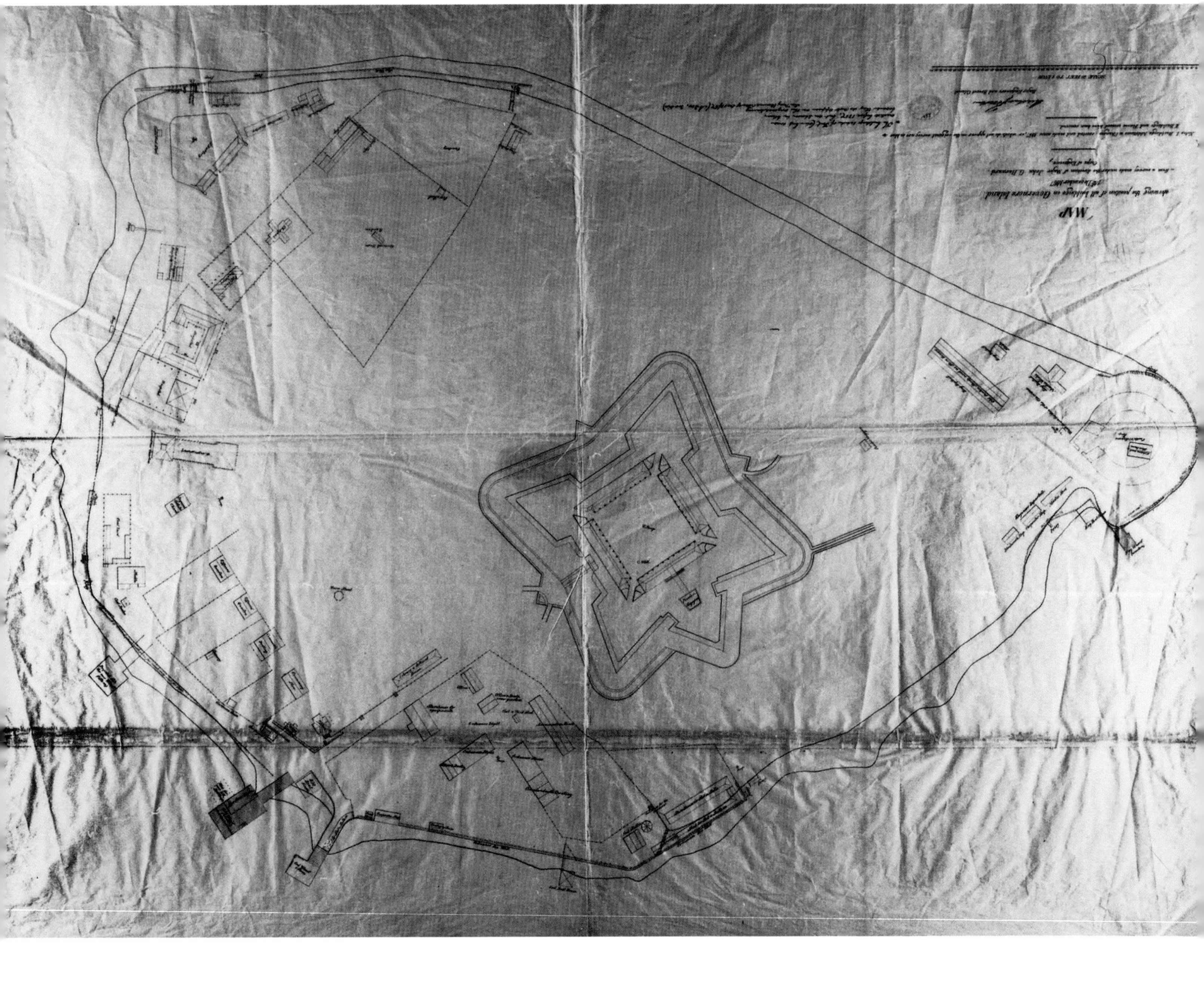

VETERAN POSTMAN TYLER, *March 15, 1890, unknown artist. Illustration in the* Illustrated American. *Author's collection.*

on the island, it was imported for special events. On July 4 and 5, 1992, a few years before the island's final closure, this band performed at the VIP Center during the dress parade. In a performance reminiscent of the nineteenth century–but without the Victorian bandstand–the Coast Guard Band also played a concert on the village green.[26]

MAP SHOWING LOCATION *of water, drain, and sewer pipes on Governors Island, August 30, 1879, unknown delineator. RG 0077, Miscellaneous Forts File. Courtesy of National Archives Architectural and Cartographic Branch, College Park, Md.*

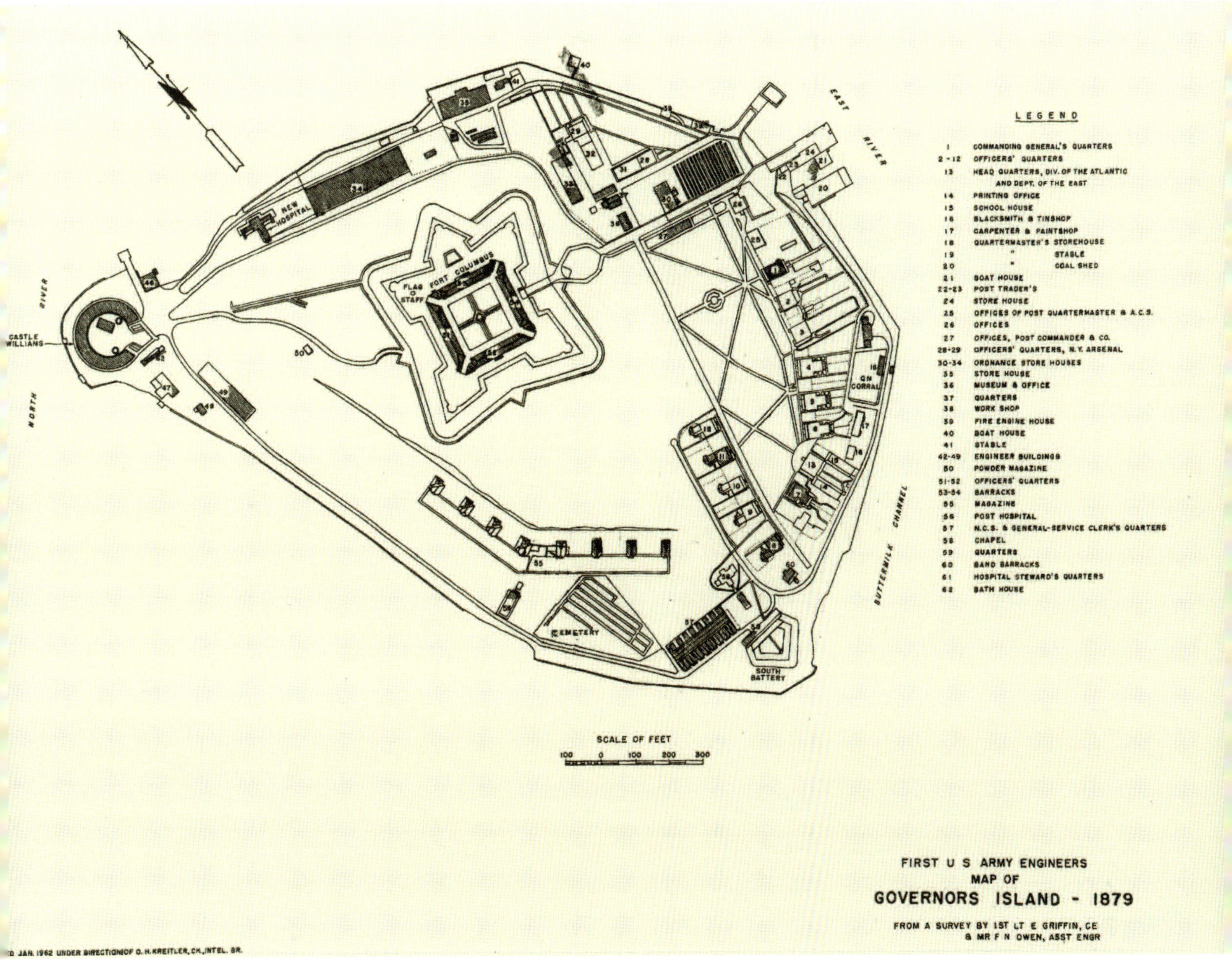

GOVERNORS ISLAND *in the year of Hancock's arrival, 1878, Currier & Ives. Portion of a lithograph entitled* New York. *Courtesy of Library of Congress, Geography and Map Division, Washington, D.C.*

ISLAND HIGHLIGHTS *The Commanders*

A flock of pigeons flapped in and out of the dark portholes in the circular fort, and a hen marshaled her brood among a pyramid of black cannon balls....The muzzles of the cannon pointed at us from the walls of the fort; but peace never seems more permanent than amid the unused materials of war.[1]

General Winfield Scott Hancock commanded the new Division of the Atlantic and the Department of the East on Governors Island from 1878 until his death in 1886. He was well qualified for this role: he'd been a West Pointer with service in three border wars and the Battle of Gettysburg, and at just more than six feet tall and 240 pounds he must have been formidable. Politically savvy and free of wartime concerns, Hancock changed the face of Governors Island, much as Jonathan Williams had done in the early 1800s and others would do at the turn of the twentieth century. A series of strolls that his chief of staff, General William T. Mitchell, might have taken during this period unveil the legacy of "Hancock the Magnificent."

William Mitchell arrived on Governors Island with General Hancock and about a dozen other officers on July 1, 1878. In an economizing mood, Congress had ordered Hancock's command to depart from its headquarters at Greene and Houston Streets in Manhattan and to settle on Governors Island, where housing, always an expensive proposition in the city, was free. The move, however, totally changed the military focus of the island from fortification and troop induction to administration.

To make room for the expanded officers' corps, participants in the forty-year-old Governors Island recruiting station were sent to David's Island in New Rochelle, New York. According to the *New York Times*, only one company of infantry, the brass band, and various mechanics attached to the Quartermaster Department–about one hundred men in all–remained at the station. They were immediately augmented by two companies of the First Regiment of Artillery under the command of Captain J. T. Sanger and Captain Thomas Ward.[2]

In the late 1880s, when General Mitchell walked to his office in the former hospital (Building 9), he probably witnessed a formidable amount of residential construction and reconstruction that would not be equaled again at Governors Island until the 1930s. His superior, General Hancock, wanted to accommodate the necessary increase in officers in a style appropriate to their rank. To do this, he apparently had the support of the War Department, which despite the fact that there was no permanent army during this

Few men have served their country better than Winfield S. Hancock....A big man with a big head, a big heart and a big brain, Hancock is the personification of honor....He would make the finest looking President who ever sat in the White House, except possibly, George Washington. His form towers above other men, and he attracts attention by his mere looks wherever he goes. His eyes are blue, and have a benignant and mild expression when in repose, but inspiring when in danger. His manner is dignified and knightly, and he is courtesy itself....He gave a man a good opinion of himself, and made each one feel he was of more importance than he ever before suspected. It was this that caused him to have so much power over his officers and men in battle, and made them prefer rather to die than forfeit the good opinion of their leader....A volume would not contain an account of all the heroic deeds of a man like Hancock....A glorious soldier, a steadfast friend, a useful citizen, he is all that is noble, manly and brave.

("OUR CANDIDATES," *WASHINGTON POST*, JUNE 25, 1880, 2.)

period, helped to finance construction and modernization of permanent installations, mainly on the frontier.[3]

On Mitchell's path were the makings of Nolan Park (Buildings 6, 7, 8, 10, 11–built for hospital steward David Robertson–and Buildings 14 through 18). These Victorian, vernacular-style, wood-frame houses known as "Colonel's Row" enclosed one side of a green, opposite from which sat the original masonry homes of the most senior of the officers, known as "General's Row." Together, these structures, their views, their carefully tended vegetable and flower gardens, and their parklike surroundings became the settings for Thursday afternoon band concerts, twentieth-century garden parties, and weddings of the socially prominent. They also set the tone for the "island village" that army and Coast Guard families remembered in the twenty-first century.

One of the modernizations taking place was in Building 25, a structure that backed onto Andes Road on the northern end of Nolan Park. Here was a splendid example of adaptive reuse, which because of the island's size constraints became more and more prevalent. According to the Library of Congress Historic Building Survey, this building was originally an ordnance storehouse. By 1863, in addition to supplies and clothing, it housed a carpenter's shop and the post's school. A library and a billiard room were added by 1867, providing one of the original recreational outlets for the soldiers. In 1870, the building became the site for courts-martial. When Hancock and Mitchell arrived in 1878, office space for the post commander and his adjutant was also among the varied uses to which it was being put.

The post's school must have been seriously overcrowded by 1880. More than a hundred children between the ages of seven and sixteen–nearly 20 percent more than the number of soldiers–were living on the island. Some may have taken the twice-daily ferry ride to classes on the mainland, but those who remained formed a group that was quite a contrast to the normal military hierarchy. Sons and daughters of American officers sat side by side with the children of Irish clerks, an Irish printer, Portuguese laborers, a Prussian barber, and a Scots tailor and druggist.[4]

On his way to the ferry for a trip to Manhattan, Mitchell probably also had to avoid ditches caused by the building of new infrastructure. Hancock had secured permission from the state legislature to lay gas and water lines from Brooklyn onto Governors Island. By 1880, for the first time in the island's history, gas lamps began to light the pathways at night, and city water–when the pressure was right–replaced the use of wells and cisterns. Among the other Hancock innovations that Mitchell might have passed were four on-street mailboxes because letter carrier pickup service had also been extended to the island in 1880.

When Mitchell arrived at the ferry dock at the end of Andes Road, he doubtless found that the private tug that had been carrying passengers for fifteen cents a ride had been replaced with a government-owned craft, complete with a heated cabin. Captain William Loring and Mate Sam Walter oversaw the disembarking of passengers from the now-free ferry from Manhattan.[5] Among those alighting might have been James Fay, the post trader who furnished meats, greens, and dry groceries to families on the island, or tailor James Craigh.

Also aboard might have been Abraham "Abe" Brokaw, the headquarters messenger, full of news about General Hancock's nomination for president of the United States on the Democratic ticket. Walking with Brokaw to the commanding officer's house were individuals

THE MILITARY SERVICE INSTITUTION, *March 29, 1890, unknown photographer. Illustration in the* Illustrated American. *This military think tank was housed in the 1850s former arsenal storehouse. Author's collection.*

THE MILITARY SERVICE INSTITUTION MUSEUM, *March 29, 1890, unknown photographer. Illustration in the* Illustrated American. *The museum held a vast collection of military artifacts, including Lieutenant General Philip Sheridan's horse Winchester. Author's collection.*

seeking positions and favors. One of these visitors described the Hancocks' parlor as an interesting but functional room:

> [It] was plainly furnished. A somewhat faded Brussels carpet, the figures upon which were anything but modern in style, covered the floor. The chairs, sofas, mirrors, and other furniture were decidedly old-fashioned. Several portraits and paintings adorned the walls, and articles of bric-a-brac were arranged upon the mantle and on a what-not in a corner. A piano with quaint, carved, crooked legs was included in

THE SIEGE OF GOVERNORS ISLAND *by hungry office seekers, September 1888, J. A. Wales. Cartoon in* Puck. *General Hancock was often the subject of derision in* Puck *cartoons. Author's collection.*

the inventory. On the floor in front of the fireplace was a curious mat, which was an imitation of the skin of a white fox, with funny little glass eyes in the head.[6]

Hancock, continuing in command at Governors Island, would soon be defeated by Samuel J. Tilden by a narrow margin. Brokaw, however, remained in service on the island until his death in 1907.[7]

On Sunday, following services at St. Cornelius Chapel, General Mitchell walked to the South Battery and the newly opened Officers' Mess. His thoughts were likely of the sermon that had just been preached by Reverend Edward H. C. Goodwin of Trinity Church, who was officiating in the absence of a permanent military pastor. Though paid by the Trinity parish, Goodwin resided on Governors Island with his wife, Mary, and their four sons and two daughters.

At the Officers' Mess, Mitchell was doubtless greeted by John Rolf, the mess steward. Founded on June 20, 1879, on orders of General Hancock, this eating establishment had grown by 1881 into a members-only eating and social club.[8] About-to-retire General James B.

LIBRARY OF THE MILITARY SERVICE INSTITUTION, *March 15, 1890, unknown photographer. Illustration in the* Illustrated American. *Author's collection.*

Fry, who for many years was the army's provost martial general, presided over the thirty-one clubmen. During the Civil War, he had the controversial role of recruiting volunteers, supplementing the draft, and catching deserters.[9]

Fry was also a vice president of an innovative military think tank formed and initially headed by General Hancock. The Military Service Institution of the United States was modeled on England's Royal United Service Institution. Designed to increase the army's professionalism, it also helped to place the military on an elevated footing through high-caliber discussions and intellectual pursuits. By December 1878, just four months after his arrival on Governors Island, Hancock had assigned "commodious temporary quarters" in Building 25 to the institution. In storage space previously used by ordnance, now there was a library with more than one thousand volumes as well as a museum filled with memorabilia, most notably General Philip Sheridan's Civil War horse Winchester, fully stuffed and mounted.[10]

With foam and with dust the black charger was gray; By the flash of his eyes and the red nostrils' play, He seemed to the whole great army to say: "I have brought you Sheridan all the way From Winchester down to save the day."

("GOVERNORS ISLAND HAS A MUSEUM OF RARE HISTORIC RELICS," *NEW YORK TIMES*, SEPTEMBER 18, 1904, SM6.)

The museum's quarters ultimately became less commodious, but never moved from Building 25. A collection of Native American arms and artifacts, a card table used by George Washington, battle flags, armor, ammunition, and more were packed away during the Cuban War to restore space to the Ordnance Department for supplies.[11] In 1899, officers sought in vain to move the museum to Manhattan, but although Winchester was always in view, the museum never fully recovered its late-nineteenth-century glory days and closed in 1922. According to Jann Warren-Findlay and Nancy Dallett's historic resource study for the National Park Service, many objects were returned to their owners, but Winchester and many other military relics now reside in the National Museum of American History.[12]

PROGRAM, *June 3, 1922, unknown artist. Winchester left Governors Island for the Smithsonian Institution in Washington, D.C., in 1922. This is the program for the departure ceremony. Courtesy of Susan Kroeger.*

The Military Service Institution also published a highly respected journal. Institution members—who paid $5 followed by $2 yearly dues or a life membership of $25—received and were among the contributors to the publication. They attended informal monthly luncheons at the Officers' Mess and thereafter meetings in Building 25.[13] There, invited papers—subsequently printed in the journal—were read on subjects ranging from "the military necessities of the United States and the best provisions for meeting them" to "camp sanitation." A paper entitled "A Military Court of Appeal," presented by General Fry in December 1881, was followed by a lively discussion about the finality of military court findings and the desirability of doing away with ultimate review by the president.[14]

It is not known how long William Mitchell remained in service to General Hancock, and there is no evidence of his presence at Hancock's death on Governors Island on February 9, 1886. Attending Hancock in his last illness—from a carbuncle exacerbated by diabetes—were post surgeon John H. Janeway and a Dr. Purley. Ever present, of course, was hospital steward David Robertson.

Contemporary descriptions of the southwest bedroom in the commanding general's house where Hancock lay in his final hours indicate that he, who had greatly improved life on Governors Island for others, lived very simply. The room was tastefully furnished. Beside the west wall of the room was an unadorned walnut bed. Opposite it was a marble mantle, to its left a walnut wardrobe, and on the right a dressing case. In one corner were some flags and a toy schooner in full sail. On the mantle were signs of the family life forbidden to ordinary soldiers: a tin locomotive and pile of small toys belonging to grandson Gwynne Hancock.[15]

Chapter Four

METES AND BOUNDS

The subject of enlarging the Island has been carefully studied, and if the question had been one of relating solely to the storage of military supplies and to the quartering of one battalion of troops, the decision would have been that the present area is large enough for these purposes. But the Board believes that the great national importance of New York Harbor makes it extremely desirable that there should be a capacious Government reservation convenient to the City and adapted to every military requirement, provided it can be obtained at reasonable cost.[1]

When New York's many islands became too crowded for commerce and comfort, our forefathers simply made more land by building out into the water. At the dawn of the twentieth century, the U.S. Army, finding Governors Island too small to carry out its mandate as a military reservation to protect New York City, embarked on a massive land-reclamation project. Before the end of the first decade, the island's size had doubled, and its profile in the harbor had changed significantly.

In many ways, the project was unique. Thanks to aggressive leadership, for the first time in the history of Governors Island the army not only made plans that looked at the island in a comprehensive manner, but also called on one of the most famous New York City architects, Charles McKim, to help. Army engineers even invented a new technology that set the pattern for the construction of seawalls in other parts of the city. The implementation of the land expansion, equal in size to Battery Park City (New York's last significant landfill), came to fruition in record time and on budget. Directing all of this was Elihu Root, the secretary of war whose political acumen finally got something done–at least partially.

PLANNING AND DESIGN

THE PROBLEM IN 1900

Despite the improvements to the island during Winfield Scott Hancock's administration, by the turn of the twentieth century Governors Island was in a derelict state yet again. A 1901 report from the U.S. Adjutant General's Office titled *Sites for Military Posts* indicated that the army base, 436 men strong, was made up of four artillery complements and one band. In addition, according to the 1900 U.S. Census, more than 120 prisoners and 100 assorted workers and family members also resided on the island.

NEW YORK, *ca. 1874, J. Bachmann, illustrator, and G. Schlegel, printer. Lithograph. This bird's-eye view of New York shows a breakwater wall on the north side of Governors Island. The unfinished south side allowed waves to spray over the houses on Brick Row. Courtesy of Prints and Photographs Division, Library of Congress, Washington, D.C.*

GOVERNORS ISLAND SHORELINE, *1860s, Mathew Brady. The uneven shoreline of Governors Island in the 1860s included debris and a sunken barge. In the distance, the spire of Trinity Church looms tall on the Manhattan skyline. Courtesy of Still Pictures Branch, National Archives, College Park, Md.*

The quartermaster's inventory of Fort Jay structures that served the men in the lower military echelons showed major weaknesses. Four barracks, Castle Williams, four noncommissioned officers' quarters housing six officers and their families, the crematory, and the powder magazine were listed in "fair" condition. Conversely, ten married officers' quarters and–probably because they were more closely scrutinized by periodic health inspections–the bake house, the mess hall, and the kitchen were listed as "good." The eighteen married officers' quarters and the stable for ten horses under the jurisdiction of the Department of the East were not rated.[2] A report from Department of the East headquarters to the army's adjutant general a year earlier put the problems in graphic perspective: "The buildings were erected at different times, to meet varying emergencies, and the final result is an aggregation of poor structures which are objectionable in many ways. With few exceptions, they are old frame buildings, only slightly raised above the soil, inconvenient, unsanitary, and inflammable."[3]

In addition to the problems on the land, the land itself was shrinking. The island that New York State had granted to the federal government in 1800 purportedly contained 93 acres, one-third more acreage than existed a century later. (A 2003 study for the National Park Service posited that the original shoreline might have been even larger.)[4] Situated in the face of waves from storms and shipping, besieged by swift currents, and subject to a tide that twice daily ebbed and flowed at least 6.0 feet, the island's shores were in constant threat of a washout. On the southwestern side, according to Edmund Banks Smith, even the new brick (or regimental) rowhouses that had been constructed between 1892 and 1895 were endangered: "[W]hen the sea was high, spray would dash upon the front of the houses."[5]

As early as 1865, the army engineers had received approval to build a seawall at or near the low-water mark and enclosing the entire island. Construction had proceeded in fits and starts,

ENLARGEMENT OF THE CITY *of Greater New York, 1905, Hart (no first name given). Lithograph. The enlargement shows how crowded Governors Island had become. Courtesy of Library of Congress, Geography and Map Division, Washington, D.C.*

first between Castle Williams and the South Battery, and later on the northwestern side. However, a letter written twenty-six years after the endorsement complained that "offal and garbage covered the shores of the island. [The debris] drifted up at high water and decayed in the sun...[I]n the summer this is a source of constant danger to the health of the garrison."[6]

Work continued on the seawall in the 1890s, mostly to replace washed-out mortar and to shore up existing foundations.[7] But the fight against the elements was a losing battle, and by 1900 the island, according to the chief engineer, had shrunk by one-third to 69.4 acres, exclusive of docks.[8] Given these conditions as well as pressure from members of Congress to return the island to the city for a park and the fact that overall expansion and reorganization of the army was under discussion, the question being asked in Washington was, Should Governors Island be abandoned, retained, or enlarged?

Assuming that it should be kept, Secretary of War Elihu Root stepped in. A highly regarded New York City attorney who was well connected politically and socially, Root had been appointed to the War Department post by President William McKinley in 1899. Described by one of his successors, Henry L. Stimson, as the most "intelligent, constructive and vital force [to occupy] the [War Department] post in American history,"[9] Root would go on to become secretary of state under Theodore Roosevelt, a U.S. senator, and in 1912 a winner of the Nobel Peace Prize. But in July 1900, using his considerable talents to the benefit of Governors Island, he appointed a board of survey to consider the island's condition and suggest plans for its improvement.

The board's membership was indicative of the division of labor in using and maintaining the island. Colonel Amos S. Kimball, assistant quartermaster general of the U.S. Army, was appointed chair. Since the early nineteenth century, the quartermaster had been in charge of repairs and new construction on the land. Colonel George L. Gillespie of the Corps of Engineers represented the service arm that maintained the marine parts of the island. Seawall and pier construction and repair, dredging, and removal of sunken ships blocking the harbor were among the tasks in his charge. The third board member, Major General John R. Brooke, stood in for the army, the actual users of the island. Brooke was serving as governor-general of Cuba and had recently been detailed to Governors Island to replace Wesley Merrit as the commander of the Department of the East.

Root set the men a fourfold task: find housing for at least one battalion of troops–in other words, double the amount of men in the regiment; provide storage space and shipping berths for all branches of the army, including the Quartermaster, Subsistence, Ordnance, and Medical Departments; rationalize and improve the existing outdated structures; and provide more space, if needed. In commissioning these officers, Root clearly had in mind a thorough overhaul of the army's preparedness, with Governors Island as the focal point. New York City provided ready access to a large network of railroads and terminals that could send troops and supplies to ships safely docked at the island; all that was needed, he wrote, were "wharf accommodations for vessels and room for trans-shipment."[10]

The board appointees were also charged with finding a way to accommodate more soldiers on the island in times of stress. The army had been sorely embarrassed during recent troop movements to Cuba and to the Philippines on an eastern route via the Suez Canal; without space on Governors Island for tent grounds, men had been forced to reside in railroad cars until their ships were ready for departure. Finally, perhaps the board of officers could covertly provide a strong rationale for the army to retain Governors Island considering that the army had grander plans for it: a possible transfer of the transport service from the Pacific Coast.[11]

THE KIMBALL PLAN, 1900–1901

Piecemeal reactions and repair had always been the order of the day for the island. In fact, not since John Montresor's maps for the British in 1755 had there been an overall vision for improvements. In order to justify keeping the island and expanding its role in the U.S. military, Secretary Root probably recognized the need for a properly planned approach. So, following a rational planning method, the board of officers visited the island, looked at alternatives, and estimated costs for their choices. The report they submitted to the army adjutant general on August 17, 1900, was thorough and comprehensive. It provided a framework for action, some parts of which proceeded immediately, although other parts would languish for nearly thirty years. The report proposed solutions for the storage problems and recommended rearrangement of some of the buildings. The main focus, however, was on the creation of a major pier facility and enlargement of the island.

Beginning a cost-cutting refrain that would be echoed repeatedly over the next decade, the board of officers focused first on unnecessary expenditures. Lack of storage space on Governors Island was a prime target. They estimated that in times of utmost stress–such as the late-nineteenth-century wars against Spain in Cuba and the Philippines–the quartermaster paid $83,600 annually for at least 178,000 square feet of warehousing and dock space in the city.[12] The officers felt that money could be saved if additional space were eked out on the island. The arsenal, which mainly held obsolete war material that everyone agreed should be sold, was a perfect alternative to the city rentals. Disregarding the desires of arsenal personnel, the officers recommended reducing that compound from five storehouses to two and adding four new rectangular warehouses located behind the seawall on the vacated property.[13]

[I]mprovement of Governors Island] is of primary importance as a matter of preparation for any exigency that may require the use of troops and of military supplies upon the Atlantic seaboard or at any point in the West Indies or Central America. If we construct the Isthmian Canal it will be especially important that we should have some point where men, ships and supplies can be readily brought together.

(LETTER FROM SECRETARY OF WAR ELIHU ROOT TO WILLIAM B. ALLISON, MARCH 1, 1901, GENERAL CORRESPONDENCE 1884–1923, RG 77, 853/71, NATIONAL ARCHIVES, COLLEGE PARK, MD.)

Having examined all of the housing and administrative buildings on Governors Island, and despite finding all of them "so old and in such bad repair that renewals will be required in a few years," the board recommended only "general repairs to all."[14] Several exceptions were made, some of which were further evidence of the hierarchical order common to army bases. A new administration building for the Department of the East commanding general was to be erected in place of one of the arsenal storehouses; more varied administrative functions no doubt required additional space, and a larger, handsomely designed main building would lend a sense of permanence to a post in jeopardy of closure. The board also recommended recladding two sets of officers' quarters in brick (probably Buildings 2 and 3), perhaps to give them more importance because they were situated next to the commanding general's house. In addition, in the construction estimate were several new homes for garrison officers. Although sites were not specified, mention was made of the island's south side, probably a proposed expansion of Colonel's Row and Brick Row.[15]

Besides living quarters for the upper echelons, the board was also concerned with the soldiers' physical health. Beginning what became a nearly three-decades-long process to replace the twenty-six-year-old medical facility, the board included in its estimate a small sum for "moving and repairing the hospital." It envisioned a "much-needed" gymnasium in the conversion of one of the five arsenal storehouses. However, no funds were listed for this structure in the more than half-million-dollar total cost estimate for buildings.[16]

Estimates of Cost of Buildings on the Island

Two Brick storehouses, Q.M. Dept.	$80,000.00
One Brick storehouse, C.S. Dept.	40,000.00
One Brick storehouse, Medical Dept.	40,000.00
One Brick storehouse and office, Ordnance Dept.	40,000.00
One Power-house and accessories	40,000.00
One Administrative Building, Hqrs. Dept. of East	65,000.00
Six double sets of quarters for officers	90,000.00
Moving and repairing Hospital	21,000.00
Buildings for C.S. and Q.M. Depts., east side	35,000.00
Constructing, repairing and moving other minor buildings	35,000.00
Raising barracks in Fort Columbus one story	50,000.00
Repairs to Engineer dock at Castle William and transfer of coal buildings	15,000.00
TOTAL	$550,000.00

(REPORT FROM THE BOARD OF OFFICERS TO THE ADJUTANT GENERAL, U.S. ARMY, AUGUST 17, 1900, GENERAL CORRESPONDENCE 1884–1923, RG 77, 853/37048, 10, NATIONAL ARCHIVES, COLLEGE PARK, MD.)

Root's instructions to the board of officers had included making provision for barracks and quarters for at least one battalion of troops. Because new structures would be a tight fit on the island, the board suggested an adaptive reuse of Fort Jay. "The four buildings should be raised one story," they wrote. Considering the aesthetic aspects, and probably in response to concerns about damaging the historic fortress's integrity, the report continued, "[this] will not mar the appearance of the post." The cost for the work was estimated at $50,000, but the money for an entirely different regimental barracks was not actually requisitioned until nearly thirty years later.[17]

The board's plan for a new wharf centered on the assumption that the most up-to-date transport carriers, some with drafts reaching 26 feet, would be home based on Governors Island. Foreshadowing the U.S. Coast Guard's coming to the island, this plan apparently was the first major attempt to change Governors Island from a land-based administrative and training facility to a depot using the waterways. As in the rest of New York, some form of water transportation to and from the island had always been in operation. But unlike the maritime commerce that formed the economic base of the city, Governors Island's vessel traffic in peacetime was strictly limited to carrying people and goods necessary for the island's day-to-day functioning.

In his military history, Edmund Banks Smith gives a brief account of the Governors Island ferry transportation from 1600 to 1913. Although all-purpose boats were open to all on the post, the Ordnance Department and the headquarters commander had their own vessels. Banks describes the first privately operated oared barges running in 1756 from the Battery in Manhattan to a stairway at the foot of Andes Road. They charged as little as "three pence" per trip. By the middle of the nineteenth century, according to Banks, "a fleet of eight to ten small boats [were also] plying to Pacific Street in Brooklyn, which was convenient for persons going to market."[18] During the Civil War, steam-powered tugs were put into service and were eventually run by the government free of charge. At the time the board of officers began its deliberations, the ferryboat *General Hancock* had joined the fleet, probably carrying, among other cargo, soldiers ready for training, secretaries, and polo ponies.

In order to introduce major military shipping to Governors Island, the board inventoried the four existing small wharves, all located on the north side. These wharves had various functions, but none had the water depth to handle the newest cadre of transport ships Secretary Root was seeking to base on the island. A small dock near Castle Williams was used for landing cargo and coal to heat the prison, but it was sorely in need of dredging and repair. The main ferry dock for the post, now significantly enlarged, was still located at the end of Andes Road, to the west of San Juan Dock. To its west sat the Ordnance Department pier, and on its southeast was the post coal dock.

Finding no appropriate structure that would allow an expansion into shipping, the officers studied three alternatives for a major new pier. All of the suggestions placed the pier facing Manhattan, just outside of the proposed new storehouses and in the approximate location of what is now Soissons Dock. One idea was to erect a single 1,000-foot-long, 50-foot-wide timber wharf parallel to the seawall. Another possibility was to build two 450-foot-long piers, 300 feet apart, which would jut out perpendicular to the island. A third version described an upside-down, U-shaped basin formed by three piers. One pier, parallel to the island, would be located out in the harbor, and the other two would run perpendicular from it to the shore. Without question, all of these alternatives required dredging the harbor to a depth of 26 feet to accommodate transport ships of the most current design.

BOAT LANDING, *Governors Island, n.d., Rotograph Co. Postcard. The Andes Road boat landings are* (left to right): *ordnance dock, San Juan dock. Author's collection.*

At the conclusion of this exercise, the board selected the first alternative, a timber-pile wharf, because it fit best with the storage improvements (and probably was the most cost effective). As evidence of the importance of this part of their recommendation, the officers separated the cost estimate for the wharf from the other improvements, specifying a $200,000 item in the next War Department budget request: $100,000 for the wharf and $100,000 for the excavation of 250,000 cubic yards of boulders, hardpan, and sand.[19]

"Governors Island to Be Much Enlarged" ran the September 6, 1900, *New York Times* headline after publication of the board of officers' report.[20] Their plan was indeed ambitious, but ambition was not unusual for this city of islands where growth routinely took place into the water. Here was an enlargement plan on the scale of the first major expansion of Manhattan Island in 1686, when Lieutenant Governor Thomas Dongan had granted the underwater land

HYDROPLANE VIEW *of Castle Williams and surrounding buildings, ca. 1912, unknown photographer. The new T-shaped pier is on the upper right. Courtesy of Prints and Photographs Division, Library of Congress, Washington, D.C.*

on the East Side from high to low tide to the City of New York. During the late seventeenth century, this grant encouraged the filling of 95 acres from Whitehall to Corlear's Hook for shipping and commerce. Here was also an early-twentieth-century expansion plan equal to the later Battery Park City, where housing and finance would take precedence on 92 new acres.

Governors Island was fortuitously positioned for expansion. A sandbar of more than 110 acres, with a depth that ranged from 9.0 to 20 feet, projected from the southern rim of the island out into the upper bay. This shoal provided a desirable shallow base for enclosure by a retaining wall and for filling the water area. By coincidence, funds had recently been appropriated under a rivers and harbors bill to dredge Buttermilk Channel, which ran along the eastern edge of the sandbar. What better dumping ground for the dredge material than a Governors Island extension? The dredging company would avoid long towage and could reduce its fuel costs, and the army could avail itself of the necessary fill at a nominal sum.

The board of officers once again studied options and costs before making their recommendation. A solid timber dyke running east to west, 300 feet south of Governors Island, would create an enlargement of 15 acres. Placing the dyke 1,500 feet out would gain 70 acres, and

GOVERNORS ISLAND PRIOR TO LANDFILL, *ca. 1903, unknown publisher. Postcard. Author's collection.*

SOUTH POINT *of Manhattan Island from Governors Island, ca. 1913, unknown publisher. Postcard. Author's collection.*

NEW YORK SKYLINE *at night, taken from Governors Island after a snow storm, n.d., Manhattan Post Card Publishing Co. Inc. Postcard. Author's collection.*

VIEW FROM GOVERNORS ISLAND, *1940s, unknown publisher. Postcard sold atop the Empire State Building. Author's collection.*

SKYLINE OF MANHATTAN. . . *view from Governors Island to lower N.Y. City, ca. 1940, R. H. Macy & Co., Inc. Postcard. Author's collection.*

NEW YORK SKYLINE *from Governors Island showing financial center of the world, ca. 1945, Irving Underhill. Postcard. Author's collection.*

placing it 2,000 feet from the shore would yield 90 acres. There are no records of the board's discussions; however, language in the report gives a hint of why they opted for the largest expansion. They and Secretary Root sought a "capacious reservation...adapted to every military requirement."[21] Because this part of the plan was the most expensive, the officers also probably surmised that the $725,000 allocated for constructing the 5,800 lineal feet of crib bulkhead that was required to encase the most expansive alternative would pass congressional scrutiny.

Using the engineering technology for the New York City Dock Department's nineteenth-century waterfront work, the planned bulkhead would consist of a crib of round piles high enough to reach a foot above mean low tide placed thickly enough to form a 10-foot-wide enclosure of the shoal. The piles would be sunk into a 2- to 3-foot trench and then bolted together. To buttress the structure from wind and waves and to provide a base for an above-water seawall, the resulting pen would be filled with stone. Engineers estimated that the 4 million cubic yards of sand fill to be placed on the shoal once the dyke was complete would cost $160,000. With the crib, the total cost came to $885,000—an amount that was acceptable to Washington and that never changed in the decade-long enlargement of the island.[22]

The War Department has already decided to spend $1,500,000 in transforming Governors Island, the famous and picturesque headquarters of the Department of the East, into the largest and most beautiful military post and transport depot on the Atlantic coast....From 60 acres the green isle will be converted into one of 150 acres, a sloping parade ground with barracks ample for a regiment covering the present shoals to the southwest.

("NEW YORK BAY TO BE TRANSFORMED BY MANY HUGE IMPROVEMENTS," *THE WORLD*, MARCH 25, 1901, UNPAGINATED.)

Having resolved the issue of placement of the timber dyke, the board of officers concluded their report with two caveats. Both were heeded. The first related to money. Experienced in the difficulties and delays in procuring congressional funds to improve Governors Island and eager to claim the nearby cheap fill, the board recommended payment in full: "An appropriation for the entire estimate of cost [$1,595,000] [should] be asked for in one lump sum, in order that the improvements may be begun and executed under contracts made favorable by the widening and deepening of adjacent channels."[23] The second caveat addressed the desire to turn Governors Island into the most beautiful of military posts. Colonel Kimball and his fellow board members—probably at the behest of Secretary of War Root, who was particularly interested in beautifying the military bases under his control—made sure to pitch architectural excellence: they recommended "that the buildings proposed for the island be erected only on plans prepared by competent architects,"[24] thus removing the design work from the purview of the quartermaster, who for the first time since the early 1800s was relegated to a position of oversight and construction.[25]

The War Department approved the Kimball plan on November 28, 1900, but there was a glitch. The choice of expansion as an acceptable way to proceed opened the door for a critique of the recommended placement of the new pier and storage sheds. Despite the fact that the majority of the images and postcards of Governors Island portrayed Lower Manhattan from the perspective of Fort Jay, Lieutenant General Nelson A. Miles, in a pro forma review of the plan for the adjutant general's office, worried that a working dock on the north side would impair the view the other way—of the island from the city. Why not locate the four storehouses to "the south side of Governors Island, in the proposed extension, or adjacent thereto?"[26] Piers could be accommodated either out into Buttermilk Channel or by cutting into the new

Dear Sirs:
The Government proposes to make extensive changes in Governors Island....The structures proposed will necessarily make a great change in the appearance of the island and, the island is so conspicuous an object in the harbor of New York that I am very desirous to have the changes made in good taste, and to have them render the island an object which will contribute to the beauty of the harbor instead of marring it....
Very truly yours,
Elihu Root.

(LETTER FROM SECRETARY OF WAR ELIHU ROOT TO MCKIM, MEAD & WHITE, JUNE 29, 1901, GENERAL CORRESPONDENCE 1884–1923, RG 77, 853/86, NATIONAL ARCHIVES, COLLEGE PARK, MD.)

land. To bolster his argument, Miles cited several cost savings obtainable by his plan. Dredging would be necessary only in the Buttermilk Channel area. Furthermore, touching on a historically sensitive subject that would not be resolved for another year, Miles pointed out that the amount of stone needed for the extension already existed in-house. "The Board," he wrote, "might also consider razing the useless batteries of Fort Columbus and Castle William and utilizing the stone and brick for filling, which could be easily done by the means of an inclined tramway."[27]

In a second report dated December 9, 1900, which argued that Buttermilk Channel was too narrow and that cutting into the landfill would use up too much of the new land, Colonel Kimball flatly rejected Miles's suggestion.[28] The controversy quelled, Root lost no time in seeking funds for the plan's implementation. On January 3, 1901, the War Department submitted to the House Appropriations Committee the entire estimate of $1,100,000 required for the engineering component for the fiscal year ending June 30, 1902. Included in this amount was funding for the new wharf and related dredging ($200,000), erection of the crib dyke ($725,000), and a larger amount than previously estimated for the fill ($200,000). A request in the quartermaster's budget for $15,000 was also added for repair of the existing wharf at Castle Williams. On January 9, 1901, six days after the engineering estimates were submitted to Congress, the quartermaster asked for his part of the pie: $535,000.[29]

The Sundry Civil Act of March 3, 1901, passed five months after publication of the board's report, appropriated $260,000 for the engineering project for the first fiscal year. The engineers went right to work on the designs for the dock, seawall, and the soundings for the dredging.

ASSAULT ON ALBANY, 1900–1901

Smoothing out the rough edges of the board's plan was the least of Secretary Root's problems. Before a post could be sunk or any bids sent out, the federal government had to procure the lands under water. This problem was not unique. As a means to fortify New York Harbor at the turn of the nineteenth century, the state–owner of New York City's waters, islands, and waterfronts since the time of the British–had ceded Governors Island to the federal government.[30] A subsequent state act, approved on May 7, 1880, had ceded some underwater lands around and to the south of the island to the United States "for the purposes of erecting and maintaining docks, wharves, boathouses, sea walls, batteries and other needed structures."[31] Now, in order to realize Root's expansive dream, the government had to go to Albany once again and persuade New York State to give up even more underwater lands. It was a race for time in which Root performed elegantly.

Prospective suppliers of fill for the Governors Island extension were quick to offer their services. On December 7, 1900, nine days after Secretary Root approved the plan, Nicholson and Company, a construction firm specializing in fireproof buildings, proposed to give the army free fill.[32] But they were told in no uncertain terms that state approval of the transfer of the shoal, or the lands under water, was required before the army could accept any offers.

Even before Secretary Root approved the board's plans, he, wearing his attorney hat, had asked for the army's counsel on the matter. Politically prescient, he hoped that the 1880 state conveyance of underwater lands around the island would suffice. He wanted to avoid a fight in Albany in which a three-quarters majority vote of both chambers was required to secure such lands. However, at the end of December 1900, when he received a negative reply from counsel, Root began a campaign to get speedy approval from the state legislature and the New York State Land Office (the ultimate provider of the deed). Time was of the essence. Congress was about to rule on providing funds for harbor dredging, and Root saw the merits of piggybacking his request for money for the Governors Island landfill. The latter would provide cost savings to both projects. In addition, nearby dredging would hasten completion of the extension.[33]

The letters to and from Root's office in January and February 1901 are indicative of his stature in the community, his political savvy, and his uncanny ability to implement an agenda for Governors Island. Probably only George Washington, who had ordered the construction of the first fort, had exerted the same impact on the island. Root, having been active in local Republican politics both as an attorney (he once represented Boss Tweed, a move that he long regretted) and as a potential office seeker, now exploited his contacts in Albany to the utmost.

His first appeal was to fellow Republican and friend Lieutenant Governor Timothy L. Woodruff. Following up on a suggestion made at a dinner party, Root immediately sent a letter to Woodruff that contained draft bills and asked him to "put [them] in the hands of a Senator and Assemblyman who will make efficient sponsors for them and will keep a lookout for them." Assuming that the bills would pass handily, Root also enclosed copies of a draft deed for subsequent action by the commissioners of the Land Office. To sweeten the pot, he extolled the business and defense benefits of the island's extension both to the city and to Woodruff's home borough, Brooklyn.[34]

But matters did not proceed as smoothly as these efforts indicated they would. On January 9, 1901, a bill proposing the ceding of lands under water at Governors Island to the United States for military use and defense purposes was introduced into the New York State Assembly by Harris Wilson, a New York City attorney whose district was downstate, and into the state Senate by Timothy Ellsworth of Niagara County, who, it was hoped, could bring in the upstate votes. According to Lieutenant Governor Woodruff, the bill was "in position to be put upon its final passage as soon as the committees in charge report it favorably."[35] Woodruff assumed that the measure would become law in a few days, but he was wrong. Despite a letter-writing campaign by Root to the governor and assorted legislators, the Assembly held up the legislation for a month.

Charges flew from Democratic legislators, in particular Brooklynites eager to protect the commercial piers along Buttermilk Channel, that the extension into the harbor would seriously impair ferry and shipping traffic. Perhaps aware of the Nicholson and Company offer, the legislators also asserted that dumping contractors who had allegedly already been hired would benefit. One legislator suggested that if the island were put up for auction, it could bring in

Dear Sir:

We are in receipt of your letter of June 29th...extending to us an invitation to act as architects, in preparation of plans for the various works, in consultation with the Engineers and Constructing Quartermasters of the Army, who will supervise the construction of the work. The problem is one which will interest us greatly, and we consider it a high honor to be associated with a work of such importance from every point of view.

[*AUTHOR'S NOTE:* THERE IS NO RECORD OF THE PAY THE ARCHITECTS RECEIVED. HOWEVER, $60,000 OF THE 1901 CONGRESSIONAL APPROPRIATION WAS HELD BACK FROM THE ENGINEERS; CONCEIVABLY A PORTION OF THIS AMOUNT MAY HAVE BEEN USED TO PAY THE FIRM.]

(LETTER FROM CHARLES MCKIM TO SECRETARY OF WAR ELIHU ROOT, JULY 1, 1901, GENERAL CORRESPONDENCE 1884–1923, RG 77, 853/87, NATIONAL ARCHIVES, COLLEGE PARK, MD.)

millions of dollars. An assemblyman from Staten Island even favored razing all structures on the existing acreage and deeding the island to the city for a park and for a tunnel from Manhattan to South Brooklyn (his home borough). Failing this measure, he allegedly proposed the island's conversion to a parade ground for the navy.[36]

On February 4, 1901, at the requests of J. F. Allds, Assembly leader and chairman of the Ways and Means Committee, and Lieutenant Governor Woodruff, Root answered these charges with equanimity. He elucidated three points. First, the project had the approval of the departments in charge of protecting the interests of navigation and defense of the city. Second, the only beneficiary of the project would be the U.S. government because the Buttermilk Channel dredging bids would be lower. Third, no contractor had been given special consideration, and none was currently engaged or had submitted bids for the work.[37]

Allds then went to work on his end, convincing the opposition to support a small change in the language of the bill. Instead of *directing* the Land Office commissioners to make the grant of the lands under water, the bill would leave the action to their *discretion*. For opponents, this wording removed the onus of voting for an item that might anger their constituencies. From Root's perspective, there was no danger in the language change: his friend Woodruff, who had shepherded the bill from its inception, was also a Land Office commissioner.[38] The records show that Woodruff was not present at the special session of the commissioners, but he must have lined up his fellow members for a favorable vote. Four days later, Assemblyman Wilson informed Root that his bill had passed the Assembly with a vote of 102 to 28, two more ayes than required. However, the bill languished in the Senate Finance Committee for several weeks more while members continued to debate the issue of the new land's alleged interference with harbor commerce.

Root was successful in his appeasement efforts. On February 27, 1901, Governor Benjamin B. Odell signed the bill authorizing the New York State Land Office to transfer "approximately 90 acres of land under the waters of New York Harbor adjacent to the westerly side of Governor's Island" to the United States.[39] Seizing the moment and without waiting for the formal transfer, Root immediately contacted the chairman of the U.S. Senate Committee on Appropriations and asked for "a moderate appropriation...for the commencement of the work."[40] A few weeks later, on March 7, 1901, the New York State Land Office commissioners conveyed the contested underwater lands and ceded jurisdiction to the United States.[41]

Seen in the context of the history of peacetime legislation regarding Governors Island, this resolution was speedy despite the aggravation. The papers were signed only three months after Secretary Root submitted language for the bill and a quick three days after Congress appropriated the money he had requested. After settling the bill of one dollar for the land and a five-dollar patent fee, Root turned his efforts toward directing the reconstruction and enlargement of the island.[42]

"THE MASTER PLAN," 1901–1907

Islands were much written about in early 1901. England's Queen Victoria died after a sixty-four-year reign, and Australia became an independent commonwealth. Closer to home, Secretary Root secured legislation stipulating that Cuba cede Guantanamo Bay to the United States. It was part of a larger agreement for a withdrawal of federal troops from Cuba, many of whom had been billeted through Governors Island.

Although New York dailies touted the magnificence of the impending transformation of Governors Island, these articles were premature puff pieces, based perhaps on army press releases. In reality, the army had much more work to do physically and politically before the "green isle" could become a reality. The confusion brought about by a lack of space as well as by the proposed functional changes had to be rationalized, and someone had to turn words into design. This meant drafting a blueprint for the placement of all recommended land improvements and generating detailed drawings for renovating or building individual structures. In the ensuing months, the design work proceeded on two tracks. The quartermaster and the chief engineer, who had worked in harmony on the overall plan, went their separate ways–the former to lead the land-based program and the latter to direct all of the water-based projects.

It seemed to us that the best plan was to conceive of a cyclone having laid the island completely waste, and that we should then undertake to establish an Army post upon the most modern plans....When these plans are fully carried out–which it will probably take some ten years to do–New York harbor will have one of the finest Army posts in the world.

(COLONEL AMOS S. KIMBALL, QUOTED IN "SWEEPING CHANGES AT GOVERNORS ISLAND," *NEW YORK TIMES*, APRIL 18, 1902, 2.)

Four months after securing the funds to start the Governors Island project, Secretary Root stepped in again to introduce the independent architect firm McKim, Mead & White to the project. This move might have seemed unusual for the army, where construction of everything, from tented camps to hospitals to the commanding general's home, had historically been undertaken in house and according to the army Quartermaster Corps' standardized plans. Yet several contemporaneous military projects were also calling on outside designers' expertise. Chicago's Daniel Burnham was advising on designs for the Presidio in San Francisco;[43] New York's Carriere and Hastings had recently completed designs for buildings at Fort Hancock in Sandy Hook, New Jersey; and the firm of McKim, Mead & White, at the behest of Secretary Root, was designing a campus for the Army War College at Fort McNair in Washington, D.C.[44] In choosing outsiders, Root made sure to maintain army tradition by delineating the architects' role. On Governors Island, they were to be responsible only for plan preparation: "[T]he construction," he wrote, "will be done under the supervision of the engineers and the constructing quartermaster of the army."[45]

Amidst talk of holding an architectural competition for the design work, Root opted for exclusivity.[46] Furthermore, in his selection of McKim, Mead & White, he went directly to the top of the profession. Established in 1879, the firm was, by 1901, the most prestigious in the country. Charles McKim and his colleagues had been central to the Beaux Arts designs of the 1893 Columbian Exhibition, where city beautification and comprehensive plans were central themes. The firm's designs for Harvard University had given its architects experience with campus settings. In New York alone, by 1900 they had completed the first Madison Square Garden, the *New York Herald* headquarters, and the University Club. They were also at work on a master plan for Columbia University, which had historic eighteenth-century ties to Governors Island.

Root's choice of Charles McKim, the principal architect for the firm, was particularly appropriate. Castle Williams and "the old fort" were to be preserved, he wrote, and "the new structures should be in harmony with them."[47] McKim's experience with visionary plans at the Columbian Exhibition and his knowledge of early American buildings and decorative elements were a good fit with the nineteenth-century architectural legacies on Governors

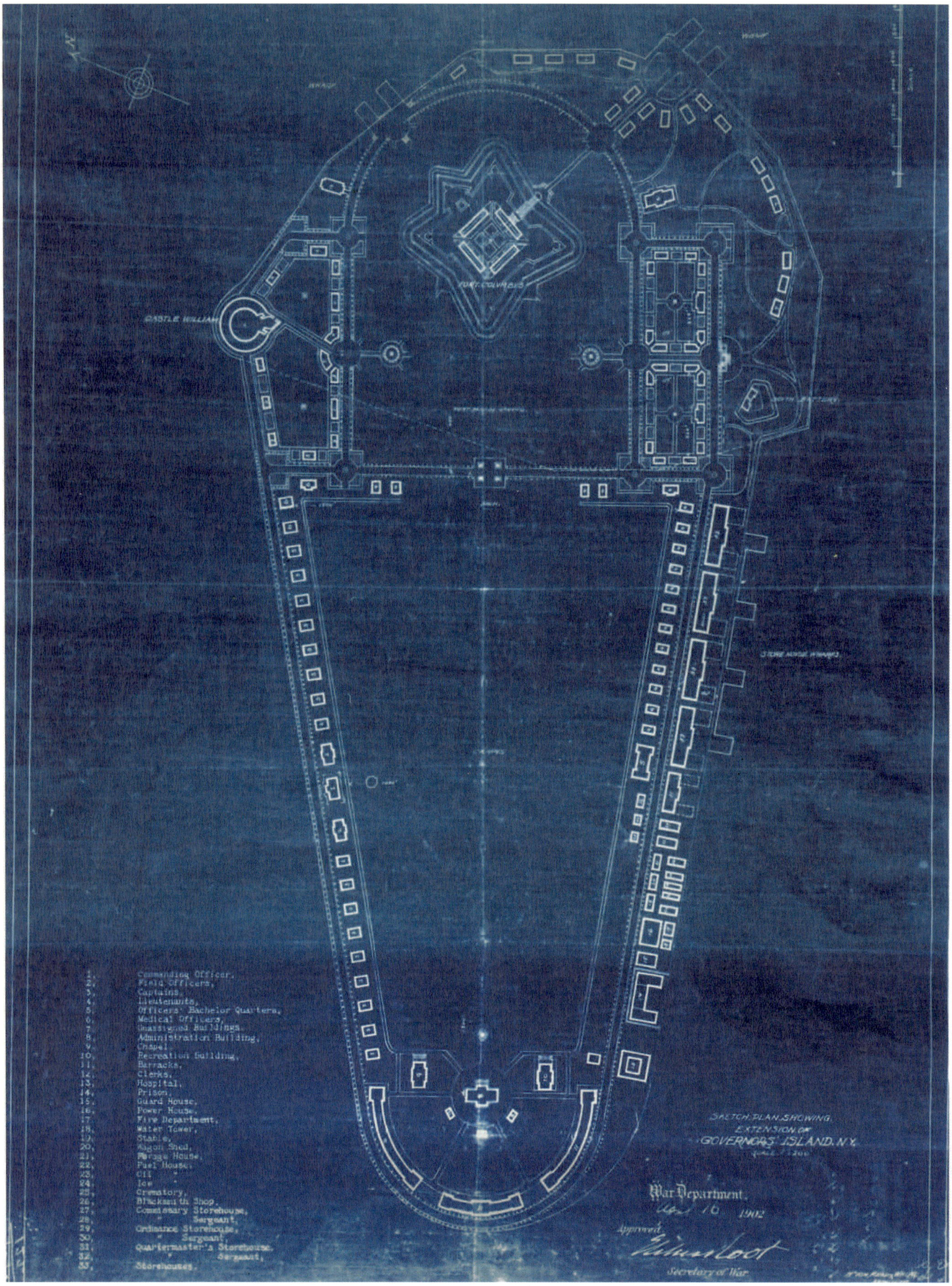

SKETCH PLAN *showing extension of Governors Island, 1902, McKim, Mead & White. The plan shows a proposed layout for Governors Island. Only three historic structures remain: Fort Jay (Columbus), Castle Williams, and the South Battery. Courtesy of Architecture and Cartographic Section, National Archives, College Park, Md.*

Island.[48]

The McKim firm replied to Root's invitation virtually overnight and immediately critiqued the shape of the landfill. The map of the 1901 land grant shows it to be an uneven, pentagonal shape with an inverted triangle on the north and a squared-off southern end. Lieutenant General Nelson Miles had begun the discussion of changing this shape in his August 1900 endorsement of the board of officers' plan, where he recommended putting the southern portion of the landfill farther out into Upper New York Bay and terminating it in a triangular point. His rationale was to enable the positioning of a battery of rapid-fire guns to protect Buttermilk Channel and the Hudson River against torpedo boats. There was also a practical reason for his suggestion. A point, he argued, would form "an excellent breakwater against the powerful surf that at times rolls in from the sea during storms."[49]

If the island were extended so as to cover all the shoals, it would have very much the appearance of a balloon, the big end of which would face the city.

("GOVERNORS ISLAND EXTENSION BENEFITS," *NEW YORK TIMES*, DECEMBER 9, 1900, 1.)

As outlined the island will be transformed into the shape of a common kite, with the tail pointing to the Narrows.

("WHAT HAS BECOME OF ALL THE DIRT TAKEN FROM THE SUBWAY?" *NEW YORK TIMES*, NOVEMBER 27, 1904, SM7.)

But Miles's suggestion was again ignored. In justifying the reasons for keeping the squared-off configuration, the original designer, army engineer Colonel W. L. Marshall, explained that he was governed by the ease of placing the necessary stone and fill at the least cost, and not by "ideas of beauty and symmetry."[50] However, Charles McKim was interested in beauty and symmetry, and he asked for an additional 19 acres to round off the tip of Governors Island properly. The appeal was to importance and fame because the island would be, as a headline in the *New York Times* eventually heralded, "the greatest military post in the world."[51]

Despite complaints that part of the already-made seawall would have to go and that there might be problems in Albany with regard to securing the additional 16.0 to 19.4 underwater acres, which the state would once again have to cede, Secretary Root approved on April 19, 1902, what might have been considered an artistic folly. However, on this go-round it was not Root, but Colonel Marshall, now in charge of constructing the reclamation project, who made the request to Albany for the land transfer. Marshall also explained the financial bind. Sufficient funds were on hand to construct the foundation for the new portion of the seawall only if it were done in the coming months. Any funds unspent by June 30 would revert to the treasury.

In Albany, this restriction meant the rush was on. Senator John Raines from upstate Ontario County and Assemblyman Frank Platt of New York County spent much of February 1903 shepherding bills for the additional acreage through the state legislature. Approval came on March 6, three days after the U.S. Congress had appropriated $150,000 for the project for the next fiscal year.[52] As before, the Land Office's actual ceding of the additional lands under water to the federal government came later, with just three weeks left in June and the fiscal year. Fortunately, this amount of time was adequate, and work on the seawall never stopped.

Meanwhile, McKim was working on a larger vision. Not unlike the development of Battery Park City, this process was iterative and thus would take place over a period of thirty years. Few records are available that provide written insight into the planning process. However, at least three drawings exist that show the McKim firm's overall plan for the island, ranging from a simple schematic view produced in 1902 to a 1906 map showing the placement of all the buildings and a three-dimensional, bird's-eye view that made its debut in the press in 1907. From these drawings, it is possible not only to see what the architects hoped to achieve, but also to determine the pattern that formed the island's eventual development.

BIRD'S-EYE VIEW *of the 1906 McKim, Mead & White plan, November 30, 1907.* Scientific American *cover illustration. This plan was unveiled to the public in 1907. Although there is probably no connection, Elihu Root's father-in-law, Salem Wells, was the managing editor of* Scientific American *in 1878. Collection of Barbara Romer.*

SCIENTIFIC AMERICAN

NEW YORK, NOVEMBER 30, 1907

As ordered by Secretary Root, the McKim firm worked with the quartermaster, and in 1902 the deputy quartermaster, rather than McKim, asked the War Department for approval for changes to the Kimball plan. Topmost on the list of needed changes was housing. Rather than knock down Fort Jay and rebuild it for an entire regiment, as Miles and others had suggested, McKim rightly focused on the quarters for a smaller group, a single battalion. These men were placed in Fort Jay, with the associated officers residing somewhere nearby. If indeed the army eventually expanded the troop size to a regiment, the scheme would locate those men somewhere on the reclaimed land. In line with the Kimball plan, an upgrade to the housing for the officers related to headquarters was also in the program.

Although Castle Williams had recently been refurbished, the McKim firm intended to construct a new prison. Whether it was to be on a new site or within the castle is unknown. As to warehousing, the firm suggested a change that was radical if one espoused the Kimball plan, but right in line with Lieutenant General Miles's original endorsement: all storehouses of the various departments should be placed facing Buttermilk Channel on the newly made land.[53]

The next plan from the McKim office that has survived shows sweeping changes, some of which differ from McKim's initial view. In this 1906 iteration is a layout of all the proposed buildings and open spaces with their associated activities. What is most striking is that the hodgepodge of the original island has been virtually wiped clean. Gone are the yellow wooden houses of Nolan Park, the old guardhouse, the department and regimental headquarters, the hospital, and the arsenal. Gone, too, are the assorted warehouses scattered around the original campus. But the two edifices that Root had ordered to be preserved, Castle Williams and Fort Jay, remain on the plan. In addition, the continued presence of the South Battery home of the Officers' Mess and the newly consecrated St. Cornelius Chapel is obvious because of these buildings' size, shape, and position on the map.

The uneven star-shaped walls of Fort Jay (to which Secretary Root had returned its eponym on January 20, 1904) stand alone in their off-center position on the island in the McKim plan, as they had since their construction a century earlier. No quarters are shown for the enlisted men. Instead, in place of the two-story structures where Confederate prisoners Alonzo Bell and Thomas Sparrow had resided and of the green where regimental officers and the band had once lined up to begin the dirge for executions are a huge reservoir and water tower. Perhaps the latter were placed with foresight in case the water pipes to Brooklyn were damaged by nature or a military attack or there was a general drought. The centrality of the tower and the water element provided by a reservoir also suggests that they were probably important decorative elements, lending beauty and extra importance to an army base that was fighting for its survival.[54]

The most striking aspect of the 1906 plan (a bird's-eye view of it was published in *Scientific American* on November 30, 1907) is the vast amount of open space. The original, slightly misshapen landform is idealized into a formal half-moon shape. In place of Nolan Park and the cluttered rows of buildings that actually made up the army post and headquarters, the plan shows a vast park with Fort Jay at its apex, around which sit dozens of houses arrayed in an orderly manner. This type of open space, typical of the City Beautiful movement, was not unique to the Governors Island plan. The army was incorporating large greens and botanical gardens into military campuses such as Fort McNair and the San Francisco Presidio at this time. Not only did a park provide beauty and breathing space, but at Governors Island it also provided extra views, perhaps to entice army officers to live on this isolated island in New York Harbor.

Parks were also reserved on the newly made land. Rather than repeat the historic pattern of Manhattan, which filled up every available acre, the architects took full advantage of the opportunity to preserve the land unencumbered. An exclusive in the *New York Times* described it best: "And this Parade–what a magnificent affair it is!" But it would require work, the writer continued: "It is as green as grass can make it, and the landscape artist who has it in charge must know his business." The journalist then gave the military rationale for providing such a space: "The Parade is the scene of the military ceremonies, such as the dress parades, the guard mounts, the reviews, the inspections, &c. It is the finest parade ground in the country–1,700 feet long and in breadth varying from 1,400 feet to about 900 feet at the southern end."[55] Curiously, no mention was made of the opportunities for training troops on this newly made ground.

In their 2004 National Park Service analysis of the McKim plans, Jann Warren-Findlay and Nancy Dallett found "thirty-three different uses around the outer edge of the expanded island."[56] An enlargement of the 1906 plan accompanying the *New York Times* article contained a description of many of the designated activities. Most involved the same uses as those that had existed on the island before its expansion. Following the model found in most military institutions at the time, however, the facilities were now organized into stricter hierarchal and greatly expanded groupings.

There were four distinct districts. At the northeast quadrant of the island were the housing and administrative offices for the top brass of headquarters. On a band across the island at the approximate juncture of the old and new land were homes for the major officers of the post in place of Brick Row. The commanding officer would reside in the center, on a line with Fort

Jay. As in other new installations such as Fort Hancock, the quarters for this cadre were large enough for families–an important feature because all of these officers were purportedly married. Twenty-seven wives, two mothers-in-law, thirty-four sons, and twenty-three daughters of undisclosed ages were listed among the island's permanent residents.[57] The regimental officers were located on a middle ground on the periphery of the landfill. Smaller houses were shown lined up in a row, like soldiers about to enter the parade.

And in response to Secretary Root's original instructions, at the southern end of the landfill were to be the enlisted men's facilities, sited in an enormous barracks capable of housing 1,200 troops.[58] This barracks can best be seen in the bird's-eye rendering: a multistoried structure of a size equal to Castle Williams, surrounded by narrow buildings. The first impression is one of monumentality. Although Fort Jay, sitting in its elevated position with the water tower rising above it, is still the primary structure on the drawn plan of the island, the proposed barracks are imposing. Perhaps to give them further importance, they are lined up on an axis with Fort Jay to the north, with a Beaux Arts ornamental structure positioned near the southern seawall.

Noncommissioned officers had their proscribed space in a dormitory for bachelors and in eight single- and two-family houses on McKim's rounded tip of the island. These houses are the smallest domiciles shown on the plan, but nothing necessary for a soldier's life was omitted. Within this compound would be the post exchange, or canteen, and a school for training the enlisted men. Though the prospective noncommissioned officers' families would be at the mercy of a foghorn announcing the enlarged island's presence, most of their homes were to be situated with perhaps the best views of the upper and lower harbor.

Industrial facilities for a major transshipment post and a ferry slip for a growing military population are also clearly delineated in the McKim drawings. The architects, apparently listening to both the Kimball board and Lieutenant General Miles's critique of their plan, positioned warehouses in two places: on the northern periphery of the original island and on the Buttermilk Channel side of the newly made land. Probably to shorten the trip to supply day-to-day housekeeping items such as food, clothing, laundry, and coal to the regimental barracks, additional square and rectangular industrial structures, along with firehouses, a lumberyard, shops, and a wagon shed, were neatly lined up on the southeastern side of the landfill. One of two stables on the island was also to be located nearby; the other, keeping even the horses in hierarchal order, was to be located adjacent to department headquarters on the north.

The new wharf on the north shore of the island is in good condition and is one of the best wharves in the harbor for vessels drawing not over 26 feet. It is not used nearly to its full capacity as a wharf....The east half of the wharf is covered with a plain steel storage shed...they are plain, unsightly buildings, not in harmony with what I understood was the real purpose in the enlargement of the island.

(Memorandum from Lieutenant Colonel W. L. Marshall to Brigadier General A. Mackenzie, May 31, 1904, General Correspondence 1884–1923, RG 77, 853/37078.197, National Archives, College Park, Md.)

Between Castle Williams and the new transport wharf, the McKim maps show a series of piers with one-story sheds. As per Root's original directive, large warehouses labeled for the Quartermaster, Subsistence, Ordnance, Engineer, and Medical Departments were lined up immediately adjacent. In a move that might have been seen as wasteful, a new main ferry terminal with slips for passengers and freight replaced the recently completed transport pier. This replacement was perhaps a face-saving move, however, because by all accounts the pier had not yet been used by large ships.

With these configurations shown on arsenal property, the ordnance commander on Governors Island, who was already feeling pushed out by the

INCINERATOR, *November 14, 1918, unknown photographer. Scrapbook photograph. The world's first incinerator was located south of Castle Clinton in 1855. This new one was constructed on the landfill. Courtesy of National Archives, College Park, Md.*

Kimball plan, had cause to worry. Despite his complaint that "it would not be possible to carry on the business of this Arsenal in the limited space apparently allotted us on this Island," nothing on the McKim plans even labels the arsenal.[59]

A comparison of the McKim plan with a map prepared by the army engineers in 1908 gives an idea of what was going to be moved. The hospital had occupied various structures on the eastern portion of the island since the 1830s. The McKim plan shows this important facility, along with barracks for the "hospital sergeants," situated on the waterfront to the south of Castle Williams (the barracks are shown at the end of the row of officers' homes, one of which was designated for the surgeons). Thus, patients could enjoy the same views of the harbor, New Jersey, and Staten Island as the prisoners in Castle Williams.

A more noxious building, the crematory, would also be moved. A scarcity of land for burying refuse and probably insufficient funds to hire scows to cart the garbage elsewhere might have led to the 1855 introduction of the first incinerator in the United States on Governors Island. Nineteenth-century photographs of Castle Williams show the crematory, as it was first called, just south of the castle. In the McKim plan, however, the structure has been moved out of the populated area to the industrial compound on Buttermilk Channel and bears the updated label *incinerator*.

Another structure that received a better home on paper was the twenty-year-old, severely overcrowded Military Service Institution. Upon learning that this section of the island was going to be razed, members with connections to the secretary of war lobbied for a permanent structure to house the august organization's offices and considerable collection of memorabilia. Secretary Root's approval of a recommendation to erect a new building "adequate to that institution" doubtless caused the architects to locate a "museum" in a prominent position, adjacent to the commanding general's house.[60]

Although the McKim plan gives an excellent picture of the elements that were important to establishing a first-class army base at the turn of the century, equally important is what is not included on the map. Despite a major commitment to elegant grounds and open spaces, the conservatory, long a place to nurture plantings on the island, has been removed. Nurses had typically been relegated to leftover living quarters in and around the old hospital; in the new plan, nurses are not specifically mentioned. A new prison was in the McKim firm's original scope of work, but the map does not show it, and Castle Williams is the only structure that is unlabeled. As for education and religion, there are no specific sites for nursery or primary schools for possibly fifty children or for a YMCA or Catholic or Jewish chapels. And most significant in view of Governors Island's historical role as protector of the harbor, there is nothing in the plan of the island that gives it the appearance of a viable fortification save for a small storage garage for machine guns on the southeast and Castle Williams on the northwest—the guns of which had long ago been removed.[61]

CONSTRUCTION

ENGINEERING A NEW PENINSULA, 1901–1906

The architects planned and drew elegant maps for the reclamation of Governors Island, but it was the engineers who actually created the ground on which the new regimental quarters and other structures would be built. As with all waterfront projects, these professionals began with soundings and borings to find the least expensive layout for the new transport pier and extension. They prepared bid documents for everything from rock blasting to rock delivery. They made blueprints for basic stone walls and for grading the new land. An enlargement of more than 100 acres was a complicated affair, involving at least six different types of vendors, among them dredgers, dock builders, carters, and stonemasons. Management involved sequencing the workers, using available materials in a timely manner, and handling delays. Most important, because money for the project was dependent on annual congressional appropriations, the engineers had to keep close tabs on expenses. In the end, save for a few legal wrangles with stone and dirt purveyors and insufficient funds to properly green the property, the project—the largest acreage of landfill in the city's history to be constructed all in one piece—was completed in a little more than a decade and on budget.[62]

The engineers, Colonel Marshall and his assistant Henry Nash Babcock, began with a pier, and their talents were immediately challenged. As outlined in the Kimball plan, the wharf would sit parallel to a portion of the island's north shore. But soundings revealed zero depth at the seawall; no ship with a draft as deep as 26 feet could possibly land there without expensive dredging. Thus, the men redesigned the pier into a two-and-a-half-block-long T shape that instead projected out into the harbor.[63]

Because of the delays in securing the landfill legislation in Albany, work did not begin in earnest until a year after Secretary Root had secured the first congressional appropriation. After July 1, 1901, however, progress was substantial. By October 12 that year, Marshall had signed a contract with the lowest bidder—dock builders Warren Roosevelt and John W. Sullivan (their firm was known as R&S)—for pier construction and related dredging.[64] In his 1901 "Report of the Chief of Engineers" for the War Department, Marshall gives a sense of the dredging task.[65]

In the eight months between November 1, 1901, and July 2, 1902, R&S removed 70,550 cubic yards of material "including one boulder of about 19 cubic yards volume" from the harbor area north of the pier. A later description of the pier work contains a comment relevant to the condition of New York City's waterfront in the twenty-first century: "None of the piles were creosoted" because the waters of the upper bay were so polluted that they were "free from toredo [a clam that eats and destroy wood piles]."[66] Although their contract specified a four-month completion, it was not until August 1902 that R&S turned over a finished dock to the army. The cost, probably counteracting the disappointment of the delay, was $72,799.10, nearly 75 percent under budget.[67]

Pending the completion of the dock, the engineers had also budgeted $35,000 to build a warehouse and shed to cover the T, or the structure's outer portion. In the past, they had used standardized plans to design this type of facility. A letter from Marshall to George Gillespie, now elevated to Brigadier General, affirms Secretary Root's interest in beautification and illuminates the role the McKim group had already established as arbiter of taste on Governors Island. It also further explains how the Governors Island extension came in on budget. "Upon consulting Col. Kimball of the Quartermaster Department [the office that would use the facility], about the character of the warehouse shed and superstructure he desires on the large dock now nearing completion," wrote Marshall to Gillespie, "with a view of agreeing upon a design that would present a pleasing external appearance, I was informed by him that a firm of architects in New York, by authority of the Secretary of War, is considering the whole subject of the improvement of Governor's Island, and that this structure which is to constitute the entrance to the island will form part of their design."[68]

Marshall went on to relate that until the McKim design was complete, no work would be done on the superstructure for the pier. But with Kimball's backing, he suggested transferring the $35,000 that remained in the budget for this item to construct part of the retaining wall around the landfill. These funds were indeed moved to the seawall budget, and others ultimately ruled regarding the pier's aesthetics. At an unknown date "under plea of emergency," the quartermaster built a temporary shed that, according to Babcock's history, "he subsequently enlarged to cover the entire floor, and the plan for a more sightly structure was sidetracked."[69]

The other major change that the engineers made to the Kimball plan involved the seawall to be placed around what would eventually become 103.5 acres of new land. Not only do remnants of this seawall still remain today, but the engineering innovation reached beyond the boundaries of Governors Island, affecting construction along New York City's waterfront. Again, depth soundings were the first order of business. This time the waters within the original 90-acre grant were examined. At least part of this information was available from a survey that Marshall had prepared for the anticipated dredging of Buttermilk Channel under the Rivers and Harbors Act of 1900. The soundings on this map, dated November 28, 1900—the same day that Secretary Root approved the Kimball plan—show water depths ranging from a shallow 3.7 feet near the South Battery to more than 30 feet out toward the lower harbor. These numbers indicated that in certain sections the crib, or traditional woodpile framework, would start from 30 to 45 feet under water, and huge amounts of stone fill would be needed to bulwark the enlargement properly against an inflow from the river.[70]

VIEW OF GOVERNORS ISLAND *from Lower Manhattan before the landfill process began, photograph, 1901, Irving Underhill. Courtesy of Prints and Photographs Division, Library of Congress, Washington, D.C.*

VIEW FROM THE WHITEHALL BUILDING *showing the completed western side of the landfill, photograph, ca. 1910, Irving Underhill. Work is still underway on the Buttermilk Channel side. Courtesy of Prints and Photographs Division, Library of Congress, Washington, D.C.*

To reduce costs, the engineers devised an ingenious alternative. Borings taken of the subsurface stratum that would hold the posts for the crib work showed a soft mud bottom on most of the area to be enlarged. Rather than use the traditional crib to confine the sand fill as recommended in the Kimball plan—and as was done without question throughout the harbor—the engineers experimented with something new. After the required bidding process, contract preparation, and army approvals, Brown & Fleming of 129 Broad Street and their subcontractors, the Toomey Brothers of Guilford, Connecticut, began work on December 17, 1901, to dump rocks directly into the mud without a frame. Marshall and Babcock took the chance that leakage through this type of wall would be minimal, and they were correct. When the riprap, as the accumulation of loose stones was called, reached 2.0 feet above the low-water line, it formed a solid foundation that both contained the fill and, after settling, held an attractive masonry wall surrounding the new land. The chief of engineers in Washington was evidently willing to experiment; the New York City Dock Department followed suit; and subsequent revetments along Rikers Island and Brooklyn's Shore Parkway were also built in this manner.

Contractors for Governors Island Extension	
Dredging	R. G. Packard Company, 130 Pearl Street October 12, 1901–July 11, 1902
Pile dock	Roosevelt and Sullivan, 80 New Street October 12, 1901–sometime after August 6, 1902
Riprap	Brown & Fleming, 129 Broad Street November 12, 1901–May 5, 1903 delivered 142,000 tons at 35 cents per ton; September 4, 1905–January 3, 1906, delivered 2,514 tons to repair settlement.
	John D. Miller, 39 Cortland Street May 5, 1903–November 1904
Embankment	New York Filling Company December 24, 1902–September 1906 (letter)
	Henry Steers Inc. July 9, 1909–May 10, 1912, delivered and placed 387,307 cubic yards of earth; February 2, 1910– October 28, 1911, cellar dirt, fertilizer, and grass seed for 79 acres
	No names were found for interim filling contracts.
Rock Removal	R. G. Packard Company, 130 Pearl Street December 4, 1902–April 15, 1903 (deepening access to wharf)
Stone Seawall	Humphrey Toomey, Guilford, Conn. June 22, 1904–November 1, 1905
	Brown & Fleming continued this work sometime after July 1906. A gap left open for filling operations was closed January 31, 1911 by Henry Steers Inc.

(FROM THE WAR DEPARTMENT'S ANNUAL REPORTS AND THE U.S. ARMY CHIEF OF ENGINEERS ANNUAL REPORTS FROM 1901 TO 1913.)

Now all that was needed to keep the more than 1.3-mile-long foundation within budget was to procure rocks at a decent price. The bid specifications give an idea of the massiveness of the material the engineers sought. Stones had to be of "hard, durable quality." The outside layer of the riprap required "shaped blocks from ½ to 2 tons in weight," and narrow stones were rejected. Smaller rocks were acceptable for the inner portion of the wall, but they, too, were hefty. Half of the stones had to weigh more than 200 pounds, and the remainder could be a mix of stones from 30 to 3,000 pounds.[71] If timed correctly, tons of rocks of all shapes and sizes could be gotten for free: just across the harbor, the Interborough Rapid Transit (IRT) Line was excavating for the city's first subway.

By July 1902, the carting company had maneuvered its heavily loaded clamshell dredges from the Battery in Manhattan to the shoal off Governors Island. Beginning just southeast of the South Battery, the company dumped 142,000 tons of large boulders and small rocks along

Buttermilk Channel, enough to complete 2,230 linear feet of foundation–equivalent to about eleven New York City blocks. The depth of the riprap was in consonance with earlier soundings, ranging from less than 1.0 foot to 26 feet. The $35,000 culled from the shed on the wharf allowed an additional 700 feet of foundation to be constructed along the Hudson River within the same contract.

No sooner had the engineers saved some money than a new expense appeared: a fog signal that was not on the original plan but would remain a part of life on the island until its closing. Governors Island's position between two navigable waterways had historically been known for its ability to protect the harbor. Now, as the new peninsula stretched farther toward the Outer Harbor, the island was becoming a hazard (especially in heavy fog) to the very port it was meant to protect. In 1902, to keep barges, scows, ferries, and other vessels from crashing into this new protrusion, the engineers erected a modest lighthouse shed on piles where the work was to end. But it was not long before this makeshift lighthouse was hit by a scow under tow and completely wrecked. Undeterred, the engineers moored a schooner with signals on its mast in place of the shed. A boat had the advantage of being easy to move as the land expanded, and its lights and foghorn protected both the land and passing vessels. But the cost of the annual rental and the burden of the boat's management had to be added to the budget.[72]

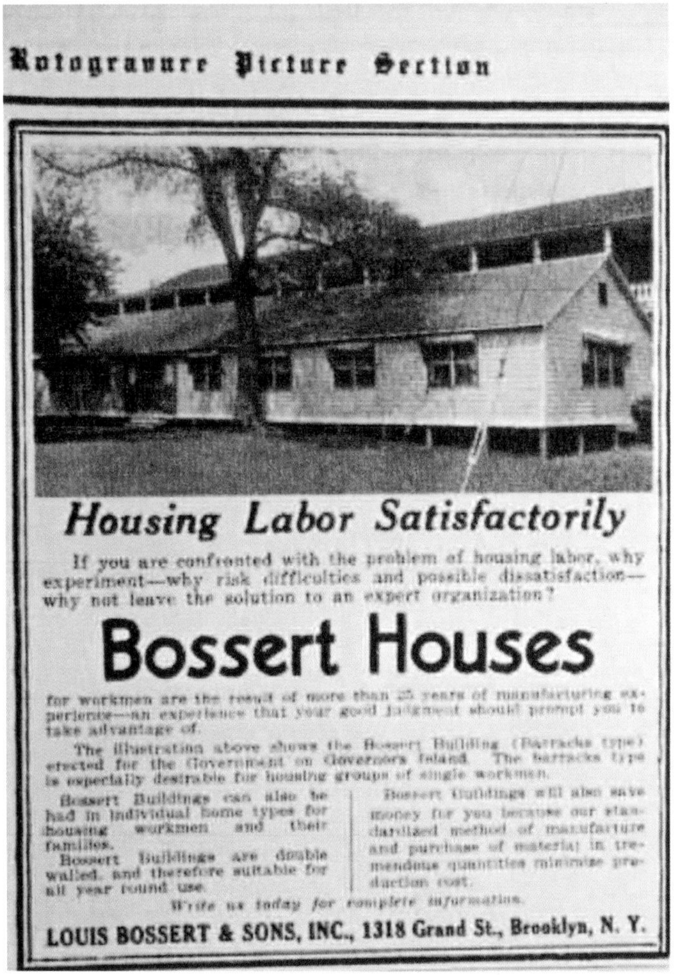

BOSSERT HOUSES *display ad,* New York Times, *February 3, 1918, no page number, unknown delineator. World War I interrupted any grandiose plans for developing the landfill. Instead, the army erected prefabricated houses. Author's collection.*

At the beginning of the expansion, the engineers had hoped for its swift completion in order to take advantage of cheap materials offered by the subway construction and the dredging of Buttermilk Channel. By July 1903, however, with work under way on the southern newly rounded end of the riprap, the price of rocks had nearly doubled to fifty-eight cents a ton; Brown & Fleming's low-cost contract had run its course; and McKim's aesthetics only made matters worse. Where the next contractor, John D. Miller of 39 Cortland Street, secured these more expensive rocks is unknown.[73] Henry Babcock and the *New York Times* reported that the stone was obtained from the subway and New York City excavations. It is also possible that diggings from the Whitehall Building, one of the early downtown skyscrapers, might have been a source. As for the higher cost, perhaps the contractor had to travel farther, or demand had escalated, and stone was harder to find. Higher prices may have been understandable, but the engineers could not easily accept a rise in cost owing to aesthetics.

In adding the extra acres to accommodate "McKim's Folly," the engineers wasted money already spent. They were forced to abandon a portion of the riprap that had already been purchased and put in place. Nevertheless, the work continued, and 169,166 additional tons of rocks were delivered. By November 5, 1904, three years after work on the outer wall had begun, the contractors had completed more than a mile of the wall. Only 4 percent of it remained to be finished.

More than a bulkhead was needed for Governors Island to grow, however. A year after the scows began dumping rocks, the task of making the actual land began. Without benefit of modern construction equipment, the landfill must have been a daunting task. The enclosed shoal sat in water ranging from 4 to 6 feet deep on the Buttermilk Channel side, and 8 to 10 feet deep on the Hudson side. The engineers estimated that the entire water mass required an average of 14 to 16 feet of fill, or approximately 4,500,000 cubic yards of dirt–nearly 10 percent more than the cubic yardage excavated for the foundations for the World Trade Center[74] and one-third more than the yardage dumped to create Battery Park City.[75] As described in the bid documents, the extension was to be composed of "sand, gravel, cellar dirt, etc.–only such as will make good, firm, solid land, not liable to wash away readily." Perhaps remembering the offal that had earlier washed up on the island's shores, limits were placed on the condition of the material to be used: "it must be free from substances liable to decay, to give off odors, or otherwise to become a nuisance." In other words, the new land would not be a garbage dump. The fill substance was subsequently altered to include a combination of mud and dry material in order to keep it from simply being swept away by the wind.[76]

By the end of 1902, the seawalls on either side of the northern third of the peninsula, beginning west of the South Battery and south of the formerly wave-washed Brick Row, were far enough along to contain fill safely. On the day before Christmas that year, the lowest bidder, the New York Filling Company of 17 State Street, signed a contract with the army to deliver the first of many loads of dirt.[77] Now came the difficult and expensive part. Contractors sitting in scows anchored in the middle of New York Harbor would have to lift a mixture of dry fill and no more than 50 percent mud over the 2-foot-high riprap wall and dump it onto the more than 100-acre shoal. Wind, waves, and traffic were most likely constant problems for the workers, who filled in all of the wet area to an elevation 2 feet above the top of the bulkheads (4 feet above where the scows sat in the harbor). Once the initial level had been reached, the contractors had three additional tasks before them: pile up additional fill along the Hudson River and Buttermilk Channel shores, push this material inward, and grade it to a crest between 13 and 15 feet high.

Of course, all of this effort came with a price tag that the army engineers had not anticipated: 8.5 cents a cubic yard, double the 4.0 cents budgeted in the Kimball plan. And like the rocks, the price rose as work progressed–to 22.6 cents per cubic yard. In addition, the engineers had not calculated the effort of moving the second deposit of fill inland.[78]

Equipment failure and weather were only two of the problems that added to the cost and delayed the work. At the outset, the contractor's mechanical equipment either malfunctioned or was inefficient. The pump, which was probably concurrently used to dredge Buttermilk Channel, washed away as much of the mud as it deposited.[79] Then the arms of the derricks that sat on the seawall, which were supposed to lift the dirt from the clamshell dredge to the land, failed because the claws were not strong or long enough to reach above the initial 2-foot elevation of the new fill. A particularly cold winter was a further irritation. In January and February 1905, with only 4 percent of the work complete, the entire surface of the area to be filled in froze solid. Despite these setbacks, when warm weather returned, the work resumed, albeit slowly. By June, the walls of another third of the shoal were ready to contain new land, and the engineers issued new bids.[80]

Although designed by the engineers and not by the McKim firm, a safety cap on the Governors Island extension was the construction of a granite wall. This wall was to provide a formal, above-ground enclosure for the land and would eventually be viewed by aviators, polo players, and generations of military men and women. On August 1, 1904, having determined that the riprap had settled sufficiently in the areas where the filling was complete, Brown & Fleming (with the Toomey Brothers again as subcontractor) was rehired to provide cement and stones and to construct a 3-foot-wide, 3-foot-high masonry wall beginning at least 2 feet below the top of the landfill. Capped by a 3-foot-wide coping, the wall rose along the new shorelines of the island. It is unknown where Brown & Fleming procured the material for the wall. The IRT dig had moved to the Bronx and Brooklyn; perhaps excavations from the Singer Building were used because it was under construction during this period.

The contractors have had two dredges and a pump employed during nearly all of the year, building this material up above low water, but with comparatively little success. The dredges are not able to cast up the material high enough to make a bank which will not be washed down by waves, and the pump apparently has not been operated to best advantage.

(WAR DEPARTMENT, "REPORT OF THE CHIEF OF ENGINEERS, U.S. ARMY," IN *ANNUAL REPORT FOR THE WAR DEPARTMENT FOR THE YEAR ENDING JUNE 30, 1904* [WASHINGTON, D.C.: U.S. GOVERNMENT PRINTING OFFICE, 1904], 1125.)

Between 1905 and 1906, there was yet another cause of delay. Legal problems beset both the decorative enclosure and the completion of the landfill. By October 1905, with just four months remaining in the Brown & Fleming contract and only 35 percent of the granite wall completed, Humphrey Toomey's reliability became questionable. Complaining about extremely high tides and difficulties in securing materials, Toomey asked for an extension of time to complete his work.[81] In a flurry of legal documents and in a letter sent by Toomey directly to Secretary of War William Howard Taft (who had succeeded Elihu Root in 1904), however, it is apparent that the delays were actually caused by Toomey's debts. He simply had not paid either the suppliers of the materials or the laborers, whom he faulted for dilatory behavior. Ever cost-conscious, however, the engineers chose to capitalize on Brown & Fleming's low rates rather than rebid the contract. The slowdown continued, and it was not until eight months later, on July 17, 1906, that everything was back in order; reliable Brown & Fleming had agreed to "rush the work through" on their own.[82]

FINISHING TOUCHES, 1907–1912

As the engineering work wound down, the quartermaster was obviously itching to put his imprimatur on the new land and finally to begin the implementation of the McKim plan. But probably because the new land required time to settle, and time and money were needed to turn the McKim plan into working drawings, the architects' vision lay in abeyance, a blueprint for the future. Between 1907, when the quartermaster began his queries, and 1913, when the landfill finally came into that department's hands, there is no evidence of either drawings or budget allotments for establishing individual structures on the expansion. Instead, the quartermaster built where he always had, on the original island, even while the engineers were kept busy more than doubling the island's size.

Nothing in the records indicates that the quartermaster's request for $535,000 in January 1901 was either granted by Congress or spent by the department. Instead of building brick storehouses and a new headquarters building or moving the hospital and adding a story to the Fort Jay barracks, the priorities were changed to more modest projects–save for one. On May 10, 1904, a major enhancement occurred that could be seen throughout the harbor: electricity replaced the fifty-year-old lighting system, which over time had evolved from whale oil to kerosene and finally to gas.[83]

Given that the Department of the East (which became the Division of the East in 1903) was headquartered on Governors Island and that many still felt the island was an important fortification for the protection of New York, the army also decided to improve the living conditions of the officers who had to live on the island while it was being enlarged. Using annual appropriations from Congress for the category "Buildings and Quarters," the quartermaster built "according to more natural dictates of expediency," thereby initiating smaller quality-of-life changes for both officers and enlisted men.[84] As usual, the funds had to be spent within the calendar year, which left no time to use anything more than the standard military plans. The space for new structures was as limited as the funds. Between 1902 and 1906, a large single-family officers' quarters was built on an unused plot at the northwestern end of Nolan Park (Building 20). In addition, now that the sea no longer washed up on Hay Road, the quartermaster continued the eastern development of Brick Row, specifically Building 403 in 1905–1906 (the brick house used for the 1988 Reagan–Gorbachev summit) and Building 404 in 1902–1904. Congressional funds also became available at this time for a category called "Post Exchanges and Gymnasiums," and the department took advantage of these funds in 1903 to supply much-needed recreational facilities in the basement of the South Battery.[85]

Meanwhile, the land filling continued until at least April 1912, during which time Henry Steers, the contractor hired at the completion of the New York Filling Company's work, was also engaged to turn the landfill into a lawn.[86] New problems continually cropped up. Some sand leaked out through the riprap; large sinkholes appeared, caused by both the wet subsurface and annual frosts; and at least 20,000 yards of dried-out fill blew away into Buttermilk Channel. In addition, windblown sand had replaced waves as an irritant to life on the former edge of the island. According to a memo from this period, it was impossible to plant grass or lay down sod on the extension, and the dirt "is also a great nuisance in the officers' quarters nearby, and often it must be raked up from the lawns on the island to prevent killing sod there."[87] The need for a "landscape artist" presaged in an earlier *New York Times* article was obvious, but one would not be hired. No sooner was the sand problem partially under control than Colonel Sigrid W. Roessler–now in charge of the project, having replaced Colonel Marshall in 1907–was forced to go begging for $15,000, a pittance compared to the work's overall price. The request was denied, and the southernmost 22 acres of the new land remained sand.[88]

Arguments over the siting of a foghorn to protect the harbor's shipping commerce revived the discussion of aesthetics begun by Elihu Root a decade earlier and are evidence that the McKim plan became the point of departure for future land-use decisions on Governors Island.

By 1910, the engineers' early-warning vessel was still in operation, located near the completed terminus of the island. But this signal was insufficient according to the Department of Commerce and Labor, which had been designated to run such facilities nationwide. Secretary Charles Nagel now insisted on placing a light and fog signal on the southwesterly end of the island. A letter from War Secretary J. M. Dickenson was polite but firm. Without specifically mentioning the planned Beaux Arts ornamental structure designed by McKim, Mead & White to line up with Fort Jay, Dickenson explained that a structure that might destroy the integrity of that plan was unacceptable.[89]

I also enclose a photograph of a plan showing the proposed improvement of Governors Island....Though the location of a *lighthouse* of proper architecture at the point marked "A" on this plan might not seriously detract from the landscape and architectural effect of this scheme, its location [anywhere else] would materially mar the artistic conception of the architects who originated the plan.

(LETTER FROM J. M. DICKENSON, SECRETARY OF WAR, TO CHARLES NAGEL, SECRETARY OF COMMERCE AND LABOR, APRIL 8, 1910, GENERAL CORRESPONDENCE 1884–1923, RG 77, 1799/75216, NATIONAL ARCHIVES, COLLEGE PARK, MD., EMPHASIS IN ORIGINAL.)

In addition, Dickenson was concerned about the effect that such a noxious sound would have on living conditions. Though a foghorn at the southern end of the island probably would not have affected homes on Brick Row, the closest quarters then in existence, what about the health and welfare of island residents once all the new housing proposed in the McKim plan was built? Perhaps also worried that the military might be deterred from serving on Governors Island, Dickenson continued: "There can hardly be any doubt that the location of a steam siren or fog horn of any kind in such close proximity to residences occupied by officers and their families and to barracks occupied by enlisted men [all shown on the McKim plan] would constitute a serious nuisance."[90]

Despite Dickenson's request that the fog device be located off island and a last-ditch suggestion that the matter be discussed with President Taft (formerly the secretary of the army) at his next Cabinet meeting, the army did not prevail. Rather, it was forced to build and run the fog device on the southwest corner of the completed landfill, using signals donated by the Lighthouse Service. Two years later, on May 10, 1912, in a consolidation of such facilities, Colonel Roessler happily turned over the foghorn's operation (and expense) to the Commerce Department.[91]

Dickenson's original letter about the matter actually envisioned a future that can be seen in contemporary drawings by schoolchildren at P.S. 26 and that many army and Coast Guard families still talk about: "this nuisance would last for all time and be of frequent occurrence" owing to the presence of fog in New York Harbor.[92] The foghorn would become as familiar on Governors Island as reveille and taps.

HANDOVER: READY AT LAST, 1913

ON JANUARY 23, 1913, thirteen years after the addition to the island was first proposed, Colonel Roessler transferred to Colonel John S. Mallory, commanding officer of Fort Jay, a masonry seawall 7,219 feet long that enclosed an area of 103.55 acres. The capacious government reservation envisioned in the Kimball board's report was now a reality. Eleven acres larger than Battery Park City and built at a cost of $10,300 per acre, the area was filled in to a height of 10 feet, or nearly one story above mean low tide. But it was virtually empty.[93]

Despite the planning, the architectural and engineering designs, more than a decade of laying stone and carting dirt, and much press hyperbole, there was still no decision about

DRAWING OF THE UBIQUITOUS FOGHORN *even appeared in teacher Carole Teller's third- and fourth-grade art class, 1990s, Stephanie Sitives. Courtesy of Carole Teller.*

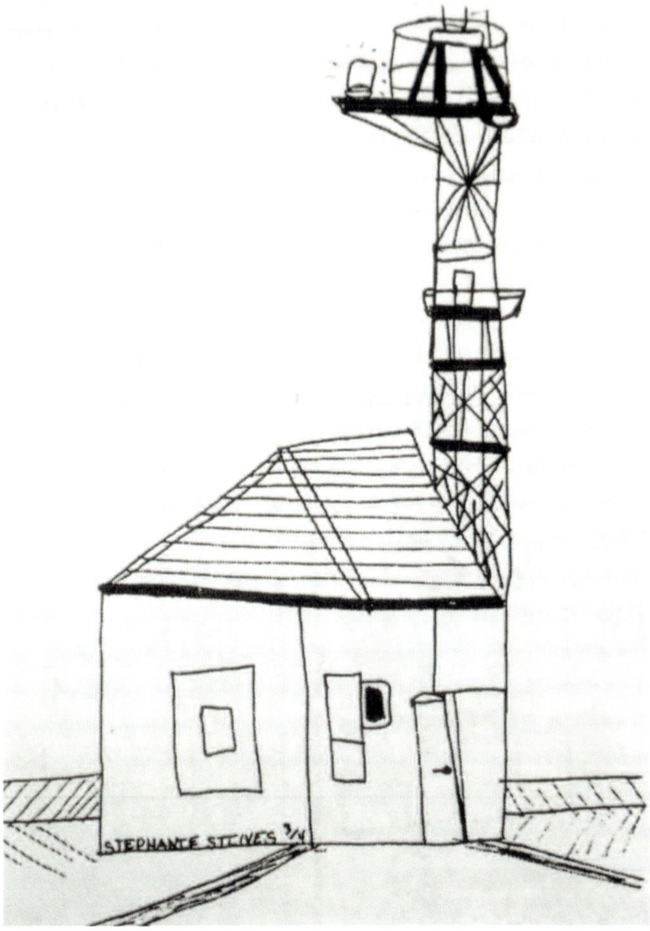

Governors Island's future. Owing in part to a period of relative peace and controversy among army officials as to the advisability of running their own money-losing transport service, the relatively unused wharf was evidence of the army's decision to abandon the island as a supply station and landing for large transport ships. By and large, save for the infantry troops drilling in flying dust and perhaps fantasizing about an elegant, grassy, McKim-designed parade ground, the island was pretty much what it had been at the turn of the century, only larger.

Would things have been different had Elihu Root remained longer in the War Department? Probably not, because the army was in the process of downsizing and closing military posts all over the country and was once again debating whether to abandon Governors Island altogether. Two questions would be asked again and again about Governors Island in the twentieth century: Should it be turned over to the city for a park? And should it be sold to the highest bidder? The ultimate decision would not come until many years later.

In January 1913, however, Colonel Roessler, Henry Babcock, and all of the military and civilian personnel involved in the enlargement of Governors Island must have been incredibly proud of their accomplishment. From a budgetary perspective, the project had been brought in at the $1,100,000 that had been estimated in 1900. As an engineering feat, the sheer size of the task and the invention of new technology for constructing bulkheads were impressive. What a sight this parachute-shaped island must have been! In a photo taken by Irving Underhill from the Whitehall Building around 1911, the details of the massive construction project are evident: the perfectly aligned stone wall; the contrast between the unfinished, sunken western portion of the land and the uneven mounds of dirt waiting to be graded; the derricks and scows in action along Buttermilk Channel. From Brooklyn overlooking Atlantic Basin, the three-dimensional landmass indeed resembles the silk of a parachute, with the flat, empty landfill looking like the strings holding an invisible soldier gently floating into the lower harbor.

It is almost certainty that ten years hence there will be in New York Harbor the finest military post not only in this country but in the whole world...transports will sail from it to the island possessions of the United States, and there will be great headquarters buildings on it and splendid mansions and imposing barracks. There will also be a wonderfully beautiful parade ground, a splendid park, and a great athletic field.

("THE TRANSFORMATION OF GOVERNORS ISLAND," *NEW YORK TIMES*, SEPTEMBER 29, 1907, SM2.)

ISLAND HIGHLIGHTS *Twentieth-Century Island Engineers*

Col. W. L. Marshall is one of the best known engineers in the Army....Under his supervision the reclamation work that is to double the size of Governors Island is being done.[1]

In charge of what was arguably New York City's most massive landfill project was fifty-five-year-old Lieutenant Colonel W. L. Marshall. A stout man, esteemed by New York trade organizations and shipping establishments, Marshall was perhaps the "brains" of New York Harbor. From his office in Room H7 of the Army Building at 39 Whitehall Street, he had for years directed the surveying and dredging of the harbor.[2] His signature appeared on the soundings and surveys for keeping navigational channels open and ships safe from dangerous rocks and sunken vessels.

Marshall's role in the Governors Island landfill probably began in the early 1900s, when he doubtless supplied maps and engineering information for the Kimball board's plans for improvements. His immediate superior was the Washington-based chief of engineers of the U.S. Army, Brigadier General George L. Gillespie, an acquaintance of Marshall and a member of the Kimball board. By 1901, Marshall was directing the construction of the recommended reclamation project.

Marshall's assistant–in charge of the day-to-day operations of the Governors Island extension–was a civilian engineer, Henry Nash Babcock of Pelham Manor. Babcock, who earned $250 a month, had modest offices in sheds that were moved with his work, first to the north end of the island and eventually to the newly made land.[3] By July 1901, Marshall and Babcock were ready to increase the size of Governors Island and to build a pier grand enough to accommodate the largest army transport vessels.[4]

Marshall's superiors apparently regarded him highly enough that on January 23, 1903, he was the one who made the request to Albany for the extra nineteen-acre land transfer needed to round off the south end of the island in an architecturally harmonious manner. In writing to New York's secretary of state John R. O'Brien, Marshall requested a speedy release of the underwater land. His appeal contained both logic and boosterism. "It is the opinion of the architects," he wrote, "that the island would be more commodious and better worthy of its conspicuous position in the center of New York Harbor, if the lower end were rounded instead of being carried straight across the shoal."[5]

But Marshall had less success with Washington politics. By July 1906, three years after the first mud and dirt had been dumped by the New York Filling Company, the northern section of the landfill was still not properly graded. Furthermore, in order to complete the job, the company had deposited more than $72,000 worth of extra material to fill in the center part of the plot. When company owner George Leary asked for payment for the overage, Marshall refused, planning to hold out until the work was complete. Instead, the grading came to a halt, and the top brass in Washington were brought into the fray. The new chief of engineers, Brigadier General George L. MacKenzie (who in late 1901 had replaced Gillespie), supported Marshall, but Leary apparently had a political contact or relative capable of overriding the engineers, so he appealed directly to the comptroller in the Treasury Department.

History shows that legal opinions on this matter were many, and in the end the lawyers

AERIAL PHOTOGRAPH *of Governors Island, ca. 1960s, unknown photographer. By the late 1960s, the army had constructed high-rise housing on the western edge of the landfill, and the Coast Guard had added three additional piers. Courtesy of U.S. Coast Guard Historian's Office, Washington, D.C.*

AERIAL PHOTOGRAPH *of Governors Island, n.d., unknown photographer. When the Coast Guard base closed in 1997, the Governors Island landfill was fully occupied. The influence of early McKim, Mead & White plans is evident in the preservation of a large, open space in the center of the island. Courtesy of U.S. Coast Guard Historian's Office, Washington, D.C.*

NEW YORK HARBOR, *Governors Island, 1906, E. Beck. Blueprint. Governors Island showing soundings taken in extension, November 2–20, 1906. Courtesy of National Archives, College Park, Md.*

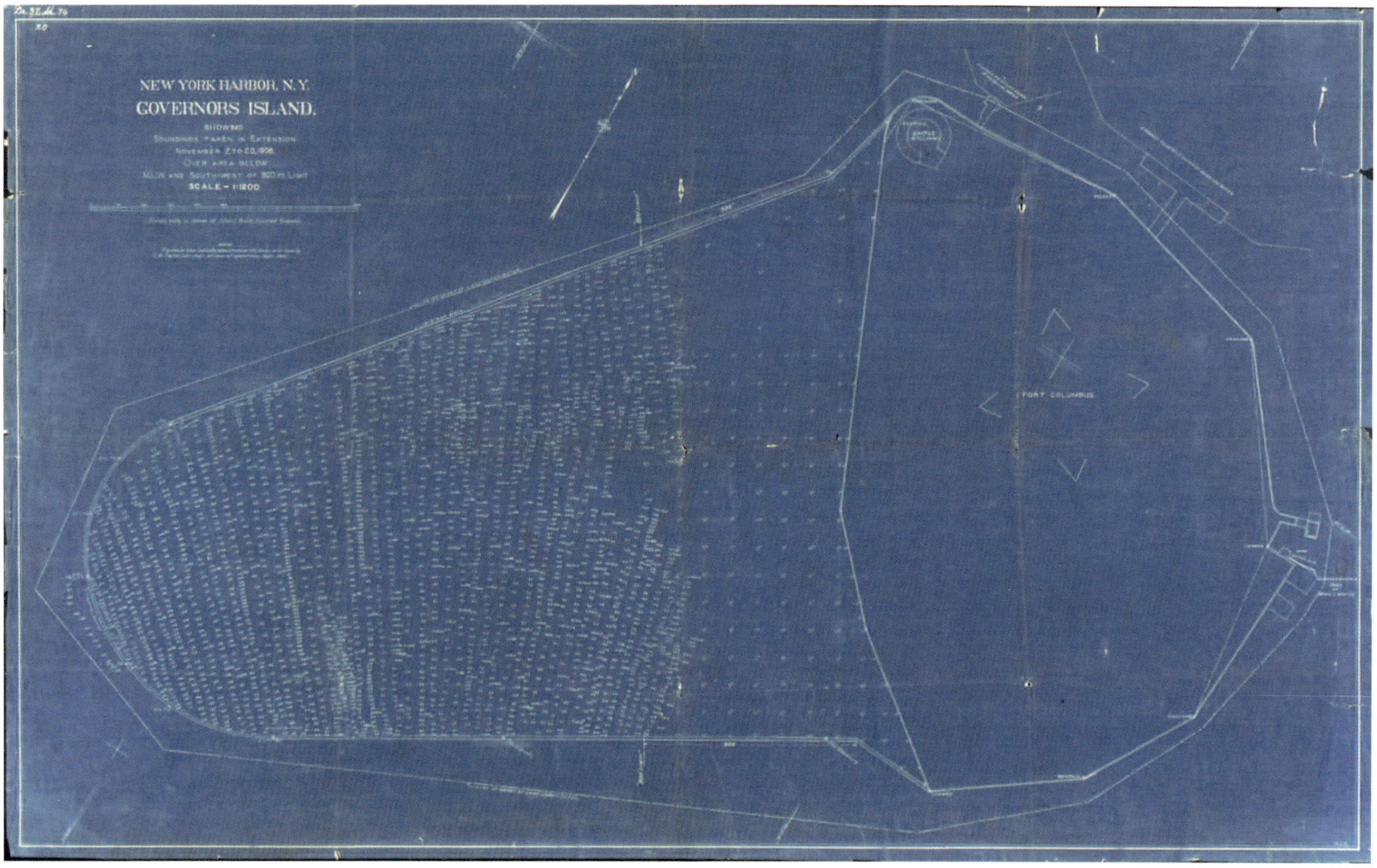

determined that if Leary sued, the costs would be higher than the outstanding invoice. Much to his dismay, Marshall came out the loser. To add to his dismay, because every last penny was budgeted a year in advance, there was no money to pay Leary. The Treasury Department footed the $72,708.70 bill, but only temporarily, thus adding to the overall tripled cost of the landfill.[6]

A year later, as the engineers checked off a long punch list, W. L. Marshall was no longer in charge. His weight—not his age, ability, or popularity—precipitated this change. In November 1907, Marshall, sixty-one years old and with three more years left to serve in the army, was forced into early retirement in a rather ignominious manner. His extreme stoutness apparently brought into question his physical fitness for active service. In order to prove himself to a board of examiners, Marshall—the man with excellent sea legs, the man most knowledgeable about New York City's waters around Governor's Island, and the man who had single-handedly orchestrated the creation of the city's largest landfill—was forced to ride a horse. He was too portly and inexperienced in horsemanship to pass the test.[7]

Henry Babcock, who remained in day-to-day charge under the command of Colonel Sigrid W. Roessler, took on the difficult punch list, which included filling the settlement in the brand-new seawall and planting grass on the windswept sand. Frequent repairs also needed to be made because ferries and other types of craft persistently ran into the new appendage to the island. In his comprehensive report titled "The Enlargement of Governors Island" published in the prestigious *Professional Memoirs* of the Corps of Engineers in 1914, Babcock complained three times about the vessels that ran into the seawall, "under conditions, as far as known, which show inexcusable neglect on the part of the navigators."[8]

ENLARGEMENT OF *Governors Island, 1903, W. C. Marshall. Map showing progress of filling to June 30, 1903. Author's collection.*

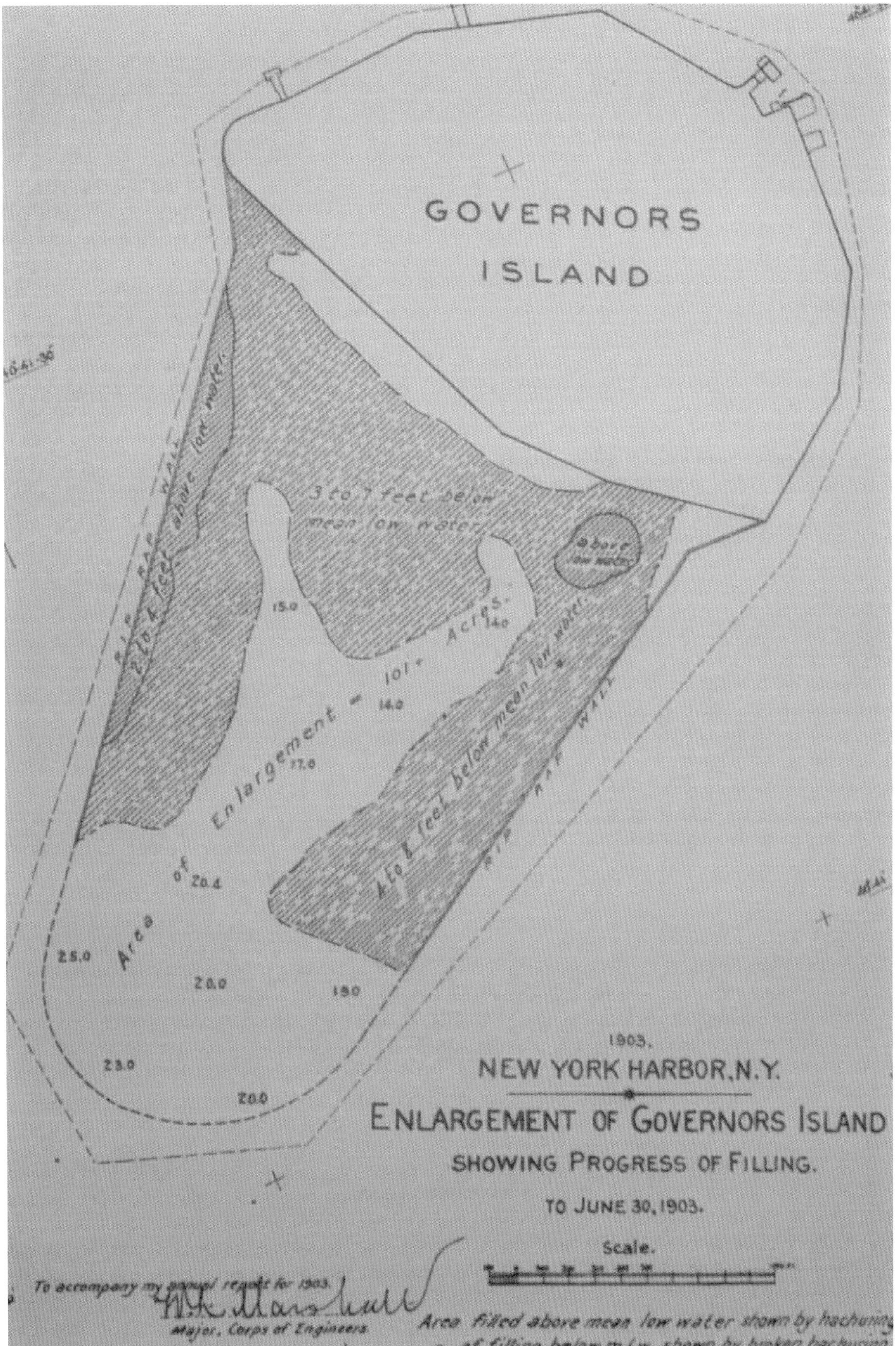

Approximately twelve years after Babcock's arrival on Governors Island, his work there ended. At his departure, he saw the new land that he had helped to create rising gently to the center. Sitting on it were only three structures. A relatively new fog light/device was complemented by remnants of an airplane shed. And on the southern periphery–ready to become quarters for noncommissioned officers someday–was Henry Nash Babcock's last field office.[9]

ISLAND HIGHLIGHTS

Where Does the Dirt from the Subway Go?

Uncle Sam himself has used many hundred thousand cubic yards of subway stone and dirt in his Herculean labor of increasing the size of Governors Island.[1]

At the turn of the twentieth century, Governors Island became the unlikely beneficiary of the budding New York City subway system. Just across the harbor, the IRT Line was excavating for the city's first underground at the very same time army engineers were seeking tons of rocks to build a foundation for more than one hundred acres of the island's new-made land. It was engineer W. L. Marshall's idea to conjoin the two projects. In a 1903 memo to his superior in Washington, he wrote:

> At this time the construction of the Rapid Transit Subway in New York City is requiring the excavation of large quantities of stone, which must be disposed of...
>
> The contractors for the bulkhead deliver and place these stones at the rate of 35 cents per ton of 2240 lbs. In effect, the United States pays nothing for the stones and only a fair price for placing them in position. Under other conditions this work would probably have cost $40,000 more.[2]

According to a Metropolitan Transportation Authority history, under a lease from the city, the privately owned Interborough Rapid Transit Company broke ground for the first electric-powered subway line in March 1900. Starting from City Hall and moving north to the Bronx, workers used picks and shovels and at times boring machines to dig trenches for what typically became a fifty-five-foot-wide by fifteen-foot-high tunnel. But the debris from the excavations had to be deposited somewhere. Some of the rocks were doubtless carted to foundations of office buildings under construction at that time, but others traveled by water to places south of Manhattan.[3]

Photographs of the time show a temporary viaduct erected by the IRT Line running through Battery Park. Carts moved the bedrock from City Hall and later the Battery loop to the waterfront. The *New York Times* described the process:

VIEW OF THE IRT CONSTRUCTION TRACK *that carried excavated stones to a Battery landing, July 21, 1904, unknown photographer. From there, the boulders were transported by barge to Governors Island* (far left), *where they became the seawall for the island's extension. Courtesy of New York Transit Museum.*

> During the four years spent in tunneling under Manhattan Island approximately 3,000,000 cubic yards of stone and dirt have been dug and blasted....[N]ecessary actors have been moving behind or below the scenes. They are an Army in themselves–the men who have been moving the dirt and stone with wagon, derrick, viaduct, tug and scow from under the feet of New York. Six to 12 dredges have recently been loaded at the battery and unloaded either at Governors Island or off Greenvill...or Sandy Hook.[4]

For Brown & Fleming, a company hired by both the IRT to remove their underground excavations and the U.S. Army to build the Governors Island retaining wall for the landfill, Governors Island was a very convenient dumping ground. The trip was short when compared to trips to New Jersey or Staten Island and thus required fewer man-hours and minimal fuel.[5] In the eighteen months from January 1901 to the end of June 1903, Brown & Fleming delivered more than 200,000 tons of free riprap to the army for a carting fee of thirty-five cents a ton. Except for a gap to allow the dirt to be brought in, the more than twenty-block-long seawall to contain the landfill was finished a year later.[6]

CURTISS LANDING *at Governors Island–winning the* World*'s $10,000 prize, May 29, 1910, L. Biedermann. Poster. Author's collection.*

Chapter Five

FLIGHT OR FIGHT?

Half way between the prow of Manhattan and the thick beam of Brooklyn, lies a smallish, roundish, flat island...it has an excellent polo field. It is also just large enough and just flat enough, in fact just right in every way, for an airport.[1]

Wars threatening New York or the larger interests of the United States were not the only events that put Governors Island under siege. From 1919 to 1941, the military on the island was under attack by merchants, politicians, and numerous interest groups who wanted the island for another use: a municipal airfield. Using words instead of guns, a roster of famous names from LaGuardia to Hoover to Roosevelt fought for their cause against the secretary of the U.S. Army and various commanding generals of Governors Island. In all, there were twenty-two years of arguing, politicking, and marketing; hearings, plans, and counterplans; two presidential commissions; and eleven pieces of legislation. Throughout these years, the army sought funding from Congress for improvements to the base, and local business groups sought ways to create an airport. Ironically, the advances in technology that introduced flight to Governors Island in 1909 ultimately saved the day for the army.

AN ILLUSTRIOUS SANDY STRIP, 1909–1918

THE HISTORY OF FLIGHT on Governors Island began in 1909 with the confluence of the Hudson-Fulton jubilee—the commemoration of the Hudson River's discovery and the launching of the first steamboat—and the availability of a barren strip of land. The island, with its polo ponies and mule-drawn supply carts, sat in the midst of a heavily competitive transportation revolution occurring around it. On the sea, the *Mauretania* vied with the *Lusitania* to become the largest and fastest passenger ship; on land, the newly minted Oldsmobile and Ford factories competed to turn out the first affordable motor cars. The launching of Orville and Wilbur Wright's motorized biplane, the *Flyer,* was followed by international air-cup races and endurance flights to promote the newest means of transportation.

A healthy competition was in process in 1909 between Wilbur Wright and another American flyer, Glenn Curtiss. Both men had created small airplane-manufacturing businesses, and Wright was even working with the army to develop a military plane. Both were also winning prizes for exhibitions and air races. In February, the Wrights displayed their flight prowess at Templehoff Field in Germany, earning $12,000. In August, Curtiss won $5,000 and the

WILBUR WRIGHT *with unidentified officer and children, 1909, George Grantham Bain. Courtesy of George Grantham Bain Collection, Prints and Photographs Division, Library of Congress, Washington, D.C.*

Gordon Bennet Trophy for the fastest speed at the Reims ten-kilometer air-race course. But their competition also moved into the legal courts. That same month Wilbur Wright sued Curtiss for patent infringement because Curtiss was allegedly using Wright's designs for his own newest planes.

The start of the two-week-long Hudson-Fulton jubilee to observe the tercentennial of Henry Hudson's discovery of the Hudson River and the centennial of Robert Fulton's steam-run water transportation system seemed, on the surface, to have little to do with once-again sleepy Governors Island. In 1909, the newly made extension to the island was an uneven, sandy, mosquito-ridden plain waiting to settle and for funds from Washington to be developed into a first-class army base. Leonard Wood, commanding general of the Department of the East at the time, was an ardent horseman, and the extension must have been an inhospitable track for his daily rides. When not reorganizing the army's training and penal systems, Wood, along with his wife, Louise, had an active social life. They presided at Governors Island's splendid spring garden parties and entertained dignitaries with parades and dances. These occasions enabled Wood both to show off the historic military base and to further his own political aspirations. Thus, it was an easy sell when the Hudson-Fulton organizers approached Wood to gain permission to use Governors Island's newly made land for an event in that celebration. What ensued catapulted the island into the age of flight.

Monday, September 20th, 1909. Weather cool and windy....A very busy morning with the annual report, work incident to the Hudson-Fulton Celebration, numerous requests for passes to see the Wrights fly, etc....Wilbur Wright and Mr. Hammer called this morning at the office. Wright is a quiet reserved chap, looks very much like his pictures. Seems to be very pleased with the opportunities furnished for his flying test.

(LEONARD WOOD, DIARIES, LEONARD WOOD PAPERS, COLLECTIONS OF THE MANUSCRIPT DIVISION, LIBRARY OF CONGRESS, WASHINGTON, D.C.)

Billed as a "memorial of a brilliant past and an inspiration to a more lustrous future," the Hudson-Fulton celebration aimed to demonstrate the growth of transportation. Naval parades would go up the Hudson with replicas of Henry Hudson's sailing ship the *Half Moon* and Robert Fulton's steam-run

WILBUR WRIGHT *aloft in the* Flyer, *n.d., unknown photographer. Those who watched this exhibition saw a man in a life jacket flying a biplane with three small American flags and a sixteen-foot-long red canoe underneath. Courtesy of Special Collections and Archives, Wright State University, Dayton, Ohio.*

Clermont.[2] The empty landfill on Governors Island also provided the perfect venue to celebrate the jubilee's flight portion. The site was situated close enough to Manhattan to transport distinguished guests easily, held a prominent position in the harbor where people in boats of all shapes and sizes could watch, and had enough clear land to establish a rudimentary airfield.

Flying machines are no longer toys and dreams...they are an established fact.

(DAVID LLOYD GEORGE, FUTURE PRIME MINISTER OF GREAT BRITAIN, AT REIMS AIR MEET, AUGUST 22 TO 29, 1909, IN DAVID H. ONKST, "REIMS AIR MEET," IN THE U.S. CENTENNIAL OF FLIGHT COMMISSION WEB SITE AT HTTP://WWW.CENTENNIALOFFLIGHT.GOV/ESSAY/EXPLORERS_RECORD_SETTERS_AND_DAREDEVILS/REIMS/EX2.HTM.)

With Wood's permission, the Hudson-Fulton committee invited aviators Wright and Curtiss to exhibit their prowess by flying over water. Besides the glory, the enticement for the flyers was monetary. A donation in honor of Joseph Pulitzer of the *New York World* assured that the pilots would be paid $1,000 for expenses; to encourage new records, whoever stayed in flight for more than ten miles would receive an additional $15,000.

By September 22, three days before the official opening of the Hudson-Fulton celebration, the committee had created a small airstrip on the newly made land, accompanied by two shelters constructed twenty feet apart on either side of the field. Curtiss and Wright had a cordial meeting (the first since the initiation of Wright's lawsuit) in front of Wright's shed, optimistically called an "aerodrome" in the press. Inside, Wright's mechanic, Charlie Taylor, who had built the engines for the original *Flyer,* assembled the 1907 Model A–type flying machine. Having also had experience assisting prior ascents from the Kill Devil Hill sand dunes in Kitty Hawk, North Carolina, Taylor created a monorail that would catapult Wright's plane from the shed, thus avoiding the possibility of the plane's wheels sinking into the soft surface of the landfill. Curtiss planned to take off in the sand.

Monday, October 4, 1909: Mr. Wilbur Wright made a remarkably fine flight in the morning, flying from Governors Island to a point well beyond Grant's Tomb and returning.... [A] large crowd of people present and much enthusiasm shown by vessels along the river.... Mr. Wright is a very interesting individual...very modest, has little to say, and everything he does say is to the point.

(LEONARD WOOD, DIARIES, LEONARD WOOD PAPERS, COLLECTIONS OF THE MANUSCRIPT DIVISION, LIBRARY OF CONGRESS, WASHINGTON, D.C.)

These landmark flights were awaited with much anticipation during the first week of the celebration, yet weather conditions made life tense among the organizers. There were dignitaries to be greeted. Prince and Princess Kunigore Kuni of Japan arrived on the island on a sunny day and were greeted by a battalion of the Fifth Infantry as they walked to Commander Wood's home

SPECTATORS WATCHING *the* Flyer *in flight, September 1909, unknown photographer. Courtesy of Special Collections and Archives, Wright State University, Dayton, Ohio.*

CURTISS'S AIRPLANE *at rest, showing construction of machine, at Governors Island, New York Harbor, October 1909, unknown publisher. Postcard. Author's collection.*

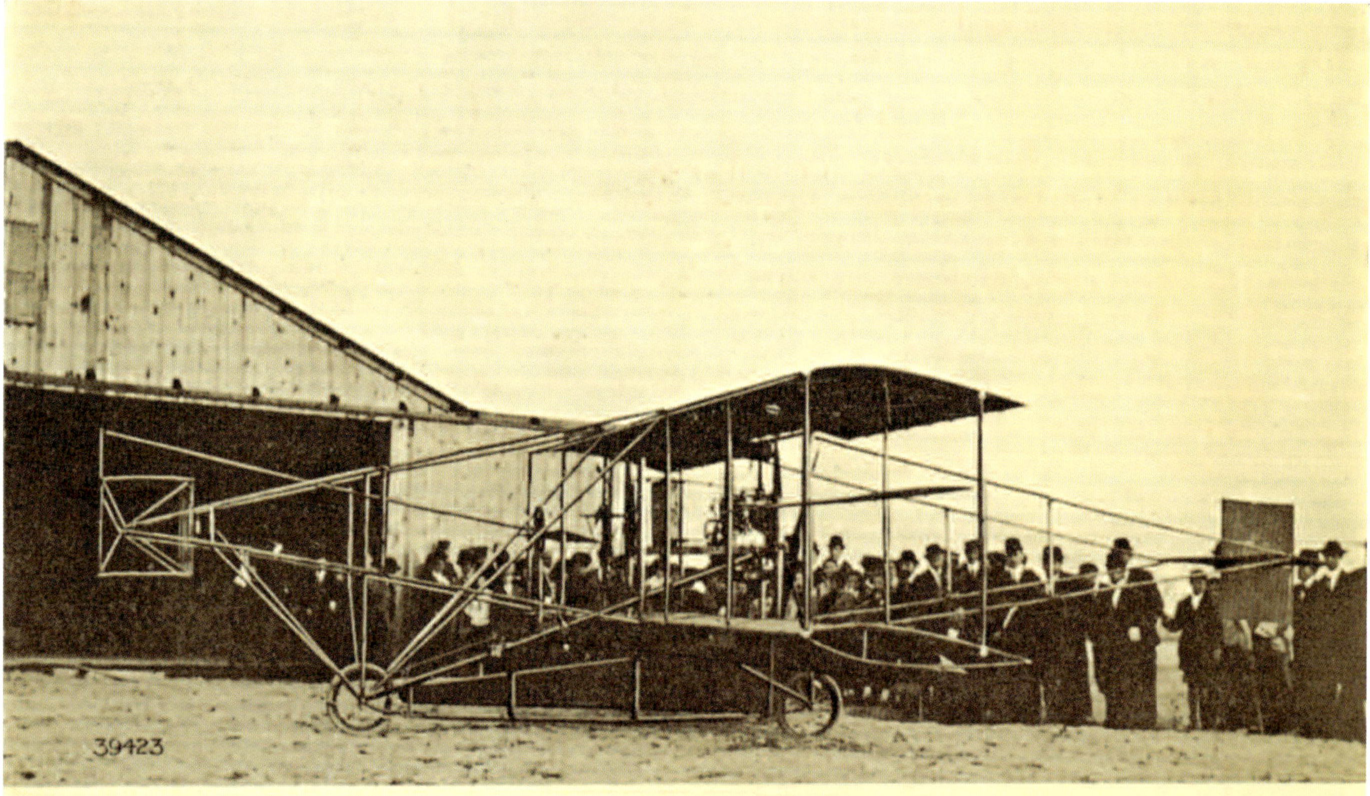

Curtiss's Aeroplane, at rest, showing construction of machine, at Governor's Island, New York Harbor, October, 1909.

for the official greeting and then to a reception at the Officers' Club. Three hundred guests arrived in a heavy rain for another event. Wood wrote in his diary about the problems they had with getting people to the island:

> The Quartermaster's department, with its usual stupidity, apparently failed to give orders for the *General Hancock* [the ferry to Governors Island] to make as frequent trips as possible. Consequently there was some delay in the people coming to the island. The British officers came on [Docks Commissioner] R. A. C. Smith's yacht, the Navy Yard people on their own boats, and a portion of the Hudson Fulton people on their own boats, so that the delay, while aggravating, was not general.[3]

Grand Admiral Hans Von Koester, the highest-ranking German naval officer, arrived in pouring rain. Nevertheless, two companies and their band greeted him, all of whom were cold and wet through and through.

September 29 was the first day of reckoning. A white flag with a red center rose over Governors Island and the Brooklyn Bridge to indicate clear skies.[4] Curtiss made a 6:00 A.M. attempt to set the record for distance over water. Reports are murky as to the results. Some say he actually flew three hundred yards, but others say he became mired in the soft surface. Wright had better success. By 9:00 A.M., a crowd had gathered, including William J. Hammer (secretary of the aeronautics committee of the Hudson-Fulton celebration, electrical engineer, and founder of a museum of light bulbs) and Guglielmo Marconi, who was poised to telegraph the results. At 9:00 or 9:15 A.M., Wright catapulted from his track, and signalmen immediately raised three flags and detonated three bombs to indicate to everyone in the harbor that a flight was finally in progress.

OFFICERS WHO WITNESSED *the landing of the first plane on Governors Island, New York Harbor, ca. 1909, unknown photographer.* Left to right: *Captain John E. Woodward, Twenty-ninth Infantry; Colonel John R. Van Huff, chief surgeon; Colonel George Andrews, adjutant general; Captain R. H. Allen; Glenn H. Curtiss, aviator; Lieutenant Allan L. Briggs, Twenty-ninth Infantry; Captain John Madden, Twenty-ninth Infantry; Colonel Isaac W. Littell, chief quartermaster; unknown; Captain Brian H. Wells, assistant to the chief quartermaster. Courtesy of Still Pictures Branch, National Archives, College Park, Md.*

In seven minutes, Wright flew twice around Governors Island. Not content with this run and failing to meet the ten-mile challenge, he took off again at 10:18 A.M. This time he was aloft for five minutes, and accompanied by the whistles of harbor craft and the *Lusitania* he circled the Statue of Liberty at fifty miles an hour. Wright made one more attempt at mileage later that afternoon, once again flying around Governors Island, this time for twelve minutes.[5] At the end of the day he had failed to win the Hudson-Fulton purse, but he had set a record for making the first flight over American waters.[6]

The competition between the two rivals continued. With a week remaining in the celebration, on October 2 Curtiss tried and failed once again to take off from Governors Island. He departed, but would return eight months later with a different kind of success. Meanwhile, Wright took off from Governors Island for the last time two days later, on October 4. To the plaudits of the press and the excitement of viewers up and down the Hudson River, Wright flew twenty miles, circled Grant's Tomb, another focal point of the celebration, and returned to Governors Island–all in thirty-three minutes. The glory and the prize money were his. For the army on Governors Island, however, Wright's trip was not only a precursor of the role flight would have in future wars, but also the first salvo in a battle to use the island for a commercial airport.

The runway and the sheds created on Governors Island by the Hudson-Fulton committee remained in use under army auspices for the next few years as a venue for endurance contests and stunt flying. In May 1910, it was Glenn Curtiss's turn for a heroic welcome. Responding to a $10,000 challenge, again from the *New York World,* Curtiss took off from a potato field in Albany and after two fuel stops landed with much hoopla on Governors Island. Greeted by Major General Frederick D. Grant, son of Ulysses S. Grant, Curtiss delivered a letter from the mayor of Albany. In the same year that the Governors Island ferry began to carry motor cars, Curtiss had demonstrated the feasibility of air mail.

By 1913, the year that the Governors Island landfill was certified as complete by the army engineers, aviation had become more than a novelty. In 1911, Congress had appropriated funds that allowed the Aeronautical Division of the Army Signal Corps to purchase five planes. Two of them were purchased from the Wright brothers' factory, and one from the Curtiss factory. Small airports, consisting of sheds for passengers and maintenance, and short runways were also beginning to appear. In Germany, there were terminals for Zeppelin airship passengers. The United States boasted twenty airports on land converted from fields or country clubs.[7]

However, the airstrip on Governors Island–now under the jurisdiction of the army quartermaster–remained unimproved. Fliers occasionally asked permission from the commanding general to use the airstrip to test individual patents. These permits were approved ad hoc, probably depending on whether the army needed the space for training, recreation, or social events. One well-connected group pressed for construction of a hydroplane hangar, but the army leadership disapproved, saying the land was needed for tents to house troops and for supplies to be sent to Texas (on the way to U.S.-occupied Vera Cruz) and China (where a new republic was in formation). In a pattern that would be repeated over the next twenty years, however, Congress overrode the army and approved the hangar. The quartermaster drew up plans and advertised for bids,[8] but nothing was built.

November 20, 1916—Out for an early morning ride. Just as we were coming in Miss Ruth Law arrived in her flight from Chicago. She got in about 9:00 A.M. Weather cool and chilly. Had been coming along at about eight thousand feet; an old style rattle trap machine of the most dangerous sort so far as our aviators could judge. She made the flight from Chicago in nine hours and twenty-four minutes with one stop. She carried a primitive map arrangement rolled up in a cigar box and turned it as she flew along, unwinding the roll. On the whole, she is a very quiet, well mannered type of woman. She looks like a school teacher rather than an aviator.

(LEONARD WOOD, DIARIES, LEONARD WOOD PAPERS, COLLECTIONS OF THE MANUSCRIPT DIVISION, LIBRARY OF CONGRESS, WASHINGTON, D.C.)

MISS RUTH LAW *being congratulated by Major Leonard Wood on completion of her record flight from Chicago to New York, January 1918, unknown photographer. Photograph from* National Geographic Magazine. *The flight was 832 miles, and the actual flying time was nine hours, one minute. Author's collection.*

BLUEPRINT *of the layout of the World War I cantonments, January 14, 1919, Major E. A. Simmons, Quartermaster Corps. Scrapbook photograph of the blueprint. Courtesy of National Archives, College Park, Md.*

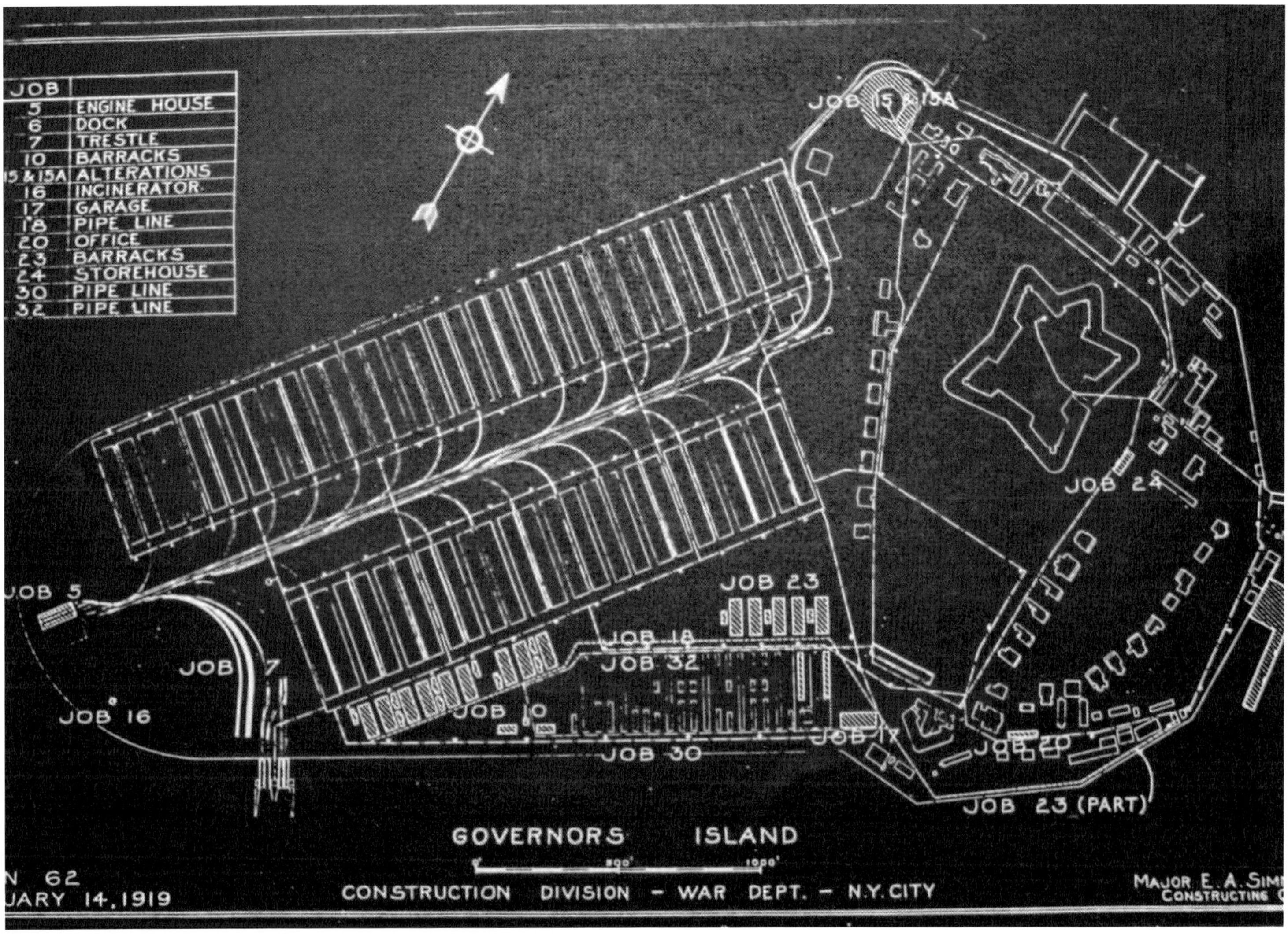

Meanwhile, the Governors Island strip continued to provide a venue for spectator sports. In 1913 and 1914, visitors to the island's annual garden parties were thrilled by the stunt flights, one of which featured a live air attack against a kite. Another highlight was a nighttime flight by Catherine Stinson, a Canadian stunt pilot who became the first woman authorized by the U.S. Postal Service to fly air mail. Stinson took off from the island's runway in total darkness with fireworks attached to her plane. Several hundred feet in the air, she caused the fireworks to ignite and proceeded to fly safely through the conflagration.[9]

Details of flight on Governors Island during the World War I years are sketchy. In Europe, the sky became the new battleground. The first air squadrons were sent to France after America's entry into the war in 1917. Governors Island was far too small to handle the volume of military traffic, so fliers from the East Coast probably departed from Glenn Curtiss's airfield in North Beach in Queens, from Mitchell Field on Long Island, and from hastily transformed baseball and polo fields on other military bases in the region.

Governors Island most likely helped the cause of flight on the ground. Civilians ran a training center on the island to promote military aviation, but this training probably took place in classrooms. There is also mention of space to test planes made for the government by the Sturtavant Company.[10] By the closing months of the war in 1918, however, any flight activity was doubtful. A January 14, 1919, blueprint of work being done by the War Department's

PREFABRICATED BARRACKS *on the unfinished landfill, November 14, 1918, unknown photographer. Scrapbook photograph. No room was left for a runway. Courtesy of National Archives, College Park, Md.*

Construction Division shows more than seventy hastily erected buildings standing on the landfill that had been virtually deserted just three month earlier. This flat, sandy area, still mosquito-infested, had been filled in with a mass of rectangular living quarters and warehouses lined up (as if at attention) in two orderly rows.[11] Running through the middle of the buildings and into each of the warehouses, on land where Wilbur Wright's *Flyer* had once taken off and landed, was another mode of transportation: the world's shortest railroad.

THE MERCHANT'S ASSOCIATION PURSUIT OF THE STRIP, 1919–1925

THE FIRST SKIRMISH OVER THE EXPANSION of the Governors Island airstrip took place at the end of World War I. It began with the army's request to Congress for construction funds to improve the landfill for use by the military base. The New York Merchant's Association countered this request with a pronouncement that the unfinished land should be used for a municipal airport. The merchants were resourceful and evidently powerful enough to wage what would become a long, drawn-out battle.

ENGINE HOUSE, *November 14, 1918, unknown photographer. Scrapbook photograph. The landfill contained railroad tracks and an engine house to store and service a locomotive. Courtesy of National Archives, College Park, Md.*

The changes to the island that Robert Lee Bullard–commanding general of the army's Second Corps Area, then headquartered on Governors Island–envisioned when he approached Congress for financing in 1919 were long overdue. They were loosely based on the master plan drawn up by McKim, Mead & White ten years earlier. A description of these plans in the press indicates that in keeping with Secretary of War Elihu Root's 1901 promise, all of the historic structures on the north end of the island, including Castle Williams and Fort Jay, were to remain intact. However, Root might have been surprised at the

GOVERNORS ISLAND, *New York Bay, showing aerial view of the cantonments on Governors Island, ca. 1918–19, unknown publisher. Postcard. The world's shortest railroad ran through the center to carry supplies. Author's collection.*

transformation of the McKim plan for the landfill portion of the island. *Concrete* was the operative word. Macadam highways would replace the hastily constructed World War I–era dirt roads. The "temporary" sheds would be razed. In place of McKim's grand "parade" would be a competitive polo field with accompanying grandstands. The barracks, large enough to house an entire regiment that Root had once ordered to be billeted there, would be moved away from the center of the landfill. A later description by *New York Times* writer Howard Mingus emphasizes maintenance over aesthetics: "Such structures as may be necessary will be of concrete, with foundations firmly placed so that the Army post may be maintained in future at a minimum of expense. Concrete barracks will be constructed on the Buttermilk Channel side of the island and the enlisted men housed there. The barracks are planned to include three buildings, each to cost $300,000."[12]

When Bullard's funding request reached Congress, the New York Merchant's Association had been expected to support the army build-out. In 1919, however, the association's aviation committee had another use in mind: the land on Governors Island should be preserved structure free because it was the only available location for a municipal airport. The association, with offices in the Woolworth building in Manhattan, had more than thirty-five thousand resident and nonresident members. With a permanent staff of experts, it prepared professional reports on issues relevant to the business community. So there was perhaps good reason for these merchants to recommend turning Governors Island into an airport: aviation was becoming an established mode of transportation, and they wanted to show that New York could reap the economic benefits of time saved both in travel and in high-cost, lightweight shipping.

Boosterism was another component of the desire to use Governors Island as a municipal airport; because the field of flight was advancing so quickly, civic associations such as the Merchant's Association were hoping to keep New York apace with the rest of the modernizing

FORT JAY GARAGE, *ca. 1920, Wells Studio. The army kept up with the transportation revolution. Courtesy of Still Pictures Branch, National Archives, College Park, Md.*

world. By 1919, the Curtiss flight had evolved into regularly scheduled air-mail service between New York, Chicago, and Washington, D.C. The first two-engine passenger plane had been constructed, and British and Dutch airline companies had been formed to transport passengers. Le Bourget Airport in Paris was open, and international flights carried about a dozen passengers daily across the English Channel between London and that city. Amsterdam–London service was in the offing, and just a year later the first formal European airport terminal would open in Croydon, England. In the United States, international flights between Key West, Florida, and Havana, Cuba, would soon begin, and a nationwide airport system was in formation, bringing together 145 municipally owned airstrips. Among these cities, Chicago, Philadelphia, St. Louis, Boston, and Los Angeles were on their way to having primitive terminals, typically with one hangar, gasoline and oil storage, a wind indicator, a telephone connection, and a location marker.[13]

Governors Island…is particularly advantageous for shipments of jewelry and precious stones, legal documents, securities, financial papers, and certain other articles of traffic which are common to the business of lower New York; and it is not too remote for passenger service.

(LETTER FROM THE MERCHANT'S ASSOCIATION OF NEW YORK TO COLONEL JAMES A. WOODRUFF, U.S. ARMY, SEPTEMBER 17, 1934, REPRINTED IN U.S. SENATE, *LANDING FIELD ON GOVERNORS ISLAND: HEARINGS BEFORE THE COMMITTEE ON MILITARY AFFAIRS ON H.R. 12009, AN ACT TO AUTHORIZE THE ENLARGEMENT OF GOVERNORS ISLAND AND CONSENTING TO THE USE OF A PORTION THEREOF AS A LANDING FIELD FOR THE CITY OF NEW YORK AND ITS ENVIRONS*, 74TH CONG., 2D SESS., JUNE 5, 1936, 12.)

Congressional inaction on the Governors Island aviation front followed the 1919 salvos. The request for funds for Bullard's improvements never left committee. Undaunted, he probably used post savings and army labor to clear some of the cantonments to build his polo ground in 1921. Leftover space became a drill field. Press reports from 1923 are equivocal in indicating that perhaps the Merchant's Association proposal was ahead of the times. The season for passenger and parcel transportation in the New York area was limited to the summer months, when existing equipment could safely fly; furthermore, there existed neither a formal licensing system nor rules of the air.[14]

Acting Secretary of the Army Dwight Filley Davis, however, remained firm in backing the army's position. In a letter to the Merchant's Association, he made it eminently clear that Governors Island was out of consideration for an

WINNER *in Dodge Motor Class, August 10, 1920, Sergeant J. H. Saum, Signal Corps. Courtesy of Still Pictures Branch, National Archives, College Park, Md.*

airport. Military and commercial uses must be kept separate, and the field was needed for military purposes. "The proposal," he wrote, "not only necessitates the removal of numerous post structures but would also isolate from each other important parts of the post and seriously interfere with communication between them. Moreover, the field would occupy practically all ground available for drill and recreation purposes."[15] Founder of the Davis Cup, Davis was an ardent proponent of recreation. Perhaps the open space that would be derived from the army's planned improvements to the landfill helped to propel his advocacy of those changes.

At this point, Merchant's Association members went to work and did what they did best: visited with flight officials abroad to see firsthand what was required for an urban airport. In January 1923, the association produced a carefully researched report that looked at costs and estimated the likelihood of commercial flights operating in the New York region. The report showed that Governors Island was the only place in New York that conformed to the requirements for an air terminus: easy access and swift, inexpensive construction. Curiously, it also recognized that Governors Island's days as an air terminal were limited: "realizing that if commercial aviation attains even a small measure of success, it will soon outgrow the facilities offered by Governors Island. [The Merchants Association] is now undertaking a further survey of possible locations in the vicinity of New York."[16]

LAGUARDIA AND HOOVER'S PURSUIT OF THE STRIP, 1925–1927

BASED ON THE MERCHANT'S ASSOCIATION report and in-house studies, Congress was finally ready to discuss locating an airport on Governors Island. Arguments followed two legislative tracks. The army pressed for passage of motions to allow construction to begin on much-needed housing facilities on Governors Island, but congressional leaders opposed this plan and rejoined with separate legislation in favor of a municipal airport. During this period, each side derived advantages from "surprise testimony" in the form of a Commerce Department report.

But even after seven years of off-and-on verbal combat, airport proponents were unable to prevail. The army, which from the start had veto power over any civilian actions taking place on military property, remained on the winning side.

In 1924, Congress had authorized a bill allowing the sale of certain army properties; the proceeds were to be placed in a housing fund for military posts throughout the United States. By April 1926, the roster of posts to benefit from this bill was ready, and Governors Island was on the list. The island was overcrowded but the potential was there to turn acres of crudely developed landfill into a glorious campus, so the army pressed for the release of these monies. New York congressman and soon-to-be New York City mayor Fiorello LaGuardia had other ideas for the landfill, however. Earlier that year LaGuardia had proposed a resolution to use Governors Island as a landing field,[17] and on March 22 and April 3, 1926, probably prompted by LaGuardia, Democratic representative Horace G. Prall and Republican senator James W. Wadsworth, both from New York, introduced bills directing the secretary of war to make the necessary arrangements to do so.

Against the historic background of Fort Jay and Castle Williams will rise wireless masts for the radio stations used in air transport. A meteorological bureau will be located there, conveying last minute weather data to the pilots of all outbound planes....Permanent hangars will be erected to house the mail planes. The mechanical force will have repair shops and other facilities for inspecting and servicing the machines....A field hospital, ambulance service and fire protection would be necessary...[in addition to] a club house where the flying men may rest between hops, a restaurant and a branch post office.

(HOWARD MINGUS, "HUGE AIRPORT FOR NEW YORK IS IN PROSPECT," FROM *NEW YORK TIMES*, DECEMBER 6, 1925, XX5.

An earlier report from a congressional select committee of inquiry gives a good picture of both state-of-the-art airport design at the time and what flight proponents such as LaGuardia were going to ask of the army on Governors Island. Instead of the grand "parade" as pictured in the 1906–7 McKim plans, what was proposed for the island was a half-mile-long, five-hundred-foot-wide landing field running through the middle of the landfill in a north-south direction. Two runways were included, each one hundred feet wide. One extended the length of the space, and the shorter one stretched fifteen hundred feet across the field at the widest part of the island. Underground gas and oil tanks were necessary appendages, as were runway lights and searchlight towers. In addition to the demolition of the structures still remaining on the landfill, facilities to be given up by the army included the red brick officers' homes on Brick Row and the officers' golf course at the south end of Fort Jay. The army's response to these details echoed Secretary Davis's 1923 remarks; in this case, a "polo ground" replaced the more amorphous "recreational" use for the field.[18]

The possibility that passage of the Prall and Wadsworth legislation might result in action improved on April 16, 1926, curiously enough in hearings about housing construction on army posts. In testimony to the U.S. Senate Committee on Military Affairs, Major General Fox Conner from the general staff of the War Department made it apparent that the army still needed to sell additional properties in order to fund all of the projects on its recently published roster. Aware that posts in his constituency were on the list, Senator Wadsworth asked Conner whether the War Department had "dreamed ahead as to the disposition and final use of the posts around New York...[namely] Governors Island?" In his response, Conner made it clear that talk about an aviation landing field had been opposed by the Second Corps Area staff headquartered on the island, but he continued: "There has been no decision on it. In fact, the matter has not been presented to the secretary of war." In his next sentences, however, Conner presented an opportunity for the municipal airport proponents: "there has been some talk–perhaps I have done most of it myself–about selling Governors Island. If we could get the money [estimated appraisal in the testimony was between $18 and $25 million], if we could put Governors Island on the market and sell it, and one other place, we could see our way clear towards financing this housing program."[19] Fiorello LaGuardia jumped right into the opening Conner had made and claimed the rights to the island for New York State.[20] For the next ten years, virtually until the groundbreaking of his eponymous facility, LaGuardia championed Governors Island as an airport.

The pace that soldiers know has returned to the army post–a placid spot where men drill, army mules graze and salutes are fired....Governors Island will return to normal, a little world in itself at the foot of a metropolis, attracting attention only when a court martial is held, a military prisoner escapes or the commanding officer gives a garden party.

("GOVERNORS ISLAND DROWSES AWAY AGAIN," *NEW YORK TIMES*, JUNE 26, 1926, SM13. COPYRIGHT © 1926 BY THE NEW YORK TIMES CO. REPRINTED WITH PERMISSION.)

But even LaGuardia was powerless to fight the army at this time. The army was even given an assist when in May 1926, with President Calvin Coolidge's urging, Congress passed different legislation involving flight. The Air Commerce Act of 1926 authorized the secretary of commerce to issue and enforce air-traffic rules–including rules regarding safe altitudes of flight and the prevention of collisions between vessels and aircraft. With six thousand airline passengers recorded for 1926, this statute was much needed. Ironically, it created another layer of bureaucracy that the army could use to its advantage. Any nonmilitary use of Governors Island now not only had to be approved by New York State (which owned the land) and by the War Department, but also had to meet the criteria for airfields and flight safety set by the secretary of commerce.[21] By June 1926, the new secretary of war, Dwight Filley Davis, vetoed the airport resolutions in both houses of Congress, and Governors Island continued in its sleepy state.

It did not drowse for long. The battle was rejoined six months later in 1927–a year in which flight was in the forefront of the news. Charles Lindbergh became the first person to fly solo across the Atlantic Ocean, and Amelia Earhart won fame as the first female passenger on a plane crossing the Atlantic. That year also witnessed the formation of Pan American Airways[22] and the construction of the first American aircraft carriers, the *Lexington* and the *Saratoga*. American cargo was delivered by air for the first time, and *Wings,* a silent movie about wartime fighter pilots, won an Academy Award. It was in this heady atmosphere that the Governors Island barracks/airport debate resumed.

In early December 1927, LaGuardia and W. W. Cohen, a newly elected U.S. representative from the Seventeenth District of New York, introduced another round of legislation to make Governors Island an airport. Before Cohen submitted his bill to Congress, he surveyed his supporters and opponents by sending out a poll via telegraph. The results and articles in the press provide evidence of the lineup of interest groups in favor of the Governors Island airport. Potential economic beneficiaries were pilots, beacon light manufacturers, labor and transportation trade groups, the editor of *Aero Digest,* hoteliers, and bank presidents. Also to benefit were such luminaries as Mayor James Walker, William Fox of Fox Movies, and newspaper tycoons, among them William Randolph Hearst and Herbert Bayard Swope, editor of the *New York World* and backer of Wilbur Wright's first flight from Governors Island.[23]

LaGuardia continued to fight on two fronts: in favor of the airport legislation and against funding for the Governors Island portion of the army housing improvements bill (by then known as the Deficiency Act).[24] In addition to using his congressional platform, he also made a

GOVERNORS ISLAND, *New York Harbor plot plan, May 31, 1927, McKim, Mead & White. PR-042, Tube 441. This plan for the new building program shows Building 100 (Liggett Hall) sprawled across the northern end of the landfill. Courtesy of Collection of The New-York Historical Society, New York City.*

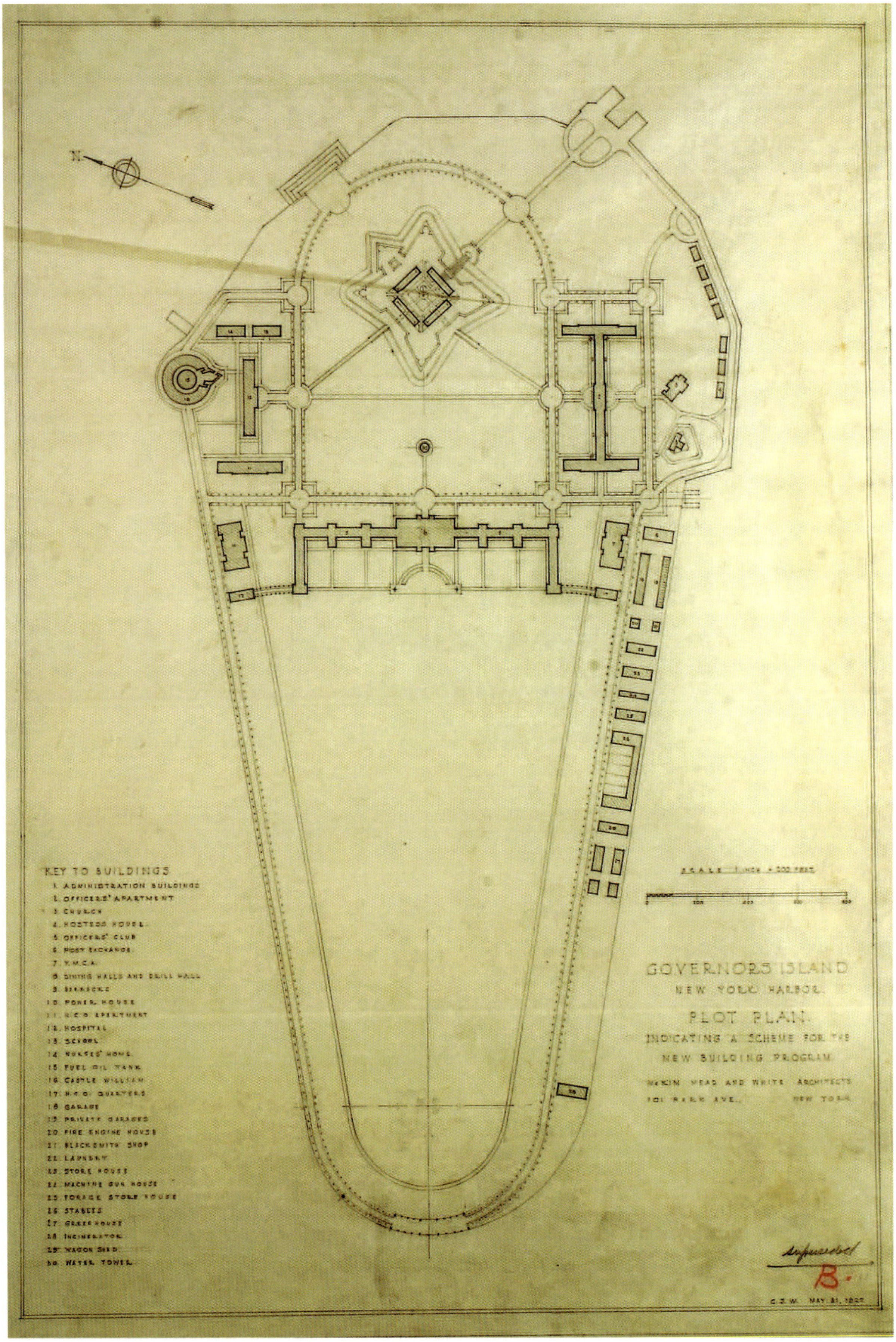

public plea for the airport in an article in the *New York Times*. The piece was accompanied by a cartoon that showed planes and seaplanes flying at different altitudes and circling a blown-up view of the razed, floating landfill. The historic portion of the island is nowhere to be seen. Hangars are depicted on the north end of the property, and a breakwater containing a seaplane base appears on the south end. "The largest city in the United States, the greatest port in the world, the biggest financial center known to history," LaGuardia wrote, "is still without a public airport." With even greater hyperbole, he continued:

> No greater monument to the life and activity of the Republic can be imagined than Governors Island as a national airport. With the background of lower Manhattan, flanked by the rising skyline of Brooklyn on the east and the Statue of Liberty on the west, bristling with the activity of planes landing and taking off in a harbor bristling with the world's commerce, the air traveler...would have impressed upon him immediately the very life, the activity and the prosperity of this country.[25]

Now the flight proponents were aided by Commerce Secretary Herbert Hoover, who, in fulfilling his new mandate, appointed a fact-finding panel called the Commission on Suitable Airport Facilities for the New York Metropolitan District. Not surprisingly, Governors Island was found to be a viable site. Assistant Secretary of Commerce for Aeronautics William McCracken presented the Hoover Commission's report at a luncheon on December 20, 1927, shortly after the introduction of the LaGuardia-Cohen airport bills. For the first time, the flight issue was approached from a national perspective. There was enough knowledge about air flight and airports that the commissioners no longer had to seek criteria abroad. They examined sites in the New York region for accessibility, meteorological conditions, property values, and the cost of conversion to an airport. The report recommended construction of airports in six locations around New York City, all designed to meet future needs. Among them were three areas that eventually housed flight facilities: Queens/Flushing Bay, Newark Bay (already under construction and opened in 1928), and Wall Street/Brooklyn. In a boost to its defenders, the report said that Governors Island, listed as "Site No. 11," "falls within the Wall Street–Brooklyn area and is recommended for this section."[26]

BARRACKS OR PLANES? 1928–1930

ALTHOUGH FLIGHT WAS PUSHED to the forefront of the debate by a second study, the Hoover Commission did include other possible locations for a New York City airport. More important, the U.S. House's rejection of LaGuardia's 1927 motion to strike Governors Island from the Deficiency Act and President Coolidge's signature of the act in January 1928 finally gave the army the go-ahead to make some of the improvements it had sought since the completion of the landfill sixteen years earlier. By 1930, instead of an airport, the island had a spanking new state-of-the-art barracks designed by McKim, Mead & White. But the victory was to be a Pyrrhic one only. Congress proceeded to erect a boundary that the army was not allowed to cross with additional construction until just before World War II.

Out of more than $6 million earmarked for improvements at military posts in general, the 1928 Deficiency Act finally allotted Governors Island $1,086,000 for the long dreamed of

LIEUTENANT GENERAL HUNTER *Liggett, n.d., unknown photographer. Building 100 was named after Liggett in 1957. Courtesy of Garret Roosma.*

This barracks that you see here...was purposely run north and south. I was in the House then, and they had the laugh on us, only it slipped out. And they said, "Now we are going to clinch Governors Island as an airport," and they had this barracks running...north and south...and the Military Affairs Committee of the House learned about it, and checked upon it....And they took that building and they just turned it around and ran it east and west.

(STATEMENT OF HONORABLE FIORELLO H. LAGUARDIA, MAYOR OF THE CITY OF NEW YORK, TO U.S. SENATE, *LANDING FIELD ON GOVERNORS ISLAND: HEARINGS BEFORE THE COMMITTEE ON MILITARY AFFAIRS ON H.R. 12009, AN ACT TO AUTHORIZE THE ENLARGEMENT OF GOVERNORS ISLAND AND CONSENTING TO THE USE OF A PORTION THEREOF AS A LANDING FIELD FOR THE CITY OF NEW YORK AND ITS ENVIRONS,* 74TH CONG., 2D SESS., JUNE 5, 1936, 69.)

"model" regimental barracks and $30,000 for architects' fees. This grant was necessary. Island housing problems since the turn of the century were exacerbated by an increase in the size of the army and by the fact that soldiers were still living in makeshift barracks constructed during World War I. By now, the physical condition of island housing had come to such a sorry state that a German visitor ironically observed that his country had provided better quarters for its military prisoners during the war.[27]

With funds finally in hand, Major General Hanson E. Ely, head of the Second Corps Area, headquartered on the island, immediately forged ahead with the construction. The army's objective was to quarter all of the Sixteenth Infantry–the Fort Jay official command–under one roof, but before work could actually begin, an internal conflict had to be resolved. There were two competing plans for the housing. The design by McKim, Mead & White, an outgrowth of their 1907 beautification program, envisioned a continuous, red brick structure 1,120 feet long, three to four stories high, and built in a U shape with the long flat side facing north and the entrance at the south in the center of the U. According to this plan, the barracks would be sited east to west across the island on a line between Brick Row and the north end of the drill field (by then formally located on the landfill) and the polo grounds. Some army officials, however, still clung to the view that the new housing should be placed lengthwise on the island, situated north to south along the shore of Buttermilk Channel, with its entrance on the drill field. In those days before air conditioning, the prevailing westerly winds provided a natural coolant, and siting the housing across the open drill and polo fields offered a grand view of the harbor that was not possible in the McKim design.

It is unclear just how the decision was made to follow the east-west McKim plan because army records on this matter have not been found. Stories that the army's decision was based solely on the desire to block construction of an airport have some validity. A new report by the Regional Plan Association (RPA), a civic group devoted to planning the New York region as a whole, gave succor to the flight proponents, however. In its Graphic Regional Plan, the RPA listed forty-six locations for units within a regional airport system. Governors Island, a "proposed airplane field" with seaplane facilities, was a highly touted number nineteen. "Although civil use of military airports is not suggested as practical or desirable under average conditions," the planners wrote, "it is suggested that Governors Island...should be assigned in part for such use because of its exceptional location adjacent to the heart of the city of New York. As a municipal airport it would be used by military planes and civil planes: in an emergency it could be readily turned over entirely to military use."[28]

Undoubtedly, introduction of the 1927 Cohen and LaGuardia airport legislation was instrumental in the decision to use the east-west siting of the barracks. In addition, the McKim design was central to the still-unimplemented overall plan for the landfill. Perhaps some felt

BIRD'S-EYE VIEW *indicating relative position of proposed buildings on Governors Island, April 18, 1927, Quartermaster Corps drawing. McKim, Mead & White Collection, PR-042, Tube 441. This shows the army's preferred location for the new regimental barracks. Courtesy of Collection of The New-York Historical Society, New York City.*

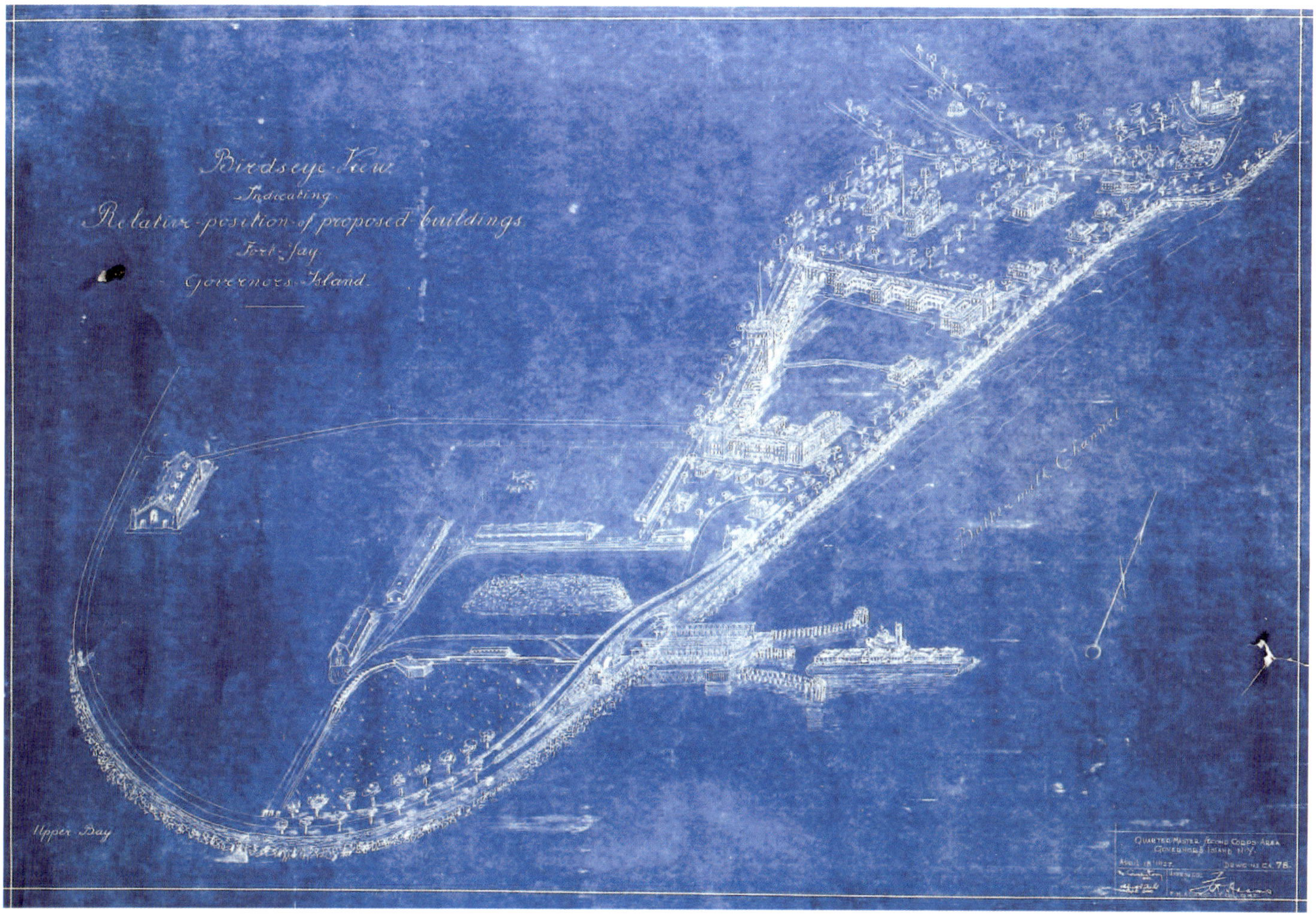

that if the island could finally recapture its physical glory, recruitment would be easier. According to a 1929 article in *The Business Week,* however, the Hoover Commission report was pivotal. "Under the threat of [these] recommendations," the article stated, "the entire military-social hierarchy at Washington moved heaven and earth to get started on new barrack construction on the precious island retreat before the transformation into an airport could get through."[29]

Having decided on the design and placement of the barracks, the army had to jump over one more hurdle before construction could begin. Immediately after President Coolidge signed the Deficiency Act, LaGuardia and others tried yet again–although unsuccessfully–to block funds earmarked specifically for Governors Island. On February 25, 1929, Representative W. Frank James, using another approach and prodded by LaGuardia, inserted a caveat into the Deficiency Act. Under this provision, no federal monies could be granted for construction on Governors Island west of an arbitrary line "running in a northwesterly and southeasterly direction across [Governors Island], and paralleling the eastern face of the regimental barracks building at a distance of three hundred feet." Shortly thereafter, the "James Line" passed both houses of Congress.[30]

Perhaps in order to avoid any further political complications, the barracks, known initially as Building 100, was constructed swiftly. In just twenty-two months, the army erected what was described in the press as "probably the longest building in the world designed solely for

SIXTEENTH INFANTRY *Barracks, Fort Jay, N.Y., n.d., unknown publisher. Postcard. Message on the reverse side reads: "My home the barracks." Author's collection.*

BUILDING 100 *(Liggett Hall) under construction, ca. 1929, unknown photographer. Courtesy of Still Pictures Branch National Archives, College Park, Md.*

LIGGETT HALL, *late 1930s, unknown photographer. Author's collection.*

the shelter of soldiers." Longer than the height of the Chrysler Building, the tallest skyscraper then extant, the structure apparently followed the James Line. But in fact, the two wings of the U encroached upon it. Again the military prevailed. On July 3, 1930, after much discussion about forcing the army to tear down the extensions, Congress moved the James Line farther to the southwest to coincide with the "two wings of the new barracks buildings."[31]

I was raised on an Army post, and of course Washington meant everything out in Fort Sully in South Dakota...and Governors Island came along just about the same time, and that was a sort of Valhalla, a "happy hunting ground," a military paradise, the very last word in a desirable assignment in the Army. That memory continued...all through my childhood and boyhood. And now I come to Washington seeking to convert Governors Island into something that is needed, and something that will be of benefit to the entire community.

(STATEMENT OF HONORABLE FIORELLO H. LAGUARDIA, MAYOR OF THE CITY OF NEW YORK, TO U.S. SENATE, *LANDING FIELD ON GOVERNORS ISLAND: HEARINGS BEFORE THE COMMITTEE ON MILITARY AFFAIRS ON H.R. 12009, AN ACT TO AUTHORIZE THE ENLARGEMENT OF GOVERNORS ISLAND AND CONSENTING TO THE USE OF A PORTION THEREOF AS A LANDING FIELD FOR THE CITY OF NEW YORK AND ITS ENVIRONS,* 74TH CONG., 2D SESS., JUNE 5, 15, AND 16, 1936, 63–64.)

THE HOME TEAM WINS, 1930–1941

THE FINAL BATTLE OVER GOVERNORS ISLAND came to a head in 1936. Straining to keep up with advances in aviation and to connect to the new infrastructure under way in New York City, proponents of an airport on Governors Island struggled on. That they were pulling back from their original grandiose schemes is evident in the hearing testimony's language. A "Grand Central Station" and "airport" for mail, freight, and passengers became "not a large airport but a 'landing' or a 'taxi station.'"[32] During six more months of congressional hearings, LaGuardia was once again the star player. Proponents tried everything from staging mock riots to designing plans that would enlarge the island with more fill, but to no avail. The military, aided by a new presidential commission, finally won. LaGuardia and others fought hard, but in the end they were powerless to beat the army.

However, it was patently obvious that New York had to embrace the transportation revolution occurring in the early 1930s in order to stay competitive with other cities. First and foremost, the municipality had to provide service for the growing number of air passengers in the United States, which in 1929 reached 172,000–greater than a twentyfold increase over the number in 1926. That number doubled a year later. Providing service entailed more and improved landing facilities. Larger and faster planes were being manufactured by the Douglas and Condor factories, as well as by the newly formed Curtiss Wright–a merger of the two factories begun by the first fliers on Governors Island. Commercial companies such as United, American, and Transcontinental and Western Air Lines (the latter soon to become TWA) were operating in the United States. They bought the new twin-engine planes that in 1932 were capable of carrying a dozen passengers and that three years later could transport fourteen people in sleeper seats and twenty-eight on day flights. Paved (instead of cinder) runways were introduced during this period to handle the new planes' weight.

By the early 1930s, the New York region had met the challenges of air travel. Pursuant to the Hoover Commission's recommendations, Newark Metropolitan Airport opened in 1928 with Eastern Airlines as its prime carrier. The following year, North Beach in Queens began to operate as a private venture on land formerly occupied by an amusement park. New York City's first municipal airport, Floyd Bennet Field, opened in Brooklyn in 1931 on landfill in Jamaica Bay. Seaplane bases were constructed on the East River at Wall Street and Thirty-first Street.

Despite all of this airport activity, or perhaps because of the tremendous strides being made in commercial flight, Governors Island continued to be on the congressional agenda. To meet the new exigencies of flight, the discussion turned this time to creating additional landfill. Aerial photographs from the mid-1930s indicate that the original landfill was now nearly back to its prewar, empty state, but it was widely recognized that if it were to be an airport, even more space was needed. The debate over adding additional land to Governors Island while making plans for a larger, six-runway airport had a sense of déjà vu. The city would add seventy acres by building an outer wall of rocks and filling the enclosure with dirt from construction–this time from the Sixth Avenue subway being built then and perhaps from an expected Second Avenue line. The cost was estimated at roughly $2,500,000, or about $35,000 per acre–more than three times the amount of the turn-of-the-century landfill.[33]

The Governors Island debate languished while engineers made further studies and New York City's new mayor, Fiorello LaGuardia, flush with funds from Washington to fight the Depression, turned his attention to building the city's infrastructure. In the works were the construction of the Triboro Bridge, the East River Drive, the Queens Midtown Tunnel, and the West Side Highway. Although LaGuardia had an option to purchase the North Beach airfield, which could be accessed by the new Manhattan highways, he continued to be single-minded about an airport on Governors Island. Access to this field would be easy if a vehicular tunnel that was under construction from the Battery to Brooklyn included an exit to the island. Air passengers and mail could be rushed to and from Manhattan in as little as five minutes.[34]

The final major hearings regarding an airport on Governors Island took place before the Committees on Military Affairs in the House and Senate between January and mid-June of 1936. More than fifty-five groups and individuals testified. The cast of speakers included many who had fought the good fight since the 1920s. The New York Merchant's Association, the RPA, and the New York Board of Trade all remained staunchly in favor of an airfield. Some new proponents had joined them–the Airline Pilots Association, the American Legion Aviators post, and TWA–and their participation was evidence of how the flight industry had matured.

Most of the issues raised during these five months had been endlessly discussed in the past. Witnesses against the airport argued over the continuing need for military defense of downtown and the effect of air currents, visibility, wind, fog, and runways on air safety because they all were incompatible with the new technology. Some cited new dangers to shipping. There was fear of a plane clipping the *Queen Mary*'s 250-foot-tall mast and of the projected landfill's negatively affecting the Port of New York's tonnage, which had reached an all-time high of 137 million, surpassing the fifteen next-highest U.S. ports. And Eastern Airlines, begun in 1928, found Governors Island much too close to Newark for competitive comfort.

Pro-aviation advocates spoke about the accessibility of Governors Island to the city and its potential contribution to the growing system of municipal airports. Several speakers made cases to back personal interests. Senator Robert F. Wagner Sr. was in favor of an airfield because it would allow him to fly from Newark to the island, avoiding automobile traffic and shortening his trip from Washington by twenty to thirty minutes.[35]

Considerable time at the hearings was occupied by the issue of the army's need of the landfill on Governors Island for two seemingly disparate activities, military training and polo. It was argued that these activities were closely related. The former instilled discipline, confidence, and order, and allowed soldiers to handle arms. The latter honed the skills of officers who in war would be assigned to mounted companies. Opponents over the use of the land for an air-

IMPORTANT AIRPORTS, *existing and proposed, that would serve the metropolitan area center, 1928, Staff of the Regional Plan Association. Courtesy of Regional Plan Association, New York.*

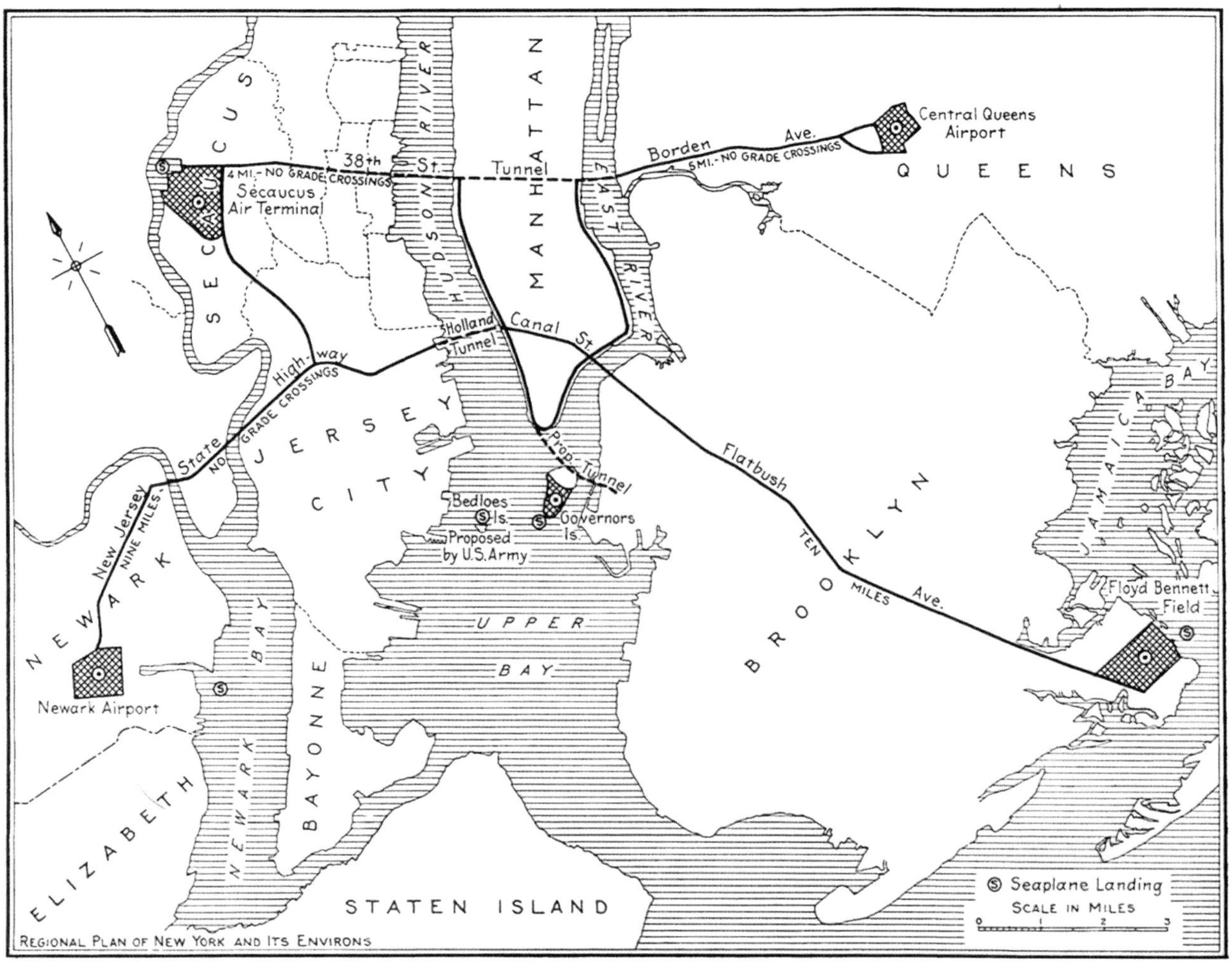

GLIDING ANGLE *for airplanes and its application to building heights in the vicinity of landing fields, 1929, Staff of the Regional Plan Association. Diagram. The Regional Plan Association created this design to allay fears that airplanes taking off from Governors Island were sure to hit Fort Jay or, even worse, a Manhattan skyscraper. Courtesy of Regional Plan Association, New York.*

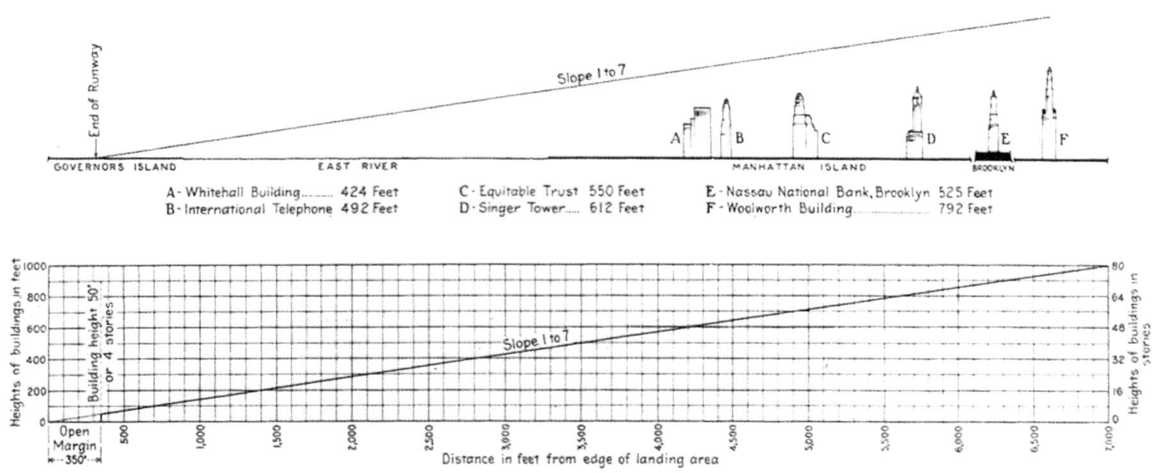

FIG. 31

GLIDING ANGLE FOR AIRPLANES AND ITS APPLICATION TO BUILDING HEIGHTS IN THE VICINITY OF LANDING FIELDS

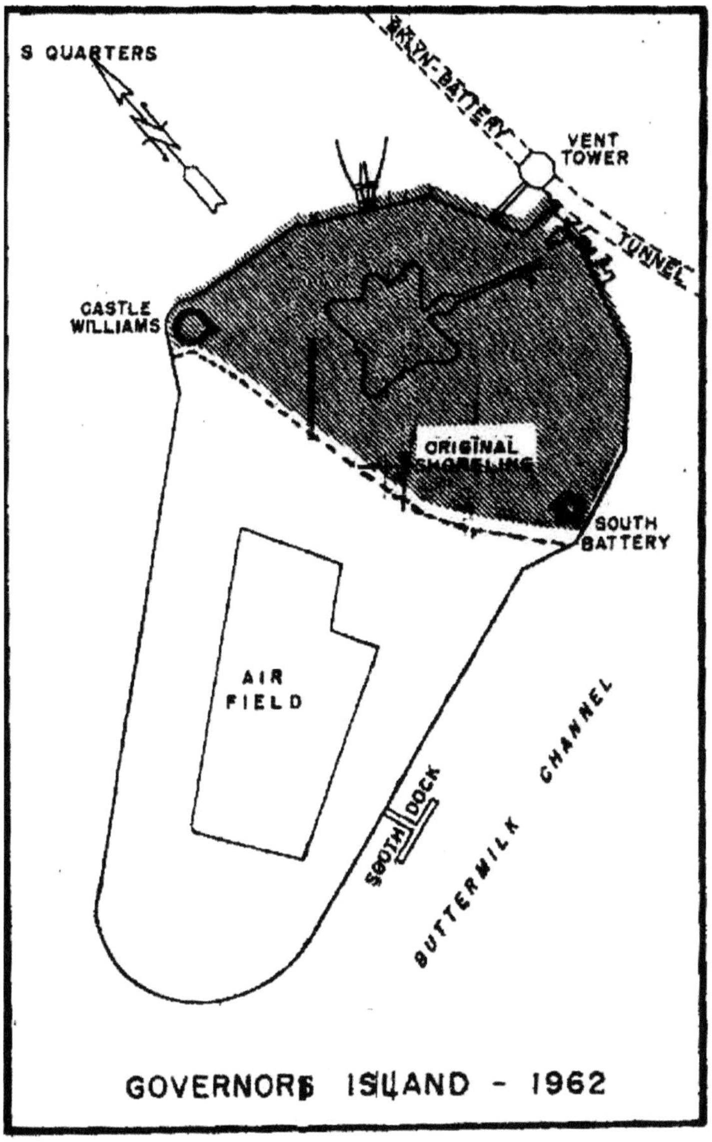

GOVERNORS ISLAND, *1962. Prepared under the direction of D. H. Kreitler. Courtesy of Michael Shaver.*

port generally agreed that training was important and that it now required more room. Soldiers no longer drilled in close lines. It was essential that they had space for "operation and functioning of all infantry weapons, grenade throwing, bayonet training, tent pitching, convoy operation, anti-aircraft combat formation, and chemical warfare training."[36]

The need for polo, however, was questionable. When General Bullard, an ardent player, was in charge, he had grabbed a piece of the coveted airport land for his state-of-the-art polo facility. By 1936, the field appeared to be an embarrassment, and the army began to back off. In June of that year, Colonel A. S. Williams, commander of the Sixteenth Infantry and happily housed in Building 100, wrote to the War Department regarding the urgent need for an easily accessible training ground for his men: "Polo is considered at this headquarters as a suitable game for Saturday and Sunday afternoons, when the ground is not needed for strictly military purposes."[37]

And I will even ask the commissioner of the Parks Department, Commissioner Moses, to find them a new polo field, if they want to play it.

(STATEMENT OF HONORABLE FIORELLO LAGUARDIA, MAYOR OF THE CITY OF NEW YORK, TO U.S. SENATE, *LANDING FIELD ON GOVERNORS ISLAND: HEARINGS BEFORE THE COMMITTEE ON MILITARY AFFAIRS ON H.R. 12009, AN ACT TO AUTHORIZE THE ENLARGEMENT OF GOVERNORS ISLAND AND CONSENTING TO THE USE OF A PORTION THEREOF AS A LANDING FIELD FOR THE CITY OF NEW YORK AND ITS ENVIRONS*, 74TH CONG., 2D SESS., JUNE 15, 1936, 70.)

But the final word against the airfield project came from a presidential board. In August 1934, President Franklin D. Roosevelt had appointed another commission to investigate the feasibility of an airport on Governors Island. On June 15, 1936, the chairman, Brigadier General James A. Woodruff of the Army Corps of Engineers and commander of the Port of San Francisco, presented the report to the assembled senators. Woodruff summed up most of the negative testimony to date and announced the unanimous conclusion that "Governors Island was not adaptable as an airport." Having been voted up in the House in March 1936, the eleventh bill on the subject, the Act to Authorize the Enlargement of Governors Island and Consenting to the Use of a Portion Thereof as a Landing Field for the City of New York and Its Environs, was dead. Beaten but undeterred, Mayor LaGuardia broke ground for LaGuardia Airport the following year.

Even though the army was victorious, it was not until 1941 that construction was allowed on the formerly contested ground.[38] On May 14, 1941, with war under way in Europe, President Roosevelt signed the congressional repeal of the James Line, and the 1929 and 1930 building restrictions placed on Governors Island by airport proponents were finally removed. But the idea of a flying field died more slowly. A map published by First Army engineers in 1962 shows the Brooklyn Battery Tunnel, the vent tower, Fort Jay, Castle Williams, and the South Battery. Attached to the landfill is South Dock, and on the otherwise blank slate is a very large rectangle labeled "Air Field." Nearly fifty years later, former Coast Guard residents used the same words as a landmark to locate their former homes.[39]

ISLAND HIGHLIGHTS *Island Public Works*

Governors Island, headquarters of the United States Army's Second Corps Area, is undergoing sweeping changes as a result of a construction program which is being carried forward rapidly.[1]

A Depression windfall came to Governors Island in the 1930s in the form of money and manpower from the federal PWA and WPA. New buildings, sports fields, flagstone pathways, and renovated historic structures were part of a public-works boom to provide construction jobs. Unemployed men performed myriad other tasks under relief programs. Artists painted murals, architects drew plans, and civil engineers and brick masons helped to execute them. Others performed much-needed office, service, and educational duties, all paid for by Washington.

What might be called the fourth wave of construction on Governors Island began in a small way in 1932 with money from New York City's unemployment relief funds. The army hired out-of-work laborers to remove some of the cantonments and an old rubbish heap on the landfill to make space for athletic facilities. Planned were three baseball diamonds, a hockey field, a volleyball court, and tennis courts.[2]

Work continued in earnest the following year under orders of Major General Dennis E. Nolan, commanding general of the Second Corps Area. In 1933, following an improvement program that had begun with the 1930 opening of the regimental barracks, the Ordnance and Quartermaster Departments used more than $1.5 million of PWA funds to complete four structures. Two were much-needed housing structures: one held fifty-one noncommissioned officers' quarters (cost: $386,000), and the other was a more expensive building (with such accoutrements as maids' rooms) that contained twelve officers' apartments ($146,000). In addition, workers completed a hospital designed by the McKim, Mead & White firm ($365,000) and nurses' quarters ($48,000).

Without assurances that completion funds would be available, work was also under way on a second officers' quarters (estimated cost: $127,000), an addition to the noncommissioned officers' apartment building (estimated cost: $104,000), and the island's roads and walks (estimated cost: $40,000). Plans for a new school and headquarters building were on the drawing boards, but their actual construction was in doubt.[3]

COMPLETED FOUNDATION *for noncommissioned officers' apartments (Building 110), April 14, 1939, unknown photographer. Scrapbook photograph. Courtesy of National Archives, College Park, Md.*

COMPLETED FOUNDATION *for one 375-men barracks building, March 15, 1939, unknown photographer. Scrapbook photograph. Courtesy of National Archives, College Park, Md.*

USA WORK PROGRAM WPA, *April 11, 1939, unknown photographer. Three WPA workers constructing a beautifully laid-out flagstone walk across the golf course, with Fort Jay in the background. Courtesy of Still Pictures Branch, National Archives, College Park, Md.*

WPA funds that became available with the advent of Franklin D. Roosevelt's administration were another boon to the army; however, these monies were allowed to be used only for repairs. Thus, with a million-dollar appropriation to be shared in part with other New York–area military compounds, Quartermaster Colonel John R. R. Hannay began the renovation of an estimated fifty to sixty buildings and three piers on Governors Island on December 10, 1936. The army was ecstatic. According to the *New York Times,* the island "will be thoroughly renovated to give it an aspect commensurate with its rating as prize post of the army."[4]

Among the prizewinners were the cottages on Colonel's Row and Brick Row and the apartments in Fort Jay. Probably the oldest structure to benefit from the WPA largesse was the nearly one-hundred-year-old General's House (Building 1). Begun at the request of Julia Nolan, wife of the resident commanding general, the work was directed by WPA architect John Slick. Once again through the use of unemployed New York City laborers, the historic structure was completely restored. By July 1937, it had become the home of the next commanding general, Tasker Bliss.

The army also took advantage of New York's unemployment relief funds and WPA programs to hire men in a variety of nonconstruction jobs. These individuals worked on Governors Island as tailors, soda jerks, waiters, blacksmiths, civil engineers, stenographers, and detectives.[5] The YMCA women's division allegedly hired a full-time Spanish instructor as part of the Y's recreational program.[6] And the army was even able to find help to beautify the

It was the source of much regret to me to learn that the most recent attrition in the ranks of the Works Progress Administration, had caused the loss to us of your most efficient and capable services...[T]he results of your technical knowledge and teaching of the crafts are definitely impressed on the department with which you were connected....I am sure that many of the men who were privileged to be in one or more of your classes will be much better equipped to face the world as a result of your teaching.

(LETTER TO MR. J. P. HAMIL FROM COLONEL CONVERSE R. LEWIS, COMMANDANT, U.S. DISCIPLINARY BARRACKS, GOVERNORS ISLAND, AUGUST 11, 1939, RG 92, 21/600, NATIONAL ARCHIVES, COLLEGE PARK, MD.)

landscape by hiring WPA worker Leo Novak to superintend the planting of trees supplied by parks commissioner Robert Moses.[7]

The U.S. Disciplinary Barracks in Castle Clinton was another employer of WPA workers. Laborers set new urinals, toilets, and shower fixtures in the lavatories and drinking fountains in the courtyard. The army also hired instructors through the WPA to train prisoners for a variety of jobs after their release. According to prison records, Jacob Macek taught music to budding bandsmen. In 1938, there were also at least five crafts teachers; Patsy D'Agostino taught tailoring, and a Mr. Hamill taught carpentry and woodworking to novice furniture makers and refinishers. In addition, ten prisoners attended a Mr. Washburn's auto mechanics classes, and an indeterminate number of men learned to fix radios from a Mr. Goldman and refrigerators from Mr. Louis Rosbach. The programs went well for short periods of time. The biggest complaint came from the instructors over the loss of equipment: the prisoners smuggled pencils from the schools and gloves from the auto mechanics class.[8]

A lasting imprint of the WPA on Governors Island was made through the Federal Art Project. In an attempt to "decorate" the interiors of the new and rehabilitated military buildings in an important way, the army commissioned two murals. On a wall in the Officers' Club at one time was Anthony Raveille's larger-than-life depiction of early engineer Jonathan Williams and his famous fortifications, Castle Clinton and Castle Williams.

At the end of October 1938, post officials and the WPA unveiled another large set of panels. Thirty-three-year-old Tom Loftin Johnson, a student at the Yale School of Fine Arts and the École de Beaux Arts in Paris, had in 1934 won a competition for a mural in the dining hall at West Point.[9] It is unclear how he was chosen for the Governors Island piece, but it might have been through a selection committee headed by Juliana Force, the first director of the Whitney Museum in New York City, who also headed the WPA arts program for a time. Johnson's work, entitled *The United States Army in War,* memorializes officers from General George Washington to General Frank R. McCoy and army battles from the American Revolution through World War I. Another lasting documentation of Governors Island's windfalls from a sad period in civilian history, the Johnson mural may still be viewed today on a wall of the main entrance to Pershing Hall (Building 125).[10]

MURAL *by WPA artist Tom Loftin Johnson, 1938. The mural hung in the Officers' Club. Courtesy of Prints and Photographs Division, Library of Congress, Washington, D.C.*

LUISITA WOOD, *n.d., George Grantham Bain. Courtesy of George Grantham Bain Collection, Prints and Photographs Division, Library of Congress, Washington, D.C.*

Chapter Six

ISLAND LADIES

[H]ow pretty is everything about military life–I am sure soldiers' wives ought to be the happiest women in the world.[1]

Wives, mothers, girlfriends, secretaries, servants, and eventually enlisted personnel and officers–all the women who lived on Governors Island were pioneers. They arrived by boat, conquered new territory, braved loneliness and often difficult living conditions, and worked hard at keeping families together and building community. But they were also protected by the island's seclusion and the military order. They could comfortably participate in local sports and in social and philanthropic activities, yet by virtue of Governors Island's place in New York Harbor, big-city events were just a short boat ride away. The stories of the pioneering women of Governors Island illuminate the inner workings of the military base and the changing strictures of the military hierarchy; they also illustrate both the close links that Governors Island once had to New York society and the changing roles of women, ethnicity, and class in the larger world.

EARLY SOJOURNERS, 1624–1848

WOMEN AND CHILDREN'S RESIDENCE on Governors Island has always been noteworthy for its impermanence. From the beginning, the original Dutch immigrants, the Palatines (refugees from the Palatinate, districts in Germany ruled by the Holy Roman Empire), and the wives of British and American Revolutionary War soldiers merely passed through. As was common in other settings, the quality of their sojourn depended on the island's physical condition and on their contacts. For the earliest visitors, living conditions were primitive at best. For others, particularly those in high places in the state, Governors Island in the eighteenth century was a bucolic retreat under government ownership. By the nineteenth century, a visit with the right military personages was quite comfortable.

In his history of Dutch Manhattan, Russell Shorto tells of eight Dutchmen who landed on Governors Island from New Amsterdam in 1624. There is no evidence of women and children accompanying them, but these pioneers did bring their cattle. The land, graced by plentiful nut trees and no open pasture, was inhospitable to livestock, however. After a day or two, the settlers sent the cattle to Manhattan Island to graze, initiating an interdependent relationship with the mainland that still exists.[2]

During the British occupation of New York, the state turned Governors Island into a rural getaway. In 1699, the New York Assembly set the island aside as "part of the Denizen of His Majestie's Fort at New York for the benefit and accommodation of his Majestie's Governors," and it became known informally as "Governor's Island." Three years later, the actual governor, Lord Edward Hyde Cornbury, used taxes imposed on "every person that Wears a Perl Ring" and others in order to build a manor.[3]

The manor house and its "smiling garden" were supposedly situated on the high ground where the current Governor's House (Building 2) now stands, but evidence of it has never been found. Although Cornbury was married, and his wife, Catherine, is buried in Trinity Church, there are no records of her on the island. But some allege that Cornbury himself was a cross-dresser, thus perhaps lending a female presence when he was there.

PORTRAIT OF EDWARD HYDE *(Lord Cornbury), early eighteenth century, unknown artist. Postcard. Courtesy of New-York Historical Society, New York City.*

The first documented families who landed on Governors Island were probably glad to leave it; in fact, the Palatines might even be thought of as the island's first prisoners. In 1708, at the invitation of England's queen Mary, they had arrived in London in droves, finally freed from years of German persecution. Probably because of their overwhelming numbers, they were not allowed to rest long in England. Some were sent to Ireland, others to Scotland, and in January 1710 a third group of more than three thousand sailed to America. The six-month voyage took a large toll, and many of those who finally arrived in June 1710—the exact number is unknown—were sickly. To prevent the spread of disease to New York City, the immigrants were unloaded and then quarantined on Governors Island for three months or more.[4]

We know little about the lives of the women who lived in huts that two city carpenters hastily constructed on the island. One woman, the widow Johanna Zangarin, was accompanied by her thirteen-year-old son, John Peter, and his brother and sister. The Americanized Peter Zenger eventually became famous. He settled in New York

City and started the *New York Weekly Journal*. In 1735, he was tried and acquitted for publishing articles exposing the poor administration of the provincial governor of New York State, William Cosby. Four decades before the passage of the First Amendment, Zenger established the principle of freedom of the press in America.[5]

But another group of eighteenth-century women lived on the island in comparative splendor. Wives and children of British soldiers who in June 1775 were billeted in New York Harbor on the ship Asia found safe haven on the island thanks to the good offices of Cadwallader Golden, lieutenant governor of the Province of New York. Writing to a Major Hamilton of the Eighteenth Regiment, Spring Hill, Golden offered the governor's country retreat to the women and children on the ship. His main concern seems to have been sloppy housekeeping: "You have my leave to encamp the women on Governor's Island and if there is any room in the House which the Family who live there do not make use of, I am willing the women should have it. You will please give orders that they by no means burn or destroy the Fences or do any kind of Injury to anything on the Island."[6]

Nearly seventy-five years later, on April 27, 1848, the wife of an American officer also stayed in a borrowed space. Socially prominent Francis Marvin Smith Webster and her two daughters arrived on Governors Island from Fort McHenry in Baltimore. She was the well-connected wife of a West Pointer fighting in Saltillo, Mexico, and she relied on the hospitality of friends and family as she awaited the return of her husband from the Mexican-American War. On Governors Island, she knew Colonel Ichabod Crane, the post commander, and was the guest of the hospital surgeon, Joseph Russell, whose house adjoined the recently constructed Chapel of St. Cornelius at the south end of Nolan Park.

Mrs. Webster spent her time in the same manner as did many Coast Guard wives years later: going to church, caring for her children–one of whom was sickly–and shopping in the city. However, in letters to her husband that she wrote while still on Governors Island, it is evident that if she cared to stay until her husband's return, her borrowed space would be in the governor's house–with strangers. The correspondence does not reveal how long Mrs. Webster remained on the island, but by August she was living with friends in Hartford.[7]

NINETEENTH- AND TWENTIETH-CENTURY CARETAKERS, 1814–1950

MANY OF THE WOMEN WHO LIVED on Governors Island had no familial relationship to the military. Some were caretakers who forged ties with the soldiers by providing supplies–some licit, some illicit. Others performed such household duties as laundry, cooking, cleaning, and childcare for soldiers, civilians, and officers and their families. They brightened and eased the islanders' lives, but were always outsiders. Still another group of caretakers worked on the island as secretaries, a position that was important to the functioning of both the administrative offices and the post's day-to-day operation. None of these roles was unusual for females in contemporary society, but on Governors Island the women made up only a fraction of a largely all-male population. Their very presence doubtless caused stares. As for the female secretaries, they were probably competing for jobs formerly held only by men.

The soldiers who were billeted on Governors Island were often the recipients of city women's patriotic largesse. Some women showed their gratitude by knitting. According to artillery orders published in Edward Banks Smith's military history, in the winter of 1814 the ladies of the Stocking, Hood, and Moccasin Society of New York sent forty-six pairs of mittens and an equal number of hoods to the soldiers and sentinels on duty. The gesture did not keep all of them warm that winter, however, for the garrison was composed of more than a thousand men and an unknown number of recruits who were being trained as artillerymen. Accompanying the woolen goods was an apologetic note: "The Society regrets that the state of their funds does not enable them to do more for those whose claims are strengthened by every consideration of Patriotism and gratitude."[8] During World War II and thereafter, women regularly visited the island to read to wounded soldiers. One of these women was Alice Berliner Greenbaum, daughter of the inventor of the gramophone.

Preparation of food was another means of caretaking. A Mrs. Libley, wife of a general in the Confederate army in Texas, spent the Civil War living with her father–the sutler William Kendall–in a house on Rotten Row. Kendall provided the post with extra food and supplies from his small store (the forerunner of the PX) and could also be called on, for a price, to provide those items not officially approved, including additional spirits. Thomas Sparrow, one of the Southern prisoners housed in Fort Jay, writes of the "[h]ome made cakes" that Mrs. Libley sent for "the officers of the C.S.A. Mess no. 2." Because prisoners were rarely allowed to have visitors, and propriety had to be maintained, she did not present the cakes in person. In her place, a "servant girl" delivered a tin canister accompanied by "a plain enameled card" with a note written in what Sparrow appreciatively described as "a very pretty female hand."[9]

Aunt Nannie's Silver Sponge Cake

(1879)

5 egg whites beaten stiffly
½ c. of flour sifted four times
¾ c. sugar
1 t. vanilla
½ t. baking powder

Sprinkle with powdered sugar.
Bake 20 minutes.

(ST. CORNELIUS ALTAR GUILD, *WHAT'S COOKING ON GOVERNORS ISLAND* [GOVERNORS ISLAND, N.Y.: ST. CORNELIUS ALTAR GUILD, 1949], 39.)

One group of female caretakers, covertly present on Governors Island, looked after the sexual and beverage needs of unmarried soldiers and prisoners. When discovered, these ladies were promptly removed. In January 1915, a girl named Mary attached herself to one of the companies of the garrison. In addition to prostituting herself, Mary was found to have conveyed whiskey to some sentinels. Although as a civilian Mary was probably not subject to court-martial action, there is no doubt that she left the island and did not come back. According to the Garrison Orders, she was "drummed off the island and never to be suffered to return."[10]

Female servants were an important part of Governors Island's caretaking force early on. Most of these women lived on the island either in dormitories or in rooms assigned to them in the homes of high-ranking officers. The 1860 census records a dozen "servants," all but one of them women. Ten, mostly in their twenties and early thirties, were Irish immigrants. Details of their actual duties are unknown, but judging from the Confederate prisoners' letters and items in the press, it is likely that some escapees of the Irish famine who settled on the Lower East Side in Manhattan rapidly found work across the harbor as laundresses. On Governors Island, soldiers and prisoners who needed their uniforms washed and ironed were eager but stingy patrons. The laundresses probably washed the clothes by hand in Buttermilk Channel or in washhouses nearby. They lived in the "camp-women's quarters," which they shared with the few married soldiers prior to 1856 (when the quarters burned down). This frame, one-story house with a basement located southeast of Nolan Park on Buttermilk Channel had twelve rooms, six on each level.[11]

In the late 1870s, when Governors Island became a military headquarters, there were new demands for domestic servants. The women married to soldiers and the wives of most civilians who worked on the island as tailors, bakers, shoemakers, and other types of tradesmen tended to their own households and children. Officers' wives, in contrast, needed workers to maintain their homes and cooks to feed their fairly large families and assist with entertainment duties. Word of mouth probably brought dozens of girls from the Manhattan Irish community to fill these very desirable positions. According to the 1880 census, Mary Flannery, Margaret Farrell, and Margaret Murphy worked for Captain and Mrs. William Mitchell and for Major and Mrs. Asa Gardner, the latter couples at least third-generation Americans.

The quarters of these and other high-level officers contained living and work spaces designed for the hired help. For example, in the commanding general's/admiral's house there were a large kitchen and pantry on the main floor, as well as an expansive laundry and two servants' rooms in the basement. Another maid's room in the attic had plain wood floors–unlike the oak floors in the family bedrooms.

Thirty years later, in April 1904, a rash of weddings of the "wonderfully good looking"[12] Irish maids working in officers' homes was apparently newsworthy, and these stories may be seen as evidence of the increasing assimilation of the Irish among the population at large. Governors Island was a microcosm of the ethnic mix in New York City at the turn of the century. The available censuses for Governors Island show a definite shift over time in the soldiers and noncommissioned officers' birthplaces.

Women's Pay

1814	**One woman in proportion to 17 men**	**A ration in kind**
1861	**Irish laundress for POWs**	**60 cents/dozen**
	Cook for officer prisoners in Ft. Jay	**$3/week**
1862	**Irish laundress for POWs**	**$1.00/dozen**
1935	**Nurses in the new hospital**	**$70–180/month**
	Cook, nurses quarters	**$1,080/year**
	Mess Attendant, nurses quarters	**$720–960/year**
1949	**Chief Clerk, Post Hospital (WAC)**	**$168/month**

(COMPILED FROM THE FOLLOWING SOURCES: EDMUND BANKS SMITH, *GOVERNORS ISLAND: ITS MILITARY HISTORY UNDER THREE FLAGS, 1637–1913* [NEW YORK: EDMUND BANKS SMITH, 1913], 71; ALONZO E. BELL, DIARIES, MF.P.48.1, 17, TRANSCRIBED BY ALEX CHRISTOPHER MEEKINS, OFFICE OF ARCHIVES AND HISTORY, DIVISION OF HISTORICAL RESOURCES, ARCHIVES, AND RECORDS, NORTH CAROLINA STATE ARCHIVES, RALEIGH; ROGER S. DURHAM, ED., *A CONFEDERATE YANKEE: THE JOURNAL OF EDWARD WILLIAM DRUMMOND, A CONFEDERATE SOLDIER FROM MAINE* [KNOXVILLE: UNIVERSITY OF TENNESSEE PRESS, 2003], 56; OFFICE OF THE SURGEON GENERAL, CORRESPONDENCE 1928–1937, RG 112, 434/000.1–400, NATIONAL ARCHIVES, COLLEGE PARK, MD.; AND "WACS CELEBRATE 7TH ANNIVERSARY," *NEW YORK TIMES*, MAY 14, 1949, 15.)

In the mid-nineteenth century, these men were mostly foreign born, as was common for the army in general because, as today, citizenship was not required, and the army provided paying jobs. Like the maids, the largest portion of privates on Governors Island came from Ireland. Of the more than twenty sergeants, more than half were foreign born, and at least half of them were from Ireland. But by 1900 there was a significant ethnic shift: 75 percent of the two hundred privates on the island were American born. The largest foreign group now came from Germany, with Ireland a close second. These ratios were duplicated among the sergeants.[13]

By 1904, given the ethnic mix on Governors Island, if an Irish maid on an island with hundreds of men were to marry a soldier, he most likely would not be an Irishman. One of the women struck by Cupid's bow that year was "tall and slender, golden-haired" Maggie Dooley, the housekeeper for the commander of Company F of the Eighth Regiment, who was swept away by one of her employer's soldiers, Sergeant Swartz, described in the press as being of

A SECRETARY *in the Department of the East working next to an unknown officer, ca. 1913–19, unknown photographer. Courtesy of U.S. Army Military History Institute, Carlisle, Pa.*

A SECRETARY *working at what is probably an Underwood typewriter, ca. 1913–19, unknown photographer. Courtesy of U.S. Army Military History Institute, Carlisle, Pa.*

German extraction. Within two weeks of meeting, they were wed by Father Henry in a chapel at 7 State Street in Manhattan.[14]

The weddings were happy endings for these women, but not for their employers, whose reactions provide an insight into early-twentieth-century gender roles. For the couples who by rank were used to having household help, and at a time when wives listed their professions as "housekeepers," the weddings and the subsequent loss of their employees caused a reversal in traditional family duties. The men—captains and colonels—were suddenly seen doing such household chores as cleaning the stove and shopping for daily provisions in Manhattan. An article in the press described these henpecked helpmates: "Capt. Stewart has been seen several times of late on the ferryboat, his fingers bound up in different colored strings. Some of his fellow officers charged him with having forgotten some of the things Mrs. Stewart told him to buy, and that she took the string method to make him remember. The Captain made no defense."[15]

By 1910, the population of servants on Governors Island had diversified. One possible reason for this change was that officers who had been stationed in Cuba, Puerto Rico, and the Philippines probably brought low-wage servants back to the United States. A Hispanic nursemaid cared for Luisita Wood, the daughter of the commanding general, in 1908. Other ethnicities were also represented. Many servants now came from the South, although their race is not listed in the census. The women housekeepers, cooks, and nannies were now also French, Hungarian, Japanese, Russian, Scottish, Swedish, and West Indian. Irish women were still in the mix, but their numbers were lower, perhaps owing to that rash of marriages a few years earlier to soldiers of the Eighth Regiment.[16] The 1910 U.S. Census also indicates that wives of civilians who worked and lived on the island were beginning to join the domestic workforce. One such woman, married to an unnamed New York–born plumber, listed herself as a laundress.

Robinson Crusoe discovered a long time ago that running an Island is a lot of hard work....The complex task of running Governors Island is also a lot of hard work. But we too have our Fridays—the unsung heroines of Governors Island, our secretaries. Typists, file clerks or whatever their titles may be, they play a vital role in the functioning of our community. They are industrious but unassuming, furnishing the behind the scenes support that keeps their offices, and their bosses, running smoothly....So this week we salute our girls Friday—not just one of them—all 55 of them.

("WHO'S WHO IN THE MANAGEMENT," *COAST GUARD GAZETTE*, AUGUST 1, 1969, 7.)

Not much is known about the secretaries who worked on Governors Island other than what can be gleaned from photographs probably taken by the army's publicity bureau. Beginning in the 1920s, daughters of some of the civilian residents of the island were listed in the census as stenographers, but whether they worked for the military is unknown. It was more likely that they took their skills to offices on the mainland and would have commuted to work by ferry.

Photographs taken between 1913 and 1919 tell the workaday story of those women who worked on the island for the Eastern Depot, the inspector general, or the post commander. They sat at a flat-topped desk that in 1911 cost

$45.[17] They dressed primly in a white, long-sleeved blouse or a dress with white collar and cuffs and wore their hair either cropped short or pulled back in a bun. Sitting in close proximity to their officer bosses, they probably typed on an Underwood typewriter, which was purchased by the military in bulk during this period. The room was lit by electricity that had come to the island in 1904. One or two telephones were within reach, although the secretary was probably not required to answer the single instrument that sat on the officer's desk, for it was a long reach.

Our secretary [in the Coast Guard clinic located in the basement of the hospital] began working for the Army directly out of secretarial high school. She had the same office space for thirty-eight years.

(AUTHOR'S TELEPHONE INTERVIEW WITH JON KEMPFER, HEALTH-CARE ADMINISTRATOR, 1992–95, WINTER 2004.)

In later years, a wider variety of paid jobs formerly held by men on the island became available for women. The post exchange hired cashiers, and eating clubs sought waitresses.[18] In 1950, Lieutenant General Walter Bedell Smith, commanding general of the First Army, dedicated a renovated reference and fiction library. In the past, soldiers (and during World War II a civilian from Queens named Harry Koch) had sat in the librarian's chair,[19] but now a woman, Mrs. George A. Harer–who doubtless lived off-island–was the post librarian. She must have been delighted to be in charge of a newly acquired col-

THE GOVERNOR'S HOUSE, *September 28, 1864, unknown photographer. Courtesy of Still Pictures Branch, National Archives, College Park, Md.*

COMMANDING GENERAL'S *residence, Governors Island (Building 1), n.d., Rotograph Co. Postcard. Author's collection.*

GENERAL GRANT'S *residence, Governors Island, with entrance to Fort Jay on the right, n.d., YMCA. Postcard. Author's collection.*

COMMANDING OFFICER'S *house, September 28, 1864, unknown photographer. Courtesy of Still Pictures Branch, National Archives, College Park, Md.*

lection of books donated by Elihu Root, the turn-of-the-century secretary of war who had masterminded Governors Island's expansion.[20]

NOLAN PARK NORTH, 1837–1908

EVEN THOUGH THE MILITARY PERSONNEL'S residence on the island was always temporary, obvious attempts were made to lend an air of elegance and permanence to the officers' living quarters. The wives and daughters of the top echelon officers–who, of course, found shelter in the best spaces–probably found this task easier to accomplish. Descriptions of the Governor's House (Building 2) in a nineteenth-century serialized romance and of the commanding general's quarters (Building 1) in an early-twentieth-century newspaper article show attempts at such permanence. In *Agnes: A Romance of Governor's Island,* published in installments in 1837, we see the heroine and her military father alight at the dock at the foot of Andes Road from a green barge used only by officers. "What a pretty island!" exclaims Agnes and then asks, "Do you

FRANCES MCCOY, *wife of Major General Frank R. McCoy, Commander, U.S. Army, Second Corps Area, ca. 1936, unknown photographer. Courtesy of Frank R. McCoy Collection, U.S. Army Military History Institute, Carlisle, Pa.*

PORCH *of the commanding officer's house, ca. 1938, unknown photographer. Courtesy of Frank R. McCoy Collection, U.S. Army Military History Institute, Carlisle, Pa.*

MRS. LEONARD WOOD, *n.d., George Grantham Bain. Courtesy of George Grantham Bain Collection, Prints and Photographs Division, Library of Congress, Washington, D.C.*

live in one of those white houses, father?–or in the Fort?" Her father replies, "My residence is in the large white house you will observe on the left of the avenue. It is the quarters of the Commanding Officer [of the post]." The inside of the apartment is not described, but according to the National Park Service's Historic American Buildings Survey it had five rooms on two stories and access to balconies on each floor that overlooked Nolan Park and New York Harbor.[21]

Seven decades later, a November 24, 1907, *Washington Post* article told of the interior of the dwelling one house away. Major General and Mrs. Frederick Dent Grant lived in the commanding general's house in extravagant contrast to the simplicity by which one of his predecessors, Winfield Scott Hancock, had arranged his home there. The sixty-seven-year-old dwelling was now heavily decorated with English, French, Chinese, and Japanese furniture, much of it gifts the Grants had received from foreign ministries during their travels. The walls

GENERAL FREDERICK DENT GRANT, *Mrs. Leonard Wood, Mrs. Frederick Dent Grant, and General Leonard Wood, ca. 1908, George Grantham Bain. General Grant turned over the command of Governors Island to General Wood on November 10, 1908. Courtesy of George Grantham Bain Collection, Prints and Photographs Division, Library of Congress, Washington, D.C.*

BRIGADIER GENERAL TASKER HOWARD BLISS *and family, ca. 1912, unknown photographer. These early-twentieth-century residents of the commanding general's house are accompanied by a military aide and a house servant* (in the background). *Courtesy of Tasker Bliss Collection, U.S. Army Military History Institute, Carlisle, Pa.*

of the reception and entertainment rooms were covered with imported fabrics and important paintings. Prized collections of memorabilia from Frederick Dent Grant's father, Ulysses S. Grant–including a comb made of wood cut from a tree under which Grant met Lee at Appomattox–rested on tables throughout the house. Although the care with which the house was furnished gave the appearance of permanence, the furnishings themselves were evidence of the Grants' peripatetic lives.[22] Another much-traveled general and his wife, Leonard and Louise (Luisa) Wood, arrived at the house a year later. It had been emptied of the Grants' collections. Wood had just returned from Manila via Rotterdam after leading the Philippine Division. Details about their living accommodations are sketchy, but, like Agnes, Wood and his wife and several children reached the island via a special tug. Upon their arrival, they found comfort: the fireplaces were lit, and the beds had been made.[23]

We fortunately have a picture of Luisa's life while on Governors Island. Like her upper-class contemporaries, Luisa employed a nanny to care for her eight-year-old daughter, Louise Barbara (known as Luisita), and her eleven-year-old son Osborne. At home, she wrote often to her other son, Leonard Jr., who was attending Groton. The letters contained little news about Governors Island, but were focused on praising Leonard's academic life.[24]

On Concert evenings and help nights after 7:00 o'clock, and Saturday afternoons between the hours of 1:00 and 7:00 o'clock, the club rooms will be thrown open for reception of the Ladies of the Garrison, their guests and friends. The south-west porch and the tea room will be open to ladies at all times.

(GOVERNORS ISLAND CLUB, *CONSTITUTION AND BY-LAWS* [GOVERNORS ISLAND, N.Y.: GOVERNORS ISLAND CLUB, 1914], NO. 25, P. 19, COURTESY OF GARRET ROOSMA.)

But Luisa Wood was not only a mother; she was also the commanding officer's wife, and in that position she had the opportunity to meet important military men and foreign diplomats. Yet like most contemporary wives of prominent men, her role was a secondary one. Luisa was always at her husband's side when guests, such as the Prince and Princess Kunigore Kuni of Japan, paid a call. She shared the receiving line with Wood and other military couples at the annual May garden party, greeting the guests as they enjoyed the special day on Governors Island. In the evenings throughout the social season, the Woods traveled to Manhattan for parties and political events, perhaps at Delmonico's or the two-year-old

COLONEL'S ROW, *n.d., unknown photographer. Castle Williams is on the far left. Courtesy of Still Pictures Branch, National Archives, College Park, Md.*

PRIVATES' QUARTERS, *September 28, 1864, unknown photographer. Courtesy of Still Pictures Branch, National Archives, College Park, Md.*

Plaza Hotel. On these occasions, a certain discrimination against early-twentieth-century women was evident. Dinners were strictly for the men. However, once cigars were lit and the speeches began, Mrs. Wood was invited to partake of the remainder of the evening.[25]

Despite her subservient role at most public events, Luisa did have an opportunity to be front and center at the garden party. Although General Wood's staff handled the details of arranging for guest transportation and for setup of the refreshment tents and the sham battles (which were an important part of the entertainment), Luisa played hostess to a small, all-female gathering. Besides its social purpose, the garden party was held to raise funds for the Army Relief Society, a philanthropic organization that gave aid to military widows and orphans. To show her support of the charity, Mrs. Wood entertained its officers at a well-publicized luncheon in her home.[26]

LESS-PRIVILEGED WIVES, 1837–1990

THE WIVES OF JUNIOR OFFICERS and enlisted men on Governors Island lived in less salubrious quarters than the women in Nolan Park. This difference was the norm on military bases because the type of family housing one lived in was determined by rank. In turn, these residences' caliber was determined by military policy and the availability of monies for a particular post. In the nineteenth century, the junior officers' and enlisted men's families lived in hardship conditions. Beginning in the 1930s, however, their quality of life began to improve. WPA funds, changes in army regulations on marriage, and additional congressional appropriations for family housing allowed for new living quarters on the island.

I lived in the barracks, a very large building that was pretty barren at the time [December 1966 to January or February 1967]. In those days you had a rack, a wall locker and maybe up to ten roommates who moved in and out as their orders dictated. The rack had two sheets, one blanket. [Later on my ships were only issued one sheet.]

(E-MAIL TO AUTHOR FROM WILLIAM P. SEIBT, CWO3, U.S. COAST GUARD, RET., A SEAMAN APPRENTICE STATIONED ON GOVERNORS ISLAND IN EARLY 1964, SENT APRIL 29, 2004.)

In the nineteenth century, junior officers with families crowded into converted barracks. In the 1837 serial *Agnes: A Romance of Governor's Island,* Agnes visits Mrs. Gregory, a lieutenant's wife. Mrs. Gregory resides with her husband and several children in an apartment in Fort Jay, which greatly contrasts with the colonel's house in Nolan Park where Agnes lives. The junior officers' compound at that time consisted of four 2-story structures with small, poorly ventilated quarters for the garrison and its officers. In keeping with the army's intolerance of marriage, there are no records of family apartments in Fort Jay at this time. The descriptions in *Agnes,* however, are probably accurate: two rooms serve as "parlor, nursery and kitchen" for the Gregory family. The furniture is shabby. "The showy sofa exhibited marks of frequent removals—the carpet and other appurtenances looked time-worn."[27] Even Mrs. Gregory's reactions to the time-honored reveille and taps are affected by the living accommodations. Agnes, who resides on the opposite side of the island, revels

WAGONER CHARLES W. HOBBIE *and his wife, 1898, unknown photographer. The couple is standing in front of the post commanding officer's quarters (Governor's House). Mrs. Hobbie was probably on Governors Island to bid farewell to her husband, who was mustered on the island prior to being sent to Cuba. Courtesy of First Regiment, New York Volunteer Infantry Collection, U.S. Army Military History Institute, Carlisle, Pa.*

in the "roar of cannon, [and] the spirit soaring drums." But Mrs. Gregory, whose apartment is probably adjacent to or not far from the guns, bemoans that "[being] awakened at daylight by cannon and drums, whether you are sick, or well, sleepy or not, is not so agreeable, I assure you."[28]

Nearly twenty years after *Agnes* was published, the women traveling with Lieutenant/Captain Ulysses S. Grant and his regiment were probably also guests at Fort Jay. Grant was stationed on Governors Island from April to July 1852. Having served in the Mexican-American War, he was waiting with his regiment for orders to tame the Oregon Territory. Grant lived in the Block House (Building 9). His pregnant wife, Julia, was at home in Bethel, Ohio. In a letter to her dated June 20, 1852, Grant describes housing conditions for a lower-level officer and his camp followers: "We are now pretty well settled in camp with the usual comforts; that is, a chest and a trunk for seats and a bunk to sleep in. The ladies have come over from the City and are living in a few vacant rooms that are not required by the Company of Artillery stationed on the Island." The "ladies" were probably wives of soldiers in Grant's regiment who were waiting to travel with the companies around Cape Horn to the northwest. The weather, "exceedingly warm for the last few days and very unpleasant for the camp," probably added to their discomfort.[29]

But the accommodations at Fort Jay improved over time. By the early 1920s, the complex was devoted entirely to officers' quarters, and some of the newly renovated apartments doubtless held families. By the 1930s, all of the soldiers were finally settled in Liggett Hall, and a subsequent WPA building program refurbished Fort Jay's interiors. Each of the four buildings was reconfigured to hold four 2-story apartments with basement rooms for the maids. As evidence that the automobile was now a recognized part of military life on the island, two-car garages were also added to the compound. Fort Jay had become very desirable family housing.[30]

In addition to the renovations to Fort Jay in the 1930s, the army used WPA funds to pay for the construction of a dwelling for fifty-one noncommissioned officers and their families. For example, Building 315, a brick and terra-cotta tile apartment house, was built on Buttermilk Channel at a cost of $393,365. Although the placement of this structure did not conform to the 1907 McKim plan, it did provide comparatively luxurious nine-hundred-square-foot living spaces. Families could enjoy an oak-floored living room and a kitchen with an enameled iron sink/laundry tray. A tiled bathroom with Eljer fixtures, two pine-floored bedrooms, closets, and a service porch were additional features. No more washing in the river: laundry equipment was available in the basement. In

Fort Jay [in 1952] was an enclave of primarily privileged [army] officers and families—we had the run of the island....The Quad is where the 5 P.M. cannon was shot every day—this was right outside our kitchen door, so we often observed it firsthand and always made a bit of a "rite" of it, even saluting.... From a seven-year-old's perspective [the apartments] were big—living room, dining room, smallish kitchen and two bedrooms affording a spectacular view of lower Manhattan every night before bed.

(E-MAIL TO AUTHOR FROM JEFF HOLMES, WHO RESIDED ON GOVERNORS ISLAND AS A CHILD, SENT SEPTEMBER 21, 2004.)

COMPLETED FOUNDATION *of eighteen-family NCO apartment building No. 111, March 15, 1939, unknown photographer. Scrapbook photograph. The apartments for the noncommissioned officers were near the YMCA. Courtesy of National Archives, College Park, Md.*

recognition that peripatetic families were going to live there, the basement featured one hundred new storerooms for much-traveled belongings and children's outgrown toys.[31]

The evolution of army policy regarding married enlisted men preceded a physical change on Governors Island that finally eliminated "temporary" World War I and II units and developed the landfill with state-of-the-art housing. The army had historically exempted married men from the draft, and the discouraging family housing conditions on Governors Island were a possible manifestation of this policy. In 1936, only nine soldiers out of eighty in the U.S. Disciplinary Guard Company lived on the post with their wives and children.[32] One former resident described their accommodations, a converted World War I corrugated iron warehouse, as a tarpaper shack.[33]

By World War II, however, circumstances forced a change. In order to fulfill U.S. obligations abroad, the size of the military had to increase at all costs. Thus, the ensuing loosening of marriage restrictions and eventual funding from Washington opened the door for new construction on the island to house the expanding rank and file.

In 1960, according the *New York Times,* there were "1,000 wives, children, and husbands in 'dependents' housing" on Governors Island, and this population explosion caused the landscape to change dramatically.[34] A year later, using congressional funds for family housing for the military, the army constructed three 7-story apartment houses on the landfill along Upper

OFFICERS' QUARTERS *with mess, ca. 1920s, unknown photographer. Scrapbook photograph. One of dozens of prefabricated structures in the cantonment. Courtesy of National Archives, College Park, Md.*

SIXTY-THREE-MEN BARRACKS *with lavatory, 1920s, unknown photographer. Scrapbook photograph. Courtesy of National Archives, College Park, Md.*

E.M. (ENLISTED MEN'S) MESS *with kitchen, 1920s, unknown photographer. Scrapbook photograph. The mess served 250 soldiers. Courtesy of National Archives, College Park, Md.*

FORT JAY, *N.Y., eighteen NCO apartments (Bldg. #111), July 20, 1940, unknown photographer. Scrapbook photograph. Courtesy of National Archives, College Park, Md.*

New York Bay, on Craig Road between Second and Sixth Roads. The Capeharts (Buildings 844, 845, and 846), named after the sponsor of the financing bill, replaced leftover two-story cantonments from the two world wars that until 1958 had been used as family quarters. The contrast must have been extraordinary. The new structures towered in comparison to the nineteenth- and early-twentieth-century historic buildings on the island. Although the Capeharts seem minuscule compared to twenty-first-century residential high-rises, according to the *New York Times* they were the second-tallest dependents' quarters ever built in the United States (a military complex twice as tall in Alaska was the tallest).[35] Constructed to capture the views, the buildings formed their own residential complex. They were centered on a skating rink and backed onto the "airfield," as the large open space with ball fields was still called.

It was into the Capeharts–number 855, apartment 5E–that Staff Sergeant Harvey L. Thompson and his German-born wife, Hildegard, moved in 1963 with six children and another on the way. The army may have finally been equipped to house families, but not large ones.

COLONEL JOHN S. AND WIFE MARJORIE ROOSMA *in front of Quarters 5-9, n.d., unknown photographer. Courtesy of Garret Roosma.*

COLONEL'S ROW, *the golf course, and Fort Jay under the first heavy snowfall of 1954, Bastinck-Wasucci (no first name given). The house on the right is the post commander's house. Courtesy of Garret Roosma.*

VIEW OF LOWER NEW YORK BAY *from the Thompsons' dining room in the Capeharts, mid-1960s, unknown photographer. Courtesy of Claudia Iannucci.*

According to Claudia Iannucci, Thompson's daughter, the family initially lived in crowded conditions similar to Mrs. Gregory's in the nineteenth century: "We only had two bedrooms. My parents had one; my brother had his bed in the living room. During the day it was folded up. The other room had us five girls, and we all shared one bathroom. I remember sleeping on a folding, metal Army cot with itchy Army blankets. While we lived there we received new mattresses and blankets because the original ones had bedbugs."[36] Unlike Mrs. Gregory's quarters, however, this apartment had electricity, running water, a refrigerator, an incinerator for garbage, washing machines on the ground floor, and the benefit of sufficient windows and fabulous views. From the building, situated on the western flank of the island–as had been prescribed in smaller scale in the McKim plan–the Thompsons' school-age children had a decent walk to P.S. 26, then situated across the landfill along Buttermilk Channel.

HILDEGARD THOMPSON, *n.d., unknown photographer. Born in Germany, Hildegard was the wife of Sergeant Harvey L. Thompson. Courtesy of Claudia Iannucci.*

Not having an inventory of larger accommodations, the army eventually moved the Thompson family to the building next door, where the now nine-member family resided in apartments 2E and 2F. The army made no attempt to join the two units, so everything was doubled: four bedrooms and two each of baths, living rooms, kitchens, and dining rooms, one looking out to the Statue of Liberty. The Thompsons used the redundant kitchen as a storeroom, but the extra refrigerator-freezer came in handy, as did the extra dining room, which became a TV room and playroom.

In 1972, less than five years after the Coast Guard moved onto Governors Island, the number of military dependents again increased, this time sixfold.[37] To meet the need for sheltering 675 families, the Coast Guard opened another residential building, the eleven-story-high Cunningham Apartments (Building 877). Designed by a small New York City firm, Leo Kornblath Associates, and named after a Coast Guardsman who in 1936 sacrificed his life attempting to rescue two fishermen during a blinding snowstorm near Charlevoix, Michigan, this structure comprised three connected towers located between Gresham Road and New York Harbor.[38]

One of the early Cunningham residents was Carolyn Masini, the daughter of a Coast Guard noncommissioned officer. She lived in the

CUNNINGHAM APARTMENTS, *ca. 1972, unknown photographer. Courtesy of U.S. Coast Guard Historian's Office, Washington, D.C.*

high-rise for six years with her mother. Within a year of her arrival on the island, the new P.S. 26 was opened and named after Frederick C. Billard, commander of the Coast Guard from 1924 to 1932. Instead of hiking across the island as the children of the past did, Carolyn was able to walk a few blocks straight up Gresham Road past the Capeharts to school. Although her family's stay on the island was relatively long, the feeling of impermanence that pervades the history of the women's lives on Governors Island was ubiquitous. Ms. Masini describes the scene on her return from school: "[My mother] was looking out of her bedroom window (because she could see my Dad's ship from there) watching the ship leave the dock. I could always tell she had been crying. You had to hold down the fort (so to say) while your husband was gone."[39]

WACS AND COASTIES, 1944–1996

WORLD WAR II BROUGHT WOMEN into the army and onto Governors Island in an official capacity, and legislation developed from the subsequent civil rights and women's liberation movements fostered their presence as members of the Coast Guard. On August 18, 1944, two years after Olveta Culp Hobby established the Women's Army Auxiliary Corps (renamed the Women's Army Corps, or WACs, in 1943), 180 female soldiers descended on the island. A comparison of the WACs' reception and roles with the female "Coasties'" reception and roles in the 1970s tells much about twentieth-century social mores and changing attitudes toward women in the military and in general.

Although nurses, laundresses, and maids had been in residence on the island for more than a century, the WACs were the first women noncommissioned officers and soldiers. The army had made structural changes in the

In 1987 we moved into the new town houses in New Brick Village [#654-B] on the eastern side of the island, between Enright Road and Craig Road South. We had a good size kitchen, a foyer, half-bath, vinyl-floored dining area next to a large living room. Upstairs were three bedrooms with two full baths. The [bedroom and linen closets were] the largest closets I have ever had. We had a full-size basement that we turned into a playroom/office/laundry room/workshop.

(E-MAIL TO AUTHOR FROM LINDA FISHER, GOVERNORS ISLAND RESIDENT FROM 1985 TO 1990, SENT MAY 4, 2004.)

THE WEEKLY PARADE *is no longer single-sex, ca. 1945, unknown photographer. At parade rest, standing next to the male soldiers and officers are the enlisted women in olive drab. The WAC officers are distinguished by what was known as the "pink" skirt, which in actuality was a light olive drab. All of the women are wearing overseas hats. Courtesy of G. S. Grunert Collection, U.S. Army Military History Institute, Carlisle, Pa.*

housing stock over time to accommodate first the regiment, then officers and their families, and finally married soldiers. Now they needed to provide quarters for an entirely new cadre of residents. At a cost of $4,095, it refurbished one-half of a detachment barracks—known in 1945 as Building 101—and added feminine accoutrements.[40] The bathrooms were improved (urinals were probably replaced with toilets) and lights were added over the mirrors for easier application of makeup and styling of hair. Because women were assumed to travel with a larger number of possessions than men, the army replaced the traditional lockers in the dormitories with shelves and rods for hanging skirts and jackets. The refurbishment even included a beauty parlor.[41] Meals, however, were taken in headquarters' mess hall.[42]

Propriety on a male-dominated island was of prime concern to Major General Thomas A. Terry, commanding general of the Second Service Command, who had to uphold the mores of the period. A two-foot-thick wall separated the male and female portions of the barracks. At a time when mixed-sex dormitories were unthought of, this wall probably deflected the need for a housemother or chaperone. For further protection of the women, the army also installed a brand-new "date room," "where men callers [could] wait for the girls."[43]

All of the WACs initially commuted to work (probably as secretaries and clerks) in the city, for there were no jobs for them on the island. By 1949, however, the army base was the primary workplace of the seventy WAC residents. As was done for the men, the army relaxed the rules against marriage for WACs during World War II. Ten additional married women—who had probably signed up during the war—lived in the city at that time because

WACS ARRIVING *on Governors Island with their duffel bags, ca. 1945, unknown photographer. They are clad in shirts and six-gore skirts based on a design by Philip Mangone, a New York City suit designer. In 1951, these uniforms were redesigned by a famous New York City couturier, Hattie Carnegie. Courtesy of G. S. Grunert Collection, U.S. Army Military History Institute, Carlisle, Pa.*

NEWLY ARRIVED WACS *unpacking in the refurbished quarters in Building 101, ca. 1945, unknown photographer. Courtesy of G. S. Grunert Collection, U.S. Army Military History Institute, Carlisle, Pa.*

dormitory life, which was all that was provided for the WACs, was hardly conducive to family living. In the late 1940s, the army tightened the rules for women's service, with regulations stricter than those for men: any new recruits had to be single. Society expected wives to stay at home with their husbands.

Few details are known of the WAC workforce in the late 1940s. Major Alice Leach commanded the Governors Island detachment. Others held clerical positions. Sergeant Ursula Cocks became the post's classification officer. Sergeant Ruth K. Seshun commuted via subway and ferry from Brooklyn, where she lived with her husband and family, to work as the chief clerk in the post hospital.[44]

The WACs were active on Governors Island in the 1950s, and some even remained there until the army's departure in 1965. In fact, the first Coast Guard resident, Commander J. S. Gracey, chief executive officer of Base New York, was quartered in a barracks with army nurses and WAC officers for a few months before the handover of Governors Island from the army to the Coast Guard. With Gracey and the ensuing decades of Coast Guard occupation, many new doors opened for women on Governors Island and in the military in general.[45]

When Anna Mae McCabe Hays became the first female general in the U.S. Army in 1970, the Coast Guard had not yet been opened to women, but reform was on its way. At that time, women could serve only in the Women's Voluntary Reserves, also known as SPARs (an acronym based on the Coast Guard motto "Semper Paratus–Always Ready"). This unit was a subdivision of the Coast Guard formed around the same time as the WACs. However, the proposed 1972 equal rights amendment and other legislation encouraged a change in military policy, and a year later Congress passed a law making women eligible for active duty in the regular Coast Guard. The regulations that had placed a two-foot-thick wall between male soldiers and the WACs thirty years earlier no longer existed. Men and women now served and resided side by side. For the 655 or so women (among 37,000 men) in the Coast Guard, this inclusion meant technical training in heretofore male disciplines and months holed up with men on a ship at sea.[46]

WAC SERGEANT JANE CANNON *delivers mail by bicycle, ca. 1945, unknown photographer. Courtesy of G. S. Grunert Collection, U.S. Army Military History Institute, Carlisle, Pa.*

The year 1975 was the turning point for female Coasties on Governors Island. Probably helped by the Title IX ban on discrimination in federally funded education programs,[47] Lauren Stagg, a native of Roseville, California, became the first woman in the armed forces to graduate as an electronics technician. With this training, Stagg was now ready to repair equipment ranging from office machines to ships' radar, sonar, and more–

Boatswain's mate Judith T. Carey...said they had shipped on for the same reasons that young men through the ages have signed on to ships—to travel, to learn and to satisfy inexplicable yearnings for the sea....[Carey and nine other female recruits and two officers] were the first women assigned as regular crew members aboard a Coast Guard cutter off the East Coast....[They] are the first deep water women sailors.

(MARY BREASTED, "COAST GUARD BOASTS OF ITS RECRUITS: THEY'RE ABLE, SEAWORTHY, FEMALE," FROM *NEW YORK TIMES*, DECEMBER 7, 1977, 31.)

work previously done only by men. Rules about where she was allowed to serve were still restrictive, however, and her first assignment was at the Coast Guard Supply Center in Brooklyn.[48]

More than three centuries after the landing of the first island ladies, twelve more women became Governors Island pioneers—only this time they were shipping out. In the fall of 1977, ten Coast Guard enlistees and two officers became the first women to trade land-based jobs for life at sea. They left off-island apartments and such segregated dormitories as Liggett Hall—with washers, dryers, and in some cases kitchen facilities and sewing machines—for "racks" (beds) in "female berthing" and "rec decks" on the 378-foot, high-endurance cutter *Gallatin*.[49] A minority among the 153 male officers and crewmen, these young women worked on board in positions ranging from menial (ship's mess) to necessary (radio operators) to crucial (navigator). Just two years after Lauren Stagg received her degree, Lauren T. Cantatore, in her twenties, supervised three men as an electronics expert. According to accounts,[50] she did a good job.

Despite the loosening of the legal strictures against women in the Coast Guard, it was hard for the men to adjust. A *New York Times* article describing the *Gallatin*'s bow to women's equality contains chauvinistic remarks. The close quarters also increased the potential for sexual contact that was not available to the early WACs. One man on the *Gallatin* feared that his attention might stray "when a woman is present."[51] But adjustment to mixed-gender crews was swift. By the 1990s, sexual relationships—heterosexual, homosexual, and lesbian—aboard ship may have been forbidden, but they were not uncommon. In many cases, the friendships fostered by months at sea in close quarters led to conventional marriages. These ships were not the "nautical dens of iniquity" that some feared they would become when the women initially reported for duty in the 1970s. Rather, women stood side by side with the men as the *Gallatin* and the *Dallas* departed from Governors Island for drug patrols, missions to intercept boat people fleeing dictatorships, or visits to European ports to promote the work of the Coast Guard.[52]

One who was not delighted with the new crewmates ...said that the women assigned to work with him at his last post, a search and rescue station...did not perform well under pressure. When asked for examples, he said that a woman radio operator had burst into tears when a report came in that a ship had capsized....On another occasion...a woman radio operator had fainted on receiving a report of a man who had got a fishhook caught in his eye.

(MARY BREASTED, "COAST GUARD BOASTS OF ITS RECRUITS: THEY'RE ABLE, SEAWORTHY, FEMALE," FROM *NEW YORK TIMES*, DECEMBER 7, 1977, 31.)

COMMUNITY OF COAST GUARD WIVES, 1965–1996

UNLIKE THE EARLY ENLISTED MEN'S WIVES who were unwanted by army officialdom, Coast Guard wives were central to the day-to-day life and the unique sense of a small town on Governors Island in the second half of the twentieth century. Like the army wives before them, these modern women—some more liberated than others, from posts up and down the East Coast and from foreign lands—followed their husbands to homes on an isolated island in the midst of a crowded city. No sooner had they arrived than the men were off to sea or upriver, leaving them companionless or alone with their children. Their reactions to this situation varied. Some women felt trapped on the island, waiting for their husbands to be promoted so they could leave. Others assimilated more easily, but were nonetheless reluctant to venture into the perceived dangers of New York City alone. For them, life centered on the island, a secure and safe haven. They relied on the Coast Guard Support Center for sports programs for their children and for rescue when they were locked out of their apartments. For friendship and a sense of purpose, they joined the Officers' Wives Club or the Enlisted Men's Wives' Club (a name that in the past may have indicated second-class citizenship). The more adventuresome women could not only lead active lives within the Governors Island community, but also explore the city that was only a four-minute ferry ride away. Museums, Broadway shows and Yankees games, shopping at Macy's or Altman's, and pizza at the Staten Island ferry terminal or dinner in upscale restaurants in Midtown were constant attractions.

Snippets of the Coast Guard wives' lives reveal that motherhood on Governors Island was no different than in any small town. As one woman wrote, "The best part is everyone knows you and your kids, and the worst part is everyone knows you and your kids."[53] During the school year, they walked their children to P.S. 26, to the Child Development Center, or to daycare in Castle Williams. In these places and on the sports field or in the movie theater, the military hierarchy still prevalent in the housing and eating arrangements was nonexistent. Wives of enlisted men, noncommissioned officers, and commissioned officers met and chatted over common interests, their children, and plans for the future.

From the school, some mothers went on to jobs. Those going to work in the city perhaps stopped first for coffee at Louie's Deli at the ferry landing. Others might venture west from P.S. 26, just across Gresham Road, to the Geedunk (Building 825), as the cafeteria was commonly called. There they might pick up a donut–five cents for cinnamon, fifteen cents for chocolate glazed–before going to jobs on the island.[54] One woman, after leaving her daughter with her mother in her Cunningham apartment, at different times during her stay went to work at various jobs needed to staff the island: cashier at the post exchange, waitress in the Non-Commissioned Officers' Club, and eventually secretary to the post quartermaster.

Others brought special training or innate talents to the island. One mother sometimes substituted for an absent teacher at P.S. 26. Because it often took days to find a substitute, the parents at P.S. 26 had prevailed upon the Board of Education to allow residents with appropriate credentials to step in. Another woman with a penchant for sewing organized the notions section at the Coast Guard Exchange (the department store). This venture was timely because beginning with the bicentennial in 1976, the Coast Guard occasionally invited the public to visit Governors Island. Families were encouraged to act as guides at these open houses and, to add to the historicity of the tours, often dressed in homemade period clothing. The notions counter provided the women with the needles, thread, buttons, snaps, and other items used for sewing the costumes.[55]

Mothers occasionally gathered with friends and caught the ferry for some time together in the city. But there were always housekeeping chores at home. All of the women knew Vaskin and Ara Martin, proprietors of the base dry cleaners located in the former post bakery, which the army had constructed in 1941.[56] The women might have picked up their husbands' new uniforms or purchased a Lacoste T-shirt at discount in the cleaner's small shop or tried on a skirt to be shortened by the tailor. After 11:00 A.M. on Tuesday through Friday, an $8 haircut was available at Shear Pleasure Styling: Your Family Haircare Center. In the 1990s, if a black

FIRST- AND SECOND-GRADE *class at P.S. 26 on Governors Island, 1966, unknown photographer. Courtesy of Claudia Iannucci.*

woman felt flush, she could avail herself of cornrows for $40 or a hair weave for $90.[57]

Events during the afternoon were no different than in any New York suburb, except there was no need to drive–unless the children were past sixth grade and therefore attending schools in the city. Instead, mothers walked their offspring to sports practice on fields that had once been proposed for an airport, to swimming in the summer (in now two available pools), and to ice skating in the winter. They ran the weekly Daisy Girl Scout meetings and watched their daughters' cheerleading or ballet practice. The after-school offerings by the Support Center were legion: T-ball, softball, volleyball, bowling, and jazz and tap dancing. As one Coast Guard brat wrote, "It was all free of charge. If you wanted to do it you just needed to show up."[58]

In the evening, there was homework, dinner, and family time. Dinner choices were plentiful. Filipino families gathered in front of barbecues stationed near the housing and cooked clams. Others ordered in a $1.25 cheese pizza from Three Flags Pizza or ate out at the only Burger King that served beer.[59] The Burger King was opened in 1983 as part of the fast food company's attempt to reach military institutions, an untapped market.[60] Other families went to the various clubs on the island for dinner, where the military hierarchy was more evident and the formality and price increased with rank. One Tuesday in October 1975, upper-level noncommissioned officer families ventured to the Chief Petty Officers' Club to enjoy a special of beef stew with hot

GIRL SCOUT *patch, n.d., unknown designer.*

RESIDENTS SHOP *at the Governors Island commissary, n.d., unknown photographer. Courtesy of U.S. Coast Guard Historian's Office, Washington, D.C.*

biscuits for only $1.50 per person.[61] Entrees on a 1990s menu from the white tablecloth Officers' Club (or officers' open mess, still located in the South Battery) were pricier, but inexpensive compared to the offerings in a city restaurant: a hot dog for $1.85, surf and turf for $20. To add to the formality, jackets and ties were required on Friday and Saturday nights.

Restaurant menus at the Geedunk are indicators of the residents' changing ethnicity and tastes. Steak, baked chicken, ribs, pastrami, knockwurst, goulash, and veal parmesan with spaghetti were listed on the menus in 1969.[62] By the 1990s, however, the Geedunk served dishes that reflected the existence of an Asian population and the general popularity of Hispanic foods. In addition to the traditional meat and potatoes, patrons could choose from a menu of egg drop soup, sesame chicken, refried beans, burritos, and enchiladas.[63] Originally serving only breakfast and lunch, the cafeteria by 1992 served three meals a day and was open seven days a week. Breakfast and lunch were initially under $2, but the cost rose to $5 by the 1990s.

St. Cornelius Chapel and Our Lady Star of the Sea Chapel were the centers of activity for many families on Sunday mornings. Unlike the army's early years on Governors Island when St. Cornelius provided the only religious sanctuary, by 1977 church services and Sunday school were not the only activities offered there. The "Chaplain's Chronicle" also listed "prayer breakfasts, Bible study, and a coffee house,"[64] as well as worship opportunities for five different religions. Episcopalians, Catholics, and Jews met in freestanding chapels, and Christian Scientists and Jehovah's Witnesses held prayer meetings in the Training Center's visitor's lounge and in an apartment in the Capeharts. Members of a sixth religion, the Church of Jesus Christ of Latter-Day Saints, had to go off island to a chapel in Lincoln Center.

The Cafeteria sells 900 cups of coffee, 40 dozen home made donuts, 700 cups of soft drinks, 300 containers of milk per day. During the summer months, 15–18 gallons of ice cream are sold to the Island residents.

("WHO'S WHO ON GOVERNORS ISLAND," *COAST GUARD GAZETTE*, MARCH 7, 1969, 11.)

The island setting was also conducive to outdoor religious ceremonies. On June 12, 1977, the Catholic parish celebrated an outdoor Mass behind the chapel, followed by a picnic, to bid farewell to Father Pilarsky, the Catholic chaplain. Families were asked to bring "a salad and a vegetable dish" for themselves; the parish provided "everything else."[65] Chaplains were no longer borrowed from other dioceses such as Trinity Church; now they were provided to the Coast Guard by the U.S. Navy.

Undoubtedly a very important part of a Coast Guard wife's day was the time spent in volunteer activities. Governors Island has a long history of volunteers, in particular those nineteenth-century women who worked to support the church or who were active in the island's beautification. In the 1880s, Almira "Allie" Hancock, wife of General Winfield Scott Hancock, was a volunteer mainstay of the St. Cornelius Chapel. She not only embroidered altar cloths, as was common among female parishioners everywhere, but also headed the women's auxiliary, organized the chapel's choir, and orchestrated fund-raising musicales. Among her cohorts was Mary Moore Robertson, the wife of the beloved hospital surgeon and daughter of the bandmaster.[66] Between the 1850s and World War I, the garden outside the Robertson home was a showcase, perhaps a model for the plantings that grace Nolan Park houses to this day. In 1935, another resident, Julia Nolan, wife of the commanding general of the First Army, initiated the island's first historic preservation project. With the help of WPA funds and workers, she secured the renovation of the Nolans' quarters and the two historic structures to the north (Governor's House and Dutch House) and the South Battery Officers' Club.[67]

Following this tradition, twentieth-century wives participated in the island community under the aegis of various clubs. The Enlisted Men's Wives' Club was by far the most active and influential. Its fund-raising work and annual holiday events encouraged the formation of friendships that lasted long after individuals left Governors Island and contributed to a sense of community on the island that the Coast Guard was anxious to foster.

Just as Luisa Wood had hosted garden parties in support of the Army Relief Society, the Coast Guard wives raised money for causes on Governors Island. Beneficiaries included the school, the Boy Scouts and Girl Scouts, and enlisted families in need. A major source of the

INSIDE BURGER KING, *viewed through a porthole, n.d., unknown photographer. Consumer Food Service Inc. of Fords, N.J., was the franchisee. Courtesy of U.S Coast Guard Historian's Office, Washington, D.C.*

THE ONLY BURGER KING *to serve beer opened on Governors Island on May 5, 1983, unknown photographer. Courtesy of U.S Coast Guard Historian's Office, Washington, D.C.*

EXTERIOR *of the officers' mess, well guarded by nineteenth-century cannons, ca. 1950s, unknown photographer. Courtesy of Garret Roosma.*

THE MAIN DINING ROOM *of the officers' mess (Officers' Club), n.d., unknown photographer. This dining room was the most formal of the dining establishments on Governors Island. Courtesy of Thomas Dunn Collection, U.S. Army Military History Institute, Carlisle, Pa.*

MATCHBOOK *cover from the Officers' Club, n.d., Lion Match Company, Inc. Author's collection.*

donations came from sales in the thrift shop located on the first floor of Building 400.[68] Outgrown clothes, toys, and lightly used household items brought in funds and outfitted homes that were constantly in flux. The club periodically also raised money through a flea market set up on tables in the P.S. 26 gym.[69]

Menu

Half-dozen Escargot	$4.50
Lumpia Shanghai	$3.25
Filet Mignon	$14.00
Surf and Turf	$20.00
Hot Dog	$1.85
French cheesecake with Strawberry Sauce	$2.00
Wines and Champagne by the bottle	$7.50 to $25.00.

(MENU FROM THE OFFICERS' OPEN MESS, 1990S, COURTESY OF CAROLE TELLER, ART TEACHER AT P.S. 26.)

Friendship and emotional support came through events that both entertained the children and occupied the women's lonely hours, regardless of their husbands' positions. In 1976, the Enlisted Men's Wives' Club inaugurated an annual talent show that, as one writer described, "would make 'Star Search' look like amateur hour."[70] Women and men with and without skills performed on the stage of the Governors Island Theater. In 1981, adults (sixteen and older) and children paid $1.50 and $1.00 respectively to watch a female and male leg contest. The admissions probably barely covered the production costs.

The Enlisted Men's Wives' Club annual Halloween party and Easter egg hunt were central to the establishment of community on the island. They also brought the different ranks of the Coast Guard families together in events centered on children. Servicemen, women, and children still remember the haunted house in Castle Williams. Phones flying through the air and pillowcases full of candy are among their reminiscences. Easter was the time for the clubs to work together in a communal spirit. Following an army legacy, the Enlisted Men's Wives' Club, joined by a diverse group of volunteers including the Filipino-American Club and the Officers' Wives' Club, delighted the children with egg hunts and egg-rolling contests on the lawn in Nolan Park.[71]

On weekends the Governors Island ferry only ran at half hour intervals. One Saturday a top island official ventured into Manhattan to replenish the family tomato supply. Having missed the ferry, he was forced to wait on Governors Island for 30 minutes. Once in Manhattan it took an hour for him to travel uptown to the nearest market and return to the ferry terminal. Again the ferry had departed. This became the officer's oft-told "three-hour tomato" story.

(AUTHOR'S INTERVIEW WITH ADMIRAL RICHARD LARRABEE, NEW YORK CITY, MAY 2004. REPRODUCED WITH PERMISSION.)

The Coast Guard wives were clearly the heart and soul of Governors Island, although the Support Center must be given credit for aiding and abetting their work as athletic directors, security forces, and constant cheerleaders. But it was a two-way street. Particularly at times when finances were strapped, the island administration needed volunteers to keep the programs working and the island in order. The wives may have individually moved in and out following their husbands' promotions or transfers, but as a group they were constantly present. Although not specifically mentioning the women, a 1975 notice from the Support Center sums up the relationship between the women and the island:

> Residents working together on projects of mutual interest which benefit our children illustrate the value of living in a community such as Governors Island. Those Coastguardsmen who must be at sea or otherwise off the Island can be assured that members of their families will have others to turn to who not only understand their problems, but who are genuinely concerned and are most willing to help.
> Volunteers make Governors Island a better place to live.[72]

COLONEL PHILLIPS *describes an outdoor kitchen to Bedford Disaster canteen women, May 20, 1942, unknown photographer. Courtesy of U.S. Army Military History Institute, Carlisle, Pa.*

ISLAND HIGHLIGHTS *A Wedding Pageant*

Katherine Corbin...plighted her troth to William Usher Parsons yesterday afternoon. From the presence of high military officials and leaders of New York Social circles, the wedding festivities partook both of the glitter of military life and the éclat of an event of the best society....The ceremony and the accompanying features were marked with a picturesqueness and freshness alien to the conventional wedding....[L]ittle save the energetic tooting of the numerous craft plying up and down the bay served to remind one of the proximity of the great city of New York.[1]

Governors Island was and still is an idyllic setting for weddings. When the U.S. Army was in residence, weddings rivaled the pageantry of weekly parades and garden parties and showed off Governors Island at its best, with men dressed in colorful military attire and women wearing silk dresses and picture hats. As the bride and groom walked from the Chapel of St. Cornelius under the traditional arch of sabers, the scene was as fine as any at West Point or the Coast Guard Academy.

These female-centered ceremonies revealed much about the island and its relationship to the world outside. Many were also a microcosm of the social scene in New York, Washington, and cities in the Midwest and California.

High-ranking officers with means took advantage of both the setting and the varied facilities on Governors Island to marry off their daughters in a glamorous and opulent manner. On

ARRIVAL OF DIGNITARIES, *n.d., unknown photographer. Such arrivals were important events in island life. Courtesy of Frank R. McCoy Collection, U.S. Army Military History Institute, Carlisle, Pa.*

THE DUKE AND DUCHESS *of Windsor are received by Lieutenant General Hugh Drum, May 21, 1943, unknown photographer. Courtesy of G. S. Grunert Collection, U.S. Army Military History Institute, Carlisle, Pa.*

PRESIDENT RONALD REAGAN *and Mikhail Gorbachev at the Admiral's house, 1988, unknown photographer. Vice President George H. W. Bush is on the right. Courtesy of U.S. Coast Guard Historian's Office, Washington, D.C.*

September 7, 1897, the marriage of Miss Katherine Corbin was the social event of the fall season. Daughter of Lieutenant Colonel Henry Clark Corbin, adjutant general of the Department of the East, Katherine wed William Usher Parsons, son of a New York City businessman and a graduate of Yale University and Columbia Law School.

The party began at the ferry dock on Andes Road. Special arrangements had been made for steam ferries and a military revenue cutter to run at frequent intervals. Guests were escorted to the front of the Corbin home, one of the Victorian cottages on Colonel's Row, where the adjutant general (a widower) greeted the invitees prior to their walk to the chapel, a short distance to the south.

The guest list was a veritable roster of military dignitaries and the civilian social register. From the island were Major Amos Kimball, the assistant quartermaster general who would soon plan the island's enlargement, and his wife. Other majors, lieutenants, and colonels came from such army bases as Fort Hamilton, Fort Slocum, Willet's Point, Fort Wadsworth, and even from the War Department in Washington. Among the civilians were old New York society names such as Van Wyck and Van Rensselaer. Senator Calvin S. Brice came from Ohio, Corbin's home state, and President William McKinley, unable to attend, sent a wire.[2]

At the Chapel of St. Cornelius, a religious hierarchy was evident. The ceremony would normally have been performed by Reverend Edward Goodwin, who was on loan from Trinity Church in Manhattan because a military chaplain had never been assigned to the base. On this occasion, however, given the celebrants' status, the nuptials were performed by Goodwin's superior, Reverend Morgan Dix, Trinity Church's rector.

The women's beauty was replicated on the island itself. Portions of its sixty-nine acres were blanketed with flowers and decorations. Masses of white rhododendrons, palm leaves, and ferns surrounded the altar and filled an alcove of the chapel. Flags, bunting, and blossoms adorned the green at Nolan Park and the front of the Corbin house. Following the ceremony, squads of blue-coated soldiers served lunch in tents that had been erected on the lawn in Nolan Park.

Anna Drum was married in the Catholic chapel on Governors Island on December 29, 1941. Her father, General Hugh Drum, Commander of the First Army[,] [which was headquartered on the island], was the first Catholic commander there. Rumor had it that he wanted Catholic servicemen to have a better religious venue than a room in the South Battery. His daughter's pending marriage may have spurred the construction of Our Lady Star of the Sea, the Catholic chapel [Building 309].

("ANNA C. DRUM, DAUGHTER OF GENERAL, WED TO LT. T. H. JOHNSON JR. AT GOVERNOR'S ISLAND," *NEW YORK TIMES*, DECEMBER 30, 1941, 16.)

In the evening, guests moved down the lawn to the headquarters building that had been transformed into a ballroom with banks of flowers and exotic plants. Here, according to the *New York Times*, "the sight of the uniformed officers and fair women whirling in the cadences of the dance was strikingly pleasing."[3] But such happy and gala events were transitory on this military base. In less than a year, the Governors Island Thirteenth Infantry, some of whom may have served at the Corbin wedding, shipped off to war in Cuba.

ST. CORNELIUS CHAPEL, *Governors Island, n.d., unknown photographer. Courtesy of Garret Roosma.*

INSIDE ST. CORNELIUS *Chapel, where the Corbin/Parsons wedding took place, n.d., unknown photographer. Courtesy of Garret Roosma.*

HENRY CLARK CORBIN, *ca. 1950s, Evelyn Beatrice Longman. Memorial plaque. Courtesy of Garret Roosma.*

POST CHAPEL *of St. Cornelius the Centurion, Governors Island, n.d., Rotograph Co. Postcard. Author's collection.*

ISLAND HIGHLIGHTS *Isle of Dogs*

There is not a piece of ground the size of Governors Island anywhere in this or any other neighborhood, outside of dog stores or kennels, where [dogs] are to be found in such numbers.[1]

Fox terriers, pugs, poodles, bull terriers, St. Bernards, and innumerable mongrels found safe haven on Governors Island at the turn of the twentieth century. Many animals came as part of commanding officers' households. During the command of Henry Clark Corbin—now a major general—dogs were in high favor. He owned a Scotch collie, and his wife owned a prize Pomeranian. Other dogs were brought in for military display, but many arrived under less-auspicious circumstances. How they actually got there and how they were received over time are little-known facts about the island and the military's attitudes.

Unlike human visitors, who required elaborate passes to gain access to Governors Island, a clever dog could probably find myriad ways to gain free entry. Although prisoners were known to plan elaborate escapes via the ferry and passing boats, some dogs probably used these vessels to find secure homes. In 1902, Lazarus, a yellow mutt, jumped from a barge into Buttermilk Channel and was rescued at the island's seawall by soldiers who heard his plaintive whine.

Many dogs—such as Sporty, a mutt who understood only Spanish—arrived on the island having been secreted out of Puerto Rico by soldiers returning to New York. Sporty subsequently learned English and military etiquette, such as standing at attention and responding to fire alarms. Oblivious to military hierarchy, animals with and without pedigree became company mascots. Rags, "blind in one eye, almost deaf and badly crippled from wounds received in France,"[2] was the pride of the First Division. A St. Bernard slept on a cot covered with regulation army blankets and ate only army food. It was a sad day for these dogs when their units departed; however, adoption by another company was likely.

The army brought some dogs onto the island to display military preparedness. These dogs, unlike the mixed breeds already in residence, were highly trained. Photographs of turn-of-the-century garden parties show Labrador retrievers jumping over twelve-foot-high barriers and rescuing a "fallen" soldier.

Neither mascots nor pets were immune to a commanding officer's order for their dismissal. In February 1905, Major General James F. Wade ordered his staff to issue a leash law. Wade was tired of seeing lawns and flowers destroyed by digging paws and other reminders of dogs' visits. In an effort to preserve the island's fast-disappearing rabbits and squirrels, the leash law also required that every dog not "tied to a string, one end of which was...tightly gripped by the guardian of the dog," should be forced to leave the island immediately. Unhappily, walking around the island with a pet at the end of a string was beneath many soldiers' dignity. According to the *New York Times,* "a procession of dogs, each one led by a stalwart soldier, [was] marched away from the island."[3]

The ambiguous relationship between man and beast on Governors Island continued under the Coast Guard. By then, stray dogs were no longer a problem because all guns, dogs, and

RAGS, *the Hero Dog of the First Division, with Sergeant Hickman, n.d., unknown photographer. Courtesy of Still Pictures Branch, National Archives, College Park, Md.*

cats had to be registered. But household pets' detritus became an issue.

"Doggie islands" were one solution. A 1973 map in the *Coast Guard Gazette* showed eight areas—mainly on the island's periphery and one in Fort Jay—reserved for "pet relief."[4] Teaching families to value and care for their pets was another path. Obedience classes were held in the school gym; ribbons were awarded to the best-trained dog. In 1975, Red Foxx, a Doberman pinscher, and Baron, a cocker spaniel, were among the winners.[5] Despite classes and relief stations, however, some owners still failed to contain and curb their dogs properly. For them, the same sanction pertained that the army had meted out decades earlier: pets were immediately removed from the island.[6]

BLACK POODLE *in front of Fort Jay garage, ca. 1918, Wells Studio. Scrapbook photograph. Courtesy of National Archives, College Park, Md.*

YOUNG BOY *with friend in front of the ordnance sergeant's house, n.d., unknown photographer. Courtesy of Still Pictures Branch, National Archives, College Park, Md.*

COLONEL JOHN ROOSMA *and sons Will* (left) *and Garry* (right) *with new puppy, 1947, unknown photographer. Courtesy of Garret Roosma.*

RED CROSS *rescue exhibition on Governors Island, ca. early 1900s, George Grantham Bain. Courtesy of George Grantham Bain Collection, Prints and Photographs Division, Library of Congress, Washington, D.C.*

GARDEN PARTY, *Governors Island, May 27, 1908, George Grantham Bain. Commanders' Row and St. Cornelius Chapel are in the background. Courtesy of George Grantham Bain Collection, Prints and Photographs Division, Library of Congress, Washington, D.C.*

Chapter Seven

"SMILING GARDEN OF THE PROVINCE"
Recreation on Governors Island

It seems to be a beneficent arrangement of nature that all great harbors are provided with small islands....[In] New York Harbor, the fairest of them all [is]...the "Smiling Garden of the Sovereigns of the Province," as the old Colonial Governor used to call it, which in its long career has done more smiling than frowning.[1]

Governors Island a park? Absurd! But twenty-first-century planners have "park" as their central theme for rejuvenation of the island. The idea is, in fact, not new. Throughout this harbor island's history, competing in a schizophrenic pattern with the military realities has been the tantalizing image of it as a park. A look back in time at the changing recreational possibilities on the island–from people watching to competitive sports, from legislative inroads and defeats to opportunities for the general public to enjoy this New York oasis–reveals that contemporary ideas reflect historical conceptions of what was and what might have been.

FOREST, FARM, AND "SMILING GARDEN," 1600–1800

IN ITS NATURAL STATE, Governors Island was ideal for a bucolic retreat. Situated at the confluence of the East and Hudson Rivers in Upper New York Bay, it was a waterfront setting par excellence. On the land were fertile forests. Native tribes named the island "Pagganck" for its abundant groves of hickory, oak, and chestnut trees,[2] so it made perfect sense that when New York's Dutch settlers first arrived on Governors Island, they renamed it "Nootten Eylandt," or "Nut Island."

By 1637, the Dutch were firmly settled–but in Manhattan. It was their cattle that were sent to Governors Island to enjoy the pastoral life. Governor Wouter Van Twiller, however, had other ideas. He purchased the island for his private use at the alleged cost of two ax heads, a string of beads, and some nails.[3] Van Twiller's ownership was cut short when he was sent home as a result of corruption, and the island reverted back to the Dutch West India Company, thus beginning nearly a century of use as a sawmill, farm, and retreat under government ownership.

The British occupation of New York formalized the island as a country getaway for the state. Lord Edward Cornbury and his successors used it as a gubernatorial mansion and summer playground. One follower, Governor William Cosby, introduced pheasants to the island, thereby rounding out the picture of a proper English retreat.

It was not long before tension arose between the island's use for pleasure and its use as a bastion to defend the growing maritime city. With the onset of the Revolutionary War, this

OIL PAINTING *of Governors Island in the mid–eighteenth century, n.d, F. Wille. This image hung in the main sitting room of the Officers' Club. It might be an imaginary vision of the British governors' summer retreat, complete with windmills from the Dutch era. Courtesy of Garret Roosma.*

debate was swept aside when the military appropriated the land. Both the Americans and the British built fortifications on the island. However, when the British Royal Navy surrendered to the State of New York in 1783, it left behind two reminders of the island's prior use: a gardener's house and a summerhouse.[4]

With peace secured, all efforts were concentrated on the postwar rebuilding of New York City, and by default Governors Island reverted to a recreational site. In 1784, the New York State Assembly formally returned the island to its former status as a retreat for the exclusive use of the governor. New York City contested this designation and in true entrepreneurial style put forth a plan laying out the land with development plots, streets, and lanes. Although there is no evidence of construction during this period, advertisements show that the state did lease the land for a racetrack, setting the stage for later recreational use of horses on the island. A newspaper described a vision for the island: "As improvements are now begun on Governors Island...we may expect soon to see it metamorphosed from a neglected spot, into a seat of taste and rural elegance."[5]

RECREATION, 1800–1888

THE U.S. ARMY CONCENTRATED ITS EFFORTS on fort building after the State of New York handed over Governors Island to the federal government in 1800. But there were also recreational opportunities for those who lived on or visited the island, which set the pattern for succeeding military pageantry, political events, garden parties, and eventually open houses. In the summer of 1812, the first garden party was held so that guests could watch the artillery take target practice. The attendees, attired for afternoon tea, applauded as gunners at Castle Williams and its Manhattan sister, Castle Clinton, shot at a sunken hulk in the harbor that separated them.

Similar events became well-attended spectator sports. In 1815, celebrants of the Treaty of Peace with Great Britain watched

September 9, 1861. I got up early this morning as is my custom and double quicked round our boundaries. It is a little cloudy and looks ominous of ugly weather.

(ALONZO E. BELL, DIARIES, MF.P.48.1, 20, TRANSCRIBED BY ALEX CHRISTOPHER MEEKINS, OFFICE OF ARCHIVES AND HISTORY, DIVISION OF HISTORICAL RESOURCES, ARCHIVES AND RECORDS, NORTH CAROLINA STATE ARCHIVES, RALEIGH.)

TENNIS PLAYERS *on resident James Lord's porch in Nolan Park, 1887, unknown photographer. Courtesy of Daughters of U.S. Army Collection, U.S. Army Military History Institute, Carlisle, Pa.*

martial salutes and rockets discharge from Castle Williams. Recreation for the troops was an extra ration of liquor. Midcentury executions were always occasions to view. During the Civil War, the regiment, residents, and visitors turned out for the death blow to bounty jumper James Devlin. One contemporary journalist noted his own distaste: "[t]he eagerness of the women to watch the shooting was most disgusting."[6]

COAST GUARD PATCH, *n.d., unknown designer. Tennis continued to be a popular sport throughout the Coast Guard's stay on the island. Author's collection.*

Active recreation for the soldiers on Governors Island is not well documented. However, diaries of Civil War prisoners hint at what opportunities might have been available for at least the rank and file. In 1861, Thomas Sparrow, one of the Confederate officers imprisoned on Governors Island, revealed that exercise was important to the prisoners' daily lives, even though it was not on the official roster. Soldiers held in Castle Williams played cards and pitched quoits in the circular yard. Officers were free to roam within proscribed limits from Fort Columbus, where they lived. They tossed a football and played truncated games of baseball, walked around the island, dug soft-shelled clams from the sand, or listened while a brass band "discourse[d] most charming music," Sparrow wrote. "After 5 in the afternoon we...congregate on the West of the Island...Here, on the lawn, the younger officers exercise themselves with throwing heavy stones over their heads backwards and at jumping leapfrog."[7]

After the Civil War, the army began to recognize the importance of recreational amenities. The South Battery, a fortress that had never fired a cannon in war, was retrofitted for an offi-

THE PARK, *Governors Island, N.Y., 1907, Post Exchange. Postcard.* Left to right: *the gazebo/bandstand, commanding officer's house, and Dutch House. Biweekly band performances were the norm. Author's collection.*

THE PARK *looking north, ca. 1915, Chas. R. Vagler. Postcard. Author's collection.*

cers' club. The post band played in the gazebo, tennis was popular, and prisoners tended the increasing number of gardens. An article in *Scribner's* in 1881 compared the island to the eighteenth-century governor's retreat. The imagery is bucolic: "sylvan calm," rippling spring grass, a hen and her chickens in the yard of Fort Jay, a "superb lawn," and "foliage hanging duskily against the gray and crimson sky."[8]

PUBLIC PARK, 1870–1920

AFTER THE DEATH OF Major General Winfield Scott Hancock in 1886, a lengthy period of peace, coupled with the lack of a constituency for creating a first-class army base on Governors Island, left a vacuum that allowed the park issue to reappear. These discussions, which endured only over a period of thirteen years, were precursors of the post–World War I airport debates; the word *park* in these earlier records may easily be substituted for *landing field* in the later records.

In July 1888, U.S. representative Francis B. Spinola of New York–the first Italian American to sit in Congress–introduced a bill in the House asking permission for the park commissioners of New York City "to improve and beautify Governors Island in conjunction with a public park to be laid out on said island."[9] The House Committee on Military Affairs reported favorably on the bill, citing a severe lack of open space in Lower Manhattan owing to such encroachments as commercial office buildings into City Hall Park, the Hudson River Railroad into St. John's Park, and the Elevated and an immigration depot into Battery Park. At a time when the influx of immigrants was at a peak, the bill implied that with diminishing recreational facilities downtown, a park on the island would be a healthful outlet for the poor.

It is to be regretted that the General Government was ever allowed to possess itself of Governor's Island. The site is most charming and salubrious for a park and pleasure ground; and had it been devoted to those purposes, its accessibility from the city would have rendered it a favorite resort of our citizens.

(TITLE UNKNOWN, *DAILY GRAPHIC*, SEPTEMBER 18, 1873, UNPAGINATED.)

No records have been found regarding the reactions to this bill from either the army or the interest groups favoring the proposition. The New York Society for Parks and Playgrounds became active at this time, and its members may have been among Spinola's supporters. An August 25, 1888, piece in *Harper's Weekly,* signed by Paul Leicester Ford, traced the history of the military decline of Governors Island and suggested "the near approach of the time when the battalion shall issue from the sally port of Fort Columbus for the last time, and Governor's Island shall become once more a sylvan haunt of peace."[10]

Although the Senate took no action on the bill, the park idea persisted in Congress. In December 1897, Representative Thomas J. Bradley from New

BILL *to turn Governors Island into a public park, December 17, 1897, U.S. House of Representatives. Courtesy of National Archives, College Park, Md.*

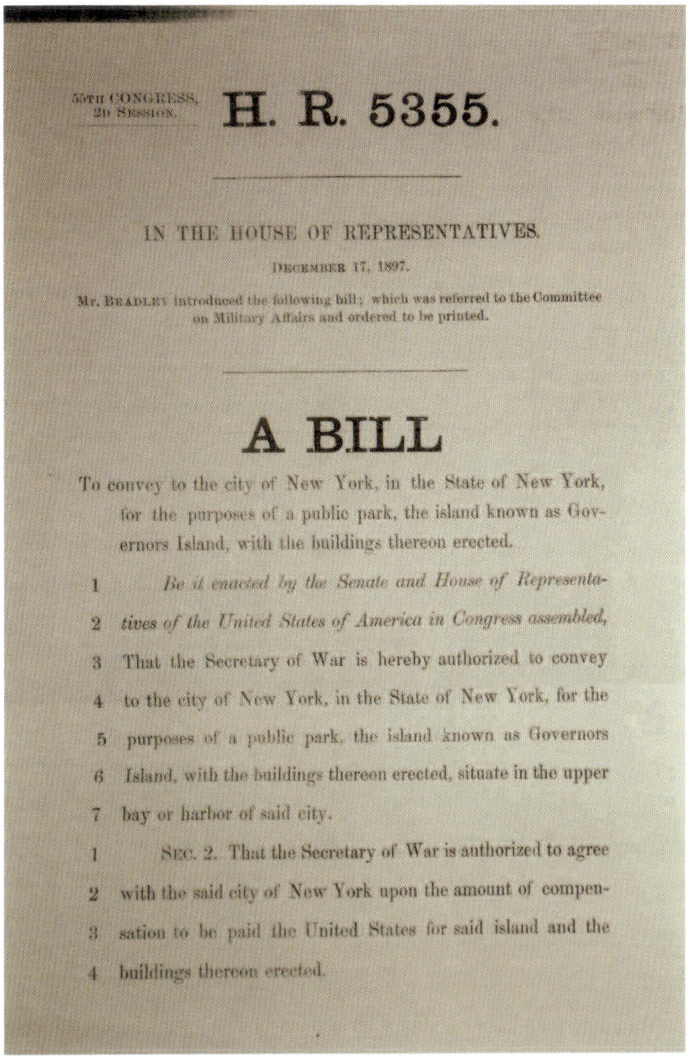

55TH CONGRESS, 2D SESSION.

H. R. 5355.

IN THE HOUSE OF REPRESENTATIVES.

DECEMBER 17, 1897.

Mr. BRADLEY introduced the following bill; which was referred to the Committee on Military Affairs and ordered to be printed.

A BILL

To convey to the city of New York, in the State of New York, for the purposes of a public park, the island known as Governors Island, with the buildings thereon erected.

Be it enacted by the Senate and House of Representatives of the United States of America in Congress assembled, That the Secretary of War is hereby authorized to convey to the city of New York, in the State of New York, for the purposes of a public park, the island known as Governors Island, with the buildings thereon erected, situate in the upper bay or harbor of said city.

SEC. 2. That the Secretary of War is authorized to agree with the said city of New York upon the amount of compensation to be paid the United States for said island and the buildings thereon erected.

York County introduced an additional bill in the House to fortify Spinola's legislative effort. This act—presaging an agreement a century later—mandated the conveyance of Governors Island from the federal government to the City of New York at a price to be agreed upon between the city and federal authorities.[11] The city's parks commissioner would have the legal authority to develop Governors Island as a park. By this time, however, the army was back in control and staking its claim. A letter from the Army Corps of Engineers used the same rationale that had been proposed earlier—that the island be transformed into a park—to justify the military's use of it: storage and residential space were at a premium, and "every other site [in the city] which could be made at all adequate for the military is already occupied for commercial or public use."[12]

In 1901, New York's lieutenant governor Timothy Woodruff put an end to the park controversy. Writing to Governor Benjamin B. Odell to support a state bill transferring the lands under water to the United States in order to increase the military presence on Governors Island, he declared: "of course the proposal to take Governors Island for the [city] government to use as a park is simple absurdity....The island is an absolute necessity for military uses, unless the defenses of the harbor and the transaction of all military business at that point is to be abandoned."[13]

Although within the military there was a growing understanding of the important relationship between recreation and performance for the rank and file, this information apparently did not translate into action for the soldiers' benefit. This deficiency is illustrated by some of the free-time activities offered mostly to the upper echelons on Governors Island prior to World War I. In 1904, the army used War Department funds to transform the South Battery clubhouse into a multipurpose recreation facility. A theater and dining room were reserved specifically for officers and their families, as were many outdoor facilities. The parade ground, when not in use for triweekly dress parades, became a "private" golf course, and a nearby tennis court provided a recreational outlet for the young people living in Nolan Park. Bike riding along the perimeter of the island was a popular sport for the wives and daughters of the military officials.

The rigorous daily drills provided enlisted men with exercise, but extracurricular recreational amenities were limited. In 1900, with a $5,000 gift from William E. Dodge, the YMCA opened one of its first military outposts on Governors Island. In praise of the group's work, the commanding officer reviewed the offerings: "You can read the papers and books and indulge in social intercourse of a helpful kind. It will make you a better, cleaner man than indulging in those enjoyments which make it necessary for us often to punish you."[14] Although having a decidedly moral bent (but believing that young soldiers would be brought to "Christian thought by way of the muscles"), the outpost did offer a gymnasium where "the

YMCA, *Fort Jay, N.Y., n.d., A. M. Simon. Postcard. Author's collection.*

YMCA, *April 17, 1902, Dunn (no first name given). Illustration in* Leslie's Weekly. *The Young Men's Christian Association opened in 1900 to provide "Christian thought by way of the muscles." Author's collection.*

A LIVELY FENCING *match in the YMCA gymnasium, April 17, 1902, Dunn (no first name given). Illustration in* Leslie's Weekly. *Author's collection.*

YMCA GAME ROOM, *April 17, 1902, Dunn (no first name given). Illustration in* Leslie's Weekly. *Here was another recreational outlet for the soldiers. Author's collection.*

RECREATION BUILDING *(250 Men), n.d., unknown photographer. Scrapbook photograph. Prefabricated post–World War I recreation building. Courtesy of National Archives, College Park, Md.*

OFFICERS' RECREATION BUILDING, *n.d., unknown photographer. Scrapbook photograph. Courtesy of National Archives, College Park, Md.*

men fence and punch the bag." There were also a billiards room, a library, and a lunchroom, where a pie cost five cents.[15]

Like the Civil War prisoners, early-twentieth-century soldiers eagerly sought opportunities for physical recreation. As part of the 1904 clubhouse construction, the army opened a bowling alley in the basement of the South Battery with its own separate entrance for the soldiers. But clearly that was not enough. That same year, absent an indoor exercise facility for the winter months, the soldiers on Governors Island took the matter into their own hands. They contributed from their own pay to equip one of the arsenal storehouses as a gymnasium.[16] In subsequent years, the men also began to play on competitive sports teams. In 1917, the Fort Jay Eleven were trounced 24 to 0 by the Naval Reserves football team, and 7 to 0 by Fort Slocum.[17] Then World War I intervened, recreation became a low priority, and prefabricated structures gradually took over the landfill/playing field added at the turn of the century. Save for the parade ground where soldiers did sit-ups and jumping jacks and a grassy area in the center of officers' housing in Nolan Park, there remained not an iota of open space on Governors Island.

Society women have ordained that Major-General and Mrs. Grant's reception and garden party on Governor's Island, next Wednesday, for the benefit of the Army Relief Fund, shall be a success weather or no. The admission ticket is only a dollar, but every dainty girl loves a soldier....To give the list of patronesses and fair matrons and maids enlisted for this noble charity would be to reprint the *Social Register*....Not to be on Governor's Island from 2 to 6:30 P.M. next Wednesday...argues yourself out of the Army set and the smartest set of society.

("TOWN TOPICS," *VANITY FAIR*, MAY 21, 1908, 6.)

GARDEN PARTIES, 1900–1965

GOVERNORS ISLAND WAS CLOSED to public visitation ever since it had become a military reservation in 1800–except for Garden Party Day. Held annually in late May or early June (except during World Wars I and II), this happy event reveals much about the island's social history. It also indicates a rare truce in the battle between the island's use for defense and its use for public pleasure. Garden parties were a means to celebrate military might–not from the point of view of the defense of New York, but rather from a national public-relations perspective. At the same time, the parties were also end-of-season outings for the cream of New York City society and the military elite.

Rain or shine, men, women, and their daughters swarmed to Governors Island on Garden Party Day. The putative excuse was to contribute to the Army Relief Society, a nonprofit organization founded in the nineteenth century to aid soldiers' widows and orphans. As with all benefit events, however, it was the organization's socially and politically connected trustees and commit-

(Left to right) **MRS. FREDERICK DENT GRANT**, *Mrs. Elihu Root Jr. (the Grants' daughter-in-law), Mrs. Francis M. Gibson, and General Fredrick Dent Grant, May 1908, George Grantham Bain. Courtesy of George Grantham Bain Collection, Prints and Photographs Division, Library of Congress, Washington, D.C.*

teewomen who raised the money for the cause, more than $26,000 in 1929, and brought guests to the island, two to three thousand people per event. Among the hostesses on the island between 1904 and 1916 were Mrs. Daniel Lamont, wife of the former secretary of war and head of the Northern Pacific Railroad, and Mrs. Robert Lee Bullard, wife of the polo-playing commanding officer. Both women were presidents of the Army Relief Society for a time.

The patrons and patronesses of the garden party, in addition to President and Mrs. [Woodrow] Wilson, include Secretary of War and Mrs. [Newton D.] Baker, Governor and Mrs. [Charles S.] Whitman... Mayor and Mrs. [John Purroy] Mitchell...Colonel and Mrs. Theodore Roosevelt, the best known officials, national, State, and municipal, here and in Washington.

("ARMY RELIEF GARDEN PARTY," *NEW YORK TIMES*, MAY 25, 1916, 13.)

Joining these ladies were Mrs. Henry Bischoff, wife of a New York State Supreme Court justice and herself a Relief Society vice president, as well as honorary vice presidents Mrs. Henry L. Stimson, wife of another former secretary of war, and Mrs. Jacob Van Vechtin Olcott, wife of the Congressman from Manhattan's Sixteenth District.[18] Olivia Sage, widow of railroad owner and financial investor Russell Sage and a noted philanthropist in her own right, was an annual contributor to the event.[19]

Governors Island's garden parties were definitely events at which to "see and be seen." Impressive high-society names (including Vanderbilt and Stuyvesant Fish) appeared on the lists of attendees, as did such political notables as New York governor Benjamin B. Odell Jr. and the wife and daughter of New York City mayor William J. Gaynor. The guests' clothing was also

FERRY PASS, *ca. 1919, Headquarters Fort Jay. Scrapbook item. Note the rules of conduct. Author's collection.*

REVERSE SIDE *of ferry pass, note by Alexander Hamilton, great-grandson of the founder of the Coast Guard, ca. 1919. Scrapbook item. Author's collection.*

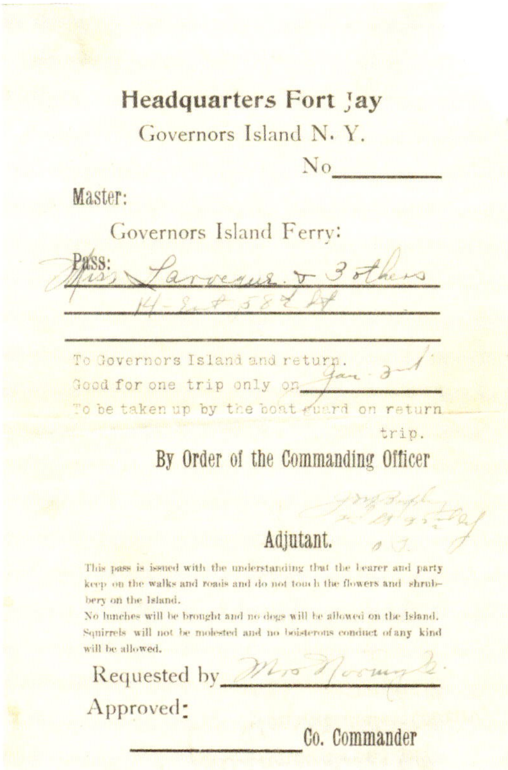

Headquarters Fort Jay

Governors Island N. Y.

No________

Master:

Governors Island Ferry:

Pass: [illegible]

To Governors Island and return.
Good for one trip only on [illegible]
To be taken up by the boat guard on return trip.

By Order of the Commanding Officer

Adjutant.

This pass is issued with the understanding that the bearer and party keep on the walks and roads and do not touch the flowers and shrubbery on the Island.
No lunches will be brought and no dogs will be allowed on the Island.
Squirrels will not be molested and no boisterous conduct of any kind will be allowed.

Requested by [illegible]

Approved:

________ Co. Commander

Party to Governors Island
for fancy dress ball
Joy, his sister, cousin,
myself.

"Wonderful Time"

noteworthy. Army personnel were resplendent in dress uniforms, but it was the women's attire that attracted attention. In 1911, Mrs. Frederick Dent Grant wore a dress of "blue marquisette over white satin." Black-and-white-striped or dotted silk dresses were popular. Black hats seemed to be the order of the day.[20]

The *General Hancock* and *Governor Meigs,* two army ferries decorated with flags, left Manhattan every fifteen minutes between 2:00 and 6:00 P.M. on Garden Party Day.[21] Once on Governors Island, patrons were treated to an afternoon of frivolity: refreshments, fortune-telling, silhouette cutting, band concerts, vaudeville shows, concerts by the Twenty-ninth Infantry band in a grandstand in Nolan Park, and dancing in the Officers' Club. The food tents run by women such as Edyth Patten Corbin, wife of the major general of the newly named Atlantic Division, and her stepdaughter Catherine Usher Parson were a highlight of one afternoon.[22]

The lemonade tent, run in 1904 by the daughter of Chaplain Edward Goodwin, was a treat to the eye as well as to the tongue. The tent was trimmed with vines, and the daughters of island residents were specially dressed to serve their patrons. *Vanity Fair* reported the details in the same vein as island weddings: "the girls wore white gowns, with small white muslin aprons, red, white, and blue belts and little silk cash bags of the same patriotic colors."[23] Over the years, other tents were added. The daughter of the New York Navy Yard admiral commandant sold cigarettes in one. A flower booth in a tent made of American flags with a fountain in its center was a particular hit. Homemade cakes were always moneymakers. One comely salesgirl, Dorothy Cronkhite, daughter of Adelbert Cronkhite, a rising star in the army, brought in eighty dollars for the Relief Fund's coffers.

An all-important aspect of the garden parties was the opportunity for the army to display its

FLORENCE KIMBALL, *Governors Island, May 27, 1908, George Grantham Bain. A girl offers goodies to Florence Kimball, daughter of Colonel Amos S. Kimball, assistant quartermaster general of the U.S. Army. Courtesy of George Grantham Bain Collection, Prints and Photographs Division, Library of Congress, Washington, D.C.*

AMERICAN FLAG TENT, *May 1908, George Grantham Bain. A flower booth was installed inside the tent. Courtesy of George Grantham Bain Collection, Prints and Photographs Division, Library of Congress, Washington, D.C.*

CIGARETTE GIRL, *Governors Island, May 1908, George Grantham Bain. Courtesy of George Grantham Bain Collection, Prints and Photographs Division, Library of Congress, Washington, D.C.*

discipline and prowess. This display initially consisted of traditional military ritual. There were full-dress parades and the escort of color. The American flag and the banners of the Governors Island regiment and others were marched in front of the soldiers lined up at attention by rank. In addition, some drills required the soldiers to follow specific musical cues and to crawl on their bellies in sham battles. In this public way, the army instilled respect for rank and authority. For the visitors, it was simply all colorful entertainment.

Between the world wars, reenactments of historical battles, polo matches, and fireworks were added to Garden Party Day. Of course, the hostilities selected for review were always ones in which the army was victorious. In 1928, the staged capture of the French village of Fleville from the Germans provided interest when one of the props, a live goat, went missing. In 1930, a two-day garden party marked the centennial of the opening of the Oregon Trail with a recreation of the battle of Red Buttes. The story told in the elaborate program describes (in language unacceptable today) a pending battle between a wagon train and "sanguinary red-skinned savages." The tale continues: "Then, at the last moment, when it would seem that the little pioneer company is doomed to extermination, scalping and worse, a body of soldiery with Old Glory floating proudly at its head, swoops down upon the attacking red-skin horde from another angle, and the aborigines are routed."[25]

Other demonstrations at the garden parties developed into shows of military might and evolving technology. These shows were helped by an active army public-relations office stationed on the island. The juxtaposition of old and new military techniques was now a painful reminder of how warfare was changing. In one afternoon, visitors applauded feathered flight in the pigeon derbies as well as popular demonstrations of air force bombardment and pursuit planes, the latter accompanied by a smoke screen prepared by the Chemical Warfare Service.[26]

Beginning in 1949, Governors Island's Garden Party Day became part of Armed Forces Day, a celebration of all the military services that had recently been united under a single U.S.

LIGGETT HALL *as the stage for the army's display of the newest military vehicles and armaments, ca. 1938, unknown photographer. Courtesy of Frank R. McCoy Collection, U.S. Army Military History Institute, Carlisle, Pa.*

Department of Defense. Lasting until 1965, the year of the base transfer to the Coast Guard (an event attended by around thirty thousand visitors), the day's activities appear to have taken on more or less importance depending on threats from abroad. In 1951, Russian satellite superiority and aggression in Korea made displays of "the latest ground and air weapons and techniques" a military imperative.[27] The army again juxtaposed the old and the new. Reenactments of Governors Island's Revolutionary War history in Castle Williams and Fort Jay were accompanied by elaborate exhibits of modern-day warfare set up in front of Liggett Hall. From pistols to Panther Jet Navy fighters, "streamlined" jeeps to Patton tanks, walkie-talkies to examples of chemical warfare techniques, all became part of the Cold War display on the island.[28]

THE EMPIRE STATE BUILDING *serves as an eerie backdrop to a tank demonstration, ca. 1938, unknown photographer. Courtesy of Frank R. McCoy Collection, U.S. Army Military History Institute, Carlisle, Pa.*

POLO, POOLS, AND CIRCUS CLOWNS, 1920–1996

SINCE GOVERNORS ISLAND'S RACETRACK days in the late eighteenth century, horses had been important to it. The army had stables for officers' horses and for mules that carted arms and supplies. Military maneuvers and reviews were always held on horseback, and some officers enjoyed a daily ride around the enlarged two-and-a-half-mile perimeter of the island. A ribbon was even awarded to the handsomest horse at the annual Fort Jay

PARADE OF HORSE CARTS *and horses, possibly part of the annual Fort Jay transportation and horse show, n.d., unknown photographer. Courtesy of Still Pictures Branch, National Archives, College Park, Md.*

Transportation and Horse Show.[29] Following World War I, peacetime and the removal of some temporary structures brought still another use for horses: polo. In contrast to a park for the poor, polo, with its hierarchical social structure and its country club aspects, seemed a fitting sport for the island. Polo also held upper-class appeal and was a way to entertain visiting dignitaries.

Inaugurated in 1921 by polo aficionado Robert Lee Bullard, commander of the army's Second Corps Area, and actively used for twenty years, the Governors Island polo field is still known for its tournaments. Teams from the regular army, the National Guard, ROTCs at eastern colleges, and private polo clubs throughout the region competed regularly against two champion Governors Island teams, the Blues and the Yellows.[30] From the season's opener in the first week of June through well into October, famous horsemen felicitously stationed on the island–J. L. Holman, W. Houghton, Harry Collins, and George W. Reade Jr.–rode the Governors Island teams to victory.[31] The events were an occasion for pomp and circumstance and for raising funds for various causes. Commanding officers–from Bullard in the 1920s to Major General Dennis Nolan in the 1930s to Lieutenant General Hugh A. Drum, commander of the First Army, in 1940–had the honor of bestowing prizes such as the military's coveted Colyer Cup upon the Governors Island victors.[32]

Some memories, however, are less happy. A former player with Squadron A in Manhattan–a team often in the news–recalled having difficulty controlling his army-issue polo pony during play on Governors Island. The rider had to spring off his horse as it made a run for the Hudson River.[33] One former "army brat," whose Olympic equestrian champion father was stationed on Governors Island in the late 1930s, hazily remembered polo games taking place "right at the time that the Germans were building tanks."[34]

INVITATION *to a luncheon honoring the international military equestrian team, November 3, 1936, unknown designer. Author's collection.*

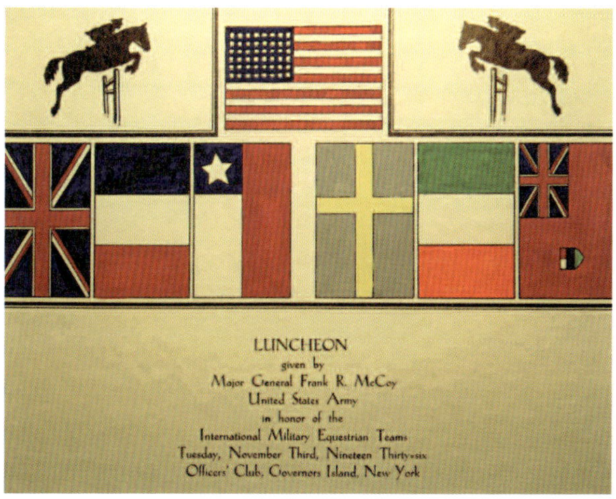

UNKNOWN POLO PLAYERS *in action on Governors Island, n.d., unknown photographer. Courtesy of Still Pictures Branch, National Archives, College Park, Md.*

Even as polo continued to be a popular sport throughout the 1930s, other athletic opportunities persisted, though they too reflected the military hierarchy. A small swimming pool, known as the "Little Pool," had been included with a new YMCA in the late 1920s and was open to all, but under the WPA a small, properly laid out golf course for officers was built into the glacis (downward slope) of nineteenth-century Fort Jay. In 1941, the army erected some recreation buildings between Craig and Gresham Roads that were assigned separately to officers and soldiers. Even the new Morris Memorial Field had facilities based on rank—football and baseball for enlisted men and the regulation polo field for officers.

The union of recreation and the military was perfectly enacted in the fall of 1941, when the last official polo game was played on Governors Island. In place of the Blues and the Yellows, the army brought in two teams of star civilian players (including Stewart Igelhart and Cecil Smith, both champion scorers) to Morris Memorial Field for one last show. The Army Relief Society was the beneficiary. For those who were not playing or watching the sport, on the north end of the polo field was an exhibit of America's modern military machines. Shortly thereafter, absent both horses and players, polo on Governors Island came to an end.[35]

Lineup for a polo game

GOVERNORS ISLAND BLUES	GOALS	FREEBOOTERS	GOALS
Lieut. Holman	3	J. Brascher	1
Capt. St. John	2	H. Barker	3
Lieut. Karlson	0	W. Erath	0
Capt. Rumbaugh	1	W. Haskell Jr.	0

Tea will be held at the Officers' Club after the game.

("GOVERNORS ISLAND TRIUMPHS AT POLO," *NEW YORK TIMES*, SEPTEMBER 21, 1925, 25; OFFICERS' CLUB, RG 92,15/080.1, NATIONAL ARCHIVES, COLLEGE PARK, MD.)

After World War II, the army built additional recreational facilities for the increasing number of families with children in order to widen the appeal of this physically isolated base. A large pool adjoined six baseball fields. An attempt was even made to return the island to a bucolic landscape. In a letter to New York

THE LITTLE POOL, *ca. 1940s, unknown photographer. Opened in the late 1920s, the pool added a family recreation facility to the island. Courtesy of G. S. Grunert Collection, U.S. Army Military History Institute, Carlisle, Pa.*

City parks commissioner Robert Moses, General Walter Bedell Smith sent his thanks for donations of trees that "bloom like a city park along the best Moses pattern."[36]

Beginning in 1947 and repeated in various guises until the Coast Guard's departure in 1996, one day a year on Governors Island was especially devoted to the children and families of the military personnel there. Organized by the army post (and later by the Coast Guard Support Center), this day provided an opportunity to raise funds specifically for island activities, such as the Boy and Girl Scout troops and sports programs. More important, unlike the garden parties—which encouraged a socially elite group of outsiders to enjoy the island—the army's circus and Coast Guard Day were designed to foster a spirit of community among island residents.[37]

In the official honors department a 6-year-old sergeant's son marched off with the military accolade…for his impersonation of General of the Army Douglas MacArthur.

("AT ARMY PARTY FOR THE YOUNGSTERS," *NEW YORK TIMES*, JUNE 2, 1951, 17. COPYRIGHT © 1951 BY THE NEW YORK TIMES CO. REPRINTED WITH PERMISSION.)

In the late 1940s and through the 1950s, the army made every effort to re-create a lively atmosphere on circus day. Wives of some of the military leaders on the island and the chaplain of St. Cornelius Chapel dressed up as clowns. One year the latter rode a white canvas horse. The sideshows, with caged house cats standing in for tigers and monkeys lent by the Central Park Zoo, were popular, as were visits by real-life stars such as Captain Video. Small children could ride a makeshift train that the engineering department had devised by using its tractors. The food booths, reminiscent of those from the

CIRCUS DAY *on Governors Island, n.d., unknown photographer. Circus Day was a popular annual event. General and Mrs. Walter Bedell Smith enjoy hot dogs with* (right to left) *Colonel Kent Lambert and clown Dorothy J. McGrew. Courtesy of Palmer McGrew.*

SANTA CLAUS *visits a sleeping soldier (regardless of rank), 1930, unknown photographer. Courtesy of Still Pictures Branch, National Archives, College Park, Md.*

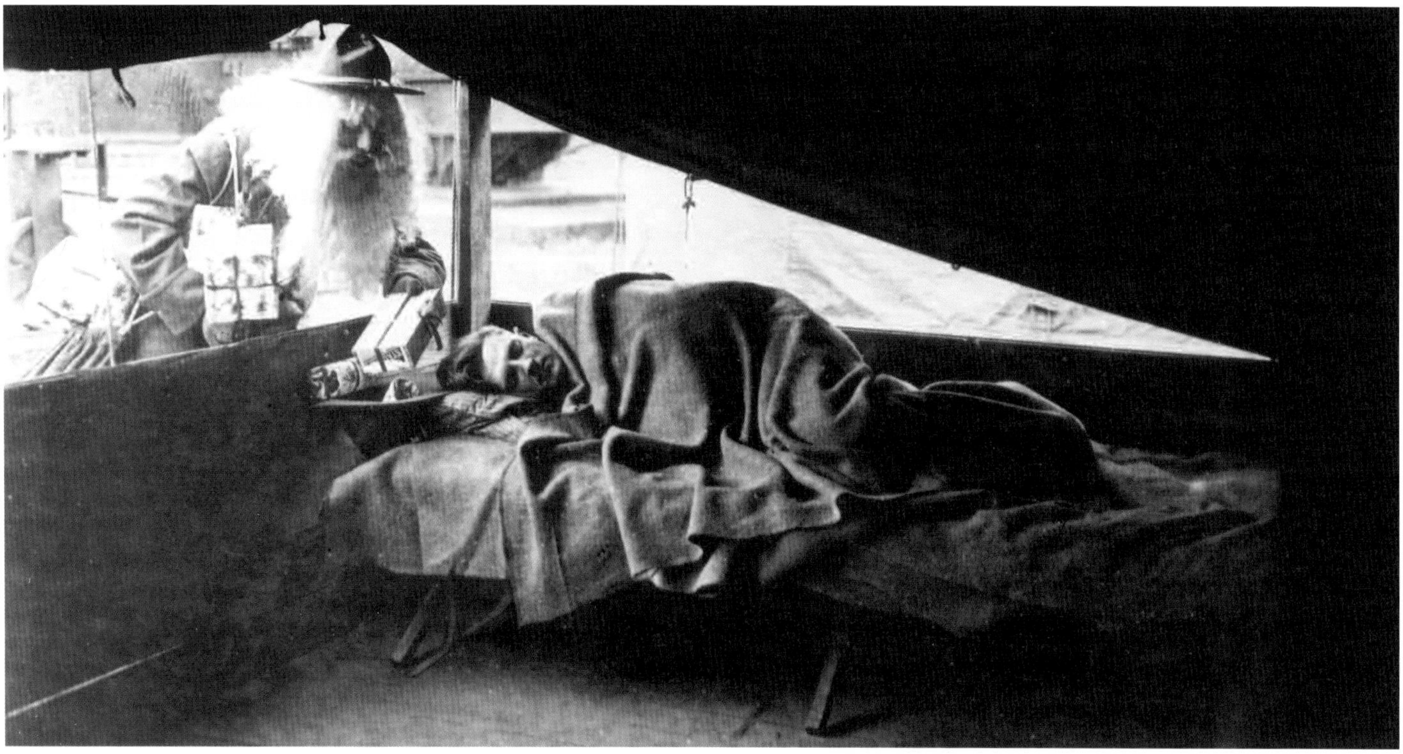

SANTA ARRIVING *by helicopter (having traded in his reindeer) on December 25, 1954, unknown photographer. He was greeted by Post Commander John S. Roosma and the children of Governors Island, each of whom was given a present. Courtesy of Garret Roosma.*

garden parties, were run by army wives. Mrs. Walter Bedell Smith's angel food cake was a hit.[38]

The military aspects of Governors Island were ever present at these events. The circus tents were the pyramid-shaped shelters used to house overflow recruits. Prisoners from Castle Williams, under the watchful eyes of armed guards, drove in the tent stakes. Yet there were modifications. Instead of military music, the Fort Jay band played "circus airs." Children marched in the obligatory parade. One year several cowboys and cowgirls, mounted on horses lent by Squadron A, were at the lead. In line behind them, doubtless showing little military precision, were hundreds of children clad as clowns, hula dancers, elephants, and even the Island Cookbook. At the end came the "perambulator parade," army mothers wheeling their costumed babies. In true military tradition, the children marched past General Courtney Hodges or General Walter Bedell Smith, commanders of the First Army. Following the review, a panel of judges awarded much-awaited ribbons for the best costume in place of Distinguished Service Medals.[39]

After 1965, the Coast Guard continued these celebrations for island residents, but on a more modest scale. On the first Saturday of August to mark Coast Guard Day, the village green in front of Building 400 (formerly Liggett Hall) was annually the scene of picnics and children's games. The playing fields were busy with competitive sports events, and decorated bicycles replaced the army's costume parade. As described by a former resident, "It [was] the best block party you've ever been to."[40]

PUBLIC PARK REDUX, 1965–2001

IN THE 1960S, NEW FEDERAL OUTDOOR open-space programs and the reinvention of New York City's waterfront allowed the vision of Governors Island as a public park to be reintroduced. As the army was preparing to deactivate the island in 1965, New York City mayor Robert F. Wagner explored the possibility of the city's purchase of the island. The expense was too daunting, but he thought there might be another way. To avoid meeting an assessed valuation of $16,250,000 for the land and buildings, dealing with the concomitant problems of demolition and development, and providing the necessary ferry transportation, Mayor Wagner suggested keeping the island in federal ownership. A relatively new program whereby excess property, such as Fort Hancock and Floyd Bennett Field, were eligible to become part of a national recreation area (ultimately known as Gateway National Park) seemed to be a perfect solution. In a letter to Defense Secretary Robert S. McNamara, Wagner used language that differed from the nineteenth-century bills that had tried to justify the island's change of use. Instead of finding a recreational outlet for the downtown Manhattan poor, Wagner aimed to please a wide constituency: "The island," he wrote, "would make available open space recreation in a centralized and attractive location easily accessible to the residents of the City and the Region."[41] But the Coast Guard had other plans.

Another decade passed with the island open only to the military. And then in 1975, fostered by the spirit of the American Bicentennial, the Coast Guard opened Governors Island to the public. On four Sundays between May and August, more than ten thousand visitors descended on the island. They simply picked up tickets at tourist venues through-

THE LAST COAST GUARD DAY *on Governors Island, August 4, 1996, unknown publisher. Envelope. Author's collection.*

out the city and hopped a ferry to learn about the Coast Guard and explore one of New York's "hidden islands." A letter to the commanding officer explained the gesture's importance: "As a Native New Yorker I have always enjoyed viewing Governors Island, but only from afar...it was with great pleasure that my wife and I took advantage of the opportunity afforded us to visit the island."[42] Although the population of visitors was far more eclectic, many of this annual occasion's offerings resembled earlier army garden parties. Coast Guard officers and enlisted men and their wives, many clad in homemade colonial costumes, guided the guests on tours of Castle Williams. The Governor's Island Band played alfresco concerts. There was the requisite bake sale, but other foods reflected the changed ethnicity within the military: Filipino and Hispanic treats and shish kebab.[43]

As in the past, demonstrations were also a part of the visitors' fare. The various Coast Guard training schools located on the island displayed their wares outside Building 400. Historic battle reenactments took place on the golf course. This time, however, instead of examining jeeps and airplanes, tourists climbed aboard buoy tenders, cutters, and

About 2 o'clock, when the head of the naval fleet appeared off the Battery, the mist had thickened so as to shut out the statue....The next puff of wind disclosed in the leader's trail a procession extending way up the North River....For the hour or more that the procession continued the crowds on Governor's Island were charmed with a series of dissolving views, the rising of the mist revealing an even prettier picture of steamers, barges, war boats, tugs, excursion floats, ferryboats, and every other kind of craft, dressed in their gayest attire....Thus, from Governor's Island visitors saw the beginning and the culmination of the greatest gathering of the fleet.

("SCENES ON THE WATER," *NEW YORK TIMES*, OCTOBER 29, 1886, 2.)

tugs to watch a Coast Guard helicopter conduct search-and-rescue exercises.

The open houses continued into the 1990s, but there are indications that the influx of visitors came at a cost, the same as in any close-knit community. Although island residents enjoyed dressing up in period costumes and showing off their neatly pressed uniforms (required attire for the day), they also had to make sure that the grounds around their homes were tended and the children were carefully watched. A notice in the *Coast Guard Gazette* on June 26, 1992, sounded an ominous note: "Although we have not had noticeable problems in the past, there is always a possibility of opportunistic criminals....Keep your doors locked, don't leave toys, bikes, etc. lying about unattended."[44]

The soil, naturally good, and consisting of about 75 acres, when improved into walks, groves and gardens cannot otherwise than present a delightful scene of recreation...particularly after the fatigues and cares of business....We may expect soon to see it metamorphosed from a neglected spot to a seat of taste and rural elegance.

(TITLE UNKNOWN, *DAILY GRAPHIC*, JULY 11, 1791, UNPAGINATED.)

By the time the Coast Guard base officially closed, Governors Island had become a place akin to a historic New England or Virginia town. Officers' children and enlisted men and women fondly remember baseball and bowling teams, playing Marco Polo in the big pool, and sledding on the glacis. In time, the public was also invited to enjoy, from the vantage point of the island, the spectacle of replicas of the tall ships in New York Harbor and fireworks–both activities reminiscent of the old nineteenth-century celebrations.

In 2003, twenty-two acres of Governors Island, including Fort Jay and Castle Williams, became a national monument under the jurisdiction of the U.S. Department of the Interior. The remainder of the island was transferred back to the State of New York for one dollar. In the deed is a requirement that might have made Francis Spinola and Robert Wagner smile: "Governors Island is to be redeveloped for public benefit purposes, including educational facilities and new public parkland."[45] The recreational legacy has finally arrived.

Coast Guard Patches

ca. 1970s

ca. 1970–1980s

1986

ca. 1980–88

pre-1985

ca. 1990s

ca. 1990s

mid-1980s

n.d.

1991

1998

pre-1993

1984

ca. 1980

ca. 1968–85

mid-1980s

ca. 1970s–1980s

1992

pre-1984

1997

ca. 1970s–1980s

1984

ca. 1980s

1990

n.d.

Appendixes

Appendix A
Major Headquarters on Governors Island, 1878–1965

1878–1891 Headquarters, Division of the Atlantic
Transferred to Governors Island July 1, 1878
Discontinued July 3, 1891

1878–1911 Headquarters, Department of the East
Transferred to Governors Island July 1, 1878
Discontinued July 1, 1911

1904–1907 Headquarters, Atlantic Division
Created January 15, 1904
Discontinued June 30, 1907

1911–1913 Headquarters, Eastern Division
Created July 1, 1911
Discontinued February 15, 1913

1913–1920 Headquarters, Eastern Department
Created February 16, 1913
Discontinued September 1, 1920

1920–1942 Headquarters, Second Corps Area
Created September 1, 1920
Redesignated Second Service Command July 22, 1942

1932–1933 Headquarters, First Army
First Army constituted as an inactive unit of the army and assigned First, Second, and Third Corps Areas August 9, 1932
First Army activated at Fort Jay more or less as a "paper" army September 2, 1933

1939 Headquarters, First Army–Second Corps Area
Second Corps Area commander assigned command of First Army September 1, 1939

1940 Headquarters, First Army–Second Corps Area
Command of First Army and Second Corps Area separated October 1940, and Headquarters, First Army, expanded to a complete staff

1941–1942 Headquarters, Eastern Theater of Operations
Activated December 21, 1941
Redesignated Eastern Defense Command, March 20, 1942

1942–1946 Headquarters, Eastern Defense Command
Eastern Defense Command, First Army, commanded by army commander March 20, 1942–October 10, 1943
First Army embarks for Europe October 12, 1943
Eastern Defense Command discontinued March 1, 1946

1942–1946 Second Service Command
Second Corps Area redesignated Second Service Command July 22, 1942
Army commander assumes command of Second Service Command June 11, 1946–July 1, 1946
Second Service Command discontinued July 1, 1946

1946–1965 Headquarters, First Army, returned to Fort Jay under reorganization of Zone of Interior into six army areas June 11, 1946

1965 Handover of Governors Island to the Eastern Area and Third Coast Guard District, New York

Source: Anastazio Carlos Mariano Azoy, *Three Centuries under Three Flags: The Story of Governors Island from 1637* (Governors Island, N.Y.: Headquarters First Army, 1951).

Appendix B
Army Commanders on Governors Island, 1755–1965

British Commanders and Troops prior to the Revolutionary War

1755 Sir William Pepperell
1755–1775 The Royal Americans
1756 Lord John Campbell
1760 Sir Jeffrey Amherst
1767 Twenty-second Foot
Forty-fourth Foot

American Commanders and Troops during the Revolutionary War

1775 Prescott's Seventh Continental Infantry
1776 Brigadier General John Nixon
Brigadier General Israel Putnam
1776–1783 Various British detachments

U.S. Army Commanders

1789–1794 No record
1794 Captain Alexander Thompson
1808 Captain Richard Wiley
1810–1813 Colonel Henry Burbeck
1810–1813 Colonel Jonathan Williams
1811 Major Amos Stoddard

U.S. Army, Eastern Department

1821 Brevet Major General (Brigadier General) Winfield Scott
1823 Brevet Major General (Brigadier General) Edmund P. Gaines
1825 Brevet Major General (Brigadier General) Winfield Scott
1827 Brevet Major General (Brigadier General) Edmund P. Gaines

U.S. Army, Division of the Atlantic

1878 Major General Winfield Scott Hancock
1883 Lieutenant General Philip H. Sheridan
1884 Major General Winfield Scott Hancock

1886 General Philip H. Sheridan (Washington, D.C.)
Major General John M. Schofield
1888 Major General Oliver O. Howard

U.S. Army, Department of the East
1891 Major General John M. Schofield
1891 Major General Oliver O. Howard
1894 Major General Nelson A. Miles
1895 Major General Thomas H. Ruger
1897 Major General Wesley Merritt
1898 Brigadier General Royal T. Frank
Brigadier General George L. Gillespie
Major General William R. Shafter
1899 Major General Wesley Merritt
1900 Major General John R. Brooke
1902 Major General Arthur MacArthur
Major General Adna R. Chaffee

U.S. Army, Atlantic Division
1903 Major General Henry C. Corbin
1904 Brigadier General Frederick D. Grant
Major General James F. Wade

U.S. Army, Department of the East
1907 Brigadier General Frederick D. Grant
1908 Major General Leonard Wood

U.S. Army, Eastern Division
1911 Major General Frederick D. Grant
1912 Brigadier General Tasker H. Bliss
Major General Thomas H. Barry

U.S. Army, Eastern Department
1913 Major General Thomas H. Barry
1914 Brigadier General Robert K. Evans
Major General Leonard Wood
1917 Major General J. Franklin Bell
Brigadier General Eli D. Hoyle
1918 Major General William A. Mann
Major General J. Franklin Bell
1919 Major General Thomas H. Barry

U.S. Army, Second Corps Area
1919 Major General Robert L. Bullard
1925 Major General Charles P. Summerall
1927 Major General James H. McRae
Major General Hanson E. Ely
1931 Major General Dennis E. Nolan
1936 Major General Frank R. McCoy

Governors Island, First Army Commanders

November 1938–October 1943
Lieutenant General Hugh A. Drum
October 1943–January 1944
Lieutenant General George Grunert
January 1944–July 1944
General Omar N. Bradley
June 1946–January 1949
General Courtney H. Hodges
February 1949–March 1949
Major General Roscoe B. Woodruff
March 1949–September 1950
General Walter Bedell Smith
October 1950
Major General Roscoe B. Woodruff
November 1950–December 1952
Lieutenant General Willis D. Crittenberger
January 1953–November 1954
Lieutenant General Withers A. Burress
December 1954–July 1957
Lieutenant General Thomas Wade Herren
August 1957–February 1960
Lieutenant General Blackshear M. Bryan
March 1960–March 1962
Lieutenant General Edward J. O'Neill
April 1962–April 1964
Lieutenant General Garrison H. Davidson
May 1964–December 1965
Lieutenant General Robert W. Porter Jr.

Sources: Anastazio Carlos Mariano Azoy, *Three Centuries under Three Flags: The Story of Governors Island from 1637* (Governors Island, N.Y.: Headquarters First Army, 1951); *A Patch of Pride: A History of the First Army* (Governors Island, N.Y.: Headquarters First Army, 1950); Letter to author from Richard J. Sommers, Chief of Patron Services, April 21, 2004, Department of the Army, U.S. Army Military History Institute, Carlisle Barracks, Carlisle, Pa.

Appendix C
Post Commanders, Fort Jay, 1794–1953

1794 Captain Cornelius R. Sedam, Sublegion
1795 Captain Alexander Thompson, Artillery
1808 Captain Richard Wiley, Artillery
1810 Colonel Henry Burbeck, Artillery
1814 Lieutenant Colonel Tallmadge, Infantry
1821 First Lieutenant Giles Porter, Artillery
First Lieutenant Peter Melendy, Artillery
Captain S. Churchill, Artillery
1822 First Lieutenant Giles Porter, Artillery
1823 Captain Milo Mason, Artillery
First Lieutenant W. Wheelright, Artillery
Captain A. C. W. Fanning, Artillery
Captain Milo Mason, Artillery
Captain A. C. W. Fanning, Artillery
1824 First Lieutenant E. Lyon, Artillery
Lieutenant Colonel William McRae, Artillery
1827 Captain R. A. Zantzinger, Artillery
1828 Major I. B. Crane, Artillery
1831 Lieutenant Colonel A. Eustis, Artillery
Major I. B. Crane, Artillery

1833 Major A. C. W. Fanning, Artillery
1834 Captain B. K. Pierce, Artillery
1835 Lieutenant Colonel A. S. Brooks, Artillery
1836 Captain William W. Tompkins, Dragoons
1837 Lieutenant John C. Pemberton, Artillery
Captain William L. McClintock, Artillery
Lieutenant William Hoffman, Infantry
First Lieutenant E. C. Ross, Artillery
1838 Assistant Surgeon Joseph Eaton, Medical Corps
Captain John Erving, Artillery
1839 Lieutenant Colonel A. C. W. Fanning, Artillery
Colonel D. E. Twiggs, Dragoons
Captain Justin Dimick, Artillery
1840 First Lieutenant Joseph Hooker, Artillery
1841 Colonel James Bankhead, Artillery
Captain Charles S. Merchant, Artillery
1842 Lieutenant Colonel A. C. W. Fanning, Artillery
Colonel James Bankhead, Artillery
1847 Captain Gabriel J. Rains, Infantry
1848 Colonel I. B. Crane, Artillery
1850 Major John L. Gardner, Artillery
1852 Major Gabriel J. Rains, Infantry
Lieutenant Colonel John L. Gardner, Artillery
Lieutenant Colonel M. M. Payne, Artillery
Captain John T. Sprague, Infantry
1854 Lieutenant Colonel J. J. Abercrombie, Infantry
1855 Major Electus Backus, Infantry
1857 Major Albermarle Cady, Infantry
1859 Major Theophilus H. Holmes, Infantry
1861 Major Samuel P. Heintzelman, Infantry
Lieutenant Colonel Charles F. Smith, Infantry
Colonel Gustavus Loomis, Infantry
1864 Captain John D. Wilkins, Infantry
Colonel J. D. Bomford, Infantry
1865 Major M. Cogswell, Infantry
Lieutenant Colonel Julius Hayden, Infantry
1867 Lieutenant Colonel Henry D. Wallen, Infantry
1869 Lieutenant Colonel Thomas H. Neill, Infantry
1871 Major M. M. Blunt, Infantry
1873 Major James P. Roy, Infantry
1874 Major R. E. A. Crafton, Infantry
1876 Major Alexander Chambers, Infantry
1877 Captain E. G. Bush, Infantry
1878 Captain J. P. Sanger, Artillery
1880 Captain Thomas Ward, Artillery
Major John Mendenhall, Artillery
1881 Captain Thomas Ward, Artillery
Captain F. L. Guenther, Artillery
1882 Captain W. B. Beck, Artillery
Major R. A. Jackson, Artillery
1886 Captain W. F. Randolph, Artillery
1888 Major M. P. Miller, Artillery
Captain W. B. Beck, Artillery
1889 Major Tully McCrea, Artillery
Captain W. B. Beck, Artillery
Major Tully McCrea, Artillery
1890 Major W. L. Haskin, Artillery
1894 Captain P. H. Ellis, Infantry
Lieutenant Colonel W. S. Worth, Infantry
1898 Captain Luigi Lomia, Artillery
Colonel Thomas H. Barber, Infantry
Captain Thomas R. Adams, Artillery
Lieutenant E. S. Fullerton, Artillery
Major P. H. Ellis, Infantry
Lieutenant Colonel John N. Coe, Infantry
1899 Captain B. K. Roberts, Artillery
1900 Major G. A. Cornish, Infantry
Major E. R. Hills, Artillery
Major A. L. Myer, Infantry
Lieutenant Colonel C. L. Davis, Infantry
1901 Major E. R. Hills, Artillery
Captain John Conklin, Artillery
Captain Archibald Campbell, Artillery
Major W. P. Duvall, Artillery
1902 Colonel W. E. Dougherty, Infantry
1904 Captain John Stafford, Infantry
Colonel F. A. Smith, Infantry
1906 Major Francis P. Fremont, Infantry
Colonel Leven C. Allen, Infantry
1908 Lieutenant Colonel Robert F. Ames, Infantry
Colonel William H. C. Bowen, Infantry
1909 Major Charles L. Beckurts, Infantry
Colonel H. K. Bailey, Infantry
1911 Colonel G. R. Cecil, Infantry
1912 Colonel John S. Mallory, Infantry
1915 Captain M. H. Barry, Coast Artillery Corps
Captain Charles L. Fisher, Coast Artillery Corps
1917 Colonel John C. F. Tillson, Infantry
1920 Lieutenant Colonel John McA. Palmer, Infantry
1921 Lieutenant Colonel William G. Doane, Infantry
Colonel Samson L. Faison, Infantry
1922 Colonel Francis E. Lacey Jr., Infantry
1923 Colonel Charles Gerhardt, Infantry
1924 Lieutenant Colonel James T. Watson, Infantry
Colonel Stanley H. Ford, Infantry
1926 Colonel Edward Croft, Infantry
1928 Colonel Stephen O. Fuqua, Infantry
1929 Lieutenant Colonel Irving J. Phillipson, Infantry
Colonel Albert S. Williams, Infantry
1932 Colonel Joseph A. Marmon, Infantry
1934 Colonel Albert S. Williams, Infantry
1936 Colonel Albert S. Williams, Infantry
1937 Colonel Karl Truesdell, Infantry
1938 Lieutenant Colonel James L. Bradley, Infantry
Colonel Charles H. Rice, Infantry
1939 Colonel Paul W. Baade, Infantry

1941 Lieutenant Colonel Leon E. Norris, Infantry
Colonel Thomas L. Crystal, Infantry
1943 Colonel George S. Beurket, Field Artillery
1946 Colonel Kent C. Lambert, Armor
1951 Colonel N. C. Shea, Artillery
1953 Colonel C. G. Blakeney, Artillery
Colonel John S. Roosma, Military Police Corps

Source: Memorandum to Deputy Post Commander from Post Public Information Officer, November 3, 1954. Courtesy of Garret Roosma.

Appendix D
Coast Guard Commanders, Governors Island, 1966–1995

Commanders, Eastern Area and Third Coast Guard District, New York

1966 Rear Admiral James A. Alger Jr.
1968 Rear Admiral Albert J. Carpenter
1969 Rear Admiral Mark A. Whalen
1970 Rear Admiral Mark A. Whalen
1971 Rear Admiral Benjamin F. Engel
1972 Rear Admiral Benjamin F. Engel

Commanders, Coast Guard, Atlantic Area, Third Coast Guard District, New York

1973 Rear Admiral Benjamin F. Engel
1974 Rear Admiral Benjamin F. Engel
1975 Vice Admiral William F. Rea III
1976 Vice Admiral William F. Rea III
1977 Vice Admiral William F. Rea III
1978 Vice Admiral William F. Rea III
1979 Vice Admiral Robert I. Price
1980 Vice Admiral Robert I. Price
1981 Vice Admiral Robert I. Price
1982 Vice Admiral James S. Gracey
1983 Vice Admiral Wayne E. Caldwell
1984 Vice Admiral Wayne E. Caldwell
1985 Vice Admiral Paul A. Yost
1986 Vice Admiral Paul A. Yost

Commanders, Atlantic Area, New York

1987 Vice Admiral Donald C. Thompson
Rear Admiral George D. Passmore, Jr. (Third Coast Guard District)
1988 Vice Admiral James C. Irwin
1989 Vice Admiral Howard B. Thorsen
1990 Vice Admiral Howard B. Thorsen
1991 Vice Admiral Paul A. Welling
1992 Vice Admiral Paul A. Welling
1993 Vice Admiral Paul A. Welling
1994 Vice Admiral James M. Loy
1995 Vice Admiral James M. Loy

Source: Courtesy of U.S. Coast Guard Historian's Office, Washington, D.C.

Appendix E
"Who's Who in Coast Guard Management, 1969"

Commander J. S. Gracey, Executive Officer, Base New York. First permanent Coast Guard resident.

Hospital Corpsman Master Chief William G. McDermott, Assistant to the Chief Administrative Officer, Dispensary.

Mr. Anthony "Tony" Forlenza, Chief of Printing Branch. Resident of Governors Island since 1948.

Yeoman Master Chief Gerald D. Partridge, Chief of Administrative Services. Responsible for all printed matter from *Governors Island Gazette* to meal cards and invitations to island events.

Lieutenant James A. Shepard, Assistant Chief of Industrial Division. Oversees repairs of all nonfloating units, boats, ships, aids to navigation, and 4,000 buoys.

Gunner's Mate First Class Virgil W. Wilson, Petty Officer in Charge, Base New York Armory. In charge of saluting battery and small arms range. Stores include over 1,000 rifles, shotguns, pistols, and machine guns.

Miss Grace Canary, Principal, P.S. 26.

Boatswains Mate First Class Edgar V. Porch, base theater manager.

Messrs. Frank Onorato and Charley Losalzo, base barbers. Have cut hair on Governors Island since 1929 and 1934, respectively. Joined by Jose Lauz and Joseph Planco in 1969.

Messrs. Cleveland Belgraves, Vaskin Martin, Ara Martin, and Robert Tripi, dry cleaners, laundry, and men's wear shop. Have dry cleaned over 450 uniforms a week. [Replaced by Post Cleaner, Inc. in 1975.]

Mr. Joseph Frank, Food Service Manager, base cafeteria. Resident of Governors Island since 1957.

Chief Warrant Officer Hopkins [no first name given], Chief of General Mess. Supervises 21 commissary men, 31 civilians, and 20 mess cooks.

Lieutenant J. E. Cutright, Treasurer, Officer's Open Mess (CPO Club, with over 1,050 members). Runs a $300,000 annual business.

Mr. Mike Cioppa, Manager, Officers Open Mess. Resident of Governors Island since 1961. Runs package store, dining room, bar, ballroom, and enlisted guest housing.

Mr. Dan Sanders, service station manager.

Mr. Eddie Green, service station chief mechanic. Performs repairs and tune-ups on 120 cars per month.

Messrs. Henry Goodman and Bob Aird, service station attendants. Pump over 6,000 gallons of gas per week.

Mr. John F. Jennings, motor pool acting dispatcher. Responsible for 160 vehicles, among them 29 sedans, 30 pickup trucks, 7 station wagons, 10 carryalls, 10 buses, 14 half-ton trucks, 3 ambulances, 6 sedans, 26 jeeps, 2 fire trucks, 4 garbage trucks, and 3 tractors.

Source: "Who's Who in the Management," *Governors Island Gazette,* various dates, 1969.

Notes

Introduction

1. "The Baseball Tourists," *New York Times,* Apr. 7, 1889, 11.

Chapter One

FIRST IN DEED AND ALWAYS READY

The Military on Governors Island

1. Anastazio Carlos Mariano Azoy, *Three Centuries under Three Flags: The Story of Governors Island from 1637* (Governors Island, N.Y.: Headquarters First Army, 1951), 99–100.
2. Alexander V. Campbell, *The Royal American Regiment, 1755–1772: An Atlantic Community* (London, Ontario: Faculty of Graduate Studies, University of Western Ontario, 2003), 123–25.
3. Azoy, 21–23.
4. Quoted in Governors Island Club, *Governors Island: Its History and Development 1637–1937* (Governors Island, N.Y.: Governors Island Club, 1937), 50.
5. Quoted in Edmund Banks Smith, *Governors Island: Its Military History under Three Flags, 1637–1913* (Governors Island, N.Y.: Edmund Banks Smith, 1913), 42.
6. George Washington, General Orders, June 19, 1776, George Washington Papers, Letterbook 1, Image 288, Collections of the Manuscript Division, Library of Congress, Washington, D.C.
7. Smith, 44.
8. A. C. Dalmas, "Fort Jay," March 26, 1934, in National Park Service, Historic American Buildings Survey / Historic American Engineering Record, 1933–Present, Collection of the Prints and Photographs Division, HABS 31-Gov I, no. NY 5715, 1, Library of Congress, Washington, D.C.
9. Quoted in Smith, 41.
10. David Hackett Fischer, *Washington's Crossing* (Oxford: Oxford University Press, 2004), 100–101.
11. Blanche Wilder Bellamy, *Governors Island,* Half Moon Series Papers on Historic New York, edited by Maude Wilder Goodwin, Alice Carrington Royce, and Ruth Putnam, vol. 1, no. 5 (New York: G. P. Putnam's Sons, 1897), 422.
12. Quoted in I. N. Phelps Stokes, *The Iconography of Manhattan Island 1498–1909* (New York: Arno Press, 1976), 5:1228.
13. Smith, 24.
14. Quoted in Azoy, 31.
15. Smith, 53.
16. Governors Island Club, 56–57.
17. Smith, 54.
18. Ibid.
19. Governors Island Club, 25.
20. Quoted in ibid., 58.
21. Throughout this book, the name "Fort Jay" is used to refer to the army post, although the fort's name changes.
22. Governors Island Club, 27.
23. Christopher Goodwin and Associates, Inc., *National Historic Context for Department of Defense Installations, 1790–1940* (Baltimore, Md.: U.S. Army Corps of Engineers Baltimore District, August 1995), 1:12.
24. National Park Service, 4.
25. "Fort Jay Scraps Many Old Cannon," *New York Times,* October 14, 1942, 18.
26. Jann Warren-Findley and Nancy Dallett, *Draft Governors Island Historic Resource Study: June, 2004* (Philadelphia: National Park Service, Northeast History Program Office, 2004), 62–63.
27. Major C. E. Dutton, U.S. Ordnance Department, "The Ordnance Department," in *The Army of the United States, Historical Sketches of Staff and Line with Portraits of Generals-in-Chief,* edited by Theophilus Francis Rodenbough, Bvt. Brigadier General, U.S.A., and William L. Haskin, Major, First Artillery (New York: Maynard, Merrill, 1896), available at http://www.Army.mil/cmh-pg/books/R&H/R&H-OD.htm.
28. Endorsement from the Office of the Chief of Ordnance, Eighth Endorsement, July 16, 1895, RG 92, 89/84234, National Archives, College Park, Md.
29. "Governor's Island News," *New York Times,* August 31, 1889, 5.
30. Survey of Army Bases, War Department, June 8, 1897, RG 92, 89/84234.
31. National Park Service, 11.
32. For a list of headquarters and commanders, see appendix A.
33. For a list of post commanders, see appendix B.
34. Joseph E. Chance, ed., *My Life in the Old Army: Reminiscences of Abner Doubleday from the Collections of the New-York Historical Society* (Fort Worth: Texas Christian University Press, 1998), 150.
35. Thomas Sparrow Collection, no. 1878, folder 7, vol. 1, September 24, 1861, transcribed by Alex Christopher Meekins, University of North Carolina–Chapel Hill Southern Historical Collection.
36. Fiorello H. LaGuardia, "A Governors Island Airport Again Is Urged," *New York Times,* August 7, 1927, XX4.
37. E-mail to author from Garret Roosma, son of Colonel John Roosma, deputy post commander in the 1950s, sent November 4, 2004.
38. Roger S. Durham, ed., *A Confederate Yankee: The Journal of Edward William Drummond, a Confederate Soldier from Maine* (Knoxville: University of Tennessee Press, 2003), 50.
39. Azoy, 69–70.
40. Jack D. Foner, *Blacks and the Military in American History* (New York: Praeger, 1974), 109–10.
41. Ibid., 188.
42. E-mail to author from Claudia Iannucci, April 10, 2007.
43. "Drill for the Army, Scorn All Excuses," *New York Times,* August 10, 1917, 5.
44. David Rockefeller, *Memoirs* (New York: Random House Trade Paperbacks, 2003), 106–7.
45. Quoted in "Newspaper Specials," *Wall Street Journal,* May 17, 1912, 2.
46. Letter from Charles C. Nicholas to Secretary of War Dwight Filley Davis, January 19, 1926, RG 92, 276/602.2.
47. Material relating to the Coast Guard's stay on Governors Island is scanty because the records, stored at a National Archives site in St. Louis, are not indexed and will not be available to the public without Freedom of Information Law requests until 2027. But the lack of an index makes any such request impossible. The stories in this section have therefore been compiled from newspapers and numerous e-mails and interviews with former Coasties and family members who were stationed on the island, as well as from papers, reports, and weekly newsletters in the possession of the U.S. Coast Guard Historian's Office in Washington, D.C.
48. "Governors Island Memories, June 1966 to September 1997," *The Coast Guard Reservist,* December 1997, 5, available at zzhttp://www.uscg.mil/reservist/mag1997/dec1997/seven.htm.
49. U.S. Coast Guard Historian's Office, "*Red Beech,* 1964, WLM-686," available at http://ww.uscg.mil/history/WEBCUTTERS/Red_Beech_1964.html.
50. Ibid.
51. E-mail to author from Richard Morris, trainee in the Radioman School, sent September 23, 2004.
52. "Governors Island Memories," 5.

ISLAND HIGHLIGHTS *Early Island Engineers*

1. John Montresor, the Montresor Journals, September 18 and 19, 1766, edited by G. D. Scull, 387, 6–7, New-York Historical Society Collections, New York City.
2. "Engineer John Montresor," available at http://footguards.tripod.com/01ABOUT/Montresor/000montresor.htm.
3. Governors Island Club, *Governors Island: Its History and Development, 1*

637–1937 (Governors Island, N.Y.: Governors Island Club, 1937), 27.
4. "Colonel Jonathan Williams," in *Portraits and Profiles, Chief Engineer–1775 to Present,* available at http://www.hq.usace.army.mil/history/coe.htm#6.

ISLAND HIGHLIGHTS *Island Vessel*

1. Matthew L. Wald, "Search Is Begun for the Wreck of the *Karen E.,*" *New York Times,* September 13, 1981, 56.
2. Unless otherwise noted, material on the *Mahoning* was derived from the U.S. Coast Guard Historian's Office, Washington, D.C., and its Web site, http://www.uscg.mil/history/WEBCUTTERS/Mahoning_1939.html.
3. E-mail to author from James M. Edwards Jr., MK3 and MK2 (machinery tech.) in the U.S. Coast Guard from 1975 to 1976, sent March 9, 2007.
4. J. J. Round, Commanding Officer, "Welcome Aboard *United States Cutter Mahoning* (WYTM-91)," July 4, 1977, courtesy of James M. Edwards Jr.
5. Ibid.
6. Wald, 56.

Chapter Two

HOSPITAL CARE *From Rudimentary to Necessary*

1. "Fort Columbus, Governor's Island, New York Harbor, Descriptions of Military Posts," in *Surgeon General's Report* (Washington, D.C.: War Department, Surgeon General's Office, 1870), 31.
2. Mary C. Gillette, *The Army Medical Department, 1818–1865,* United States Army Historical Series (Washington, D.C.: Center of Military History, U.S. Army, 1987), 4–6.
3. Quoted in Edmund Banks Smith, *Governors Island: Its Military History under Three Flags, 1637–1913* (New York: Edmund Banks Smith, 1913), 52.
4. Quoted in ibid., 49.
5. Quoted in ibid., 51.
6. Gillette, 138.
7. Ibid.
8. Ibid., 38.
9. Smith, 67.
10. Charles E. Rosenberg, *The Cholera Years: The United States in 1832, 1849, and 1866* (Chicago: University of Chicago Press, 1962), 13–54.
11. Gillette, 64.
12. Ibid., 82.
13. Ibid., 87.
14. National Park Service, Historic American Buildings Survey / Historic American Engineering Record, 1933–Present, Collection of the Prints and Photographs Division, HABS 31-GOV I, no. NY 5715-5, 1–5, Library of Congress, Washington, D.C.
15. Gillette, 87. Dr. Russell held the title *post surgeon,* which replaced the former title *regimental surgeon.*
16. "Fort Columbus," 29–30.
17. Gillette, 30–31.
18. "You Think You've Been Here Long?" *Coast Guard Gazette,* March 11, 1976, 3.
19. Smith, 110–11.
20. Gillette, 65.
21. Memorandum from Joseph Russell to the War Department, ca. 1861, Reports, RG 112/12, National Archives, College Park, Md.
22. Ibid.
23. Gillette, 76.
24. Thomas Sparrow Collection, no. 1878, folder 7, vol. 1, September 30, 1861, 201, transcribed by Alex Christopher Meekins, University of North Carolina–Chapel Hill Southern Historical Collection.
25. Fred C. Ainsworth, Leslie J. Perry, and Joseph W. Kirkley, eds., *War of the Rebellion: A Compilation of the Official Records of the Union and Confederate Armies,* series II, vol. 2 (Washington, D.C.: U.S. Government Printing Office, 1898), no page.
26. Ibid., no page.
27. "Fort Columbus," 29–30.
28. "The Governors Island Epidemic: Rise and Progress of the Disease–List of the Deaths," *New York Times,* November 13, 1870, 1.
29. "Consolidated Sick Report (White Troops), Fort Columbus, New York Harbor, 1870–74," Descriptions of Military Posts, in *Surgeon General's Report,* 19. There is a discrepancy in the numbers. The Sick Report lists forty-three deaths. However, the *New York Times* lists the names and ranks of the dead, and they number fifty.
30. Ibid., 18.
31. P. M. Ashburn, *A History of the Medical Department of the United States Army* (Boston: Houghton Mifflin, 1929), 317–18.
32. Memorandum from the Surgeon, Fort Jay, New York, to the Surgeon General, U.S. Army, Washington, D.C., November 11, 1918, Report on the Influenza and Pneumonia Epidemic, RG 112, 153/710.1.
33. Ibid.
34. Reports to the Surgeon General, 1918–19, RG 112, 152/3.
35. Congress created the CCC in 1933 to provide jobs for the unemployed in land-conservation efforts. The administration of the Middle Atlantic camps was coterminous with the Second Corps Area, and CCC staff was headquartered on Governors Island.
36. Monthly Sanitary Reports for 1942, RG 112, 753/240.
37. Monthly Sanitary Reports for 1944, RG 112, 753/330–399.
38. Annual Report of the Fort Jay Hospital for 1950, RG 112, 108/319.1.
39. Annual Report of the Fort Jay Hospital for 1953, RG 112, 108/319.1–2.
40. Annual Report of the Fort Jay Hospital for 1956, RG 112, 108/319.1.
41. "Who's Who in the Management," *Coast Guard Gazette,* n.d., 1968, 12.
42. E-mail to author from Jon Kempfer, Ph.D., health care administrator on Governors Island from 1992 to 1995, sent September 22, 2004.

Chapter Three

AN EASTERN ALCATRAZ

1. Alonzo E. Bell, diaries, Mf.P.48.1, September 4, 1861, 23, transcribed by Alex Christopher Meekins, Office of Archives and History, Division of Historical Resources, Archives and Records, North Carolina State Archives, Raleigh.
2. Edmund Banks Smith, *Governors Island: Its Military History under Three Flags, 1637–1913* (New York: Edmund Banks Smith, 1913), 69.
3. William Best Hesseltine, *Civil War Prisons: A Study in War Psychology* (New York: Frederick Unger, 1964), 36.
4. Lonnie R. Speer, *Portals to Hell: Military Prisons of the Civil War* (Mechanicsburg, Pa.: Stackpole Books, 1997), 38–40.
5. "Ralph's Flight from Governor's Island," *Red White and Blue Weekly* (New York), November 6, 1897, 2.
6. Bell diary; Thomas Sparrow Collection, no. 1878, folder 7, vols. 1 and 2, September 4, 1861–October 9, 1861, transcribed by Alex Christopher Meekins, University of North Carolina–Chapel Hill Southern Historical Collection.
7. Sparrow Collection, folder 7, vol. 1, September 4, 1861, 115.
8. Bell diary, 17.
9. Ibid.
10. Sparrow Collection, folder 7, vol. 1, September 23, 1861, 169–72.
11. Ibid., 171.
12. Roger S. Durham, ed., *A Confederate Yankee: The Journal of Edward William Drummond, a Confederate Soldier from Maine* (Knoxville: University of Tennessee Press, 2003), 58.
13. Sparrow Collection, folder 7, vol. 1, September 23, 1861, 171.
14. Ibid., 183.

15. Ibid., 7.
16. Fred C. Ainsworth, Leslie J. Perry, and Joseph W. Kirkley, eds., *War of the Rebellion: Compilation of the Official Records of the Union and Confederate Armies,* series II, vol. 6 (Washington, D.C.: U.S. Government Printing Office, 1899), 990–91.
17. Smith, 100–101.
18. "Military Execution at Governor's Island: Tragic Ending of a Bounty Jumper," *New York Times,* February 4, 1865, 8.
19. William Henry Rideing, "Garrison Life at Governors Island, New York Harbor," *Scribner's Monthly* 21, no. 4 (February 1881), 14.
20. Quoted in "Disease among Soldiers: Precautions Deemed Necessary in Military Quarters," *New York Times,* April 11, 1884, 8.
21. Leonard Wood, diaries, July 1, 1909, Leonard Wood Papers, Collections of the Manuscript Division, Library of Congress, Washington, D.C.
22. Draft Mission Statement, United States Disciplinary Barracks, undated, General Correspondence, 1925–1940, RG 407/7, n.p., National Archives, College Park, Md.
23. "Working to Redeem Soldiers in Prison," *New York Times,* December 14, 1915, 8.
24. Memorandum from the Surgeon, Atlantic Branch, United States Disciplinary Barracks, to Adjutant General of the Army, July 19, 1919, General Correspondence, 1925–40, RG 407, 152/253.1, National Archives, College Park, Md.
25. K. T. Smith, Office of the Commandant, *Annual Report of the Atlantic Branch, United States Disciplinary Barracks, Governors Island, New York, House Documents,* vol. 114, 64th Cong., 2d sess., 1925, 9–19.
26. "Ralph's Flight from Governors Island," 25–28.
27. Draft Mission Statement, n.p.
28. Draft Mission Statement, ca. 1929, United States Disciplinary Barracks, undated, General Correspondence, 1925–1940, RG 407/13, n.p., National Archives, College Park, Md.
29. Office of the Commandant, Annual Report of the Atlantic Branch, United States Disciplinary Barracks, FY 1923, General Correspondence, 1925–40, RG 407, 7/253.2, National Archives, College Park, Md.
30. Office of the Commandant, Annual Report of the Atlantic Branch, United States Disciplinary Barracks, FY 1937, General Correspondence 1925–40, RG 407, 15/391.1, National Archives, College Park, Md.
31. Ibid.
32. E-mails to author from a civilian who resided on Governors Island from 1927 to 1943, sent 2004–2008.
33. [Records of] Prisoner of War Camp Fort Jay, December 3, 1943, RG 389, 461/2481, National Archives, College Park, Md.
34. Ibid., February 24, 1944, RG 389, 461/2664.
35. Major Frank L. Brown, report of visit to POW camp, Fort Jay, New York, to Chief, Operations Branch, POW Division, Office of the Provost Marshall General, Washington, D.C., February 24, 1944, [Records of] Prisoner of War Camp Fort Jay, RG 389, 461/2664.3.
36. Ibid.
37. "Court Martial Opens in Fort Jay Disorder," *New York Times,* December 6, 1951, 54.
38. E-mail to author from Wanda Hinkel, wife of an electronic technician first class on the U.S. Coast Guard cutter *Dallas* and mother of two children, all of whom resided on Governors Island in the 1990s, sent April 14, 2004.
39. E-mail to author from "An Army Brat," sent May 6, 2004.
40. Photograph, *Coast Guard Gazette,* July 1, 1976, 3.

ISLAND HIGHLIGHTS *Island Music*

1. "Governor's Island, Movement of Troops," *New York Times,* December 5, 1853, 2.
2. Rudi Williams, "Air Force Sergeant Traces Bugle's History," November 8, 2000, available at http://www.defenselink.mil/news/Nov2000/n11082000_200011084.html.
3. *U.S. Army Bands in History,* available at http://bands.army.mil/history/.
4. Anastazio Carlos Mariano Azoy, *Three Centuries under Three Flags: The Story of Governors Island from 1637* (Governors Island, N.Y.: Headquarters First Army, 1951), 16, 19.
5. Ibid., 32–33.
6. "Bands from 1830–1860, Rise of the Brass Band," in *U.S. Army Bands in History,* available at: http://bands.army.mil/history/default.asp?chapter=9.
7. "West Point," in *U.S. Army Bands in History,* available at http://bands.army.mil/history/default.asp?chapter=6.
8. Quoted in "Bands from 1830–1860, Rise of the Brass Band."
9. Quoted in "The School of Practice," in *U.S. Army Bands in History,* available at http://bands.army.mil/history/default.asp?chapter=10.
10. U.S. Bureau of the Census, 1860 census, Governors Island, July 3.
11. Conversation with Michael Shaver, National Park Service, February 22, 2007.
12. Thomas Sparrow Collection, no. 1878, folder 7, vol. 1, September 24, 1861, 167–68, transcribed by Alex Christopher Meekins, University of North Carolina–Chapel Hill Southern Historical Collection.
13. Edmund Banks Smith, *Governors Island: Its Military History under Three Flags, 1637–1913* (New York: Edmund Banks Smith, 1913), 100.
14. "Yellow Fever: The Governors Island Epidemic," *New York Times,* November 13, 1870, 1. The dead were George Fogarty, September 6, followed by his son and wife; Peter Creamer, September 10; Private Henry Bennet, October 1; and George Einselle, date of death unknown.
15. Surgeon J. J. Milhau, United States Army, "Report on Fort Columbus, Governors Island, New York Harbor," Description of Military Posts, in *Annual Report of the Surgeon General* (Washington, D.C.: U.S. Government Printing Office, 1872), 16.
16. Azoy, 70.
17. "The Army Regains Its Bands," in *U.S. Army Bands in History,* available at http://bands.army.mil/history/default.asp?chapter=16.
18. "Partnering with Civilian Institutions," in *U.S. Army School of Music,* available at http://schoolofmusic.army.mil/History%20of%20The%20US%20Army%20School%20of%20Music.pdf.
19. "The Army Regains Its Bands."
20. Memorandum from 2nd Lieutenant/Infantry William C. White to Commandant, Atlantic Branch, United States Disciplinary Barracks, n.d., RG 407, AS32294, 15,322.6, National Archives, College Park, Md.
21. Letter from Joe N. Dalton, Chairman, Entertainment Committee, to unknown recipient, n.d., RG 407, AS32294, 15,322.16, National Archives, College Park, Md.
22. Memorandum from Adjutant General of the Army to Commanding General, Eastern Department, October 22, 1918, RG 407, 152,322.16.1, National Archives, College Park, Md.
23. "Army Band Leader Honored at Ceremony Marking Retirement Here after 41 Years," *New York Times,* July 30, 1948, 2.
24. "WAC Band in Salute on Governors Island," *New York Times,* August 31, 1951, 18.
25. Conversation with Michael Shaver, February 22, 2007.
26. [No title], *Coast Guard Gazette,* June 26, 1992, 3.

ISLAND HIGHLIGHTS *The Commanders*

1. William Henry Rideing, "Garrison Life at Governors Island, New York Harbor," *Scribner's Monthly* (February 1881) 21, no. 4: 14.
2. "The Troops at Governor's Island," *New York Times,* July 6, 1879, 8.
3. Jann Warren-Findley and Nancy Dallett, *Draft Governors Island Historic Resource Study: June, 2004* (Philadelphia: National Park Service, Northeast History Program Office, 2004), 104–5.
4. U.S. Bureau of the Census, 1880 census, New York City, as enumerated by William S. Connell, titled "Inhabitants in the City of New York, in the County of New York, State of New York, enumerated by me on the first day of June, 1880."
5. Edmund Banks Smith, *Governors Island: Its Military History under Three Flags, 1637–1913* (New York: Edmund Banks Smith, 1913), 124.
6. J. B. McClure, *Life of General Hancock* (Chicago: Rhodes and McClure, 1880), 105–6.

7. "General's Messenger Dead," *New York Times,* September 4, 1907, 11.
8. Governors Island Club, *Constitution and By Laws: With List of Officers and Members, 1914* (Governors Island, N.Y.: Governors Island Club, 1914), courtesy of Garret Roosma.
9. "James B. Fry (1827–1894)," in *Mr. Lincoln's White House,* available at http://www.mrlincolnswhitehouse.org/inside.asp?ID=696&subjectID=2.
10. "Governors Island Has a Museum of Rare Historic Relics," *New York Times,* September 18, 1904, SM6.
11. "Military Service Institution," *New York Times,* December 2, 1878, 8.
12. Warren-Findley and Dallett, 108.
13. "Army Officers Uniting," *New York Times,* September 29, 1878, 5.
14. "What the Militia Needs," *New York Times,* December 18, 1881, 7.
15. "A Brave Soldier Dead: The Last Hours of Gen. Winfield S. Hancock," *New York Times,* February 10, 1886, 1.

Chapter Four
METES AND BOUNDS

1. Report from the Board of Officers to the Adjutant General, U.S. Army, August 17, 1900, General Correspondence 1884–1923, RG 77, 853/37078, 8, National Archives, College Park, Md.
2. U.S. Adjutant General's Office, *Sites for Military Posts* (Washington, D.C.: U.S. Government Printing Office, 1901–1903).
3. Headquarters of Department of the East, Report to the Adjutant General of the Army, 1900, General Correspondence 1884–1923, RG 77, 853, National Archives, College Park, Md.
4. Shannon Wright and Timothy Binzen, *Archeological Overview and Assessment of Governors Island National Monument, New York, New York* (Amherst: Archeological Services, University of Massachusetts, 2003), 69.
5. Edmund Banks Smith, *Governors Island: Its Military History under Three Flags, 1637–1913* (New York: Edmund Banks Smith, 1913), 156. Smith is referring to Buildings 405 to 408.
6. Press copies of letters relating to fortifications of the seawall on Governor's Island, June 1891 to December 1906, RG 77, 809/vol. 1, 9, National Archives, New York.
7. Ibid.
8. Letter from W. C. Marshall to Brigadier General G. L. Gillespie, Chief of Engineers, 1903, General Correspondence 1884–1923, RG 77, 853/37078.159, National Archives, College Park, Md. In his article "The Enlargement of Governors Island" (*Professional Memoirs* 6, no. 27 [May–June 1914]: 410–22), Henry Nash Babcock cites the island's size in 1900 as 69.8 acres (410).
9. Quoted in Century Association, ed., *Addresses Made in Honor of Elihu Root* (New York: Century Association, 1937), no page number.
10. Letter from Secretary of War Elihu Root to William B. Allison, March 1, 1901, General Correspondence 1884–1923, RG 77, 853, 71, National Archives, College Park, Md.
11. "Governors Island Extension Benefits," *New York Times,* December 9, 1900, 1.
12. Letter from Root to Allison, March 1, 1901, 71. In this letter to chairman of the U.S. Senate Committee on Appropriations requesting funds for implementing the plan, Secretary Root's estimate for rentals "in and about the harbor" was $97,000.
13. Report from Board of Officers, 7.
14. Ibid., 17.
15. Ibid., 8.
16. Ibid., 10.
17. Ibid., 2.
18. Smith, 122.
19. Report from Board of Officers, 5.
20. "Governors Island to Be Much Enlarged," *New York Times,* September 6, 1900, 1.
21. Report from Board of Officers, 8.
22. Ibid., 8–10.
23. Ibid., 10.
24. Ibid.
25. R. Christopher Goodwin and Associates, Inc., *National Historic Context for Department of Defense Installations, 1790–1940* (Baltimore: U.S. Army Corps of Engineers, Baltimore District, August 1995), part 2, 153–90, available at http://aec.Army.mil/usaec/cultural/docs.html.
26. 1st Endorsement from Lieutenant General Nelson A. Miles to Acting Assistant Adjunct General H. A. Greene, August 20, 1900, General Correspondence 1884–1923, RG 77, 853/37078, National Archives, College Park, Md.
27. Ibid.
28. "Governors Island Extension Benefits," 1.
29. Babcock, 411.
30. U.S. Congress, *Laws of 1800* (Washington, D.C.: U.S. Government Printing Office, February 15, 1800), chap. 6, no page number.
31. U.S. Patent [and Trademark] Office, *Books of Patents* (Washington, D.C.: U.S. Patent Office, May 7, 1880), no. 44, 604.
32. Letter from Nicholson & Co. to Secretary of War Elihu Root, December 7, 1900, General Correspondence 1884–1923, RG 77, 853/37078.11, National Archives, College Park, Md.
33. Letter from Secretary of War Elihu Root to Timothy Woodruff, Lieutenant Governor of New York, January 7, 1901, General Correspondence 1884–1923, RG 77, 853/37078.47, National Archives, College Park, Md.
34. Letter from Secretary of War Elihu Root to Timothy Woodruff, Lieutenant Governor of New York, December 28, 1900, General Correspondence 1884–1923, RG 77, 853/37078.33, National Archives, College Park, Md.
35. Letter from Timothy Woodruff, Lieutenant Governor of New York, to Elihu Root, Secretary of War, January 9, 1901, General Correspondence 1884–1923, RG 77, 853/37078.46, National Archives, College Park, Md.
36. "Governors Island Plans," special to the *New York Times,* January 29, 1901, 5.
37. Ibid.
38. State of New York, Commissioners of the Land Office, *Proceedings of the Commissioners of the Land Office for the Year 1901* (Albany: Oliver A. Quayle, Department Printer, 1901), 66.
39. State of New York, "Laws of 1901," chap. 46 in ibid., 65.
40. Letter from Root to Allison, March 1, 1901, 71.
41. Although the legislation allowed the conveyance of "approximately 90 acres" of underwater lands, several other numbers appear in the files. The original Metes and Bounds sent to Albany by Root say "75 acres more or less." All of the engineers' reports describe the water area that was enclosed during the initial construction of the landfill as 82 acres. Babcock, in his history of the project, uses the figure "about eighty-four ½" acres.
42. State of New York, 67.
43. Erwin N. Thompson, *The Presidio of San Francisco: A History from 1846 to 1995,* Historic Resource Study, Golden Gate National Recreation Area (Denver: Denver Service Center National Park Service, July 1997), NPS-330.
44. Jann Warren-Findley and Nancy Dallett, *Draft, Governors Island Historic Resource Study: June, 2004* (Philadelphia: Northeast History Program Office, National Park Service, 2004), chap. 7, 121.
45. Letter from Secretary of War Elihu Root to Messrs. McKim, Mead & White, June 29, 1901, General Correspondence 1884–1923, RG 77, 853/86, National Archives, College Park, Md.
46. Letter from Elihu Root to I. N. P. Stokes, August 20, 1901, General Correspondence 1884–1923, RG 77, 853/77, National Archives, College Park, Md.
47. Letter from Root to McKim, Mead & White, June 29, 1901, 86.
48. Charles Follen McKim, William Rutherford Mead, and Stanford White worked together on their projects. McKim was the designer, White concentrated on residential properties, and Mead ran the office. All of them signed the plans. For simplicity, the

name "McKim" refers to the firm throughout this text.
49. 1st Endorsement from Miles to Greene.
50. Memorandum from W. L. Marshall to Brigadier General G. L. Gillespie, March 16, 1902, General Correspondence 1884–1923, RG 77, 853/111, National Archives, College Park, Md.
51. "The Transformation of Governors Island," *New York Times,* September 29, 1907, SM2.
52. The acreage numbers again vary. In *Governors Island: Its Military History under Three Flags, 1637–1913,* Edmund Banks Smith cites a 103.55-acre extension and an island land mass totaling 173.35 acres (156). The total amount of land turned over to the Coast Guard in 1965 was 204.5 acres.
53. Memorandum from Chas. Bird, Deputy Quartermaster General, to the War Department, n.d., General Correspondence 1884–1923, RG 77, 853/37078.6, National Archives, College Park, Md.
54. "The Transformation of Governors Island," SM2. The McKim, Mead & White map, signed in 1906, was shown to the public for the first time in this article.
55. Ibid.
56. Warren-Findlay and Dallett, 128.
57. U.S. Bureau of the Census, 1900 census, Governors Island, June 1.
58. "The Transformation of Governors Island," SM2.
59. Letter from Lieutenant Colonel of Ordnance [name indecipherable], Governors Island, to the Chief of Ordnance, U.S. Army, March 25, 1901, General Correspondence 1884–1923, RG 77, 853/87, National Archives, College Park, Md.
60. Letter from unknown author to Elihu Root, Secretary of War, May 20, 1902, General Correspondence 1884–1923, RG 77, 853/134, National Archives, College Park, Md.
61. The War Department approved the McKim, Mead & White plan in 1908.
62. The description of the work is well documented in Babcock's 1914 article "The Enlargement of Governors Island." In addition, the reports of the chief of engineers, U.S. Army, in *Annual Report for the War Department* for the years 1901 to 1913 provided material for this section.
63. Babcock, 416.
64. U.S. Engineers office to Mssrs Roosevelt and Sullivan, June 4, 1902, Relyea Family Papers, 18–39, New-York Historical Society, New York City. The unit prices in the R&S bid are informative. Bearing piles were estimated at $9.75 to $11 each, depending on the length. Fender piles were $13 to $16 each, and crib work was 5.5 cents a cubic foot.
65. War Department, "Report of the Chief of Engineers, U.S. Army," in *Annual Report for the War Department for the Year 1901* (Washington, D.C.: U.S. Government Printing Office, 1901), 1298.
66. Babcock, 412.
67. Ibid., 414.
68. Memorandum from W. L. Marshall to Brigadier General G. L. Gillespie, March 27, 1902, General Correspondence 1884–1923, RG 77, 853/113, National Archives, College Park, Md.
69. Babcock, 414.
70. Major W. L. Marshall, *Survey of Buttermilk Channel, New York Harbor* (New York: Engineer Office, U.S. Army, November 28, 1900).
71. U.S. Engineers Office bid specifications for stone, October 2, 1901, General Correspondence 1884–1923, RG 77, 853/106, National Archives, College Park, Md.
72. Babcock, 411–12.
73. War Department, "Report of the Chief of Engineers, U.S. Army," in *Annual Report for the War Department for the Year 1903* (Washington, D.C.: U.S. Government Printing Office, 1903), 1126.
74. Angus Kress Gillespie, *The Twin Towers: The Life of New York City's Trade Center* (New Brunswick, N.J.: Rutgers University Press, 1999), 64.
75. Author's conversation with the Battery Park City Authority Public Relations Office, May 2006.
76. Unknown author, "Proposal for Furnishing Materials and Building an Embankment Southwest of Governors Island, New York Harbor," December 8, 1905, RG 77, 853/97–102, National Archives, College Park, Md.
77. War Department, *Annual Report for the War Department for the Year 1903,* 922.
78. Babcock, 419–20. The New York Filling Company's initial estimate must have been a compromise because the real costs were 7.4 cents for sand and hard material, which had to be transported from Manhattan or Brooklyn, and 3.6 cents for added mud, which was dredged and pumped virtually for free from Buttermilk Channel.
79. War Department, "Report of the Chief of Engineers, U.S. Army," in *Annual Report for the War Department for the Year 1904* (Washington, D.C.: U.S. Government Printing Office, 1904), 1125.
80. Babcock, 420.
81. Letter from Humphrey Toomey, Contractor, to Colonel W. L. Marshall, October 14, 1905, 809 Letters Received, RG 77, vol. 2, 65, National Archives, New York City.
82. Letter from Brown and Fleming to W. L. Marshall, July 17, 1906, Letters for U.S. Engineering office, RG 77, 13/781, National Archives, New York City.
83. Smith, 101.
84. Ibid., 35.
85. Material for this paragraph was derived from "Proposals" in the *New York Times,* October 1903 to May 1906; Wright and Binzen, 75; and War Department, "Report of the Quartermaster-General," in *Annual Report of the War Department for the Year 1901* (Washington, D.C.: U.S. Government Printing Office, 1901) and *Annual Report of the War Department for the Year 1912* (Washington, D.C.: U.S. Government Printing Office, 1912).
86. War Department, "Report of the Chief of Engineers, U.S. Army," *Annual Report of the War Department for the Year 1911* (Washington, D.C.: U.S. Government Printing Office, 1911), 1222.
87. Memorandum from S. W. Roessler to Chief of Engineers, U.S. Army, July 24, 1909, General Correspondence 1884–1923, RG 77, 853/37078.218, National Archives, College Park, Md.
88. 2d Indorsement from the Quartermaster General, August 18, 1911, General Correspondence 1884–1923, RG 77, 853/37078.241, National Archives, College Park, Md.
89. Letter from J. M. Dickenson, Secretary of War, to Charles Nagel, Secretary of Commerce and Labor, April 8, 1910, General Correspondence 1884–1923, RG 77, 853/1799.75216, National Archives, College Park, Md.
90. Ibid.
91. Babcock, 412.
92. Letter from Dickenson to Nagel, April 8, 1910.
93. Memorandum from S. W. Roessler to Chief of Engineers, U.S. Army, October 17, 1912, Transfer of New Fill at Governors Island to the Troops, RG 77, 853/37078.250, National Archives, College Park, Md.

ISLAND HIGHLIGHTS *Twentieth-Century Island Engineers*

1. "Want Marshall Retained," *New York Times,* November 25, 1907, 5.
2. Ibid.
3. Receipt indicating Henry Nash Babcock's pay, 1903, RG 77, 399.90, National Archives, New York.
4. Henry Nash Babcock, "The Enlargement of Governors Island," *Professional Memoirs* 6, no. 27 (May–June 1914): 410–22.
5. Letter from W. L. Marshall to John R. O'Brien, RG 77, 853/37078.59-61, National Archives, College Park, Md.
6. Babcock, 420.
7. "Want Marshall Retained," 5.
8. Babcock, 418.
9. District Engineer Officer to Chief of Engineers, October 17, 1912, Transfer of New

Fill at Governors Island to the Troops, RG 92, 853/37078.250, National Archives, College Park, Md.

ISLAND HIGHLIGHTS *Where Does the Dirt from the Subway Go?*

1. "What Has Become of All the Dirt Taken from the Subway?" *New York Times,* November 27, 1904, SM7.
2. Memorandum from W. L. Marshall to Brigadier General A. Mackenzie, n.d., 1903, RG 77, 159, National Archives, College Park, Md.
3. "NYC Subway Centennial," available at http://www.mta.info/mta/centennial.htm.
4. "What Has Become of All the Dirt?" SM7.
5. Ibid.
6. Henry Nash Babcock, "The Enlargement of Governors Island," *Professional Memoirs* 6, no. 27 (May–June 1914), 417–19.

Chapter Five
FLIGHT OR FIGHT?

1. "Polo Field or Airport?" *The Business Week,* October 19, 1929, unpaginated.
2. Hudson River Maritime Museum, *1909 Hudson-Fulton Celebration: The Fourth Annual Report on the Hudson-Fulton Celebration Commission to the Legislature of the State of New York, May 20, 1910,* available at http://www.ulster.net/~hrmm/quad/1909hudsonfulton/intro.html.
3. Leonard Wood, diaries, Monday, September 27, 1909, Leonard Wood Papers, Collections of the Manuscript Division, Library of Congress, Washington, D.C.
4. "Wright Airship Here for Fulton Flights," *New York Times,* September 21, 1909, 3.
5. Noah Adams, *The Flyers: In Search of Wilbur and Orville Wright* (New York: Crown, 2003), 128.
6. Wood diaries, September 29, 1909.
7. Judy Rumerman, "Airport Design," in the U.S. Centennial of Flight Commission Web site at http://www.centennialofflight.gov/essay/Social/architecture/SH15.htm.
8. Memo from Office, Chief, Quartermaster Corps, January 22, 1914, RG 92, 7679/37471, National Archives, College Park, Md.
9. U.S. Senate, Committee on Military Affairs, *Landing Field on Governors Island: Hearings Before the Committee on Military Affairs on H.R. 12009, an Act to Authorize the Enlargement of Governors Island and Consenting to the Use of a Portion Thereof as a Landing Field for the City of New York and Its Environs,* 74th Cong., 2d sess., June 5, 1936, 43.
10. Ibid.
11. Construction Division–War Dept.–N.Y. City, Plan 62, January 14, 1919, RG 92, Completion Reports 1917–1919, 109/Binder 2.
12. Howard Mingus, "Airport or Army on Governors Island?" *New York Times,* April 13, 1924, SM12. (Copyright © 1924 by The New York Times Co. Reprinted with permission.)
13. Rumerman.
14. Mingus, SM12.
15. Quoted in "Governors Island May Be an Airport," *New York Times,* November 26, 1925, 2.
16. Letter from the Merchant's Association of New York to Colonel James A. Woodruff, U.S. Army, September 17, 1934, reprinted in U.S. Senate, *Landing Field on Governors Island,* June 5, 1936, 12.
17. U.S. Senate, Committee on Military Affairs, *Construction at Army Posts: Hearings Before the Committee on Military Affairs on S. 3558,* 69th Cong., 1st sess., April 16, 1926, 17.
18. Mingus, SM12.
19. U.S. Senate, *Construction,* 17.
20. "LaGuardia Seeks Return of Governors Island under State Act Preventing Federal Sale," *New York Times,* April 27, 1926, 2.
21. Federal Aviation Commission, "A Brief History of the Federal Aviation Commission," available at http://www.faa.gov/about/history/brief%5Fhistory/.
22. "Pan American: The History of America's Chosen Instrument for Overseas Air Transport," in the U.S. Centennial of Flight Commission Web site at http://www.centennialofflight.gov/essay/Commercial_Aviation/Pan_Am/Tran12.htm.
23. "Airport Poll Backs Governors Island," *New York Times,* August 1, 1927, 7. Curiously, three men were noncommittal: Charles A. Lindbergh, Harry F. Guggenheim of the Guggenheim Foundation for the Advancement of Aeronautics, and Jesse I. Strauss of R. H. Macy & Co. (who during World War I had been an active volunteer with the army on Governors Island).
24. Testimony of Representative Fiorello LaGuardia in U.S. House of Representatives, *Hearing on the First Deficiency Bill,* 69th Cong., 3d sess., December 8, 1927, 272.
25. Fiorello H. LaGuardia, Member of Congress, "A Governors Island Airport Again Is Urged," *New York Times,* August 7, 1927, XX4.
26. U.S. Senate, *Landing Field on Governors Island,* June 5, 1936, 12–13.
27. Waldo Walker, "Model Barracks for New York," *New York Times,* January 15, 1928, 128.
28. Staff of the Regional Plan Association, *The Regional Plan of New York and Its Environs: The Graphic Regional Plan,* vol. 1 (New York: Regional Plan Association, 1929), 37.
29. "Polo Field or Airport?" *The Business Week,* October 19, 1929, unpaginated.
30. *An Act to Authorize Appropriations for Construction at Military Posts, and for Other Purposes,* 45 Stat. 1302, U.S.C. The island points in a northwesterly direction. The line's actual position ran across the landfill and the widest part of the island, several hundred feet beyond the entrance to the new barracks.
31. *An Act Making Appropriations to Supply Deficiencies in Certain Appropriations for the Fiscal Year Ending June 30, 1930,* 4 Stat. 908, U.S.C. When the army renumbered all the buildings on the island, the barracks became Building 400. It was renamed Liggett Hall in 1957 in honor of General Hunter Liggett, who replaced General George Pershing as commander of the First Army during World War I.
32. U.S. Senate, *Landing Field on Governors Island,* June 5, 15, and 16, 1936, 63–64.
33. U.S. House of Representatives, *Increase Flying-Field Area of Governors Island, N.Y.,* 71st Cong., 3d sess., February 26, 1931, 1–3.
34. This exit never materialized. Instead, the historic northern part of the island was saddled with an unattractive tower to vent air from the tunnel.
35. Statement of Honorable Robert F. Wagner, United States Senator from the State of New York, in U.S. Senate, *Landing Field on Governors Island,* June 5, 1936, 28–29.
36. Memorandum from Colonel A. S. Williams, Sixteenth Infantry, Commanding Officer of Fort Jay, New York, to Brigadier General George E. Spalding, Assistant Chief of Staff, G-4, War Department, in ibid., June 11, 1936, 116–17.
37. Ibid., 117–18. By 1936, out of the 165,000 men authorized by Congress to serve in the army, 1,200 combat troops were stationed on Governors Island. Before World War I, the troops had been convoyed off to Plattsburgh, New York, for training. This practice was no longer followed, and basic training at such bases as Fort Dix had not yet been established.
38. "Contested Ground" is used as the title for chapter 8 in Jann Warren-Findley and Nancy Dallett, *Draft, Governors Island Historic Resource Study: June, 2004* (Philadelphia: National Park Service, Northeast History Program Office, 2004).
39. E-mails to author from assorted Coast Guard wives and brats, 2004.

ISLAND HIGHLIGHTS *Island Public Works*

1. "Governors Island Has Building Boom," *New York Times,* November 26, 1933, N3.
2. "Many Idle Get Jobs at Military Posts," *Washington Post,* October 23, 1932, A10.
3. "Army Housing Fund Set at $54,708,358," *New York Times,* September 21, 1933, 20.
4. "Governors Island to Be Renovated," *New York Times,* January 11, 1936, 32.
5. "Many Idle Get Jobs," A10.
6. "Y.M.C.A. Women's Division Brings Homelike Atmosphere to Fort Jay," *New York Times,* February 1, 1942, D4.
7. "Bird-Bath Building Latest Task for Army: Governors Island Is to Become a Refuge," *New York Times,* June 27, 1937, 32.
8. Schools in the Atlantic Branch of the United Sates Disciplinary Barracks, Record

Group 92, 20/600.1, National Archives, College Park, Md.
9. "The Washington Hall Mural," available at http://www.usma57.org/Mural-corrected%20060820.pdf.
10. "Big Mural Exhibited at Governors Island," *New York Times,* October 30, 1938, 48.

Chapter Six
ISLAND LADIES

1. *Agnes: A Romance of Governors Island,* serialized novel in *The Ladies' Companion, a Monthly Magazine* (May 1837), 11.
2. Russell Shorto, *The Island at the Center of the World* (New York: Doubleday, 2004), 45, 47.
3. Edmund Banks Smith, *Governors Island: Its Military History under Three Flags, 1637–1913* (New York: Edmund Banks Smith, 1913), 29.
4. E-mail to author from Mike Shaver, a Palatine, October 4, 2004.
5. Blanche Wilder Bellamy, *Governors Island,* Half Moon Series Papers on Historic New York, edited by Maude Wilder Goodwin, Alice Carrington Royce, and Ruth Putnam, vol. 1, no. 5 (New York: G. P. Putnam's Sons, 1897), 416.
6. Quoted in Smith, 39.
7. Van R. Baker, ed., *Websters: Letters of an American Army Family in Peace and War, 1836–1853* (Kent, Ohio: Kent State University Press, 2000), 236–40.
8. Quoted in Smith, 65.
9. Thomas Sparrow Collection, no. 1878, folder 7, vol. 1, October 1, 1861, 203, transcribed by Alex Christopher Meekins, University of North Carolina–Chapel Hill Southern Historical Collection.
10. Quoted in Smith, 64.
11. John Shaw Billings, *A Report on Barracks and Hospitals with Description of Military Posts* (Washington, D.C.: U.S. Government Printing Office, 1870), 30.
12. "Cupid Is in Command on Governors Island," *New York Times,* April 9, 1904, 9.
13. U.S. Bureau of the Census, 1880, 1900, and 1910 censuses, Governors Island, all June 1.
14. "Cupid Is in Command," 9.
15. "Officers Helpless; Maids All Married," *New York Times,* April 9, 1904, 9.
16. "Cupid Is in Command," 9.
17. Office of the Quartermaster General, DOC File, 1890–1914 Index, Governors Island, RG 92, 320, National Archives, College Park, Md.
18. E-mail to author from Andrea Morningstar, daughter of an army sergeant and employee at the Post Exchange from 1965 to 1966, sent November 7, 2004.
19. "Three Hostesses Named at Fort Dix," *New York Times,* December 4, 1940, 17.
20. "Governors Island Dedicates Library," *New York Times,* February 2, 1950, 25.
21. *Agnes,* 11; National Park Service, Historic American Buildings Survey / Historic American Engineering Record, 1933–Present, HABS 31-Gov I, no. NY 5715-4, 1–2, Collection of the Prints and Photographs Division, Library of Congress, Washington, D.C.
22. "The Grant Mementos," *Washington Post,* November 24, 1907, F2.
23. Leonard Wood, diaries, November 9, 1908, 4, Leonard Wood Papers, Collections of the Manuscript Division, Library of Congress, Washington, D.C.
24. Letter from Leonard Wood to Louise Wood, no date, Letters to Mrs. Louise Wood 1908–14, Personal Correspondence, Leonard Wood Papers.
25. Leonard Wood, diaries, September 21, 1916.
26. "Sham Battle for Army Garden Party," *New York Times,* May 26, 1909, 8.
27. *Agnes,* 10–11.
28. Ibid., 12.
29. Quoted in Governors Island Club, *Governors Island: Its History and Development, 1637–1937* (Governors Island, N.Y.: Governors Island Club, 1937), 30.
30. National Park Service, Historic American Buildings Survey, HABS 31-Gov I, no. NY 5715-K, 3.
31. Office of the Quartermaster General, Completion Report, Fort Jay, vol. 203, 1931–33, RG 92, 137.
32. "Number and Status of Enlisted Men in the Army of the United States...Stationed at Governors Island, N.Y.," June 9, 1936, RG 92, 13/291.1.
33. E-mails to author from a civilian who resided on Governors Island from 1927 to 1943, sent 2004–2008.
34. Peter Braestrup, "Governors Island Apartments Provided for Married Soldiers," *New York Times,* July 5, 1960, 63.
35. Ibid.
36. E-mail to author from Claudia Iannucci, September 1, 1906.
37. Laurie Johnston, "Best of Two Worlds on Governors Island," *New York Times,* January 2, 1972, 37.
38. U.S. Coast Guard, "Governors Island Memories June 1996 to September 1997," *The Coast Guard Reservist,* December 1997, 5, available at http://www.uscg.mil/reservist/mag1997/dec1997/seven.htm.
39. E-mail to author from Carolyn Masini, July 25, 2004.
40. Records of the Signal Office, 1945–46, RG 407, 4441/625–633.5, National Archives, College Park, Md.
41. "180 WACs Are Moved to Governors Island," *New York Times,* August 19, 1944, 14.
42. Records of the Signal Office, 1945–46, RG 407, 1469/31, National Archives, College Park, Md.
43. "180 WACS Are Moved," 14.
44. "WACs Celebrate 7th Anniversary," *New York Times,* May 14, 1949, 15.
45. "Who's Who in the Management," *Coast Guard Gazette,* June 6, 1969, 10.
46. John A. Tilley, "New London Goes Co-Ed," in *A History of Women in the Coast Guard,* available at http://www.uscg.mil/history/h_womn.html.
47. 20 U.S.C. 1681, Title IX of the Education Amendments of 1972 to the Civil Rights Act of 1964: "Title IX of the Education Act of 1972 forbade gender discrimination in education programs, including athletics that received federal dollars," available at http://www.archives.gov/education/lessons/civil-rights-act/.
48. "News of the Training Center," *Coast Guard Gazette,* March 7, 1975, 16.
49. E-mail to author from Robin E. Brian, radioman third class on the Coast Guard cutter *Dallas* from 1993 to 1996, sent October 7, 2004.
50. Mary Breasted, "Coast Guard Boasts of Its Recruits: They're Able, Seaworthy, Female," *New York Times,* December 7, 1977, 31.
51. Ibid.
52. Ibid.
53. E-mail to author from Wanda Hinkel, wife of an electronic technician first class on the U.S. Coast Guard cutter *Dallas* and mother of two children, all of whom resided on Governors Island in the 1990s, sent April 14, 2004. Other stories were gleaned from Web sites, e-mails, telephone conversations, and the weekly *Coast Guard Gazette.*
54. "Island Cafeteria Menu," *Coast Guard Gazette,* September 18, 1975, 7.
55. E-mails to author from Jeffrey Freeman, chief warrant officer (W4), ret., stationed on Governors Island from 1975 to 1978, sent March–September 2004.
56. "Who's Who in the Management," *Coast Guard Gazette,* July 11, 1969, 8.
57. Advertisement in *Coast Guard Gazette,* February 7, 1992, 19.
58. Masini, e-mail, July 25, 2004.
59. Ibid.
60. "Food Chains Try New Markets," *New York Times,* December 12, 1983, D1.
61. "CPO Club," *Coast Guard Gazette,* October 27, 1975, 13.
62. "Who's Who in the Management," *Coast Guard Gazette,* March 7, 1969, 11.
63. "Island Cafeteria Menu," *Coast Guard Gazette,* April 13–19, 1992, 7.
64. "The Chaplain's Chronicle," *Coast Guard Gazette,* February 10, 1977, 9.
65. "The Chaplain's Chronicle," *Coast Guard Gazette,* May 26, 1977, 13.
66. Smith, 145.
67. "Relief Workers Find Paint Hides Colonial Brick," n.d., Governors Island File, Museum of the City of New York.
68. Hinkel, e-mail, April 14, 2004.
69. "Flea Market and Fun Fair," *Coast Guard Gazette,* March 5, 1993, 3.

70. E-mail to author from Linda Fisher, wife of a chief warrant officer and Governors Island resident from 1985 to 1990, sent May 5, 2004.
71. Hinkel, e-mail, April 14, 2004. The Easter egg hunts were mentioned in countless e-mails to the author and were well advertised in the *Coast Guard Gazette* around Easter time.
72. "To the Community," *Coast Guard Gazette,* October 2, 1975, 2.

ISLAND HIGHLIGHTS: *A Wedding Pageant*
1. "Corbin-Parsons Nuptials," *New York Times,* September 8, 1897, 7.
2. Ibid.
3. Ibid.

ISLAND HIGHLIGHTS: *Isle of Dogs*
1. "Governors Island Dogs," *New York Times,* February 17, 1902, 6.
2. "Dogs of War Will Meet," *New York Times,* March 27, 1927, 25.
3. "The Dog Is Banished from Governors Island," *New York Times,* February 13, 1905, 7.
4. Map, "Doggie Islands!" *Coast Guard Gazette,* March 2, 1973, 2.
5. "Is Governors Island Going to the Dogs?" *Coast Guard Gazette,* January 24, 1975, 5.
6. Edwin H. Daniels, "To the Community," *Coast Guard Gazette,* April 18 1976, 2.

Chapter Seven
"SMILING GARDEN OF THE PROVINCE"
Recreation on Governors Island
1. Edmund Banks Smith, *Governors Island: Its Military History under Three Flags, 1637–1913* (New York: Edmund Banks Smith, 1913), 5.
2. Ibid., 11.
3. Ibid., 19.
4. Shannon Wright and Timothy Binzen, *Archeological Overview and Assessment of Governors Island National Monument, New York, New York* (Amherst: Archeological Services, University of Massachusetts, 2003), 25, 31.
5. Quoted in Anastazio Carlos Mariano Azoy, *Three Centuries under Three Flags: The Story of Governors Island from 1637* (Governors Island, N.Y.: Headquarters First Army, 1951), 30.
6. "Military Execution at Governor's Island: Tragic Ending of a Bounty Jumper," *New York Times,* February 4, 1865, 8.
7. Thomas Sparrow Collection, no. 1878, folder 7, vol. 1, September 4 and 23, 1861, 115, 173, transcribed by Alex Christopher Meekins, University of North Carolina–Chapel Hill Southern Historical Collection.
8. William Henry Rideing, "Garrison Life at Governors Island," *Scribner's Monthly* 21, no. 4 (February 1881): 593–602.
9. U.S. Congress, House Committee on Military Affairs, *Report No. 3136 to Accompany House Resolution 176,* 20th Cong., 1st sess., July 31, 1888.
10. Paul Leicester Ford, "Governor's Island," *Harper's Weekly,* August 25, 1888, 681.
11. *A Bill to Convey to the City of New York, in the State of New York, for the Purposes of a Public Park, the Island Known as Governors Island, with the Buildings Thereon Erected,* H.R. 5355, 55th Cong., 2d sess., December 17, 1897.
12. Letter from James N. Allison to Brigadier General John M. Wilson, Chief of Engineers, U.S. Army, December 22, 1897, RG 77, 809/282-3, National Archives, College Park, Md.
13. Letter from Lieutenant Governor Timothy Woodruff to Governor Benjamin B. Odell, February 4, 1901, United States Engineer Office, RG 77, 583/61, National Archives, College Park, Md.
14. Quoted in "General Chaffee Praises Y.M.C.A. Army Work," *New York Times,* March 29, 1903, 12.
15. "Miss Helen Gould and the Boys in Blue," *Leslie's Weekly Newspaper,* April 17, 1902, 376–77.
16. "Soldiers' New Clubhouse," *New York Times,* September 4, 1904, 9.
17. "Sailors Down Soldiers," *New York Times,* November 15, 1917, 10.
18. Names were found in "Town Topics," *Vanity Fair,* various issues, 1904–13.
19. "Fashion's Fads and Fantasies," *Washington Post,* May 27, 1910, 7.
20. "Notes of Army Relief Garden Party and Other Entertainments," *The World,* May 28, 1911, 4.
21. "Town Topics," *Vanity Fair,* May 8, 1913, 5.
22. "Rain Fails to Spoil Soldiers' Garden Party," *New York Times,* June 3, 1904, 7.
23. "Town Topics," *Vanity Fair,* May 27, 1909, 4.
24. "Sham Battle for Army Garden Party," *New York Times,* May 26, 1909, 8.
25. "Military Tournament for Army Relief," in the Garden Party Day program for June 21, 1930, 25, private collection of Barbara Roemer, president of the New Globe Theater.
26. Ibid., 14.
27. "Civilians Get Peek at New Weapons," *New York Times,* May 19, 1951, 4.
28. "Army Exhibit Opens Armed Forces Week," *New York Times,* May 9, 1965, 13.
29. "Soldiers Compete for Coveted Prizes," *New York Times,* May 5, 1927, 19.
30. Material for this section was derived from assorted *New York Times* articles from October 8, 1923, to May 15, 1939.
31. "Governors Island Triumphs at Polo," *New York Times,* September 21, 1925, 25.
32. "Governors Island Takes Polo Series," *New York Times,* October 14, 1935, 26.
33. Telephone conversation with George Haas Jr., champion civilian polo player, May 2005.
34. E-mail to author from Richard Kahan, nephew of former army brat, sent October 6, 2004.
35. "5,000 Attend Fete for Army Relief," *New York Times,* September 7, 1941, 45.
36. Letter from General Walter Bedell Smith to Robert Moses, June 28, 1950, Department of Parks and Recreation, 102851/41, New York City Municipal Archives.
37. Conversations with Garret Roosma, son of post commander John Roosma, September–December 2004.
38. "Governors Island Like Coney for a Day," *New York Times,* June 3, 1949, 27.
39. "Governors Island Is Circus Bargain," *New York Times,* June 2, 1950, 25.
40. E-mail to author from Wanda Hinkel, wife of electronic technician first class on Coast Guard cutter *Dallas* and mother of two children, all of whom lived on Governors Island in the 1990s, sent April 24, 2004.
41. Letter from Robert F. Wagner to Robert S. McNamara, March 15, 1965, Department of Parks and Recreation, 103309/051, New York City Municipal Archives.
42. "From the Command," *Coast Guard Gazette,* July 10, 1975, 2.
43. Ad for open house, *Coast Guard Gazette,* May 17, 1981, 7.
44. "From the Command," *Coast Guard Gazette,* June 26, 1992, 2.
45. Governors Island Preservation and Education Corporation, Public Open Space Professional Design Services, Governors Island, New York City, "Request for Statements of Qualification," issue date: October 23, 2006, 5.

Selected Bibliography

Archival Resources

National Archives and Records Administration, College Park, Md.

RG 77, Records of the Office of the Chief of Engineers, 1900–1945.

RG 92, Records of the Quartermaster General's Office, 1890–1945.

RG 94, Records of the Adjutant General's Office, 1860–1965.

RG 112, Records of the Office of the Surgeon General (Army), 1861–1965.

RG 389, Records of the Provost Marshall General, 1942–45.

RG 407, Records of the Adjutant General's Office, 1925–45.

National Archives and Records Administration, New York.

RG 77, Records of the Office of the Chief of Engineers, 1868–1906.

RG 156, Records of the Office of the Chief of Ordnance, 1861–1921.

RG 407, Records of the Adjutant General's Office, Recruiting Publicity Bureau, Governors Island, 1940–45.

New York City Department of Parks and Recreation, 1950–65, New York City Municipal Archives.

Diaries, Letters, Collections, Memoirs

Babcock, Henry Nash. "The Enlargement of Governors Island." *Professional Memoirs* 6, no. 27 (May–June 1914): 410–22.

Baker, Van R., ed. *Websters: Letters of an American Army Family in Peace and War, 1836–1853.* Kent, Ohio: Kent State University Press, 2000.

Bell, Alonzo E. Diaries, September 15–November 11, 1861, Mf.P. 48.1. Transcribed by Alex Christopher Meekins. Office of Archives and History, Division of Historical Resources, Archives, and Records, North Carolina State Archives, Raleigh.

Century Association, ed. *Addresses Made in Honor of Elihu Root.* New York: Century Association, 1937.

Chance, Joseph E., ed. *My Life in the Old Army: Reminiscences of Abner Doubleday from the Collections of the New-York Historical Society.* Fort Worth: Texas Christian University Press, 1998.

Durham, Roger S., ed. *A Confederate Yankee: The Journal of Edward William Drummond, a Confederate Soldier from Maine.* Knoxville: University of Tennessee Press, 2003.

Montresor, John. The Montresor Journals, various dates. Edited by G. D. Scull. New-York Historical Society Collections, New York City.

Relyea Family Papers. New-York Historical Society, New York City.

Rockefeller, David. *Memoirs.* New York: Random House Trade Paperbacks, 2003.

St. Cornelius Altar Guild. *What's Cooking on Governors Island.* N.p: n.p, 1949.

Stokes, I. N. Phelps. *The Iconography of Manhattan Island 1498–1909.* 6 vols. New York: Arno Press, 1976.

Thomas Sparrow Collection. No. 1878, folder 7, vols. 1 and 2, September 4, 1861–October 9, 1861. Transcribed by Alex Christopher Meekins. University of North Carolina–Chapel Hill Southern Historical Collection.

Washington, George. General Orders, June 19, 1776, Letterbook 1, Image 288. George Washington Papers, Collections of the Manuscript Division, Library of Congress, Washington, D.C.

Wood, Leonard. Diaries, January 1, 1908 to December 31, 1911, and January 1, 1913, to December 31, 1918. Leonard Wood Papers, Collections of the Manuscript Division, Library of Congress, Washington, D.C.

Secondary Sources

Adams, Noah. *The Flyers: In Search of Wilbur and Orville Wright.* New York: Crown, 2003.

Ashburn, P. M. *A History of the Medical Department of the United States Army.* Boston: Houghton Mifflin, 1929.

Azoy, Anastazio Carlos Mariano. *Three Centuries under Three Flags: The Story of Governors Island from 1637.* Governors Island, N.Y.: Headquarters First Army, 1951.

Bellamy, Blanche Wilder. *Governors Island.* Half Moon Series Papers on Historic New York, edited by Maude Wilder Goodwin, Alice Carrington Royce, and Ruth Putnam, vol. 1, no. 5. New York: G. P. Putnam's Sons, 1897.

Bonner, William Thompson. *New York: The World's Metropolis 1623-4–1923-4.* New York: R. L. Polk, 1924.

Campbell, Alexander V. *The Royal American Regiment, 1755–1772: An Atlantic Community.* London, Ontario: Faculty of Graduate Studies, University of Western Ontario, 2003.

Clay, Steven E. *Blood and Sacrifice: The History of the 16th Infantry Regiment from the Civil War Through the Gulf War.* Wheaton, Ill.: Cantigny First Division Foundation, 2001.

Fischer, David Hackett. *Washington's Crossing.* Oxford: Oxford University Press, 2004.

Foner, Jack D. *Blacks and the Military in American History.* New York: Praeger, 1974.

Gillespie, Angus Kress. *The Twin Towers: The Life of New York City's Trade Center.* New Brunswick, N.J.: Rutgers University Press, 1999.

Gillette, Mary C. *The Army Medical Department, 1775–1818.* United States Army Historical Series. Washington, D.C.: Center of Military History, U.S. Army, 1981.

———. *The Army Medical Department, 1818–1865.* United States Army Historical Series. Washington, D.C.: Center of Military History, U.S. Army, 1987.

Governors Island Club. *Governors Island: Its History and Development, 1637–1937.* Governors Island, N.Y.: Governors Island Club, 1937.

Hesseltine, William Best. *Civil War Prisons: A Study in War Psychology.* New York: Frederick Unger, 1964.

McClure, J. B. *Life of General Hancock.* Chicago: Rhodes and McClure, 1880.

Rosenberg, Charles E. *The Cholera Years: The United States in 1832, 1849, and 1866.* Chicago: University of Chicago Press, 1962.

Shorto, Russell. *The Island at the Center of the World.* New York: Doubleday, 2004.

Smith, Edmund Banks. *Governors Island: Its Military History under Three Flags, 1637–1913.* New York: Edmund Banks Smith, 1913.

Speer, Lonnie R. *Portals to Hell: Military Prisons of the Civil War.* Mechanicsburg, Pa.: Stackpole Books, 1997.

White, William C., ed. and comp. *Unisonic Chords, Scales, and Rhythm Studies for Bands.* New York: Carl Fischer, n.d.

Newspapers

The Business Week, October 1929

Coast Guard Gazette, 1969–92

The Coast Guard Reservist, December 1997

Daily Graphic, September 1873

Leslie's Weekly Newspaper, April 1902

New York Daily Times, December 1853

New York Times, 1853–1998

Richmond Examiner, March 1865

Wall Street Journal, May 1912

Washington Post, 1880–1932

The World, March 1901, May 1911

World Telegram, June 1936

Magazines

Harper's Weekly, August 1888

The Ladies' Companion, a Monthly Magazine, May 1837

Red White and Blue Weekly, November 1897
Scientific American, November 1907
Scribner's Monthly, February 1881
Tow Line, fall 1969
Vanity Fair, 1904–13

Reports, Studies, Documents

Ainsworth, Fred C., Leslie J. Perry, and Joseph W. Kirkley, eds. *War of the Rebellion: A Compilation of the Official Records of the Union and Confederate Armies.* Series II, vol. 4. Washington, D.C.: U.S. Government Printing Office, 1899.

Annual report of the Atlantic Branch, U.S. Disciplinary Barracks, Office of the Commandant, 1923–37.

Annual report of the Chief of Engineers, U.S. Army, 1900–1915.

Annual report of the Quartermaster-General, War Department, 1901–12.

Annual report of the Surgeon General, 1870–76.

Annual report of the War Department for the years ending June 30, 1901, to June 30, 1913.

Billings, John Shaw. *A Report on Barracks and Hospitals with Description of Military Posts.* Washington, D.C.: U.S. Government Printing Office, 1870.

Garman, J., and H. Herbster. *Phase 1A, Archeological Assessment of the Governors Island Historic Landmark District.* Pawtucket, R.I.: Public Archeology Laboratory, 1996.

Governors Island Club. *Constitution and By Laws. With List of Officers and Members.* Governors Island, N.Y.: Governors Island Club, 1914.

Governors Island Preservation and Education Corporation, Public Open Space Professional Design Services, Governors Island, New York City. "Request for Statements of Qualification." Issue date: October 23, 2006.

Lewis, Harold M. *Regional Survey of New York: Transit and Transportation.* Vol. 4. New York: Regional Plan Association, 1928.

Marshall, Major W. L. *Survey of Buttermilk Channel, New York Harbor.* New York: Engineer Office, U.S. Army, November 28, 1900.

National Park Service. Historic American Buildings Survey / Historic American Engineering Record, 1933–Present. Collection of the Prints and Photographic Division, Library of Congress, Washington, D.C.

Quartermaster General. *Description of Posts, Governors Island, New York, Headquarters of the Department of the East, 1901–1902.* Report. Washington, D.C.: U.S. Government Printing Office, 1902.

Regional Plan Association. *The Regional Plan of New York and Its Environs: The Graphic Regional Plan.* Vol. 1. New York: Regional Plan Association, 1929.

State of New York, Commissioners of the Land Office. *Proceedings of the Commissioners of the Land Office for the Year 1901.* Albany: Oliver A. Quayle, Department Printer, 1901.

Thompson, Erwin N. *The Presidio of San Francisco: A History from 1846 to 1995.* Historic Resource Study, Golden Gate National Recreation Area. Denver: Denver Service Center, National Park Service, July 1997.

U.S. Adjutant General's Office. *Sites for Military Posts.* Washington, D.C.: U.S. Government Printing Office, 1901–1903.

U.S. Bureau of the Census. Censuses of Governors Island for 1860, 1880, 1900, 1910, 1920, and 1930.

Warren-Findley, Jann, and Nancy Dallett. *Draft, Governors Island Historic Resource Study: June, 2004.* Philadelphia: Northeast History Program Office, National Park Service, 2004.

Wright, Shannon, and Timothy Binzen. *Archeological Overview and Assessment of Governors Island National Monument, New York, New York.* Amherst: Archeological Services, University of Massachusetts, 2003.

U.S. Congressional Hearings and Reports

U.S. House of Representatives. *Hearing on the First Deficiency Bill.* 69th Cong., 3d sess., December 8, 1927.

———. *Increase Flying-Field Area of Governors Island, N.Y.* 71st Cong., 3d sess., February 26, 1931.

U.S. House of Representatives, Committee on Military Affairs. *Construction on Governors Island.* 77th Cong., 2d sess., April 29, 1941.

———. *For the Erection of an Airport on Governors Island.* 74th Cong., 2d sess., March 5, 1936.

———. *Report no. 3136 to Accompany House Resolution 176.* 20th Cong., 1st sess., July 31, 1888.

U.S. Senate, Committee on Military Affairs. *Construction at Army Posts: Hearings before the Committee on Military Affairs on S. 3558.* 69th Cong., 1st sess., April 16, 1926.

———. *Landing Field on Governors Island, Hearings before the Committee on Military Affairs on H.R. 12009, an Act to Authorize the Enlargement of Governors Island and Consenting to the Use of a Portion Thereof as a Landing Field for the City of New York and Its Environs.* 74th Cong., 2d sess., June 5, 15, and 16, 1936.

Web Sites

"Another NYC Isle's Prisons: Fort Jay, Castle Williams." Available at http://www.connectionhistory.org/civilwar/governorsisland.

Changes in the Uniform of the Army, 1774–1895. Washington, D.C.: U.S. Army Quartermaster's Department, 1895. Available at http://www.qmfound.com/changes_in_the_army_uniform_1895.htm.

Christopher Goodwin and Associates, Inc. *National Historic Context for Department of Defense Installations, 1790–1940.* Baltimore, Md.: U.S. Army Corps of Engineers, Baltimore District, August 1995. Available at http://aec.Army.mil/usaec/cultural/docs.html.

"Colonel Jonathan Williams." In *Portraits and Profiles, Chief Engineer—1775 to Present.* Available at http://www.hq.usace.army.mil/history/coe.htm#6.

"Engineer John Montresor." Available at http://footguards.tripod.com/01ABOUT/Montresor/000montresor.htm.

Federal Aviation Commission. "A Brief History of the Federal Aviation Commission." Available at http://www.faa.gov/about/history/brief%5Fhistory/.

Hudson River Maritime Museum. *1909 Hudson-Fulton Celebration: The Fourth Annual Report on the Hudson-Fulton Celebration Commission to the Legislature of the State of New York, May 20, 1910.* Available at http://www.ulster.net/~hrmm/quad/1909hudson-fulton/intro.html.

Koehler, Franz A. "Early Army Rations." Chap. 1 of *Special Rations for the Armed Forces, 1946–53,* in *QMC Historical Studies,* series II, no. 6 (1958), http://www.qmfound.com/army_rations_historical_background.htm.

Mr. Lincoln's White House. Available at http://www.mrlincolnswhitehouse.org/inside.asp?ID=696&subjectID=2.

Rodenbough, Theophilus Francis, Bvt. Brigadier General, U.S.A., and William L. Haskin, Major, First Artillery, eds. *The Army of the United States, Historical Sketches of Staff and Line with Portraits of Generals-in-Chief.* New York: Maynard, Merrill, 1896), available at http://www.history.army.mil/books/R&H/R&H=FM.htm.

Tilley, John A. "New London Goes Co-Ed." In *A History of Women in the Coast Guard.* Available at http://www.uscg.mil/history/h_womn.html.

U.S. Army Bands in History. Available at http://bands.army.mil/history/.

U.S. Army School of Music. Available at http://schoolofmusic.army.mil/.

U.S. Centennial of Flight Commission. "'Airport Design' by Judy Rumerman." Available at http://www.centennialofflight.gov/essay/Social/architecture/SH15.htm.

———. "Pan American: The History of America's Chosen Instrument for Overseas

Air Transport." Available at http://www.centennialofflight.gov/essay/Commercial_Aviation/Pan_Am/Tran12.htm.

U.S. Coast Guard. "Governors Island Memories June 1996 to September 1997." *The Coast Guard Reservist,* December 1997, 5. Available at http://www.uscg.mil/reservist/mag1997/dec1997/seven.htm.

U.S. Coast Guard Historian's Office. "*Red Beech,* 1964, WLM-686." Available at http://www.uscg.mil/history.html.

"The Washington Hall Mural." Available at http://www.usma57.org/Mural-corrected%20060820.pdf.

Williams, Rudi. "Air Force Sergeant Traces Bugle's History," November 8, 2000. Available at http://www.defenselink.mil/news/Nov2000/n11082000_200011084.html.

Graphics Sources

Astor, Lenox and Tilden Foundations, Picture Collection. Branch Libraries, New York Public Library.

Bettmann Collection. Bettmann/CORBIS, Carlisle, Pa., available at http://www.pro.corbis.com.

Cartographic Branch, Still Pictures Branch. Map and Photographic Collections, National Archives, Washington, D.C.

George Grantham Bain Collection; Mathew Brady Collection; Underhill Collection. Collection of the Prints and Photographic Division, Library of Congress, Washington, D.C.

McKim, Mead & White Collection. Museum of the City of New York.

McKim, Mead & White Collection. New-York Historical Society, New York City.

New York Transit Museum, Archives, Brooklyn, N.Y.

Quarter Master Museum, Archives, Fort Lee, Va.

Thomas W. Dunn Collection; Eastern Depot Collection; 1st Regiment, New York Volunteer Infantry Collection; G. S. Grunert Collection; Tasker Bliss Collection. U.S. Army Military History Institute, Carlisle, Pa.

U.S. Coast Guard Historian's Office, Archives, Washington, D.C.

Wright Brothers Collection. Special Collections and Archives, Wright State University, Dayton, Ohio.

Index

Page numbers in italic indicate a photograph, map, or table.